# Love, Sweat & Tears

## ZELIE BULLEN

### WITH FREDA MARNIE NICHOLLS

ALLEN&UNWIN

SYDNEY · MELBOURNE · AUCKLAND · LONDON

First published in 2013

Allen & Unwin
83 Alexander Street
Crows Nest NSW 2065
Australia
Phone:      (61 2) 8425 0100
Email:       info@allenandunwin.com
Web:        www.allenandunwin.com

Cataloguing-in-Publication details are available from
the National Library of Australia
www.trove.nla.gov.au

ISBN 978 1 74331 1 516

Internal design by Darian Causby, Highway51
Set in 12/18 pt Sabon by Midland Typesetters, Australia
Printed and bound in Australia by the SOS Print + Media Group.

10 9 8 7 6 5 4 3 2

*Zelie Bullen* (for...rly Zelie Thompson) has worked as an animal trainer and stu... ...f...  and television for over twenty years. She has been ... ... ...h ...ain a large range of both exotic ... ... ...nts ...d ...iraffes to pigs, donkeys, dogs and horses.

Zelie grew up on the outskirts of Perth, Western Australia, and was surrounded by animals from a very young age. Throughout her school years, she collected as many animals as her mother would allow, and unwittingly began learning about their communication and hierarchy systems just by being with them whenever time permitted. Her daily life today is her childhood dream come true, working and living with animals she loves and being paid for it.

Zelie lives on the Gold Coast with her husband, son and various animals. She has particularly enjoyed writing her story with her sister Freda.

*Freda Marnie Nicholls* began her writing career with a letter to the editor of a dirt bike magazine, complaining about the fact that she was being left to bring up three little children while her husband was off riding his bike. This tongue-in-cheek letter led to a monthly column and gave her the courage to pursue her dream of writing.

Freda has written for various national magazines and newspapers, even working as editor for a regional paper for a short time, before common sense prevailed and she realised it was more fun helping her husband on the farm and writing on a freelance basis. She has written articles for *Style* magazine, *The Land*, *Canberra Times* and various publications of RM Williams Outback Publishing and regional newspapers, writing mostly about rural people and their lives.

Freda lives on a farm in southern New South Wales with her husband and their three great teenage children.

*I dedicate this book to my devoted mum,*
*who taught me how to love.*
ZELIE


*For Bert and our beautiful children Hayley,*
*Charlotte and Sam. You are my world.*
FREDA

'I figure if a girl wants to be a legend, she should go ahead and be one.'
CALAMITY JANE

# Contents

# CHAPTER 1

# What you see is what you get

What you see is what you get. I always liked that about animals—the simplicity, the straightforwardness. When I was young, animals were easier to understand than adults, or even other kids.

I used to ride my little grey pony bareback to Beenong, which the state school kids liked to call 'that loser hippy school'. As I pushed Candy into a trot, they would line up and hurl abuse at us through their chainmail school fence, calling me a 'Beenong bastard' as I bounced off down the road away from them.

Arriving at my school, I would tether Candy out to graze. I'd pull out the bucket I kept stashed under the school foundations, fill it with water and place it beside her. Then I'd give her a quick pat and tell her I'd be back soon.

Schooling at Beenong was far from conventional. It was an independent alternative to the state school system, run predominantly by the community. We had qualified teachers, but we addressed them by their first names and everything was very casual. Lessons weren't as structured as at other schools. Contrary to what the state school kids used to taunt me with, we weren't taught to smash windows, but it wasn't uncommon for a maths class to finish early so we could go and climb trees, or for English to be interrupted so we could learn how to make cumquat jam, just because someone's cumquat tree had an oversupply of fruit. To me it was a mixture of standard schooling and real-life skills.

At the time, my family lived in the village of Darlington in the Darling Ranges, the escarpment that rises sharply to the east of Perth. Surrounded by dry spiky bushland, where we had lots of adventures, it was a great place to grow up.

Materially we didn't have much, but I didn't really dwell on that—in any case, it was all I knew. Dad had left when I was eight months old, leaving Mum with three little girls to bring up by herself. When he left, my oldest sister, Freda, was five, and Julie was two.

The first memory I have of our father was when I was about five years old. There was a knock at the door. Freda got there first; as she swung it open, I popped under her arm to see who it was. She called out, 'Dad!' and I thought, 'Who?' I had no idea who this man was. Feeling a combination of embarrassment and fear, I watched her hug him. He was a stranger—why was she being so familiar with him? If Dad had ever visited us before then, I don't remember.

Life when I was growing up was often insecure and uncertain. Mum had been left in a hideous situation, with very little support from my father, and I think she did an amazing job raising us. Even though she did her best, money was often tight and sometimes we found ourselves in bad situations. I know what it's like to be scared—and I mean really scared. Scared for my own safety and for that of my sisters; but, most of all, terrified for my mother. We watched as she struggled through several violent relationships, including an attempted drowning at the hands of one particularly nasty partner, and various beatings. I also know what it's like to be hungry, to truly crave a complete meal and a full pantry. And I know what it's like to be hopeful—hopeful that tomorrow will be easier.

These early memories were my first lessons in feeling gratitude and appreciation for what I have; as a result, as awful as some of these experiences were at the time, I'm grateful for them. I will always feel compassion and admiration for my mum, and honour her for what she lived through—the shame, the embarrassment, the bad decisions, but also her survival instincts, her sheer determination and the way she always strove to do her best for us three kids.

Mum had been born in Malaysia, from Australian and English parents. Her father was a successful exporter of tin and rubber to the ever-expanding British Empire, and ended up serving three years in Changi prison after fighting the Japanese in World War II. Grandma, together with Mum as a nine-month-old baby and my three-year old uncle, escaped on one of the last boats to leave Singapore harbour before it fell to the Japanese. They eventually made their way back to Grandma's family in Darlington.

After the war, Grandma and Grandpa were reunited and they went back to Malaysia to start their lives again. They sent Mum to boarding school in Western Australia for her secondary education, and then finishing school in Switzerland, before she came back to Australia to study art. It was then that she met and married a tall dark handsome man who swept her off her feet, my father. When Dad left and for many years after, my grandparents were still living and working in Malaysia, and Mum felt ashamed being a divorcee, and was too proud to ask for help.

But no matter what was happening in our lives at any particular moment, I always felt deeply loved and immensely important. I was raised thinking I was better looking than I actually was, smarter than I was, a better singer than I was— the list goes on. I may have been shy, but I wasn't lacking in confidence. Despite all the distressing emotions my mum must have been experiencing herself, she clearly did a great job in providing me with self-worth.

Like most mothers, she did some things wrong, but she did an awful lot of things right too. Perhaps the most important thing she taught me was how to communicate, how to express myself, how to love and how to be loved.

Another great gift she bestowed upon me was a love of animals. I grew up with an assortment of chooks and an aviary full of birds, plus two cats, called Easter and Christmas (because that was when they first decided to arrive at our house). And of course we always had dogs. Whatever was happening in my life, animals were always there for me.

The first animal I thought of as actually belonging to me was one I found when I was six. I thought I was the luckiest little girl in the world when I found some puppies just after they were born, hidden among some rocks and long grass behind a friend's house. I felt even luckier when Mum let me bring one of them home six weeks later when they were old enough to be weaned.

I called him Snoopy, after the character in the *Peanuts* comics. He was a funny little kelpie–corgi cross with an adorable, gentle personality, and he became an incredibly important member of our family for the next twelve years.

My introduction to the wonderful world of horses came later, through one of my sister Julie's school friends, who had an old white mare called Princess. When we visited, someone would catch her for us and we would climb all over her, jumping on and off, standing on her back. I became obsessed with her. She was a kind, patient playmate. Animals were my friends.

In early 1977, when I was just six, we moved from Darlington, to the Porongurups, a mountain range four hours south of Perth. Here a community had sprung up on Harriet Lemann's family farm. Mum and twenty-one-year-old Harriet had met at a party, and they soon became firm friends. Harriet was one of six children and it was her parents who owned the hobby farm in the Porongurups that turned into our home. Mum felt that there she could give us a more relaxed country lifestyle, which was what she had always wanted too. There was a big old concrete-brick homestead, a wooden apple-packing shed and an old dairy Harriet had converted into makeshift homes, which filled with different people at different times, including our little family. She and Mum grew an enormous veggie patch between the house and the old dairy to feed everyone.

The founder of Beenong School, Lance Holt, started an alternative school on the property. There were four or five kids living on the farm at any one time, and together with a handful of local kids whose parents wanted to try out the school for their sometimes troublesome children, became the pupils of 'Freewheels'. Lance called it 'Freewheels' in reference to the two buses on the property. One, a stationary blue bus, was used purely as a classroom, and the other was an old yellow double-decker that served as both occasional sleeping quarters and a means of transport to parties and excursions around the district, complete with a piano, which Harriet would play as we drove along.

Our community was very easygoing and laid-back, though there was little or no routine and life could be chaotic. But for a kid it was a whole lot of fun. Between our intermittent schooling, we'd explore the old wooden farm buildings and abandoned overgrown piles of wood and rusty steel that lay around the place, or just go out and experience the beauty of nature. If it was hot we went nicky swimming in the dam. There was a great community feel and there were always lots of fun things to do.

A local farming couple, Ruth and John Bush, sent their youngest son Robert to Freewheels for his schooling. Robert and I were great friends, and I used to go and stay with them on weekends and work on the farm, following Ruth around and doing whatever she did. I couldn't get enough of it—in fact, I remember wanting to stay there forever. People would say to me, 'So, you're going to marry a farmer,' and I would reply, 'No, I'm going to *be* a farmer.' Even then I knew that was what I wanted to do—to be with animals and work outside.

John Bush is a talented musician and music teacher, and consequently all four of their children are musical, with Robert being an accomplished saxophone player and drummer. Music filled our lives when we were in the Porongurups, and this family was a beautiful influence on me.

There was always a smattering of farm animals agisted at Harriet's place, but life changed for us when she was given an ex-racehorse called Star. He must have been well over sixteen hands and was a mad bolter, prone to galloping off with little or no warning, but we would still clamber up and ride him, normally against the advice of the adults. Freda used to dink me on the back of him. One day, as we went for a canter up the gravel hill behind the main house, Star took off and galloped into the bush—we both fell off spectacularly.

After a time, he was the first horse I rode by myself. It was pretty scary whenever he took off. I jumped off one time near the house and one of the adults told me you should never jump off a horse—you should hang in there and try to control it. I don't know if that was particularly good advice to give to a little kid on a bolting racehorse, but it's stuck with me ever since.

But then Mum bought Freda a big gentle gelding called Ben, and after a few rides I decided it was fun. We played endlessly with the horses, leading them around and riding them. We knew nothing about horses or safety, and had no equipment, just bits of rope that we strung together, but we were bumped around until we gradually worked out how to handle them and ride a bit.

After a couple of years, Freewheels School closed down and we moved back to our Darlington house, with Ben in tow. Freda spent hours on him and I'd follow her around, begging for a turn. Finally I nagged Mum until she agreed to buy me a pony for my upcoming tenth birthday.

We went to see a few horses but most were out of our reach financially, or weren't what we were after. Then we heard about a former riding-school horse that was for sale. We turned up at a grotty riding school to look at her, a grey pony called Casper (for Casper the ghost). I thought she was the most amazing pony I had ever seen in my life, because I thought she could be mine. We took her home and I promptly changed her name to Peppermint Candy, because she seemed sweet, not scary. But we soon found out why the riding school wanted to get rid of her. The first thing Candy taught me was how to hang on—she was very good at shying, and unseated me whenever she could.

Mum initially couldn't afford a saddle or bridle, so I rode Candy bareback, with just a halter or head collar (a piece of basic harness which fits behind the ears and around the muzzle), and a short length of rope attached with a single clip. I remember falling off a lot and crying. I often felt frustrated and disappointed—I just wanted to ride. I'm not sure how much pleasure I got learning to ride Candy, but eventually I managed to stay on more often than not.

Despite the difficult start we had together, I felt as though I could never love anything as much as I loved that pony. If someone irritated or upset me, I would go and see Candy and say to her, 'You wouldn't do that to me, would you?' I would hug her and tell her I loved her. I felt she understood me.

I turned to animals because they made me happy. And I suppose that was how I became so good at reading animal body language—because I spent so much time sitting with them and watching them. I loved it.

Around this time, Mum and Freda were fighting a lot. I was only ten and didn't really understand what was going on. Freda blamed Mum for many things she wasn't happy with as teenagers often do. She went to live with Dad and his new family in Perth. A short time later, they moved to Canberra, then Sydney with Dad's work as a manager for Perth entrepreneur Kerry Stokes.

I missed Fred a lot when she left, but Julie promised me that she would never leave me. More than once, she held my face between her hands and told me she would always be there. It was comforting for me, and I'm sure for her too.

I felt safe and comfortable when Julie was with me. She always seemed confident and outgoing, whereas I was the baby of the family, a mummy's girl. She would rush up and give someone a cuddle or sit on their lap, while I would hang back.

A couple of times Julie and I went to visit Dad by ourselves, taking the three-and-a-half-day bus trip across the great empty expanse of the Nullarbor Plain to Sydney. I hated not being with people I knew—without Mum, without my animals—but I did enjoy getting to know our stepmother Jan, and our two adorable little half-sisters, Cloud and Kate, as well as spending some time with Fred before she finished high school and moved out.

Julie also wanted to establish a relationship with Dad, but I couldn't have cared less. I have early memories of Mum comforting Julie at night as she lay on the bottom bunk of our bunk bed and she sobbed, saying that she wished she had a dad like the other kids at school. I didn't understand her pain.

Dad was a stranger to me, and I felt little emotion towards him. When we went to visit, I could see that Dad was trying to be nice and I felt I was supposed to be nice too, but all I really felt was discomfort. Julie often wrote long letters to him, Jan and the girls and she made sure I signed birthday cards for Cloud and Kate, calling them her babies when talking about them to her friends. She would be so excited at the prospect of going over to see them when we were asked to visit, but I was always reluctant. Our relationship with him was almost non-existent.

During our visits I remember him arriving home from work, eating dinner and sitting down in front of the television. He seemed emotionally detached from the family. I don't remember him being affectionate, though he did try once, calling me over while he was watching television; I went over and sat stiffly with him while he patted my knee. Then I jumped off the first chance I got.

There was another reason I felt uncomfortable around my father. At home in Darlington, we struggled financially. When Julie and I arrived in Sydney in our worn, hand-me-down clothes, we would be taken to Dad's expensive house on the upper north shore, full of modern appliances and abundant food. My little half-sisters pottered around in spotless outfits and seemed to own endless stuff. Knowing that Dad didn't even pay Mum maintenance I couldn't help feeling hurt. Over time, my attitude towards him became almost belligerent and when I was old enough to say so, I refused to visit him, even though Julie continued to go.

I had such mixed feelings about him. I always felt uncomfortable around him and I think he was uncomfortable around me. For many years I thought: 'Why doesn't he want us? Why did he leave? Why doesn't he have anything to do with us?' The end result of all this was that I thought, 'Bugger you—I don't want anything to do with you either.' I understand the hurt that caused that feeling and I don't blame myself for that.

When Julie and I returned to Darlington, to Mum and the animals, I was happy. But other aspects of my life in Darlington weren't going so well. Mum had seen how far behind academically Julie was when she started high school and she began to worry that I would have similar problems, so she pulled me out of Beenong for my last year of primary schooling. Up until then, I had always been to independent alternative schools which were friendly and casual. As unstable and insecure as my childhood had been, I'd had an awful lot of fun at both Beenong and Freewheels. Now, though, Mum enrolled me at a private school. Not only did I feel like a total misfit, I was bullied both emotionally and physically. I had never experienced anything like it before. On top of that, I found it strange and scary to be sitting in a class not being allowed to talk. The teacher wasn't your friend; they didn't come and say something nice to you when they walked in. They would say, 'Sit down, Zelie, be quiet,' and I used to think, 'What have I done?'

My unhappiness didn't stop when the school day ended. Three boys in particular used to grab me on the way home and push me around, trying to intimidate me. Sometimes I tried to avoid them by taking the back way home, instead of walking down the main road, but somehow they always seemed to know which route I would take and would wait for me there. It was horrible. They used to say, 'You tell anyone and we will say you are a liar.' So I never told.

I did tell Mum I hated the school, but rather than let me go back to Beenong, she sent me to Darlington state primary. I was horrified to think I would have to face the same kids who had taunted me as I rode past on Candy. To my surprise, though, Darlington Primary was a relief, because I didn't get the same amount of physical bullying there. But I still hated it—I didn't make any friends and I felt like I was different to everyone else.

In my unhappiness, I again turned to my animals. People let me down; animals didn't. Snoopy and Candy were my best friends and I thought they knew how I was feeling. I decided that you couldn't trust people—they could be liars and bullies, and were frightening and unpredictable. With animals, I felt comfortable and peaceful. Animals made me happy.

# CHAPTER 2

# Beautiful friends

I didn't have many friends at school, but I did have my horsey friends. This was a small group of six or seven girls who lived in the area and went to pony club together. To get to the monthly pony club rallies, we would either ride the nine kilometres along the old railway line to Mahogany Creek very early in the morning, or get a lift with someone who had a float or trailer. The parents took turns to be the transport person for each rally, delivering a pile of halters as well as a bale of hay and buckets for water for the horses; they would also hand out our lunches.

Our little group went everywhere on our ponies. Sometimes all of us met up, while at other times only two or three of us would ride together. On weekends, it wasn't unusual to get up in the morning, ride bareback to whoever's place we were meeting at and go for a ride. We would then rock up at someone else's place for lunch, putting all of our ponies together in their paddock. We might go for a swim or jump on the trampoline or just play with the ponies. They were such fun days.

I love the adventurous memories I have of that time. There were some hair-raising rides. I thought it was hilarious to pull the bridles off the other girls' horses as we were cantering along—they would be left holding an awful lot of rein with only the bit pressing against their horse's chest, which eventually slowed them down. Thankfully, all our horses were very docile, because they were being handled and ridden all the time. Still, the others would swear at me and ask me why I thought that was funny. In retaliation, they would try to get Candy's bridle off, but no one ever did. I'd yell, 'You can't catch me!' We found the steepest hills to go up and down, and jumped our horses over everything we could. I always wanted adventure.

One day two trainers came to our pony club to perform a vaulting display with their horses. They were from El Caballo Blanco, a centre that had been opened in Perth a few years before by a Spanish classical rider, who had imported several Andalusian horses from Spain, and whose intention was to showcase the first classical dancing horses in the southern hemisphere. I was in total awe of their skills that day at pony club and thought, 'I want to do that!'

Vaulting can best be described as ballet on horseback. It is typically performed on a big solid horse with a slow, smooth rocking-horse canter, moving in a circle of twenty metres diameter. The horse is 'lunged', meaning someone stands in the middle of the circle holding a long lead line, and the rider or riders perform a series of acrobatic manoeuvres on the horse's back. It is athletic and beautiful to watch. It can involve jumping on and off the horse as it moves along, as well as holding various positions, including sitting backwards and standing in arabesque poses on the horse's big strong hindquarters or back. It is thought to originate from Roman times and was often seen in circus rings throughout Europe in the nineteenth and twentieth centuries, and is still seen today in some of the top circuses around the world.

Afterwards the trainers taught us some basic vaulting moves, and we were then allowed to practise on their beautiful Andalusian horse as he walked around in a circle. I was captivated—riding home that day along the bridle trail, I started jumping on and off my own pony, trying to mimic what I had just seen.

From then on, I used to try all those vaulting moves on Candy as we rode along. Of course, more often than not I would hit the ground with a thump rather than land safely back in the saddle. Candy would often unseat me and trot off to munch on the nearest patch of grass, waiting for me to dust myself off and hop back on. I was no gymnast, but I would just try my best and see what happened. Sometimes I would just sit in my saddle facing backwards for a while as we rode along—anything for a bit of fun. I couldn't recall all of the vaulting moves we'd been shown, but I practised what I did remember and often just made up stuff that I thought might look good, showing off to my riding buddies.

We were a very close little gang of friends. Even when we started to grow up and got interested in boys and going out, horses continued to be a massive part of our lives.

There was not enough land to constantly graze Candy at our place, so she lived with a dozen or so other horses at Tisa Lawrence's property, about a kilometre down the road. I couldn't afford to pay Tisa agistment, so I would scoop up horse poo, muck out the stables or clean her show tack, all of which I was happy to do.

By the time I was fourteen, I was too big for Candy, so, with Tisa's help, I started looking around for a larger horse. We found a beautiful Arab cross chestnut mare called Angel's Glory.

Angel was a very special horse to me. Aside from the fact that I fell in love with her, as I do with most of my animals, I also learnt a lot from her. I think she was the first horse with whom I had a relationship of mutual respect.

Candy had been my first pony and I'd fallen off her every day until I learnt to hang on. Basically she did what she wanted and I was happy just to go along with it and simply be with her. Like my dog Snoopy, she was my friend. But by the time Angel came along I knew a bit more about horses and how to handle them.

Angel was a bit sour at first, pinning her ears back at me and with a bad attitude. I felt she was being rude, and I thought, 'Hang on, I've just paid money for you and you're being mean to me.' I quickly let her know I wasn't taking any bad attitude from her. It was weird, because I didn't really understand the concept of what I was doing. But during the first few months, my relationship with Angel turned into a very respectful one; as a result, I felt that she enjoyed my company and wanted to be with me.

At Tisa's I would watch the relationships between the horses in the paddock—which pony was boss over who, and where they all fitted within the herd. I was really interested in their social network and I felt like I wanted to be a part of it. Like them, I needed to find where I belonged in the herd.

Understanding animals' natural instincts and interactions is an important part of training animals, and I was learning this at a rapid rate, just by being with them every moment I could. For example, a dog wants to please you, and even birds need to feel that you are 'family' and safe if you want to work with them or be around them. Candy had probably seen me as beneath her, but I didn't mind that, because I was inexperienced and just enjoyed having her as my friend. But my relationship with Angel showed me that horses can like being with you even if they are not in the dominant position. If I called out to Angel in the paddock, she would call back to me and come to the fence; once she was caught, she would listen to me. This discipline was very different to what I had had before; I was always relieved if I actually managed to catch Candy. What I learnt from Angel was invaluable.

Even now, with any animal I train or bring into our family or 'herd', I realise the importance of them feeling happy with me and comfortable with their place within the group. And, as in any family situation, it is always difficult when the time comes for me to separate from an animal I have trained, because of the rapport and understanding that has been created between us.

By now I was a teenager, and I had begun to ask Mum for some boundaries, just as Angel wanted to know hers. But when I asked Mum for some rules she said, 'What for?' I tried to explain that I needed some chores or responsibilities—other kids had jobs, like taking out the rubbish. So she replied, 'OK then, take out the rubbish.' I couldn't get her to understand that I needed her to tell me on rubbish day that I needed to do that job.

It took me many years to see the similarities, but just like teenagers, animals need to know their boundaries so they can feel comfortable. Angel and I were looking for ours at the same time.

Once she knew what I expected of her and what I would accept, Angel was a very easy horse to train. When I was fifteen I taught her to rear on cue—well, most of the time! At first we were just playing together. She was an excitable Arab cross mare, and when I stirred her up she would often squeal and lift her front feet a foot or so off the ground and hop back on her back legs, using her body language, her ears and eyes to communicate her joy and excitement. Whenever she did this I praised her. Then I started to add a cue to the routine: I'd raise my arm and she would rear up onto her back legs. However, I very much doubt I could have got her to do this if we had been under pressure or on a movie set where she could have been distracted by a foreign environment. And it is not something I would encourage inexperienced people to try, because reading an animal's body language incorrectly can be dangerous. Animals react quickly, often instinctively; a situation can turn nasty very easily.

Over time I also taught Angel to bow and to lie down. But I wasn't just teaching her—I was hanging out with her and enjoying her company, having fun, and training her came naturally out of that pleasure. Even today, I still get a kick out of communicating with animals, out of knowing that we understand each other. I really enjoy spending time with a new animal and seeing them begin to trust me and want to be with me. As with Angel, whenever I am working or just hanging out with my animals, I feel comfortable and I often don't notice what else is going on around me.

CHAPTER 3

# Fancy Pants

Ever since I first started looking after animals, I have wanted
to provide a nice environment for them. I will happily wash
out a water trough, clean up poo, pull out weeds, clean tack,
anything that makes it more comfortable for them. As a child I
thought these things were all part of the fun of riding and being
with the animals; it wasn't until I was older that I realised that
many people saw only the riding as fun, not being with the
animals and caring for them.

One day in 1985 Julie's then boyfriend rang me at home and
told me that some land nearby was being sold. The lady who
owned it had dementia and she had a paddockful of skinny little
ponies who hadn't been well cared for. The RSPCA had been
called in and the ponies were in need of rescuing—would I be
interested in taking one? I thought, 'Wow, that would be so cool.
But I've got two horses—I can't be having another pony, can I?'

I called the RSPCA and asked them how much it would cost.

They told me they were just looking for good homes for them; if I could take one, it would be free. I instantly agreed to take one; not long after, this tiny grey pony arrived. I called her Fancy Pants, because of the way she acted when I first put her out in the paddock with the other horses at Tisa's—she went crazy, prancing around and carrying on. She was a very pretty little thing, but she was half wild, so I had a pile of fun taming her.

I'd had her delivered to Tisa's thinking that she could just slot into the free agistment arrangement I had going. But Tisa brought me right back down to earth—there were no more hours in the day when I could pick up poo, so I would need to pay for my new pony's feed. The stark reality was that I simply did not have that kind of money. I'd thought that I could rescue Fancy Pants, but that dream was fast dissolving.

However, I knew Dad had money. I had never before asked him for anything, but now, desperate to keep Fancy Pants, I wrote him a letter. I told him as briefly as I could about the situation I found myself in. I explained that I still had my first pony, Candy, whom I would never sell and Mum had promised I never would have to, but that I had grown out of her and bought another horse, Angel, whom I wanted to do some eventing with. Then I had been given the opportunity to save a little pony from the RSPCA; but in all of this, I hadn't really thought through how I could afford it. Would he be able to help me?

He said yes, and every fortnight for a year he sent me a cheque for thirty dollars. The first couple of cheques came with a little note which said *Love, Dad*, but after that he must have organised it with his secretary because the accompanying envelopes were written out in a lady's handwriting, with only a cheque inside and no note.

Those cheques helped me look after the horses, and with lots of other things too. I thought, 'Wow, what do you know? You don't know what you can get until you ask.' I was really glad for that and I felt grateful. If he ever asked to see me again I realised I would need to make an effort to.

When I told Mum that I had written to Dad and he had sent me a cheque she just said, 'So he bloody well should.'

So I was able to keep Fancy Pants. I knew she was unbroken and I had never seen anyone break in a horse from start to finish.

I had never mouthed a horse—teaching it to respond to having a bit in its mouth—but I had used my intuition and instinct to quieten horses and build a bond between them and myself. I would run my hand down a horse's leg and teach it to pick up its foot as a response to touch, and get it used to being handled all over. I had taught Angel to have some manners and some respect for my personal space.

Using some of the methods I'd learnt for myself over the last few years, I taught Fancy Pants to stand still when asked, to be gentle when being hand-fed, and never to show aggression towards me or treat me like I was lower in the pecking order. Eventually I got onto her back. If she didn't cope well emotionally with that, I would get off and handle her from the ground some more. If she misbehaved I would reprimand her with my voice; and I would reward her with my tone and soothing physical contact if I thought she felt uncertain and to encourage desirable behaviour.

I had a lot of fun breaking in Fancy Pants, but then I

wondered what I was going to do with her, I already had two other horses to ride.

In the end I sold her to a really sweet girl who lived just up the road. Her name was Isla Fisher and she would later become an actor and marry the British comic actor Sacha Baron Cohen. Isla used to come and hang around with me, wanting me to give her pony rides just as I had once followed Freda. I sold Fancy Pants cheaply because I was happy for her to have a home and for Isla to have her first pony. I wasn't a horse dealer; I was a kid who'd seen one of my beautiful dreams come true—rescuing an undernourished skinny thing, turning her into a plump, happy and broken-in pony, and finding her a great home.

Candy and Snoopy continued to be my best friends, until they both passed away in my eighteenth year. Each time it was a heartbreaking loss. Both of them had helped me through my childhood, more than words can ever explain. But little did I know what more was to come.

## CHAPTER 4

# Love and loss

Study was never really my thing, but I had made up my mind to work with animals and the conventional line of thinking was that if you wanted to be paid to work with animals, you needed to be a vet or a zoologist. Both these careers meant going to university.

I had battled through high school hoping to achieve the marks needed to get into either of these courses, but I didn't get the chemistry mark I needed for a vet science degree. Instead I gained entry into an agricultural diploma at Muresk Agricultural College, ninety kilometres east of Perth, thinking it would be a stepping stone into a veterinary course, and into a career that I was sure I'd love—working with animals.

In October 1988, Mum went travelling for a few months to have a much-needed break from raising us kids. Julie and I stayed behind at our Darlington house; we were joined there by my boyfriend, Paul Stanley, and Tamzin Lloyd, who had been a friend of mine since my earliest days at pony club. This was a bit of a steep learning curve for four teenagers. But Anita, Paul's mum, helped by teaching us how to look after ourselves. We suddenly had to grow up and be self-sufficient.

Paul was my first love. We were young and we sometimes talked about getting married, with him building us a house where we would live happily ever after. He was the youngest of Anita's three boys, and he absolutely idolised his eldest brother Mark, a seasoned boxer who was planning to train for the next Olympics.

At the beginning of the year, before my diploma course was due to start, I had been exercising racehorses for a trainer. But I had an accident when the horse I was riding reared, hit the side of my head with its neck and knocked me unconscious; then the horse flipped backwards onto me. When I regained consciousness and tried to pick myself up off the ground, I noticed my right leg wasn't working—a terrible pain hit me and I saw my leg was bent as if it had two knees. I had suffered a compound fracture of both bones in my lower right leg, which had to be encased in a metal external fixture for six weeks, to realign the smashed bones; then I was in a cast for another six weeks.

Freda was now living in Gundagai, south-west of Sydney where she had just become engaged to a fourth-generation farmer, Bert Nicholls. Because of my injured leg I deferred my diploma; with some time on my hands I decided to fly over and visit her. I had been there for a few weeks when, out of the blue, Paul, together with his two brothers, Mark and Dean, and Mark's girlfriend Roslyn, turned up in a little yellow Ford Escort van. They'd just crossed the Nullarbor Plain so they stayed for a few days; when the time came for them to get back on the road, Paul asked me to go along with them. Though I was initially hesitant, because it was such a small vehicle, I jumped into the van.

Mark was a very dominant elder brother. He had suggested a trip around Australia because he wanted to spend some time bonding with his two younger brothers before he started into more serious training for the Olympics. As plans progressed, he had invited his gorgeous girlfriend Roslyn along as well. There was only seating for three people in the front of the van so a mattress was laid out in the back, which two of us had to lie down on and share with Mark's bull terrier, Seb, who suffered terribly from wind. It wasn't the most pleasant trip.

Nobody wanted to spend any money (not that we had any) and Mark made all of the decisions, for all of us. Typically, he would pull up at some sort of park and we would pull out sleeping bags, doonas and whatever bedding had been stuffed into the back and camp out on the ground. By the time we had reached Townsville, I could no longer cope with Seb's flatulence, with the cramped conditions and the seemingly constant rain, as well as the condensation in the little van.

It had been raining for days. In the evening we pulled up just before town, and the boys broke into a sports hall. I didn't feel comfortable with that at all—I thought it was a really wrong thing to do. But they just wanted somewhere dry to sleep. I slept in the van with Seb that night, while the boys and Roslyn slept in the hall. I knew then and there that I didn't want to be in that environment anymore.

Leaving them to head home was difficult. Paul was torn between his brother and me, with Mark trying to get him to stay. But Paul finally decided to go with me, and we caught a succession of buses over four days and nights to make it back to Perth.

We returned to the house at Darlington and began to get back into our old routine. But shortly after we arrived back, something horrific happened. The phone rang just after dinner. It was Paul's father. I couldn't hear what was being said, but I could tell the news was bad.

Mark had been electrocuted. They had been picking fruit in Cairns and staying in a caravan. Mark was showering in the caravan when Roslyn heard him cry out her name. She rushed in and found him lying in the shower recess with a burn mark on his chest from the detachable metal showerhead. Apparently the caravan had bad wiring and was not earthed properly. Roslyn called an ambulance immediately, but when they arrived they told her nothing could be done to save him. Roslyn and Dean left the car in Cairns and flew home with Mark's body for the funeral.

Seeing Paul and his family go through that tragedy, I thought I understood how they felt. Even though we'd had our differences along the way, Mark had been like my big brother too. I felt terrible that my last memory of him was the struggle over whether Paul would stay on or return to Perth with me.

After Mark was buried, everyone tried to go back to life without him. Paul himself fell into a big wasted heap—he drank a lot and it was horrible. I tried to support him, but it was really hard trying to help him to keep his head above water.

My philosophy on drugs and alcohol has always been zero consumption, and seeing Paul drink so much was soul-destroying for me.

As nerdy as it might seem, I've never been interested in drinking or taking drugs. My attitude is probably a result of the large number of unpleasant scenes I witnessed as a child. I saw lots of things from an early age that turned me off both drugs and alcohol; I was simply furious that anybody would willingly choose to inflict so much damage on themselves.

When we were teenagers, everyone started to drink. Many of them thought it was cool to sneak off from school at lunchtime and go and drink wine down at the river. At parties they would get extremely drunk. I felt angry and disappointed with my friends, and the more I came under peer pressure, the more I wanted to go my own way.

When people find out I don't drink they usually react in one of two ways. There are those who belligerently say, 'Oh, you don't know what you're missing,' and then there are those who say, 'That's the smartest thing I've ever heard.'

As an adult, I have never felt that I missed out. I don't feel that I need any sort of substance to relax, to have fun, to wind down. There has never been a point in my life when I have thought I might just try what everyone else is doing. It's just not for me.

# CHAPTER 5

# Snoopy Two

**M**um arrived back in Perth to be with us after Mark's death, but she was talking about travelling again for a while. She had fallen in love with Cairns in particular, the people and the place. In 1989, I started my diploma course at Muresk. I was again riding racehorses on weekends, and working as a barmaid at night to earn enough money to live on. I would drive down to the closest bank at Midland to bank my wages cheque each week.

One afternoon on the way to the bank, I was standing beside the busy Great Northern Highway waiting to cross, when I felt something on my foot and looked down. A little pup was sitting there; he looked to be about six weeks old. I thought, 'That's the cutest thing I've ever seen.' I picked him up and looked around to see who he belonged to. I asked people nearby but none of them knew where he'd come from. Finally one lady told me there was a pet shop in the nearby arcade—maybe he'd come from there.

Sure enough, when I went in, there were eight other pups just like him, though he had a different patch on his face. I went up to the sales lady and told her I'd just found this puppy right next to the busy highway. She thanked me, explaining that she'd had all the puppies out for a couple of little girls to look at; he must have walked out the door and they hadn't noticed. I handed him over, but almost as soon as I walked out the door, I thought, 'I want that dog!' By then it had been nearly a year since Snoopy died, and I hated not having a dog. Then I stopped myself—I was studying and I was riding racehorses and working nights. I didn't have time for a puppy.

But still I drove home thinking, 'I want that dog; I want that dog. Why did I walk away from him?' A struggle was going on in my head.

When I got home I told Mum the story and she said, 'Oh, for God's sake, go back and get it.' It was just before my nineteenth birthday and Mum handed me the twenty dollars he cost and said he could be my birthday present.

I drove straight back to the pet shop in my old white Holden WB ute. I couldn't drive there fast enough. What if someone else had already bought him? He was there; I paid for him and we walked out together. It was one of the best things I ever did.

Snoopy Two was a blue heeler–kelpie cross, but he had floppy ears, so there was something else going on there as well. He was a beautiful happy little mate and very well trained. He went everywhere with me, and everyone used to comment on how polite and loving he was. At the time I thought I was just lucky to have a good dog. But I now know that, because Snoopy Two went everywhere with me, he learnt boundaries. He learnt what were nice manners and what weren't—that was why he became .

such a polite dog. Yes, he had a lovely temperament, definitely, but at the time I didn't understand completely why he was so well behaved.

Snoopy Two taught me a lot about training, because he could communicate his feelings so well—he had such an expressive face. If I got grumpy at something he had done, I would tell him off. But he was so expressive that I knew when I had gone too far, because he showed me how upset he was.

A large part of being an animal trainer is trial and error. There's no way you can go out and become an amazing trainer on the first animal you train; it takes time and you learn how to read an animal as you go.

Snoopy taught me about how long and how regular each training session should be. I taught him to sit, lie down, stay, heel, jump over an obstacle or onto the back of the ute, and to never get down unless he was asked. I learnt from him how simple the cues needed to be. I would babble on in his ear and he would have no idea what I was on about; but then I would give him a simple command, like 'Get up', and he would understand immediately. No one showed me how to do this—I was just playing with my dog. He was having fun and I made a fuss, and you could see how proud he became of himself.

# CHAPTER 6

# Julie

In 1989 Mum went back to Cairns. Tamzin and Julie were still living at Darlington with me, but Paul had moved back in with his parents.

Julie had always been proud of me and my ability to handle and ride horses; she would tell people how good I was, and it made me feel good about myself. I was proud to be her sister as well—she was so popular and vivacious—and I felt more confident when we went to the pub or parties together. But at around this time she got a new boyfriend, Tim.

Julie's previous boyfriends had all been lovely passive guys. Tim was more assertive. Early in their relationship, Julie confided to me that she liked going to parties with him, knowing she would be looked after. Some of Julie's friends didn't like Tim and she didn't like some of his friends. They decided to go travelling around Australia, and one of the reasons was so they could have a fresh start together, away from other people's judgement. We talked about it and, although it was hard to see her go, I wanted her to be happy. I knew I'd miss her, but we were young and we agreed that in the near future we would get back together somehow.

They took off in Tim's ute, travelling north. Julie phoned after they had worked their way across the Top End, picking fruit and doing other odd jobs, and told me they were going to see Mum, as she had heard Cairns was beautiful.

When she arrived there, I talked with her on the phone and noticed that she sounded different, distant. She told me she was fine and not to worry—she was really enjoying spending time with Mum again.

Then she rang and told me she was coming back to Darlington, but she hadn't told anyone else. She planned to be home for her twenty-first, which was only a few weeks away. I was so happy. She was coming home!

Mum rang a few days later to tell me that Julie had been in an accident. I asked her what sort of accident. Mum's reply was short: 'A bad one.' I asked to speak to Julie, but Mum said that wasn't possible. My heart sank.

Mum explained that she was in a coma. All I could ask Mum was when she would be better—I didn't realise then how bad it was. Mum started sobbing and told me that the doctors were operating on her. I kept repeating down the phone, 'She'll be alright, Mum, she'll be alright.' I think Mum was in shock, but I kept thinking that this was Julie, my tough invincible sister— nothing was going to happen to her.

When I got off the phone from Mum I immediately rang Anita Stanley. When she and Paul arrived, I was walking in circles. Poor Anita kept hugging me. She of course had recently lost her eldest son. She held my hand and we waited.

Mum rang again to tell me Julie was out of surgery. She was still sobbing. The doctors had told her that, even if Julie did wake up, she wouldn't be the person we knew, as the damage to her brain was so extensive. They were going to take her off life support. I screamed and pleaded with her, 'They don't know! Don't let them, Mum! Don't let them tell you what to do!'

I was really angry and frantic. I felt the distance between Cairns and Perth even more than I thought possible. Mum kept saying to me that Julie wasn't there anymore, and I felt like I was dying inside. Anita and Paul held me as Mum kept saying quietly, 'She's coming home, darling, I'm bringing her home. She's coming home to you.' Then she gently hung up.

For the first time in my life, I was truly inconsolable. When Mum rang again I kept yelling down the phone, 'Is she dead? Is she dead? Is she dead?' I didn't want to give Mum a chance to answer as I couldn't bear to hear what I knew was coming.

Mum sobbed as she said, 'Yes, darling, she's there with you.'

I screamed back at her, 'No, she's not. She's not here! She's not here, Mum.'

Poor Mum—she kept trying in vain to tell me that it wasn't Julie lying there in Cairns, it was just an empty body. I didn't care—I didn't want to hear that. I would have held onto anything, even a lifeless body. Julie had always told me she would be there for me, and now she wasn't.

I learnt that Mum and Julie had been at a picnic lunch at the beach with a few of Mum's friends. One of these friends, Annie, had left some pottery in a kiln and so she and Julie decided to drive back to check on it. As they drove away neither of them had seatbelts on—Annie's ute was so old that there were no seatbelts fitted.

A drunk young man driving a sports car started to overtake them, but then he saw a four-wheel drive coming the other way and he pulled back in behind Annie's ute. Instead of waiting, he tried to overtake them on the inside, on the shoulder of the road, but he clipped their ute at the back and pushed them into the path of the oncoming car. Julie had hit her head on the front windscreen on impact and then on the back window of the ute. For a long time I was very sad, thinking about how scared she must have been in those last few seconds. I tortured myself by imagining what it was like. Annie had been killed at the scene of the accident.

Mum brought Julie's body back to Perth. We held her funeral, which went past in a blur. But I do remember that when we viewed her, one of her bandanas had been tied around her head—all her beautiful long brown hair had been shaved off. The make-up the mortician had put on her, trying to cover the swelling and discolouration on her face, was ridiculously wrong. I looked down at her and the only part of her I recognised was her hands. I wanted to touch her, but I was too scared that it wouldn't feel like her, that it would make it true; that Julie really was lying there dead.

At the end of the crematorium service, her coffin glided away behind the curtain. I wasn't ready for that—there was no way I was ready to let her go. I sat on the front of my chair and for a moment I considered standing up and going and stopping the coffin. But I froze, and sat there in horror watching her disappear.

Dad, Jan and the girls had flown over for the funeral. He sat with Mum, Freda, Bert and me at the front of the chapel; it felt odd—he had been such a minor part of our family. I barely acknowledged him. As we were walking out of the chapel, he came up to me and put his arm around me. I remember thinking, 'What do you want?'—not aggressively, but just because it felt so unfamiliar. It was such an extremely raw time for us all that I felt I needed love and comfort from people I was close to, and that wasn't him. He half whispered to me that he was sorry he had missed out on so much of our lives.

I had a sudden urge to be brutally honest with him, to tell him it was Julie who had wanted a relationship with him, not me, and he was too late. But I couldn't find the words to express my feelings so I remained silent. I was angry—I just wanted him to go away and leave me alone.

In the next few weeks, Mum, Freda and I were surrounded by family and friends who all wanted to help us in our grief. But they eventually had their own lives to go back to, and we were left alone to deal with the hideous empty space Julie had left in our lives. Mum was grieving while trying to hold me together. I was trying to lean on Paul, but he wasn't yet strong enough after Mark's death. I felt let down and it ended our relationship.

Tamzin moved out of our place. Tragically, she lost her own sister, Felicity, in a car accident on New Year's Eve. It was a strange and terrible coincidence that Paul, Tamz and myself had all lost an older sibling within a year. We each continued on as best we could but we all grieved very differently. Paul would get drunk and violent; I would sob and cry; and Tamzin seemed remarkably calm. As Paul and I grew apart, my friendship with Tamzin grew stronger. We understood each other's pain.

I didn't want Julie's ashes to be put into a wall, so we had purchased a plot to bury them in. Her plot was close to Mark's. I had to drive past the cemetery every day on my way to college. It was a difficult and messy time for me. I would go to her grave a couple of times a week and tell her that I missed her. I've not held onto a lot of emotion in my life—I am usually able to let it go. But I couldn't believe I was sitting at my sister's grave at the age of nineteen. However, after collapsing in total grief on the loose gravel beside her grave a few times, I tried to avoid turning into a blubbering mess at the cemetery—it was so hard to get back on my feet afterwards and to compose myself enough to get on with my day. From then on I tried to steer away from the emotions that took me to that emotionally unstable place. I could release all that at home in my bedroom, or when I was talking to someone about Julie, but not at the graveside. When I was there, I'd try to be matter-of-fact—just thank her for looking after me when I was scared or I'd tell her what had been happening.

It was a long time before I truly let her go. The denial, the grief, the fear of being without her—these emotions were so intense. I felt that by not letting go of her, by holding onto our bond, I could somehow keep her close. I felt that letting go was betraying her. I didn't want it to change.

The memory of her holding my face after Fred had left and saying she would never leave me was so vivid and strong. I held an image in my head of her saying that and it seemed to be stuck on replay. Time and again in my grieving process, I'd scream out, 'You said you'd never go! I know you didn't mean to go, but you said you wouldn't go!' I felt so messed up, and I didn't know who to trust. Abandonment was the dominant emotion I felt.

It wasn't her fault, obviously, but I used to think a lot about whether or not I should join her, which was a hideously scary thought for a teenager to have. I would think, 'What am I supposed to do, Julie? What am I supposed to do? Why did you leave?'

# CHAPTER 7

# Dad

At the end of 1990, I got my ag diploma from Muresk and was now ready to start a Bachelor of Science degree, hoping to get into veterinary science eventually.

Over the months, Dad's words to me at Julie's funeral had played on my mind. I'd be lying on my bed thinking of Julie and the thought would come into my head that maybe I should get to know him. I put it off, though, asking myself why I would bother contacting him when he hadn't bothered to get to know me.

My boyfriend at the time, Paul Pernechele, was shocked when I announced in bed one morning that I wanted to go and catch up with my dad. I explained that I wanted to get to know him as a person, that I felt I should do that for Julie.

By some kind of incredible coincidence, which still amazes me to this day, the phone rang in the middle of that conversation, and Dad was on the line. I think it was the first time he had ever called me. In my surprise, I told him that I had just been talking about going over to see him. He was quiet for a while, and I thought he was holding back tears when he said, 'That would be great, kid.' Then he explained that he had been diagnosed with lung cancer and that it had spread throughout his body. He said he would really like to see me as well. I went back to bed and told my boyfriend I was heading east. I knew it was now or never.

I flew to Gundagai to stay with Fred, Bert and their new baby daughter, Hayley, at their family farm. We would travel up to Sydney every weekend to spend time with Dad at the home of his best mate, John McGarry. Jan and Dad had separated at this stage and he and his girlfriend Leah had lost most of their money in the property meltdown in Queensland in the late eighties and early 90s, and then he had spent what was left looking for various treatments and cures around the world. None of them had worked, and he was now a very sick man.

John and his wife Coral were wonderful. They opened their home and their hearts to us all at a difficult time, and gave each of Dad's four surviving daughters time alone with him. I was grateful to be able to spend that time with Dad, and for some of the things he said to me. I felt I finally achieved closure before he died.

He wanted me to know that he was proud of me and he was sorry that things had been hard, both financially and emotionally, because he had left. He expressed his remorse for not having spent much time with either Julie or me; he particularly felt that he and I had had a very superficial relationship, which I agreed with, and he wished that hadn't been the case. He said, 'When you have children, they are a part of you, and even when you're not with them, you feel that you carry them inside.' He apologised for leaving it so late to try to change things, and thanked me for agreeing to see him. All of this was said between attacks of coughing and gasping, and he often had to lie back on the couch to regain his breath. Sometimes he had a tear in his eye, or a small smile on his face.

He and his girlfriend, Leah, had been living in the Cook Islands on and off for the last year. In early 1992 they headed back there. Ostensibly they were going because Leah was doing some work for the Cook Islands government, but we all knew that Dad wanted to die there. He loved the islanders, the weather, the fishing, the lifestyle—he wanted to be there at the end.

I will always remember the last time I saw him. It was so different from Julie's death, where we didn't get an opportunity to say goodbye. Freda, Bert and I went to see him at John McGarry's house. Our sisters, Cloud and Kate, had also come down from their home on the Gold Coast and he had an arm around each of them, both for support and out of affection. We said goodbye; as we drove away, I looked out the back window. I remember looking at him and thinking, 'You're done.' He could hardly stand up, he looked like a skeleton, and I knew it was the last time I would see him.

Bert was driving, Freda was in the front passenger seat and Hayley was beside me in a baby seat. I looked back one last time and saw Dad walking back into the house, still with an arm around each of the girls. I turned to face the front; Freda was looking at me and she asked if I was OK. I said, 'No. I kind of was—until you asked.' And then I started crying. I said I was scared. What if I wanted him in the future?

Then Fred said something to me that has stayed with me ever since. It is one of the things that I think of when times are tough. She simply said, 'Don't worry about the future.' I have turned those words around in my brain so many times, both for myself and when talking to others who are worried or scared of something that hasn't happened yet. Such simple words, but so precious.

I was still living with Fred and Bert when we heard Dad had died. It was a hard time for everyone, but I was dumbfounded at how upset Mum was. She was in Holland with her partner at the time, Alderbertos, a Dutchman she had met when he was backpacking around Australia. They were together for three years and would spend the European summer at his home in Holland, then fly back to Australia to avoid the European winter. I thought they were a match made in heaven, but eventually they went their own ways.

We called to tell her, and as I listened to her sob, I realised with some shock that she still had love for Dad—it revealed to me the intensity of the love they had once shared. I found some peace within myself to realise that they had shared real love at some point.

Leah brought Dad's body back from the Cook Islands to Sydney, where his funeral was held. Then his ashes were taken back to Perth for a memorial service with his mother and siblings. I was the only one of his children at that service in Perth; it felt very strange—I didn't know most of the people there.

When the council had gone to use the plot next to Julie's, they had hit a shelf of granite rock so they had abandoned it and started another row. Now, when Fred, Leah and I approached them and asked if we could purchase that plot and pay to drill through the granite to place Dad's ashes there, they agreed. We buried his ashes in the plot right next to Julie and I have always felt good about that—she finally has her dad.

CHAPTER 8

# Taking risks

With everything that had been happening, I decided I didn't want to be starting another course—all I wanted was to work with animals. As luck would have it, I saw an ad on TV for the newly opened Warner Bros Movie World on the Gold Coast; the ad showed a rearing palomino horse, and I thought, 'Someone trained that horse, and I want to meet them.'

I had also become worried about Cloud and Kate—they were only eleven and nine and they had just lost their dad. I wanted to hang out with Jan and the girls and maybe bring some happiness into their lives because I knew that, if Julie had been alive, that's what she would have done. I decided to go over and spend time with them. If it didn't work out, I told myself, I could just head back to Perth. So I deferred my degree for six months and made plans to head east again.

Paul Pernechele was very compassionate and supportive about my move, but he told me he wanted me to come back to him. I had to tell him there was no guarantee that that would happen.

He was a mechanic and he helped me get my ute prepared for the journey. He even organised for his brother-in-law, who was an interstate truck driver, to give me a lift to Melbourne. We loaded my ute onto the tray and he drove me across the Nullarbor Plain to the outskirts of Melbourne, ending up in an industrial truck lot where he unloaded my ute and unceremoniously left me and my faithful dog, Snoopy, to continue our journey. By then Snoopy was starting to get more miles under his belt than most people I knew.

I had no idea where I was, but we found our way to Freda and Bert's farm in Gundagai and stayed there for two weeks. I then drove the thirteen hours to the Gold Coast and moved into the lounge room of Jan's home. Jan was warm and welcoming, as she had always been. I think she was pleased to have some family company at such a difficult time for her; she was very supportive to me during a period when I know she was struggling as well. The girls were very excited to see me.

It was the beginning of a new relationship with my sisters and enabled me over the next twenty or so years to watch them grow up. I loved sharing their lives and spending time with them. It was also the beginning of a great adventure in my own life—of taking risks, travelling by myself and (I hoped) finding out more about animal training.

I saw a classified ad in the paper just after I arrived for 'casual chaperones' at Movie World over the Christmas holiday period. I had no idea what a chaperone was, nor what prerequisites were required for such a job, but, as Jan pointed out, it would be a foot in the door to the place with the rearing palomino!

I put in a résumé, along with two thousand other applicants, and twenty of us got interviews.

My wardrobe consisted of nothing but jeans and T-shirts, so Jan lent me some clothes for the job interview. On the day she even did my make-up for me. Despite being twenty-one years old I still had no idea how to even apply foundation or mascara; we all had a bit of a laugh about it.

Off I went to my interview. I was told that the role of the chaperone was essentially to act out scripts and to assist the visitors to Movie World at the various attractions. We were also involved with the parades and escorting the Looney Tunes characters through the crowds, often having to lead them through the public by the hand and have to be the actors' eyes, ears and voice as they were encased in cumbersome costumes.

As with most workplaces, there was a hierarchy at the park, with chaperones being seen as below the show and entertainment department, which included the actors, dancers and stunt performers. I knew I had the chaperone job as soon as I walked in; I was very confident and I just thought, 'I have a good feeling about this.'

Sure enough, a short time later I got a phone call. I was one of twelve successful candidates.

Work at Movie World started with one week of induction and orientation, where we were trained in public speaking and learnt how to present the spiels for the different attractions. I practised endlessly at home—I'm sure Jan and the girls could probably recite the scripts word for word to this day, after having heard me repeat them so many times.

One thing they drummed into us all that week was that we had to be happy, friendly and bubbly—the kind of people who want visitors to enjoy the experience that was Movie World.

I thought, 'Man, I've ended up in the right place—I'll be good at that!' By then I was sick of studying and I was thrilled to be finally out in the world.

On our first day of orientation, I asked a staff member where the stables were and they waved a hand vaguely and said, 'Somewhere over there.' When we finished for the day and were given our pass and uniforms, I went up to a staff door and with much excitement thought, 'I can go through that.'

I made my way to the stables where I saw a man driving a small green open-topped utility called a Gator; he was feeding hay to the horses off the back. I walked straight up to him and said, 'Hi, my name's Zelie Thompson and I'm looking for the boss of the horse department.'

'That's me, I'm Tony,' he said.

'I'm so happy to meet you—I've come all the way from Perth to meet you.'

As I explained my interest in working with animals, his polite smile widened into a grin that covered his big friendly face. Tony Jablonski was in charge of the horses and involved with their training for the Western Action stunt show. He is still involved with Movie World with the RM Williams Outback Spectacular and from that moment on he has always tried to help me in any way he can. He was the first person I'd met (other than vets or zookeepers) who was paid to work with animals.

I volunteered to work at the stable outside my normal hours. I'd turn up there hours before the park opened and do anything I could, whether it was taking rugs off the horses or assisting Tony to train a horse. Then, in the afternoon, when I'd finished chaperoning for the day, I'd get changed back into jeans and go and help out some more.

Chaperones' shifts were rotated so we worked at all the different sites around the park. I particularly used to love the days when I was rostered on at the Western Action show. I thought it was so much fun. The Western Action stunt show was an American-style cowboy and Indian knock-'em-down theatrical performance, with larger than life characters and lots of comic relief. Actors and stunt people played the characters, but it was the live animal action, the horses and dogs, that really excited me.

To my utter surprise, on about my third roster the show's stunt coordinator walked up to me and asked if I'd like to train to be in the show. He said they needed a spare Calamity Jane for the holidays and that he'd heard Tony mention me. Something weird happened to my voice and I said, 'That would be great!' in a falsetto. I was transferred permanently to the Western Action stunt show and from then on I became one of the Calamity Jane performers.

As well as my role as Calamity Jane I also performed alongside the beautiful down-to-earth country and western singer Lee Kernaghan. Back then he was just starting out—around the time he released his first album, *Three Chain Road*—and during the school holidays he had a gig at the Western Action arena. I played one of his 'ute girls' in the show. The ute girl would drive a ute into the arena and stop, get out and walk towards Lee while he sang about the tough decision he had to make, because his girl was jealous of his ute and he had to choose between them. He is a lovely guy.

Working in the Western Action show meant I was working with stunt people. Approximately half of them were already involved in the film and television industry. Our work day began, before the park opened, by catching a bus from Movie World to a local gymnasium, where we were required to work on our strength and fitness. When we returned, we would usually attend rehearsals and then all have lunch together. I wanted to learn everything I could.

Soon after starting in the Western Action show I decided I wanted to be a stunt person too. I thought it was a whole lot of fun—not easy but fun—and it seemed second nature to me. I began training with the 'stunties' to become a qualified stunt performer, doing weekly sessions in gymnastics and trampolining. I really enjoyed all the recommended courses, such as precision driving, abseiling, rigging and scuba diving.

Once I'd done this training I was graded as 'Stunt Action Personnel', which is similar to an apprenticeship. It allowed me to do bit parts, action roles and doubling roles for film and television. To be graded as a fully fledged 'Stunt Actor', you have to show competence in five areas of expertise—heights and body control, water, vehicles, animals and fire. As a child and teenager, I had only had exposure to animals and some limited gymnastics, but now I made the most of the opportunity that had presented itself and learnt everything I could in all those different areas. Many stunt roles include some acting, so I also took acting classes.

At the time, Mark Eady was a stuntman in the Western Action show. He'd started in the business as an actor, and had then decided to do a bit of stunt work to get more acting roles. I enrolled in one of his acting courses and it changed my life. I found myself out of my comfort zone several times. It was an interesting process that eventually led me to think, 'What's the worst that can happen?' You might be embarrassed, but you learn it really doesn't matter, because everyone else is in the same position.

People have often asked me how I had the courage to do certain things in my career or approach people at certain times. I simply say that sometimes it could be intimidating, embarrassing or even a bit weird, but I reminded myself that people don't think any less of you in the end.

It had been great living with Jan and the girls, but I knew I couldn't stay on their loungeroom floor forever and I also wanted to find somewhere with a bit more land so I could bring my mare Angel across from Perth. She was now pregnant, having jumped over two fences to visit a friend's Arabian stallion. I started looking for a place with Melody Brutnall, a stuntwoman I was working with. We found a gorgeous rental property on two acres at Creekside Court in Worongary in the beautiful Gold Coast hinterland, about half an hour south down the Pacific Motorway from Movie World. It was a bit scary having to pay so much rent, but it was such a great house and location that we easily found people who wanted to move into the other two bedrooms. I had a home at last.

Life was so exciting; so many terrific things were happening. And then my heart well and truly went to another—I started going out with Grahame.

# CHAPTER 9

# Angel's Halo

Grahame and I were the same age. He was in the Police Academy stunt team. We all found him hilarious, especially when there was a bit of a crowd and he was playing up to it. His dry sense of humour and perfect timing often had us all laughing out loud. As we laughed he would smile quietly, sitting back with his barrel chest softly chuffing as he held back his own laughter. It was his rugged good looks and humour that attracted me to him at first. And his walk—I loved his walk. He moved with purpose and energy, and the more I saw of him, the sexier I found him. I was in love, and it was wonderful to feel so complete again.

Once I got involved with Grahame, he moved into Creekside Court fairly quickly, as he had endured a volatile separation from his previous partner; she had cut up all his clothes, plus a couple of belts, and left them on the front lawn of the house they had shared.

Grahame wasn't only cute, he was also very good at what he did, which always attracts me to someone. We had fun together and he was a fantastic help with my stunt training. I wasn't particularly good at stunt or precision driving when we first met, but Grahame came along to my training sessions; he would egg me on and encourage me when I was learning something new. He sometimes drove alongside in another vehicle so I had someone to drive against. He also taught me about working with fire—he loved that area of stunt work—and with body control; we practised together daily on our mini trampoline.

But his real speciality was heights. He had very little fear of heights, and he used to goof around on high things, enjoying seeing people's nervous reactions. I couldn't watch. I often told him I didn't like it, but he couldn't understand why. To him it was no different to walking along the ground. He said that he never got to the edge of a building and experienced vertigo or a falling sensation—he felt perfectly safe.

Grahame had wanted to perform stunts ever since he was a kid. His photo albums were full of pictures of him trying to do daring things, like back flips on an old BMX bike or jumping out of a tree onto mattresses. At twenty-three, he had already worked on several movies and various television productions, and he had spent a lot of time and money on training. Collin Dragsbaek, my housemate Melody's boyfriend, was our stunt trainer and one of Grahame's best friends. He told me once that he had been very proud watching Grahame develop over the last couple of years and that he knew there would be much more to come. He felt Grahame had really made it. Collin and Melody eventually had a little boy together, but three years later Collin was killed performing a stunt in a high fall off a concrete wheat silo in the movie *Love Serenade*. It was a big shock to our close-knit stunt community.

Grahame and I began to talk about getting married, but we were a bit unsure. A lot of the time we both thought we were too young to get married—we were just having too much fun being big kids. Then we'd say, 'Well, we are twenty-three—we should probably get married. That's when everyone gets married; better not leave it too much longer.' But we could never quite make up our minds to do it.

We both wanted three kids, a horse, and a motorbike each. He had a really nice road bike and he wanted to get me one, but I was having way too much fun riding on the back of his. He was a talented motorbike rider and he was a show-off; I loved it and he knew I loved it.

We would sometimes go to work on his bike, me sitting on the back with my arms around his waist. At a set of traffic lights it wasn't uncommon for him to tap me on my hand and say, 'Hang on,' from which I'd know we were about to go an impressive distance on the back wheel. That sort of thing was a thrill to both of us. We were young and ready for everything. I usually made a half-hearted effort to act responsibly, but he knew I adored and applauded his craziness. He wasn't egotistical and he wasn't big-headed—just a whole lot of fun.

Of course, it wasn't always perfect—like any relationship, we had our ups and downs. He knew my opinion on alcohol and I hated it when he drank too much. He sometimes did stupid things when he was drunk, like hanging from the rafters by his toes, and he could become obnoxious and a smart-arse.

Early in our relationship, before he moved in with me, we almost split up. He had a couple of rostered days off and was going nightclubbing in Nerang with one of his housemates. I had work the following morning so I didn't go.

He called at about two in the morning. When I answered the phone, half asleep, he said, 'Hey, babe, it's me.' He was clearly drunk. I informed him that it was two in the morning and his response was, 'Yep, yep, sorry about that. Anyway, can you come and get me?' When I asked where he was, he said, 'Oh, just at the lock-up.'

'Where?'

'Just the lock-up in Southport—you know, where police hold people until someone can come and get you.'

Now I was very awake. My heart was thumping. I thought he must have been beaten up, because I felt certain he couldn't possibly have done anything wrong. I asked him if he was OK.

'Oh yeah, I'm fine,' he said. 'I just had a little accident on my bike.' I gasped. He went on, 'But I'm fine. The police just brought me here because that's what police do.'

I could feel the anger welling up inside me. 'You were driving your motorbike while you were drunk?'

'Yep,' he admitted.

That was it. I let fly. 'So you were riding drunk and you call me, when you know my sister was killed by a drunk driver.'

'Yep, yep, sorry about that,' he slurred in response. 'Would you be able to come and get me?'

I tried to calm myself down. 'Oh God, tell me what happened.'

'Well, I didn't do anything wrong. I went around a roundabout and this loser came around the corner in his SLR or something, completely on the wrong side of the road, and ran into me.'

'That's terrible.'

'I know, I know, and then he got out of his car and ran off.

So when the police arrived, I was the only idiot there, and they took me in. It wasn't my fault; I've told them it wasn't my fault. They have the rego of the car and everything.'

After I hung up on Grahame, I woke my housemate Tina and told her what was happening. She asked what I was going to do and I said, 'I guess I'd better go and get him.' She told me I was mad. As I left, she rolled over to go back to sleep.

When I arrived at the Southport lock-up forty-five minutes later, Grahame had fallen asleep. The police had to wake him up to get him out of the cell. I could hear him as they came down the corridor—he was being vile, obnoxious and arrogant to the police. When I looked through the reinforced window, I could see him staggering and pulling at the policemen, who each held him by an arm. I thought, 'What am I doing here?'

When they finally made it through the door, he yelled out, 'Let go of me!'

One policeman looked at me, shook his head and walked off; the other one looked at Grahame and said, 'Sign here, cowboy.'

Grahame took the pen and signed with a big cross as if he was Zorro. He threw down the pen and went to walk off.

'Yeah right, mate,' the cop said. 'Not so fast—sign it properly.'

Grahame said, 'What? What?', pretending he hadn't heard.

The cop tried again. 'Mate, we need your signature here or you're not allowed to walk through those doors.'

'That's my signature,' Grahame slurred.

The policeman leaned over and said slowly, 'I need a signature—not a mark, a signature.'

'That's it, that's it,' Grahame kept repeating. He could hardly keep his eyes open. I was ready to punch him, but finally he signed and we got out of there.

As we drove along, I really told him off; but halfway through the lecture I realised that he was snoring in the seat next to me. He'd totally passed out. So I dropped him off at his mate's place in Nerang.

On my way home I saw his motorbike on the side of the road, smashed up. By the time I got home it was about five in the morning. I woke up Tina again and asked her to go back there with me and help me lift his bike onto my ute, because I couldn't lift it by myself. The whole way there, she was lecturing me about him being a loser and that, if I kept seeing him, she'd move out of the house. All I could say in return was 'I know.'

We arrived back at the roundabout to find two guys already there in Iron Maiden T-shirts and with long greasy hair; they were lifting Grahame's bike into the back of their ute. I stopped so I had my headlights on them, then got out and walked over towards them.

'How you going there, fellas?'

'Uh, hi,' one of them replied.

'That's my boyfriend's motorbike.'

'Oh yeah, right,' the talkative one responded. 'We were just going to, um, take it down the copper shop.'

'Oh right—that's nice. But could you lift it onto my ute instead? That would be really great.'

So I had these two guys lift it onto the tray of my ute, much to Tina's amusement. When we got back to my place, I backed up to a slope and Tina and I pulled it off the back and just threw it down, leaving it where it fell. By this time I was late for work and angry.

But of course he wormed his way back into my heart.

Grahame and I started to make a home together at Creekside Court. By then I had brought Angel over from Perth—I wasn't going to let her become a mum without me. I had Snoopy Two with me, we had a cat one of my former housemates had left behind, and I now gave Grahame a pet lamb, which he called Bart.

Grahame was very excited about my love of animals. He didn't ride horses and he didn't know much about animals, but when he met me and we became so close, he wanted to know more. He totally adored Angel.

Because of his enthusiasm I decided to buy him a lamb for Christmas. I didn't know how it would go down, so I didn't give it to him right away. First of all, I presented him with just a baby's bottle wrapped up—he was a bit confused by that! Next I gave him a big bag of powdered milk I'd got from the produce store. Finally, I took him outside to where Bart was sitting in a box with tinsel around his neck. Grahame totally loved it—he was blown away.

I was a little concerned about how a twenty-three-year-old stuntman would react to this gift, but he was like a little kid in a candy shop. He loved playing with that lamb, putting on stupid voices, rolling around on the grass with him. Of course, Bart soon grew into this huge sheep and became our yard mascot. He was a beautiful big fat thing who used to go everywhere, except onto our bed.

Bart was a character. He liked to chase people or head-butt them. He was playful, not wild or crazy, but the stories people told about Bart got bigger and more outrageous as time went on. Grahame loved it. It became a joke at work that we had an attack sheep.

On rostered days off together, I'd often go with Grahame out to Warwick on his bike so I could practise trick riding with Graham Heffernan. We'd met Heffo at Movie World when he was brought in to teach trick riding to some of the stunt people. He brought with him Elijah and Moses, his two paint horses (a solid stock-horse type with distinct brown and white pinto markings). We'd spent two weeks practising on them, and once again I thought, 'This is for me!' I remembered learning about vaulting all those years ago at the pony club. Now, with Heffo's training, I was able to incorporate trick riding into my role as Calamity Jane in the Western Action stunt show. Trick riding can best be described as gymnastics on a fast-running horse. It orginated in America as a rodeo sport, where judges gave fifty per cent of the score based on how the rider performed and the degree of difficulty per trick, and the other fifty per cent of the score was based on how fast the horse ran.

Heffo had recently broken up with his wife and trick-riding partner, and he was keen to train someone else to perform with him. Whenever I could, I'd grab my trick-riding shoes and we'd head up to Heffo's. Grahame would watch us train, or go for a ride on his bike while we practised. Heffo and I trained and talked.

He told me about a woman he considered a trick-riding legend—Connie Griffith. Connie was renowned for being the world's most capable and athletic female trick rider. She had sufficient strength and skill to do many of the tricks that are usually only performed by men, and was able to perform many jaw-dropping tricks including 'Under the belly', when the rider leaves the saddle, climbs down one side of the horse's body, goes underneath the galloping horse and climbs back up the other side. The 'Billy Keen Drag' showed her incredible strength. She would sit backwards and grab the back of the saddle, push into a handstand as the horse was galloping along, and while still holding onto the saddle, lower herself down behind the horse's tail with her feet dragging in the sand, she then pulled herself back up with her stomach muscles and was again sitting back on the horse. She also performed the 'Ted Elder Drag', which was the same as the Billy Keen but went even further with the rider's head going between the horse's hind legs in the drag, with the use of extension ropes attached to the back of the saddle so she could be dragged further back. One of the most impressive tricks she performed was while in a full shoulder stand with her head on the horse's neck and shoulder, she put the horse over a one-metre-high jump shaped like a half moon. She sounded awe-inspiring. I knew I wanted to meet her one day.

In July 1994, Angel gave birth to an adorable chestnut filly. She had a big blaze, like her mum, and she had white 'lipstick', which extended from her nose snip around her lips, including the corners of her mouth and under her chin. Grahame and I called her Angel's Halo. With this beautiful new foal, our little family of animals was growing.

Grahame and I had a very nice little domestic life going on. On our rostered days off, we'd go and party in Surfers, or ride out to Heffo's. It was the first time I had felt I had a routine and some kind of normality. We had our own little world, we had our own dreams. We thought we'd live happily ever after together and be successful stunt people.

Even though we rented the house at Creekside Court, it felt very much like ours—our space, our animals, our adventure together. It was a really fun safe time, and I guess I felt the way everyone feels when they think they have found the person they want to spend their life with.

# CHAPTER 10

# *Ocean Girl*

Once I was graded a fully fledged Stunt Actor, I went to my first union meeting with Grahame. It was held in a large auditorium. At that stage, I didn't really know anyone outside of Movie World. Chris Anderson, a well-respected stunt coordinator, was sitting just behind us with his assistant, Mitch Deans, both of whom would later become our good friends. We could hear Chris and Mitch speaking behind us and Grahame whispered to me that he thought they were talking about me.

Finally they leant over and introduced themselves. I was so excited to meet some actual stunt coordinators that I became giggly. I had quite long hair and Chris asked if I would mind cutting off a few inches. I didn't understand why he was asking such a question but Grahame kept urging me, 'Yes, yes! Say yes!' Somewhat bewildered, I said yes, and Chris laughed and asked me to come to his office the following morning for a meeting. That was the beginning of my stunt career outside of Movie World and what a start it was.

My first job as a stunt performer was in a new Jonathan M. Shiff children's television series, *Ocean Girl*, with the possibility of the role continuing for more than one season. I was to double the lead actor, fourteen-year-old Marzena Godecki, whose character could swim like a dolphin, powerfully and fast, and whose best friend was a humpback whale. It was to be shot out on the Great Barrier Reef at Port Douglas, near where Mum lived in Cairns, with some studio work in Melbourne.

Many people were very excited for me, though some were jealous. Most of my peers at Movie World counted themselves lucky if they got a day on a television series or half a day on a commercial, and here was I, a lead double on a prominent series that employed a lot of people. It was an exciting start to my career. Grahame was incredibly proud of me.

I had such a fantastic experience on all the series of *Ocean Girl*, but particularly on the first one. That was when I found out how well film production companies look after you. We were accommodated in self-contained apartments or expensive hotel rooms, complete with swimming pools and gymnasiums. I was young and enthusiastic and I was having so much fun and getting paid well. I'd never really had that sort of money before and I was very good at saving it. I was thrown in at the deep end, but it was a fantastic way to learn about the film industry; I was literally an information sponge, asking whoever I could about all aspects of the film industry, wanting to know everything from various job descriptions to questions about different camera lenses. I was having the time of my life.

Port Douglas made the most beautiful backdrop for the series—the Great Barrier Reef, beautiful waterfalls and of course the Daintree rainforest. We were sometimes out on the reef for five days at a time; rather than coming back in, we would sleep out on the boat. On that first series, the boat was a medium-sized ocean-going cruiser, with tiny cabins below on either side. Each cabin had two sets of triple bunks, which didn't leave much room. The galley and sitting area was located between the cabins, with a shower and toilet under the back deck. With all of the crew working on deck with scuba and camera equipment, it was very cramped, but it was a great adventure.

One Friday afternoon we were on our way back to the jetty at the end of a day's filming. We were all tired and were looking forward to getting back to our apartments and relaxing for the weekend. Just as we were coming in, someone asked me, 'Isn't that Grahame?' I looked and there he was, standing on the jetty. He had a very distinctive way of standing—one leg slightly forward, resting and looking very cool at the same time. I was pleased to see him, but there was something strange about him arriving out of the blue.

When the boat pulled in, I jumped off and hugged him, then introduced him to all the people in the crew he didn't already know. He told me he'd come to spend the weekend with me and I was so excited.

We went out to dinner with a few of the crew and then returned to my apartment. When we were alone, he looked at me and told me he had something to tell me. My heartbeat filled my ears. I knew someone had died. All I could think was, 'Not Snoopy! Please, God, not Snoopy!'

He told me that Angel had been put down. My initial relief that it wasn't Snoopy was overtaken by a wave of grief. I was so upset; I had been so close to that horse. I couldn't believe it, because she'd been lively and healthy the last time I saw her.

He told me that our neighbours had come over because he had told them he was worried about her; then they had called in a vet. Angel had apparently retained some of the foetal membrane after Halo's birth and this had caused a toxaemia that had poisoned her. When Grahame discovered how seriously ill Angel was, he couldn't get hold of me because we were out on the reef. Before she was put down, he called out another vet for a second opinion. The second vet agreed with the diagnosis, and Grahame had no choice but to have Angel put down. It was pretty tough on him; he knew how much I loved that horse. He told me that a friend of ours who had raised an orphan foal before was caring for Halo.

I had never heard of a retained foetal membrane before this, and I didn't know how to check the afterbirth or the placenta to ensure it had been expelled. After Halo was born I had phoned a local vet, to see if there was anything I should do. She had only asked if they both seemed OK and if the foal was drinking. Checking the foetal sack and placenta were never mentioned.

I cried a lot as I lay in Grahame's arms; I told him I was sick of feeling like this. My head was resting on his beautiful strong chest as he told me that he'd never before known anyone who had had so much death in their life but that it was going to stop now. He knew this would be the last one. There would be no more death—I had had my share and it was going to stop.

I believed him; I wanted to believe him. We talked about raising Angel's foal together and told each other that everything would be fine, with all our animals and with our lives together.

# CHAPTER 11

# Grahame

Twelve days later I was at the hairdresser's in Port Douglas, having my hair lightened and re-permed for my role in *Ocean Girl*. But instead of a production runner coming to pick me up, as was usual, the production manager arrived. I thought that was a bit weird, but she told me the runner was caught up doing something else.

She then drove me back to my hotel room and insisted on walking me in. I didn't understand what was going on. My front door suddenly opened and Mitch Deans was standing there; Mum was just behind him. Mum had obviously been crying and when I saw that my heart thumped in my ears—*kaboom, kaboom, kaboom*.

I walked in, anxiously demanding to know why she had come up from Cairns and what was going on. She could only repeat one word: 'Darling'. Filled with dread and foreboding, I asked, 'Who is it?'

Not for one minute did I think it could be Grahame. But then she softly said his name.

I was stunned. I yelled out, 'Who? Who? Who is it?'

And she said, more loudly, 'Grahame.'

'Is he dead?' I yelled at her. I still couldn't believe it.

And she sobbed, 'Yes.'

I spun away from her and tried to run for the door. But Mitch grabbed me and held me tight. I remember punching him and screaming, 'No!' Ultimately we collapsed at the bottom of the nearby stairs and I sobbed into his chest, while Mum rubbed my back. I could hear her crying as I half sobbed, half yelled, 'No, no, no.'

I felt as though I had been sucked into a vortex and was the only person left on earth; it was as if everything around me had vanished. I don't remember the trip from Port Douglas to Cairns, but when I got there they had already packed up my things for me. At Cairns airport I became hysterical and violent, and had to be restrained by security; I was given some sort of sedative, which made me nauseous.

They had cleared out most of business class for us and I remember trying not to scream or make a scene. All I could think was, 'Where am I going? What am I going home to?' I just wanted to go home, but I didn't know where home was. Was it where Grahame and I had lived? Was it Darlington?

We arrived at Brisbane airport and they collected me in a wheelchair and wheeled me away with a sick bag on my lap. Someone asked me where I wanted to go. It was the same question I had been asking myself, and I just didn't know. I was driven back to Creekside Court with Mum.

Ironically, Grahame had died in a high fall.

He was with a bunch of mates on the Gold Coast. They had gone out to the casino that night and then went back to a friend's apartment at about four in the morning. The apartment was on the eleventh floor. Grahame had hopped up to sit on the balcony rail, and somehow he slipped backwards. As he fell, he tried to right himself and grab another balcony rail on the way down, but he couldn't.

It was less than two weeks since I had lain beside him and he had told me that I had now had my fill of death and it was all going to stop. I had believed him. I had wanted to believe him and I had told myself that everything would be fine.

Aside from the grief, shock and despair, I now felt that I could no longer trust anyone. It wasn't that Grahame was supposed to be right all of the time; it was just that what he had said made sense. It was what I had wanted to hear.

# CHAPTER 12

# Killing myself

At Creekside Court the time leading up to Grahame's funeral was a blur. I must have had a few more sedatives during that time, and when Tamzin arrived from Perth (she was now a trained nurse), I told her I didn't want any more drugs. She agreed, saying it was just putting off what I had to live through.

I knew that grieving for Grahame was going to be hard and I was still grieving for Julie. Grahame's death came close to pushing me over the edge.

I had no concept of time. I remember Mum freaking out about me not eating or drinking. I remember my hissy fits. I remember Tamzin telling me I smelled and both of us laughing about it. I remember Tamzin telling me I had to drink water and me drinking some through a straw. I remember not wanting to have to go through the grieving process again—it was all too hard.

Fortunately, there were always people around. I found out later that my one-in-a-million friend, Diane Rainnie, whom I loved working with at Movie World, had put up a visiting roster in the staff area so I would never be alone. If it wasn't a staff member, it was one of their friends or family members.

If I had been left alone during that time, I don't think I would be alive now. I remember, clear as anything, thinking quite matter-of-factly and unemotionally that I'd have to wait until everyone had gone back to their homes before I could take my own life. Then I would try to think of exactly how I would do it. It was very stressful, but I remember just wanting to escape from the grief.

One of the things I worried about was whether killing yourself got you out of that feeling or whether you took it with you. I remember asking a couple of people what they thought, but I didn't ask too many questions because I didn't want to draw too much attention to my suicidal thoughts.

My thought processes, obviously, were not that stable. But sometimes they were very clear, and then it all became so unbearable that I would break down again.

When you grieve you go numb, then stupid, then hysterical, then numb. A good friend and colleague of Grahame's, Glenn Suter, a lovely married man with a deep faith, was so supportive and compassionate. Once, after we'd had a big crying session, I looked into his eyes and asked him to tell me what he thought about suicide. Not what his church thought or what he had been taught—I wanted to know what he himself thought.

He was hesitant and very careful with his answer. 'My church thinks one way, but I don't feel like talking about that right now. Don't think I'm condoning this, and I certainly will not help you with it—I'm here to help you get through this, not to escape from it. But, in all honesty, Zelie, I have to tell you what

I feel in my heart right now—I think that, if you killed yourself, God would say, "I gave her too much grief to cope with; I was a bit careless with that one—I will look after her now."'

That was a precious thing to say to me and I remember feeling a little bit of shame and guilt. I began to think, 'Life is not all about you, Zelie.'

About six weeks after Grahame's death, I woke up one morning with that familiar wave of grief crashing over me and the feeling that I just wanted it all to end. But then I began to feel so sad for everyone. Not for me, but for Mum, who had already lost one daughter, and for Freda, who had already lost one sister. And then I realised I couldn't hurt them all over again.

My sadness became very intense as I imagined the grief they would feel when I died. But then I thought, 'Hang on—I haven't done it yet.' So I sat up and thought, 'Oh my God, I care!' It was like I'd been hit by a truck.

I don't know how long that process took, but I went from sadness to intense grief to shock and then to true horror when I realised that I was trapped—I had made the decision to live. And it was then that I cried for myself, realising I still had to go through this process. I wondered how long it would last. Would it get worse? Would it get better? But then I made myself go and feed Halo, or play with Snoopy. That was my way out—I thought of something fun I wanted to do. I thought, 'I'm spent, but, if I'm still in the world and I haven't killed myself, I may as well do what I feel like doing.' It didn't matter if I couldn't make it across the floor before collapsing in a sobbing mess;

I had stopped that destructive thinking. It slowly became easier to do something fun, and such distractions stopped the destructive process.

Distraction—focusing on things that made me happy—helped me. But I can't say for sure that it would help someone else in a similar situation. When I hear of people who have attempted suicide, I don't necessarily think that I have the solution for them, but I certainly understand what they are going through. I just want them to hang in there, because who knows what life has in store just around the corner.

I'm very lucky, and I've had a very lucky life. In particular, I was lucky at this stage of my life to have so many people babysitting me so vigilantly—by the time the babysitting stopped, I was starting to climb back out. I had begun to get glimpses of having fun again.

When Grahame died, I felt that I'd been left behind, but it wasn't that I wanted to die with him exactly. Recovery was a very gradual process and there were times when I hung onto fear-filled memories. But, as I began to let go of things, it became easier.

My advice is to live for the moment. Find a tiny spark of happiness—a memory that once brought you joy and maybe still can. Choose to focus on that tiny spark, or else you will remain in despair. That tiny moment of remembered happiness can grow and grow and grow as you keep focusing on it.

Not long after Grahame died I decided to bring Halo home and raise her myself. I thought it would be good for me to have something to do. I had a foal that was also possibly grieving for her mum. I would look after her and comfort her. She became my main reason to get up and go outside.

The house continued to be full of people—so many offered to come and support me. One of my close pony club friends, Jean Wearmouth, came all the way over from Perth to babysit me. She told me she wouldn't leave until I was better.

In the middle of all this, Mum suddenly received a call from Perth telling us that Harriet Lemann, with whom we had lived in the Porongurups, had died in a car accident, leaving two little girls without their mother. Mum and I decided to head back to Perth to be with the family, and Jean offered to stay on at Creekside Court to look after the animals.

Harriet's memorial service was held on the top of Wattle Hill, the property where we had all lived together at the Porongurups. It was a lovely service and everyone was in reasonably good spirits as we made our way back down to the old house after her ashes had been scattered. But when we got there, a phone call came through for me from Jean. She was hysterical, and I could hardly understand her.

At first, I thought she was saying the foal had broken her leg, and I asked her to repeat herself, slowly. Halo had broken her leg; the vet was there; and they had just put her down.

I don't know why life is so unpredictable, or why some people have to endure so much heartache. Many people around the world find the answer in their chosen religion; some people believe in karma and others believe things happen for a reason.

I don't fully trust any of those theories. What I have become expert in is working out how to deal with certain circumstances.

Even though we don't have control over deaths, tragic events, car accidents and so on, we can choose how we want to live. It's not that I'm a stranger to sadness; in fact, I think it is very important that, if there is sadness, you allow yourself to feel it. Don't try to suppress it. I have allowed myself to express sadness along the way—to cry openly, without being embarrassed or self-conscious—and I think that is one of the key strategies that has allowed me to work my way through it.

I don't allow my emotions to build up, one on top of another. I think the loss of Julie triggered my ability to be like that— because that experience was so horrific and occurred fairly early in my life, I didn't care how anyone judged me. I didn't feel that I had to hold myself together when I grieved.

# CHAPTER 13

# *In Pursuit of Honor*

People were telling me to get back to work, that it would help with the grieving process, but I didn't want to go back to Movie World—there were too many memories. Still, after Harriet's funeral I flew back to the Gold Coast.

When I returned, Jean told me for the first time that she and her husband Dave had been fighting. Now she wanted to stay on the Gold Coast; she enjoyed people treating her nicely for a change. She was offered a job at the Movie World stables and kennels helping with the animals, which she happily took.

We moved out of Creekside Court, because of the memories and because the rent was getting too expensive. I moved in with Mark Eady and his girlfriend Geraldine; Mark had become a good friend after the acting course I did with him, and Jean rented a room near Movie World.

I was talked into working on an upcoming Don Johnson film, *In Pursuit of Honor.* They needed horse grooms to look after the three hundred or so horses. At the time I didn't even feel like getting out of bed, but everyone urged me to take the job; they said it would get me out of the house, out of my thoughts.

This was my first job on a movie, and it was here that I met two people who were to become very important in my life, Heidi Mackay and Wayne Glennie.

Pre-production—all the planning, building and rehearsing that needs to happen before filming can begin—was at Biddaddaba, just inland from the Gold Coast. When I first arrived, I didn't want to talk to anyone—I was there to do a job and that was it. There was a bunch of wranglers and grooms I hadn't met before and a couple of people I knew already from Movie World, but I wasn't there to socialise.

On the third day I was paired with a petite blonde girl to muck out a large paddock the horses had been in. She was annoyingly chatty and I felt like saying to her, 'Can't you see I'm not interested in talking to you?' But I couldn't be bothered, and just tried to ignore her.

Then we both arrived back at the wheelbarrow at the same time and she said bluntly, 'I heard your boyfriend died.'

I looked at her, wanting to ask her if she was right in the head. I managed to get out, 'Yeah, he did,' then turned my back on her and walked away, thinking she was an idiot. Everyone had been tiptoeing around me and the subject of Grahame; I couldn't believe anyone would be so insensitive.

We kept working. The next time we met at the wheelbarrow she said, 'The reason I mention it is that my dad just died too.'

I turned around and looked at her, and there were tears in her eyes. I said, 'I'm very sorry to hear that.' But again I walked away, not wanting to be friends.

When we met up at the wheelbarrow for the third time, she asked, 'How did he die?' She obviously wanted to talk about it, and something now stopped me turning away. She was grieving too, and I empathised with her. From that day on, Heidi and I were inseparable.

She was a couple of years younger than me, and so innocent. Even though I was in a horrid place as well, I wanted to say to her that it would be OK. She wanted to talk about Grahame, and I ended up talking about him so she wouldn't feel so alone. I don't think I would have opened up to anyone else at that particular point, but Heidi's need for comfort and my hope that I could make her feel better started me talking. In that way the grieving journey became a bit easier for me. I relaxed a bit more, instead of blocking everyone out and thinking no one else could understand.

Wayne Glennie was a polo player who had managed to land the job on the film of taking the horses between locations, using a flash Chevy pick-up and a horse trailer he'd hired off a mate at the end of the polo season. The other horse trucks were just standard jobs, but Wayne was driving a very nice truck that was comfortable to ride in and—more importantly in a humid Queensland summer—was air-conditioned. Heidi and I used to jostle to get in his truck and Wayne would joke about us being his own personal grooms, calling us over as though we were a couple of beer wenches, and we'd play along, giggling as we went.

Towards the end of that movie, I talked to Wayne about what I was going to do next and he offered me a job as a polo groom. I didn't know anything about polo, but it was another professional horse job and I could tell Wayne was a nice guy. At the time, Wayne and Jean were both looking for a place to live, so they became housemates not long after meeting each other, and they got on really well too.

Jean continued to work at Movie World, but I don't think she particularly liked anybody there. All the people I thought of as friends she found Gold Coasty and superficial, not at all like the Perth scene she was used to. She didn't really fit in and I think she missed me when I was away on that film.

After a few months Wayne and I started seeing each other and he was a great support for me, without expecting any long-term commitment. I warned him that I didn't want anything serious; I had sworn to myself that I didn't want to fall in love with anyone ever again—it hurt too much. Wayne was four years older than me, he had twelve horses of his own, he was a professional horseman and he ran his own business. It was now twelve months since Grahame had died and I missed physical contact. Wayne was just what I needed. He was such a perfect healer—a big warm teddy bear. There were no promises and no pressure, but tons of spontaneity and a life full of animals again—stuff I felt I could deal with.

The experience taught me another important lesson. When I felt like I was drowning in grief and there was nothing else for it than to give up, I just let go. I stopped needing to feel in control. I don't know if that would work in every situation, but my advice is that, when you're consumed by that feeling of wanting to control your life, to bring back everyone you've lost and to make it how it was before—just let it go. That's what I have done every time something has turned bad.

# CHAPTER 14

# Jean

The third series of *Ocean Girl* started and the producers asked me if I was ready to come back as the lead stunt double. They had used another stunt double for the start of the second series when I hadn't initially felt up to it, but I eventually went up to Port Douglas to shoot some of the scenes towards the end of that second series, after working on *Pursuit of Honor*.

I headed to Port Douglas once again. Filming went on for several weeks, and both Wayne and Jean came to visit me at different times. After we finished filming in Queensland, the unit had to head to Melbourne for some studio work. While the film trucks drove back to Melbourne—a journey of two or three days—the cast and crew were allowed to fly off to our homes for a couple of days.

Wayne organised a barbecue so I could catch up with everyone for the short time I would be there. Mum flew in from Cairns. I was shocked and hurt when Jean phoned and told me she couldn't come because she just didn't feel up to it. I tried to insist that she come, but she wouldn't be swayed. She promised she'd see me the following day.

We had a great party. Late that night there were a few people left singing on the veranda when the phone rang. It was Jean. She was crying. I kept asking her what was wrong and she finally said she had done something stupid, but she wouldn't tell me what she had done. She just said that she was sorry, and that I was the only person she wanted to talk to and apologise to.

My heart sank. What did she have to apologise for? I eventually got out of her that she had slashed her wrists.

I felt great fear and confusion. I kept her talking for a couple of minutes and then I asked her to hold on for a moment so I could go to the loo and that I would be straight back—could she wait? She agreed.

I knew Wayne had been drinking, but Mum had gone to bed early, so I ran down the hall and woke her up, gave her the keys to Wayne's Pajero and asked her to go over to Jean's as quickly as possible. Mum reacts well in a crisis situation, and she quickly woke up from her deep sleep and took off.

I went back to the phone and kept talking to Jean. She and Dave had got married just after Julie died; I had been her bridesmaid, but things hadn't turned out well. At the time, I had felt that their marriage was wrong. They had a strange relationship, where they would call each other cruel, destructive names all the time. The name-calling didn't even stop when Jean was living on the other side of the country. I had also noticed that she would constantly put herself down, unlike the Jean I used to know.

I told her on the phone this sort of relationship wasn't worth it. She told me it wasn't because of Dave—fuck him, she said, and I could hear the anger in her voice. But then she sighed and said that it was her—she was just useless.

There was finally a noise in the background and then Jean was yelling, 'No, no, no!' and I heard her drop the phone. Mum picked it up and said she was with Jean, and that she would bring her to me. She hung up.

Mum managed to bandage Jean's arms. She told me later that when she went into the bathroom it looked like a war zone— there was blood everywhere. When she went to get a towel, several were soaked with blood. Jean refused to let Mum take her to hospital but agreed to come to my place.

When they arrived, I made Jean show me her wrists; I didn't believe she could have done anything like that, but she had. Wayne and I couldn't sleep; the two of us lay on top of our bed hugging Jean, who lay between us. She was limp and ashamed; she was at rock bottom. She kept saying that it was because of me that she wasn't dead. I asked her to think about how her death would have affected her mum and the rest of her family. She said she knew they would be devastated, but she felt that they would somehow cope without her. Everything I asked her, she had an answer to. She said that there was simply nothing to live for anymore, and she was in debt to the tune of seven hundred dollars, of which two hundred was owed to Wayne.

Wayne couldn't believe it. He said he didn't give a shit about the money. He would have said the same thing even before he realised how depressed she was—she was our friend and you help friends when they need you.

Jean was a proud independent woman and she calmly told

Wayne she couldn't take his money. I then asked about her dog and she said that she knew I'd look after it. I think she could see I was starting to struggle—what she was saying felt so familiar to me. I was looking into her eyes and thinking, 'I know where you are and it's not a nice place to be.' I knew that when you're that low nothing anyone says can make a difference.

Then she said to me, 'Can you think of a reason I should wake up tomorrow?' I couldn't think of anything to say to make her think, 'Oh yeah, good point,' and that was awful. I ended up saying, 'Yes—me. Don't you do that to me.'

She said, 'That's why I'm here.'

I didn't really care what the reason was, as long as she was still alive. I had to fly to Melbourne the following day and I told her that I wanted her to come with me. She said no, she had work at Movie World. I yelled at her, 'Bugger Movie World!' But she argued that she wanted to pay back the money she owed—how would she do that if she wasn't working?

We argued back and forth. I offered to pay for her flights, and the accommodation in Melbourne was all paid for; I told her it would be fun. But she wouldn't buy into any of that. She explained that she found the thought of us having to save her torturous.

I argued that I wouldn't be able to relax if we were apart. She had come and helped me when I was at a low point, so why wouldn't she let me help me? In the morning, Mum offered to move in with her, but she wouldn't have that either.

Finally, we agreed that Wayne would check up on her every day, and she and I would speak at least once a day. I flew out to Melbourne that morning, still worried but glad that we had a babysitting arrangement in place.

About a week later, Jean's housemate called and asked for Wayne. I thought that he must want a hand moving something, so I gave him Wayne's number and hung up. I didn't think for a minute anything could be wrong with Jean, because I'd had a good conversation with her the night before. She had seemed so happy. We had already spoken during the day, but she rang again that night to tell me Dave had finally agreed to a divorce and it meant she was free. She was on top of the world, saying she could take back her maiden name and that she didn't have to be associated with that man anymore. She could get her life back and she could start all over again.

The coroner estimated her time of death to have been about midnight, two hours after we had had that phone conversation. She had asphyxiated herself by connecting the hose from her vacuum cleaner to her exhaust and filling her car with carbon monoxide.

My biggest fear was that she hadn't meant to kill herself—that it was an attempt to get attention that had gone wrong. But then I read the letters she had left behind.

One was to her landlord, apologising for owing him money; one to her parents, thanking her mum for everything and apologising if she was hurt; one to me, saying she hoped I understood and could forgive her and asking me to look after her dog. The final one was to her husband Dave, five pages of pure venom.

Wayne and I took her body back to Perth for burial and I did the eulogy. I remember seeing Dave at the funeral, wearing large sunglasses and a black suit. He looked straight at me, but I looked away because it was too much.

When I looked at him again, he was still staring straight at me. I started making my way towards him, not knowing whether I was going to punch him or hug him. He watched me coming closer and his chin started to quiver. I put my arms around him and he hugged me back very tightly and sobbed.

All of a sudden, I heard Jean's voice say, 'Can you let him go now, please.' So I let him go, turned away and walked off.

Jean had severe self-worth issues, and she was going through depression, loneliness and despair; but I know that life can change very fast and I wish she could have survived to see that. Since then, I have pined for Jean and wished she was here to share so many different things with me. Several times over the years I have known that she would have been the perfect person to fill various positions. Such a waste. I miss her.

CHAPTER 15

# Sled

I've taken a lot of risks in my life, and I've found they usually pay off. Sometimes I've taken those risks because I was in grief and I thought, 'What the hell—what have I got to lose?'

When I returned to Melbourne after Jean's funeral, I returned to *Ocean Girl* producer Jonathan Shiff's beautiful family home to stay with them for a while. I was very lucky because it would have been hard for me to be going back alone to a hotel room every evening.

When filming was completed, Jonathan was still worried about me and he asked if I would like to travel to North America with himself and Marzena, as her chaperone on a promotional tour; *Ocean Girl* had been sold to Disney Channel and was to be released that spring in America.

Wayne was terrific about it and encouraged me to go, so I said yes. It was only for ten days, and we spent the whole time in Los Angeles. It was great fun; we stayed in a lovely hotel in downtown LA and they spoilt us rotten. Both Marzena and I were quite new to the industry—I was twenty-four and she was fifteen—and they dressed us up in ridiculous teenybopper clothes so they could film us walking along a Californian beach in winter. We were freezing. When we weren't busy, they sent us off shopping with a limo driver.

Early in our stay, I decided to take another risk—I would ring the world-renowned animal trainer Paul 'Sled' Reynolds.

It took quite a bit of courage to ring Sled; it was the first time I had done something like this without any support. I'd at least had Jan and the girls there when I began work at Movie World. However, it was the beginning of a time when I took bigger risks and didn't care so much about what happened, because what did it matter anyway.

Sled's movie career went all the way back to the 1981 version of *Tarzan, the Ape Man*. He had also worked on movies as big as *Dances with Wolves* and *Indiana Jones*. At that time he had worked on about forty films, many of them very famous. I knew he had trained horses for some big films, but I was unaware that he worked with other animals too.

Just after Grahame died, Sled had come to Australia to work on *The Phantom Legacy*, a new attempt to put the famous old comic hero up on the big screen. Sled had brought four stunning Andalusian horses out from America for the movie and they were stabled in Sydney. At the time, Chris Anderson was one of the people who were worried about me. He told me that I needed to get my act together—I needed to start eating and getting fit again as he was planning on using me to double the female lead on *The Phantom Legacy*. During this time, Sled travelled around Australia meeting people and looking at other animals they could possibly use, so I heard a bit about him.

After millions had already been spent in pre-production, *The Phantom Legacy* was put on hold, as can sometimes happen. Eventually, it was filmed and released fourteen years later in 2009. When I knew I was going to America, I asked Chris for Sled's number, which he happily passed on. By now, too, I'd realised I didn't want to head back to Australia after the promotional tour—polo work didn't start for another four or five months and I thought this might be a good time to explore the United States.

I called Sled from my hotel room and told him I was an animal person from Australia who was really interested in meeting him. I said I had been disappointed when we hadn't met while he was in Australia. In reply, he was very direct, asking me what it was I wanted, so I told him straight out that I was hoping to meet him while I was in America. He asked if I was free to come out and visit his ranch—naturally, I said that would be great.

He then told me, to my utter amazement, that he had to take a zebra and a camel to a studio in downtown Los Angeles for a photo shoot the next day. He said he would swing past my hotel on the way back, pick me up and take me to his place for the day; one of the girls who worked for him could then drop me back after work. I almost fell over, I was excited about seeing a zebra and camel up close— up until then I had only been around horses, dogs and cats.

Marzena had interviews lined up so she didn't need me that day, and it all fell into place beautifully. I remember pacing in the foyer prior to his arrival. He pulled up in a cool Chevy pick-up (my dream truck) towing an amazing-looking aluminium animal trailer. I remember thinking, 'Wow, is this really happening?'

His girlfriend at the time jumped out of the passenger side. She offered her hand with a great big smile and said, 'Hi! I'm Deanne, really nice to meet you.' I felt a little relieved to know that a friendly woman was with him. I had begun to think that perhaps this wasn't the safest thing I'd ever done, planning to drive off with a stranger in a foreign country (hoping he wouldn't shoot me or rape me or cut me up into tiny bits!). But they were both very warm and I instantly felt safe; I had a good feeling about meeting these people.

As we drove away, I had to ask, 'What do you mean, a zebra and a camel? I thought you were a horse trainer.'

He smiled and said, 'Oh yeah, we do a bit of this and a bit of that.'

We drove for a couple of hours, chatting, before we arrived at Sled's ranch. As we drove up his driveway, we passed lions, tigers, wolves, a kangaroo, a small bear, and some other amazing animals.

We parked in his lot, and I looked around in wonder. There were about twenty dog runs and kennels in a U-shape. Along one wing of the U-shape were a few enclosures with three or four house cats in each. In the distance, I could see the most stunning Andalusians, Friesians and Quarter Horses in various yards with shelters. In another area, I saw long-horn cattle, a zebra and several camels. I was thinking, 'Where am I?'

Deanne gave me a tour of the place and took photos of me with all the different animals. At the end of the day, Sled told me that if I wanted to extend my trip to California I was very welcome to stay in the house with Deanne and himself as they had a spare room. They were both incredibly hospitable and it was a fantastic day. I was learning fast to take one day at a time, to enjoy and appreciate every hour I could. Later, as Sled had promised, one of the girls who were working there gave me a lift back to my hotel.

On another day, when Marzena and I had no commitments, Sled picked us both up and took us to lunch. He teased us, about pretty much anything—he knew we were just two young kids out seeing the world.

He drove us around all day, introducing us to people; it was such a treat for both of us. We went onto the set of *Batman Forever*, and I met the stunt doubles for both Batman and Robin. Marzena met Chris O'Donnell, who played Robin. She was horrified that I didn't know who Chris O'Donnell was, but I told her that I thought the stunt guys were very cute—I was more interested in them than the actors. Sled also took us onto the set of *Dr Quinn, Medicine Woman*, a western drama TV series, where I met a bunch of horse people and wranglers and trainers.

I told Jonathan about Sled's offer to have me stay. At first Jonathan was wary and asked if I was sure. Did I think they seemed alright? Did I want him to call Sled? He was like a protective father. I told him he was welcome to do so, but I didn't think he needed to as I felt safe. Jonathan accepted my decision. He had the production company change the departure date on my airline ticket; I could change my ticket again later if I wanted to. He also generously gave me five hundred dollars when we hugged goodbye.

Sled picked me up after the end of the promotional tour for *Ocean Girl*, and he and Deanne looked after me very well over the next three weeks. I just wanted to spend time with them; and I was lucky, as I caught them in the right mood and at the right time, when they had time to spend with me.

After my time with them, Heidi rang from the Gold Coast and said she was missing me. I told her I was heading for New York to visit a childhood friend, who had owned the patient horse 'Princess' from my childhood. I was taking the opportunity to explore a bit more of the US. Heidi decided to join me there and we later flew on to Dallas, Texas, in time for the Fort Worth Stock Show and Rodeo. It was cowgirl heaven.

We met and travelled with some wonderful cowboys and -girls, shopped for great western gear, and went to some of the world's biggest rodeos, before Heidi had to return to Australia. I went back to Sled's for the last few weeks before my three-month visa ran out.

## CHAPTER 16

# Movie stars and happiness

Iarrived back in Australia in 1995. I was now twenty-five, and I felt like a different person from the girl I'd been when I left. I had seen some of the world, and I'd briefly removed myself from the circle of grief. Sometimes in America it had seemed quite surreal—I would feel the depths of grief creeping in, but no one around me knew or understood what I was going through. So sometimes it was a scary place to be grieving and, as much as I could, I resisted falling into that state. But when I finally arrived home, I knew I still had stuff to work through.

Wayne picked me up at Brisbane airport. I was happy to go back into Wayne's world and work as a polo groom. It gave me an escape from the constant reminder of Grahame, although I missed many of my old friends from Movie World and the stunt world.

A few months after my return I decided I wanted to get back into the film industry and resume stunt training, but I was reluctant to do so in and around the Gold Coast, where every corner held painful memories of Grahame and I training together. However, I kept picturing myself working on movie sets. I believe that by imagining certain possibilities, you can make them happen. As if on cue, a Sydney-based stunt agency asked me to train with them and offered to represent me. I enthusiastically accepted and became part of their team. On training trips to Sydney I would either stay with friends or would be accommodated by production or stunt teams I was working with.

Wayne was very supportive and quite proud of me, I think, telling his polo mates that I was away on a movie somewhere, doubling some famous actress or being hit by a stunt car. Even though I wasn't at Movie World anymore, I also felt very supported by the people I knew there.

One of the films I worked on was *Dark City*, a sci-fi movie that has subsequently become a bit of a cult classic. I had my hair cut short and dyed dark red so I could double the lead actress, Jennifer Connelly. I was also the right height and build to have a prosthetic head, neck and shoulders attached to the top of my head for a scene in which one of the male actors is decapitated and then falls down the stairs. On days when I wasn't in front of the camera, I worked in the rigging team. It became my job to fit harnesses to the actors so they could be attached to the flying cables and rigging equipment.

This was my first experience of working with actors whom I had seen in other movies. It was fascinating for me to discover that William Hurt, Richard O'Brien and Keiffer Sutherland were nothing like the characters I had seen them play. I had teenage memories of watching Keiffer play a rugged cowboy in both *Young Guns* movies, and Richard had co-written *The Rocky Horror Picture Show* and played the quirky character Riff Raff. In my innocence I hadn't realised how well they could act!

*Dark City* involved three months of purely studio work at Sydney's Fox Studios in the middle of winter. As much as I appreciated the whole experience, I hated not seeing the light of day. Since then I've turned down jobs like that, because I know what it will be like and I'd rather be outside riding horses, or falling off horses, or just working with animals in general.

After *Dark City*, I worked on Bruce Beresford's *Paradise Road*, a film about a group of women imprisoned in a Japanese prisoner-of-war camp during World War II. There I doubled a few different actresses, including the lead, Glenn Close. It was a really fun movie because it was the first time I'd worked with an all-female stunt crew. We were beaten up by the Japanese guards, and we had to jump off ships and run through gunfire—I found it a lot more fun being outside, playing war, than cooped up in a studio.

As a stunt performer, what you do physically can either make or break the shot; particularly if it's a big set-up, there can be a lot of pressure on you. If you're at the top of a waterfall and you have to fall down it, say, you know you're going to ruin the shot if you start the drop unconvincingly or if you over-dramatise the descent.

In *Paradise Road*, we had to react to being hit with fake bullets. Timing was crucial for a realistic image. The special-effects team would rig us with squibs—a small explosion that goes off under the clothing to look as if you've been hit. There was padding under the squibs to protect us, because they can burn skin and cause bruising. Stunt performers 'pad up' whenever possible; however, sometimes wardrobe doesn't allow for this—for example, there was one time on a movie when I played a scantily clad prostitute who was beaten up and left bleeding on the bathroom floor.

Wayne was the perfect person to see me through that time in my life. He was secure, relaxed and non-judgemental, and I could come and go as I needed to. We spoke regularly on the phone, but sometimes several weeks would go by between seeing each other. Occasionally, if I couldn't get home to see him and the animals, he would catch a plane to wherever I was working and would enjoy his time hanging out on set with me. It was fun for both of us.

People often ask what certain movie stars are like to work with. Some are beautiful and others can be spoilt brats; the knowledge that a brat is starring in it will often ruin a movie for me.

One amazing actor I was glad I got to know was Kate Winslet. Lawrence Woodward, a stunt coordinator I had just worked with on *The Matrix* and some other productions, called me and told me he had a pretty good job coming up for me. I was to double Kate Winslet on the movie *Holy Smoke*, which was being filmed in outback South Australia. I said, 'Great, who's that?'

Lawrence laughed and asked, 'Did you see *Titanic*?' As usual, I didn't know who the famous actor was.

I went down to South Australia in 1998 and had an unforgettable time; it was one of the nicest jobs I have ever worked on. Lawrence is one of my favourite Australian stunt coordinators and he's a good friend as well. I respect his opinion and experience, and often call him for advice, with both financial queries and advice on the political issues that inevitably occur within our industry. He had put together a fantastic stunt crew for this job, and it was a terrific film crew as well.

I have wonderful memories of the camaraderie within the stunt team and the rest of the film crew. We looked forward to work each day; the atmosphere and attitude on set was both productive and a lot of fun. The script was quirky and unpredictable, and it was relatively straightforward hazardous action work, there were no cables or explosions. When we weren't doing something silly in a car or rolling down a hill, the stunt crew would go bushwalking or explore the dormant volcano near Hawker, a delightful South Australian town with lovely people.

Kate Winslet is beautiful. I loved that she couldn't care less about her weight—even though she wasn't at all overweight, she was being criticised in the Hollywood tabloids. She said to me that, having found herself in the public eye and therefore held up as a role model for young girls, she felt proud about the fact that she wasn't emaciated. I thought that was a pretty noble thing to say—maintaining a healthy weight and being a positive role model was far more important to her than what movie role she would get next. She was a good laugh, as was her co-star Harvey Keitel.

The actors I know are those I have worked with. So, when I see them in any role, I associate them immediately with the personal memory I have of them. This is also the case with other work colleagues. It can be a strong association, positive or negative. Many in the film industry feel they can't be choosy about the jobs they accept, but I want to enjoy what I'm doing, so I'm careful about who I work with. It's so simple—money is important, but happiness more so.

# CHAPTER 17

# Connie

With Wayne I saw a whole other world, which revolved around polo. I didn't think it was a particularly honourable world, but I had a lot of fun for a while and I met some lovely people. Some individuals spent vast amounts of money on their establishments and it was incredibly hierarchical, which I didn't like—the wealthy were on top and the grooms at the bottom. There also seemed to be a lot of non-horsey people wanting to get involved with that scene; they used the games as places for networking with the wealthy. Pretentious women would occasionally flirt openly with Wayne in front of me which I found revolting. The film industry can be like that as well, but I don't think to the same extent.

Fortunately, due to my stunt work, I didn't spend a great deal of continuous time in the polo world. If movie work in Australia was slow, Sled would often ring at an opportune time and I'd head off to America and help him out. He was always welcoming, and a lot of fun, and I found the work I did with him truly fulfilling. I was enjoying the stunt work and the success I was achieving with it, but my real love was still working with animals.

Sled was generous with his knowledge, and through him I met various people in the American film industry. I sometimes went to the Universal Studios theme park in LA with Sled's older brother Jug, who was the horsemaster for their Wild West show. One day Jug showed me some photos of him trick riding. There were photos of him as a nine-year-old standing backwards on a galloping horse, photos of him Roman riding two horses at a time, one foot on each horse. In one photo he was Roman riding while jumping both horses over a car. He talked about riding as a child with Dick Griffith and his wife Connie, and I thought, 'There's that name again'—Heffo had also spoken about Connie.

Dick had long since died, but Jug did some research and found out that Connie and her son, Tad, were trick riding in a nightly live show at the Excalibur Casino in Las Vegas. I was suddenly filled with a great urge to see them perform, so it looked like I was going to Las Vegas.

I hired an old bomb of a car and headed off on the six-hour drive. I was a bit scared being by myself—I didn't want to get run off the road and mugged by a lunatic. I knew that America, where many people have a gun under their sun visor or their seat, was different to Australia, and I'd been warned not to respond to any road rage—it wasn't worth it.

I made it to Vegas without incident and found a cheap hotel room. That night I turned up at the Excalibur Casino to see the King Arthur's Tournament show, where Connie was performing. I had no idea what to expect and was nervous about how I would go about meeting her, but now that I was there I wasn't about to beat a retreat. As it turned out, I was absolutely blown away by what I saw.

I had never seen a live show like it before, there were trick riding, jousting, fight scenes, all acting out the story of King Arthur and the Knights of the Round Table. At around the halfway mark, the trick riding commenced. In single file three women came galloping into the arena with fantastic energy. They each performed confidently, beginning their 'run' with a big smile, a clap or a wave. Then, before you knew it, one would flip upside down, hanging from the horse by one foot, her hands and hair dragging in the sand. Another would roll around to sit backwards on the horse's neck; then with a quick flick she would bounce down onto the ground and vault back into the saddle. Another stood on the saddle, both arms stretched out above her head, body arched backwards in an almost superhuman position. I watched in awe as these women performed smooth gymnastic moves on their beautiful fast-running horses. I wasn't sure which one was Connie, but I thought they were all incredible—what I had learnt with Heffo back on the Gold Coast suddenly looked simple and easy.

At the end of the show, I told the door staff that I would like to meet one of the trick riders. They advised me to leave a message at reception and then they ushered me out the door. I was outside before I knew it and had no choice but to head back to my dingy hotel, thinking, 'Damn it!'

I came back the following night and bought another expensive show ticket, but this time I cased out the staff on each of the doors until I saw a friendly-looking face. At the end of the show, I went up and introduced myself to her. I exaggerated a bit and told her I was there to meet Connie Griffith, and that I thought she was expecting me. The girl finished ushering the crowd out and then went backstage to find Connie for me, but she returned with an apology that the trick riders had already left for the night.

So I paid again for a third night, but this time I spoke to a different staff member before the show. I said I'd come all the way from Australia to meet Connie, and this time I said that I was pretty sure she knew I was coming. When the show finished, I rushed straight down to the front and the person I had been talking to said she would go and remind Connie. I stood nervously waiting, my heart pounding. What if Connie told the girl she wasn't expecting anyone? What if she didn't want to come out? What if she came out and told me off for lying about our meeting?

Finally, Connie came out. She had a small frame and a brisk walk. The sweat on her face had smudged her show make-up. I saw now that she was in her fifties, and yet she was still performing the type of gymnastics on horseback that I didn't know was humanly possible. I couldn't believe I was suddenly meeting a real-life hero of mine.

She said, 'Hi, how can I help you?' and I said, 'I don't know.' I tried to gather my thoughts and told her I had met Jug Reynolds, whom she remembered. I then explained that I had heard so much about her, and that I had done some trick riding and would like to do more.

At that point in my career I had no idea how exhausted you feel after a late night performance; she explained that she needed to go home and have a shower, but suggested I meet her at her ranch the following morning. She told me to visit about nine or ten in the morning as they rose quite late, and then gave me the address, saying she would see me out there.

She certainly would. I think I danced all the way back to my horrible, smelly hotel room.

The following morning I drove out to the ranch, arriving far too early. I sat out on the road in my car and waited for the clock to reach nine o'clock. Then I knocked on the door and Connie welcomed me in. We sat in the kitchen talking. There was a big pot of stew on the stove and she dished herself up a big bowl and ate it; then she dished up another big bowl and ate that too. I couldn't believe that this tiny little woman had just eaten two big piles of stew for breakfast!

She was chuffed that I'd come all that way to meet her, and now that she wasn't so tired she was very warm. When I told her where I was staying, she was mortified. She insisted I go back that day, get my bags, and stay in her spare room before I was mugged.

After my first night there, I woke up in the morning to a *tink-tink-tink-tink* sound. I opened the curtains to see Connie in a bikini top, jeans, chaps and boots shoeing a horse on the veranda, and I thought, 'Who is this lady—Superwoman?' I went out to join her; I didn't say anything, but I thought she was the coolest lady in the world. I spent the day helping on the ranch, cleaning out the yards, filling up water troughs, plaiting manes. Together we washed a couple of horses. I had the world's best day just being with her. We talked as we worked, and she said it was a shame her son Tad wasn't there. She told me that he was a better trick rider than her, and I thought, 'He must be something.' He was away in Mexico doubling Antonio Banderas on the first Zorro movie, *The Mask of Zorro*. Connie told me that she rarely trained people to trick ride anymore—Tad had taken over as instructor. She suggested that I come back another time to meet him.

But I had only been there two days when Connie got a phone call from Tad saying they had had so much rain in the area of Mexico where they were filming that the producers were sending everyone home for about ten days until it dried out. Tad and his girlfriend Wendy were leaving their horses in Mexico and coming home. Connie hung up the phone and smiled at me. She said, 'You just got lucky.'

I was nervous before they turned up, but when I met them I relaxed straightaway. Wendy is such a beautiful, bubbly, warm, friendly person. Tad was a bit more reserved at first; I think he was wondering who I was and what I was doing there. His mum and I explained to him that I was interested in learning more about trick riding, and he agreed to give me some lessons. Connie told him how much work I had been doing at the ranch and they never accepted any money from me for lessons or board.

I stayed with them for ten days, but it seemed like I'd been there forever. They made me feel so comfortable. I didn't like Las Vegas or Nevada (I didn't like the sand or the dry heat), but I knew I could live with this family, wherever they were.

The minute Tad turned up, so did everyone else; there was a stream of visitors all day every day—all kinds of different people, some of them trick riders camping on their way to their next performance. It was just a really thrilling place to be. Tad also did some animal training, which I enjoyed watching as it was different to how Sled worked.

That was an amazing turning point in my career. I am still so grateful for how warmly they welcomed me. I've been in plenty of beautiful homes with plenty of lovely people, but on the Griffiths' ranch we were all the same sort of people—it was as though we had grown up together. They seemed to like me and to be impressed with what I'd been through and with the fact that I'd got off my bum and gone to meet them. It was such a big thing for me—at last I was in the world I really wanted to be in.

## CHAPTER 18

# A place of my own

I returned from America and after almost three wonderful years with Wayne, I decided to end it. It was one of the worst things I have ever had to do. He'd helped me through one of the darkest times in my life and now I was hurting him.

He had half-jokingly talked about getting married and having kids, but I knew I never wanted children—after all the loss I had already been through the thought of losing a child was too horrific. I really did care for him, and, because I was so grateful to him, I had thought that the least I could do would be to marry him. But when I talked it over with Tamzin, she pointed out that gratitude was probably not the strongest foundation for a long-lasting marriage. So I ended it.

Breaking up with him was just awful. I knew I was crushing him and Wayne is such a gorgeous man. He had given me his whole heart, but after what I'd been through I think I had shut down emotionally—I truly didn't think I could ever love again.

Later in 1997 I headed off to Port Douglas for the filming of *The Thin Red Line*, to work for the first time as an assistant stunt coordinator. I went from *Paradise Road*, a war movie with an almost entirely female cast, to a war movie that had an all-male cast.

I went into the lunch tent late after a busy morning and walked up to the food table, where one other person was serving himself. Both of us reached for a spoon at the same time, so I said, 'Oh sorry, you go.'

He said, 'No, you go,' and we looked up at each other.

I thought I recognised him from somewhere—maybe another film we'd worked on—so I said, 'Oh, hi!'

He looked at me and slowly replied, 'Hi . . .', but he said it cautiously.

I asked, 'Don't I know you?' He said that he didn't think so. 'That's strange,' I said, 'because you look really familiar.'

At that he laughed and said, 'Hmm, a lot of people say that.'

'You've got one of those faces or something,' I explained.

'I guess so,' he said. I then asked him his name. 'Woody,' he replied.

'You mean, like Woody Harrelson?' I knew Harrelson was working on the movie. 'Do you know Woody Harrelson?'

He said, 'Yeah, that's me.'

I laughed. 'That's why you look familiar!' He could have been rude and embarrassed me, but he was kind instead. He seemed genuinely amused, rather than annoyed.

I said, 'Sorry I didn't recognise you,' and he said, 'It's quite refreshing actually.' We developed a good working relationship—and I did recognise him again after that first meeting in the lunch tent! Sean Penn was another actor on that film who I thought was a great guy.

When I arrived back at the Gold Coast from *The Thin Red Line*, I realised that I had nowhere to live. It wasn't a major issue as I was doing so much film work, and Snoopy and I could usually stay with friends, but for the first time in a while I felt like I wanted a home of my own, somewhere all of my animals could call home too. I had five horses agisted at Wayne's, three ex-racehorses, Bullet, Cassity and Tilly, a pretty paint gelding I called Avatar and a gelding Nakota bred by Wayne and me from one of his polo ponies. Jan had given me an Abyssinian-cross cat I called Cougar. I felt we needed a home.

I found a place in the hinterland at Maudsland, not far from Movie World, with beautiful acreage though in need of some work. I had just received an unexpected inheritance as a result of the recent death of my dad's stepmother—it covered a quarter of the deposit I needed. Mum, her mum and Freda each put in five thousand dollars to make up the balance of the deposit, so now all I needed was to convince the bank that I was able to make the repayments, which I thought might prove a little difficult because of my intermittent income.

Even though we'd broken up, Wayne was awesome. He and his polo patron, Johnny Fitzgerald, both wrote letters to the bank saying they would agist twenty-five horses on the property, which just covered the weekly repayments.

It was Wayne who helped me move in; he helped me move all of my gear and horses—he was wonderful, and still is. As it turned out, fifteen of Wayne's horses went to my property, but Johnny's didn't, so I still needed to cover the mortgage somehow.

Wayne didn't get angry after we split up until Alex moved in, and then he decided it was best to stay away from me for quite some time, which I thought was fair enough. I met Alex Kuzelicki through a mutual friend I'd worked with on *The Thin Red Line*. Alex was also a stunt person, specialising in acrobatics. He was a very good martial artist, dancer, writer, creative artist and filmmaker. He and I were very different, but we still had a lot of fun together.

Alex and I were in Nerang picking up horse feed one day in February 1998 when I received a call from Sled. All he asked was: did I want to go to Africa and could I leave the following day? A few times in the past he had rung with a work offer and only given me a week's notice, but this was extremely short notice. It was a Saturday and I was still sorting out my loan for the Maudsland Road property. I told him the earliest I could leave would be Monday night; he said he would have the girls book my flight for the Monday, and then he hung up. I looked at the phone, then turned to Alex and said, 'I think I'm going to Africa.'

Later that day I received a call from a girl who worked for Sled's company, Gentle Jungle, explaining that the job was on a big horse film called *Running Free* which was being shot in Namibia, and that I would be gone for four or five months. We were going to be in a remote community and she suggested that I take enough supplies of toiletries to last me that time because I wouldn't be able to buy anything there. My role would be as an assistant trainer, but not to Sled, which made me a bit apprehensive. I wondered who it would be; but then I thought, 'Who cares? You can't worry about the future.' The girl gave me my flight details, and that was all I knew.

Meanwhile I had been running over in my head how I could get away and leave Snoopy, five horses, a cat and a new mortgage. Alex had previously suggested he move in and he repeated that offer now. I said no, but I had to relent when I couldn't find anyone else at such short notice. I wasn't sure about it, but I just thought it would be a short-term solution, I was hesitant because I hadn't known Alex that long. I suggested he move out when I returned. He agreed, and Heidi said she'd also check the animals for me once a week.

When I arrived in Namibia, I learnt that Sled was the animal coordinator for the film; he told me I would be assisting the horse trainer, Bobby Lovgren. At the time, I didn't realise how lucky I was. The knowledge and skills Bobby passed on to me, and continued to teach me through the years, are largely responsible for making me the horse trainer I am today.

Part of the way through filming, I had a message on my phone from Wendy and Tad. Connie had passed away. I think it was two days before I could compose myself enough to call them back and find out what had happened.

She had died trick riding at an amateur rodeo. She was doing a trick that was simple for a rider of her calibre; she was seated backwards on the horse's neck and about to vault off when her pony slipped on a corner of the soft surface, dug up from the rodeo and barrel racing which had preceded the trick riding. Her pony had carried her in over six thousand performances and it was the first time he had fallen down. He came down shoulder first into the ground, rolling over Connie and crushing her. She died on her way to hospital, at fifty-six years of age. I was incredibly upset. I'd only known her a short time, but she was my ultimate trick-riding hero and a warm, kind-hearted woman.

Unbeknown to me, while Alex was looking after my home Mum was ringing to check up on things, and Alex told her he was missing me. Meanwhile I was having a blast working long hours in Africa with great people and I didn't have time to miss anyone at all.

Mum thought it would be a nice birthday surprise for me if she flew Alex out for a visit. When he turned up, he was offered a job in the grips department, who look after the equipment the camera is moved on. Alex stayed for the remaining three months of filming, but he did it tough and didn't have nearly as much fun as I did.

When we arrived home, I still wasn't planning on spending my life with anyone. I simply didn't want that domestic lifestyle, with any partner. I had resigned myself to a future with no partner or children, but Alex couldn't understand that. It was all too hard, and I let Alex stay.

I didn't want to go back to working as a polo groom, but I still wanted to work with horses so I started riding racehorses for trainers again to make money. Then in 1999 I received a call from Tony asking me to go down to the studios at Movie World to meet a man who was working with a tiger on an upcoming TV series called *BeastMaster*. Apparently he wanted to meet me and have a chat.

I hadn't done any work with exotic animals in Australia before—I hadn't even been aware that there were any big cats here outside of zoos or circuses—and I thought it sounded like fun. I dropped everything and went to the studios to meet Brenton Bullen.

# CHAPTER 19

# Bullen Bros

My initial opinion of Brenton was that he was a lovely man with a good sense of humour. I didn't know that he came from a circus background; I don't think I had ever heard of Bullen's Circus before. Brenton's grandfather Perc' had started Bullen's Circus in 1922, with just a couple of acts, which grew into one of Australia's largest circuses in the 1950s and 60s, and continued for three generations. Bullen's stopped travelling in 1969 but remained in the public eye with seven Safari Parks throughout Australia and New Zealand, and their famous 'Bullen's Animal World' at Wallacia in Sydney, which closed down in 1985. Their last Lion Safari Park closed not long after that.

Brenton wanted to know what experience I had with big cats and who I had worked with. I told him I wasn't a tiger trainer, but he said that was OK, because he wasn't looking for a trainer—he just needed someone who had been around them before.

He was stoked, because I lived locally and had some experience with tigers, and he asked if I could help him for the week. He wanted to get Sasha, the tiger, used to the sets and different environments, to see how she handled them before shooting started. I worked with him for a week and then he asked if I could help during the first week of filming. Before I knew it I was working full-time on *BeastMaster*.

*BeastMaster* was about a man who could communicate with all animals; with his animal friends, he would fight baddies and save damsels in distress. Both *BeastMaster* and another television series, *The Lost World*, were being filmed simultaneously on the Gold Coast by a joint Canadian and Australian production team. It was a good opportunity for me to gain experience not only with exotic animals but in paid stunt and trick-riding work as well.

After a couple of weeks of filming, I called Sled and told him what I was up to. After our phone call, he went away and did some research. He came back to me and said, 'Be careful—Brenton's from a circus background and they usually don't know the film business.' I now know what he meant—circus trainers are good with their animals in an environment where both the animal and its handler are comfortable, but taking them out of the circus ring and onto a film set can be a very different thing.

Sled was looking after me. He called regularly to check on how I was going and to remind me to be careful. He asked what the tiger was like. I said Sasha was lovely, a very gentle tiger, but that something weird was happening that I hadn't seen happen at Sled's place. The tiger would sort of bark at Brenton and he would jump back and stand there; eventually, the tiger would lie down and pant for a while, before getting up and making her way back to the trailer.

Sled swore. He could see how much Brenton didn't know. I asked him why Brenton allowed this to happen and he said, 'Because Brenton doesn't want to be eaten!' He told me to listen—I was not to get myself killed. Brenton and I were out of our depth.

But Brenton was careful, and because he knew his and the animal's limitations, he didn't get either of us killed. The smart thing about Brenton was that he didn't push Sasha to get exactly what was specifically outlined in the script. If the tiger didn't want to do something, filming would revolve around what she *did* want to do. If the script called for the tiger to stand majestically under a tree in the distance, they would make do with the tiger lying under the bush she liked. The script may have read that the tiger walked through or jumped over a creek, but if Sasha didn't feel like it, the script would be rewritten to read that she walked along the creek. The entire crew would simply adjust to suit the whims of Sasha the tiger.

With animal training, you get what you pay for. A Hollywood trainer like Sled, used to working under the pressure and demands of top directors, would have been able to ask one of his tigers to stand majestically under that tree, but he would have definitely been an expensive alternative to Brenton. However, I learnt a lot from Brenton too. He's not a Hollywood trainer, but he's a good animal handler, and he has a lot of compassion for his animals.

Over the years, I've been very fortunate to learn from many different people, in different situations, with different sorts of animals. One of the most important things I've found with animal training is to always be aware of how much you have yet to learn.

Fortunately, Sasha was a well-behaved tiger. She was very good with Daniel Goddard, who was the lead actor. But there were times when Daniel would become a little complacent with her. He would be caught up in the moment and he would squat down in front of her (making him seem smaller and more vulnerable); then you'd see her lift or lower her head, or she'd stop panting and start staring—all of that tiger hunting behaviour.

A lot of big cats, particularly lions, will take possession of things—maybe a ball, a bit of carpet or a bone. They can even take possession of a piece of ground. They also have a tendency to lock onto something or someone. When they have gone into this instinctive hunting mode, you need to know what to do to get them out of it. Thankfully, Sasha was a very good tiger and was easy to distract. Brenton would say, 'OK guys, I just need to take her for a walk.'

Safety is paramount when dealing with any animal, but particularly something that can kill you. There were certainly times when we had to have our wits about us. If Sasha was suddenly in a foul mood, she might threaten one of us. If she wanted to be left alone, we would give her some space and let her go back to her trailer, which was her personal territory. She'd go in there and we'd roll the canvas cover down over her enclosure to give her some privacy, if that was what she wanted, then walk away and leave her—you didn't go in there with her, ever.

We always carried canes and pepper spray as a precaution. Sasha was always on a very thin rigging cable with a high breaking strain—if it ever appeared in the shot, production would colour it out afterwards. Sometimes we would attach a double cable to her, with me holding one cable and Brenton holding the other. That way, if she went for Brenton, I would hold her, and vice versa. Tigers are strong, but Sasha was a small tiger and she did have a fair bit of age on her by then; she'd had many years to prove herself as being about as trustworthy a tiger as you can get.

I don't say that lightly, because I remember something Sled said in an interview about the making of the film *Gladiator*: 'The only thing predictable about a tiger is its unpredictability.'

A number of different animals appeared on *BeastMaster*. Sometimes they were written into the script because we had access to them; on the other hand, if the producers required a certain animal, they would talk to Brenton, who had contacts with various animal owners. Brenton's dad, Stafford, provided Cecil the baboon; another circus owner, Frank Gasser, brought his gorgeous black leopard; Mogo Zoo in southern New South Wales supplied Tom the puma; and the Bullen elephants were written into the script.

Brenton's younger brother, Craig, had been travelling around Australia with their three elephants for four years—two years on the Moscow Circus, then two with Lennon Bros Circus. When the elephants first arrived at the *BeastMaster* set, Brenton and I were still on location. We arrived back at the studio lot just as it was getting dark.

I was excited when Brenton pointed out their silhouettes to me early the following morning at 'crew call', the time the crew are called to location. I saw the elephant truck and thought it probably needed cleaning out. I was about to jump in and start cleaning when I heard someone already in the truck; I hesitated for a moment but then I thought, 'No, I'm sure they'd appreciate some help.'

It was early morning and still dark inside the truck. When I climbed in a male voice asked, 'Who are you?'

I said, 'I'm Zelie, and I work with Brenton,' then started cleaning up poo.

He said something like, 'Bloody hell, where do I get one of you from?' and I laughed.

It was Craig, but at the time we couldn't actually see each other clearly in the dark.

The first time I saw Craig properly was a little later that morning. I was at the big cat enclosures talking to Brenton; when I looked down the lot, I saw a man step out of a caravan and walk briskly over towards where the elephants were housed. He didn't look anything like Brenton, and I wondered who he was.

I asked Brenton if that was his brother and he said, 'Yeah.' I said lightheartedly that he was cute, and Brenton scoffed and replied, 'Yeah, everyone says that.'

I enjoyed working with Craig, he was friendly, easygoing and I was fascinated and impressed with his obvious rapport with each elephant. We had a great week together with Sasha and the elephants; but then I didn't see Craig again until the second series of *BeastMaster*, when the elephants were written into the script again.

# CHAPTER 20

# The Olympics

W hile I was working on *BeastMaster*, whenever stunt or other animal work came up on another TV show or on a film, Brenton was very good about replacing me for a day or two. When Tony approached me about some troop drill work at the opening ceremony of the 2000 Sydney Olympics, Brenton was excited for me and happily gave me some time off work.

A few of the people I'd worked with at Movie World were involved too. I didn't know what to expect from the experience. I thought it would be fun—we would take our horses down to Sydney, mess around, perform in front of a crowd and go home, just like other live performances. But it ended up being an even better experience than I'd hoped. What blew me away was working with a hundred and thirty-nine other people and their horses, most of whom had never done anything like this before. So many of them were genuine horse people from the country who had never before experienced the high of performing in front of a live crowd and feeling 'famous'. They were buzzing and I was thrilled to be there to witness and be a part of that on such a scale.

These volunteer horsemen and -women felt truly proud to be representing Australia. The details of the opening ceremony were a huge secret. First, we had two week-long boot-camps at Scone in northern New South Wales. Then, for ten days before the opening we rehearsed every afternoon at the Castle Hill showground, where we camped, and would then transport our horses to the stadium twenty-three kilometres away each night. We trained the horses in the stadium at two in the morning so no one could see us. We would then load them back onto our floats and trucks and transport them back to the showground just before dawn and try to get some sleep before getting up and starting the day again at about lunchtime.

The atmosphere at the rehearsals was electric, but it couldn't prepare us for the actual night itself when the roar of tens of thousands of people filled the air above and around us and the cold air hit our faces as we galloped out from underneath the warm stadium and performed an intricate troop drill choreographed and taught to us by the then head of the New South Wales Mounted Police, Senior Sergeant Don Eyb.

It began with waves of horses and riders galloping into the stadium, all carrying the Olympic flag, to the theme music from *The Man from Snowy River*. Each row of horses and riders would peel off single file and canter around the ring before lining up four abreast to trot down the length of the stadium. Horses with their riders dressed in Driza-Bone coats and Akubra hats, Australian flags flying, broke away and cantered around their designated circle, to form the five Olympic rings. Horses and riders then made their way to the edge of the stadium for the national anthem which we sang as loudly as we could with all of the audience. We left the arena at a gallop in the same formations we entered, but this time holding Australian flags, which had been swapped around for us by volunteers while the anthem was being sung. The entire experience made me feel far more patriotic than I ever imagined I would be.

One of the most valuable aspects of that experience for me was meeting Lydia Emery. We met at the first boot camp. Freda had auditioned as a rider in Goulburn, two hours south of Sydney, several weeks before the first camp, and at the audition she had met Lydia and her lovely supportive mum, Penny. Because they lived only forty kilometres away from each other, after the audition Lydia and Fred used to get together and train regularly with their horses.

At Scone, Freda introduced me to this quiet, reserved girl. What a beautiful beginning to a long friendship. I liked Lydia immediately; she seemed to be a nice country girl. I knew that my older sister got along well with both her and her mum, and I guess my heart opened up a little bit faster because of that.

After the opening ceremony, Freda had an idea. She told me that Lydia was sick of the sports medicine degree she was studying; all she wanted to do was to be around horses, but she didn't know where to go or how to start. Lydia had trained and competed in dressage, but she didn't know if it was her thing or not; Fred suggested she stay with me for a couple of weeks to help out with my horses and observe my work. I thought that would be OK—I was busy, and she could come and help me out if she wanted to.

At first I would just ask her to take the horses' rugs off each morning and put them back on at night and maybe give them some hay and wash them. After a couple of days, I asked Brenton if I could bring her with me to the *BeastMaster* set. I thought she might enjoy it and it would be a good experience for her.

She started coming down to the studios, and soon she was spending far more time at work with me than at home working the horses. I liked having her around, and she was helpful, cleaning cages and chopping meat for the animals. She was in among it all and wasn't any trouble. When the monkeys arrived from Sydney, we found she was very good with them and put her in charge of their care.

Lydia and I also had many wonderful horse rides together, which reminded me of my pony club days. She came for three weeks and stayed for two years, and we had a great time in that house on Maudsland Road.

# CHAPTER 21

# Arjuna and Aura

Brenton told me that a litter of lion cubs had been born on his family's property in Sydney. He asked how I would feel about bottle-raising one of the cubs. I almost wet my pants with excitement at the thought! He said he would bring it up to the Gold Coast and we would raise it together, taking turns with its care.

When that little cub arrived, I did all of the bottle feeds and just loved him. I called him Arjuna and I used to take him to work every day in the little Nissan ute that Brenton had supplied me with; then I'd take him home and bottle-feed him through the night. His family were me, Snoopy, our cat Cougar, Alex and Lydia.

When he was very young, he lived in my bedroom ensuite. As he got a bit bigger, he lived in the laundry; and when he got bigger still, he spent the nights in a large cage that was bolted onto the back of the ute and had a roll-up canvas canopy cover. Wherever he was, he was always very good at going to sleep whenever it was dark.

I continued to take him back and forth with me to work. One morning I was driving Alex's sedan instead of my ute. Arjuna's favourite place in that car was on the parcel shelf behind the back seats. I was stopped at a set of traffic lights when the people in the car behind us went crazy—I could hear them yelling, 'The toy in the back of that car just moved!' They were trying to signal to me; but the lights changed and I drove on, thinking, 'Lion cub? What lion cub?'

Arjuna had been written into the first series of *BeastMaster* but when the second series began, Arjuna started acting strangely. He seemed slightly uncoordinated and he'd look at you as though he couldn't quite see you properly. Lions are often a bit vague and lethargic, but now with Arjuna it was particularly noticeable. He was still very affectionate and beautiful, but it was like he was trying very hard to focus on you. He'd sometimes 'talk' in yowls and then he'd lie down on his side.

Brenton and I didn't know what was wrong with him, and we couldn't tell if he was sick or in pain. We took him to the university, to different vets, and other animal people, who all gave their two cents' worth; we researched on the internet, but we couldn't figure out what was wrong. The best the vets could come up with was that it was an unknown neurological disorder. The *BeastMaster* production team started to write Arjuna out of the script.

Wayne had started working in the animal department on *BeastMaster*. One day he was giving me a lift home from work and we called in to the vet to collect some medication for Arjuna. Wayne waited in the car while I went inside. When I walked into the waiting room, it was full of people and no one was at reception, so I took a seat.

When I sat down, my eyes went straight towards a beautiful half-grown blue heeler pup. She was the prettiest bitch I had seen in a long time, and I thought, 'Far out—that's a nice dog.'

The owner was sitting reading a magazine. When the vet nurse came out and called his name, he went up to the counter. The dog was looking insecure and hanging close to him, and the nurse said to the owner, 'Are you sure you want to put her down? Are you absolutely sure?'

I couldn't believe what I'd heard. He was going to have this beautiful dog put down?

The vet nurse said, 'She looks like a really nice dog.'

'She's friggin' useless,' said the bloke. 'She was nice as a puppy, but now she has to live on the chain. She does everything wrong—she bites everyone.

I was looking at this dog, who by now had sat down and wrapped both front paws around the man's leg. He tried to shake her off and yelled, 'Get off!' but the rougher and more annoyed he got, the more she hung on.

The vet nurse said, 'Alright, we just wanted to make sure it's what you wanted.' She left and he sat down again.

I went over and sat beside him and said, 'I'm sorry, I couldn't help overhearing. Do you mind if I ask you: are you really putting that dog down?'

He said, 'Yeah.'

I asked him if he would be open to the idea of giving her away instead, and he said, 'Oh, you don't want this dog, love. If it's not biting, it's pulling your washing off the line. If it's not doing that, it's eating your plants or digging up your footpath. It's a real pain in the arse.'

I said, 'I've got an old blue heeler dog, and I'd really like a pup from him.' This man's bitch was still young and, if Snoopy could hang in there long enough, maybe it might work out.

'Oh no—I wouldn't give her away, love. She'll bite someone and I'll get sued.'

'I'm happy to sign anything you want to say that you have no responsibility.'

'I'll have to call my wife and check,' he said.

'I'm happy to wait,' I assured him and then I left him alone to call his wife on his mobile. I was thinking, 'Please don't put that dog down; please don't put that dog down.' I felt instantly attached to her. I could see she wasn't a foul dog, she was just a terrified little half-grown pup.

I went outside and told Wayne I was trying to get this blue heeler bitch, and he laughed. Then I said, 'But apparently it bites. Can you come and get it?'

'I'm not going to get it!' he replied, laughing some more. But when I persisted he came in with me and said quietly, 'Shit, bloody good-looking dog.'

The guy returned and said, 'You sure you want it? I just need to get something clear—you're not getting her papers.'

'That's OK.' I'd never had a dog with papers.

'I'm not having anyone make money out of breeding her.'

'Oh no, you misunderstood me. I don't want to breed from her for that reason. I have an old geriatric blue heeler-cross-mongrel that I would really love a puppy from.'

'All I can tell ya is you're on your own, if she bites you . . .'

'That's OK. I do biting dogs.' Secretly I was starting to wonder if this was a good idea, but I couldn't let her be put down.

I wasn't even sure how to take her from him, because by now she was retracting her lips and baring her teeth; she was terrified. 'If you put her in my car, I'll deal with her from there,' I told him, and he agreed. So I climbed into the passenger seat and he placed her in the foot well between my legs. He shut the door and she looked at him very forlornly—she no longer looked like biting anyone.

He said, 'Alright then, good luck.'

When we drove off, Wayne was still laughing at me. I said, 'I'm not moving, for fear of her taking a nip at me,' and he said, 'Yeah I can see that!' She was sitting there looking at me, looking at Wayne, looking up at the window. Then she lay down and stayed like that for the twenty minutes it took to get back to my place.

I looked at Wayne and said, 'How are we going to get her out of the car?'

'I don't know. That's your problem—it's your dog.'

I stepped out of the car very carefully, because I still didn't know if she was going to bite me. 'You alright, girl?' I asked her. She was looking at me totally expressionlessly—that real blue heeler stare. I had no idea what that dog was thinking and I decided I was going to let her do her own thing. All she had on was a choker chain, and I thought she might get out and run away—still, I wasn't going to risk touching her to put a lead on her.

I tried to call her out of the car, but she wouldn't be in it; so we left her and I sat down on the blue metal on the driveway. Wayne said, 'Bloody hell, how long are we going to have to wait here?' because he couldn't go home until she was out of his car. He went off and made a cup of coffee, and I just sat there.

When all was quiet, I saw her begin to lower her barriers a little bit. She started to look around; she stood up, put her paws on the seat, and then carefully went back down again. I called again, but she wouldn't come.

Finally she tippy-toed out of the car and then tippy-toed over to me and sat on my lap and sighed, and my heart just melted for her. I still didn't touch her, because I was still a bit wary. I put my hand where she could see it and she didn't do anything; she was just sitting in my lap and I was talking to her, calling her 'little girl'. From that evening on, I don't think she ever did leave my side, unless she was prised off.

I called her Aura. At the beginning she was very bitchy to Snoopy, but I said, 'Oh no, we're not having that—he's the king around here. You mind your manners!' She had a very strong character and she really wanted to be dominant, but I wouldn't stand for it. If she snapped at him when food was around, she would have to wait for him to eat first—that sort of stuff. She learnt that he was the king and she eventually treated him like that.

She was awesome with Arjuna. He was about labrador size when she came along, and Aura was still a pup—she wanted to play. Obviously she was scared when she first met him, like all dogs are with lions, but once they learnt to be friends, they were great together.

Brenton and I really loved to see Arjuna playing with a fellow 'cub'. When they played a little rough, one would yelp and the other would bark, and they'd go off and sulk until the next time they thought it would be fun to play. They were just young animals growing up together.

Snoopy really loved her too, and I was happy for them. Ultimately they did have puppies, just as I'd hoped. I didn't let them mate on her first season, but waited until her second and they had six puppies. Lydia kept one and called him Ankie. He bites like Aura and yet is loving like Snoopy.

## CHAPTER 22

# Raising big cats

With the second series of *BeastMaster* now in production, Craig came back up to the studios with the elephants, and I became aware of two things—that Craig and his partner were not getting on, and that he was taking a lot of interest in me. But, although I thought he was very cute, I also thought, 'That is *not* going to happen!' I didn't want to complicate my job by having a relationship with one of the Bullens. I reminded myself that Craig had children and I didn't want any part in being the reason he left them. I needn't have worried, he moved back in with his parents regardless.

Arjuna was getting sicker and I was emotional. Craig went back to Sydney after they had finished filming with the elephants and started calling me. I would get butterflies when he called and I had to remind myself that this was a no-go. No way. He was seven years older than I was, and I wasn't looking for a serious partner. At the time, I was trying to remove Alex from my life, as much as I loved him, and I still wasn't planning on spending my life with *anybody* on a permanent basis. The fact that Craig and his partner had children was another issue for me. I had been raised in a broken home and I didn't want to be responsible for causing his children any emotional discomfort. It was all just too complicated.

Alex and I had had a fantastic time together over the last three years. I don't regret the time I spent with him. He was fun—an amazing athlete, incredibly talented and creative—but ultimately he was looking for more than I was prepared to give. The thought of potentially losing another partner, or a child, was too much, so I fought against any instinct towards settling down. I was emotionally scarred, deep in my soul. In 2001, Alex moved out.

Production for the second series of *BeastMaster* was about to end. My lovely housemate Lydia was heading to France to take up a job Wayne had organised for her as a polo groom. Meanwhile, the plan had been for me to go to the Bullens' property to help with Arjuna and the other animals, who were taken back to Park Road for the eight-week break before the third series started up. But then, out of the blue, Brenton put a stop to that. I asked if it was about money—we had already discussed that I would be on a lower wage at his place than I got for my work on *BeastMaster*. I told him I didn't care—I just wanted to keep a relationship going with Arjuna and to look after him. But Brenton wouldn't budge.

I was hurt, confused and angry. I had just spent fourteen

months raising Arjuna, and I knew he needed consistency in his training; Brenton had previously told me he felt that there was no one who could work well with Arjuna in Sydney—so who was going to look after him? Now, Brenton flatly told me that he would.

I couldn't understand why Brenton had changed his mind. I was aware I didn't own Arjuna, but Brenton had said that the two of us would raise the lion together, and I felt that he was reneging on that.

With his characteristically impeccable timing, Sled called to tell me he was working in pre-production on a film called *Scorpion King*. He told me I should stop working for that circus fella, who was going to get me killed, and come over for a visit—he had a lot of stuff happening in LA. It was very tempting, but I was worried about Arjuna, and didn't want to leave Australia.

Eventually, Brenton called and said the day had come—Arjuna was no better and they were going to put him down. I said I would fly down and begged him not to do it before I got there. He said, 'Zelie, I don't want you here. I'm no good at this sort of thing anyway. If I need to grieve, I want to be alone—you being here will make it harder for me.'

Selfishly, I told him that I didn't care what he said—if he didn't let me come down to Park Road, I would never speak to him again. 'I know about death, Brenton, and I want to be there when he goes.'

Credit where credit is due—Brenton did wait for me to come down. When I arrived in Sydney, Arjuna was far worse than

I had seen him before. He was in the back of the Nissan utility, about to go to the vet's. I crawled in there with him. It suddenly seemed small with both me and this large fourteen-month-old lion in there.

I lay next to him, and hugged him and cried. Both Craig and Brenton were there, and both were very upset. Arjuna knew we were there. He was yowling to me, and he gently grabbed my hand in his mouth and held it, but he seemed very disorientated.

Brenton didn't make it to the vet's. It was Craig who drove us there in silence, to have Arjuna put down. I held that beautiful lion in my arms as he slipped away.

I stayed on at the Bullens' for a couple of days. I didn't really want to be anywhere else; I wanted to sit outside and just be near the big cats in their enclosures, and watch them play and interact with each other. I asked Brenton if that was OK and he said, 'Absolutely, you do what you need to do.'

In the afternoon, I was sitting down the back, near the mountain lion enclosure. No one else was around. Suddenly I heard this high-pitched *eeeep-eeep* and I realised it was a cub all on its own in the grass in the enclosure. One of the female mountain lions was anxiously pacing up and down quite some distance away. She was a first-time mother and it was clear she had abandoned her newborn cub.

I ran up to the main house and grabbed Brenton and Craig. We went back to the enclosure and watched from a distance for hours, waiting to see if the mother would go back to the cub or not.

When the mother finally went back she picked up the cub in her jaws, dragging it through the water trough and then dropping it onto the cold concrete beside the trough, which obviously wasn't ideal for the tiny cub. Then she went back to pacing. By now Brenton and Craig, afraid for the cub's life, had decided to get it out. They manoeuvred the mother out of the way and scooped the cub out of the enclosure. Immediately I began hand-raising the cub, whom we called Koda, on a bottle.

Two tiger cubs, Shamarna and Indira, were born within a couple of days of Koda. I couldn't believe it: I had just lost Arjuna, but now there were three more cubs to raise. After one death, there were three more beautiful beings who had come into our world.

But then Brenton said something that just blew me away. He said, 'OK, you'd better go home now. We'll take them to the vet's to be hand-raised by their staff.'

I was stunned and asked him how he could say that when he knew my heart was broken over Arjuna and I wanted to put all of my love into these new babies. He simply said, 'No, not this time.'

So that is what we did—we dropped them at the vet's. Unbelievably hurt, I went home.

## CHAPTER 23

# Running away

When I arrived back at Maudsland Road, Sled called again and asked if I could help him at Gentle Jungle while things were so busy. This time I dropped everything and flew to the US.

Before Arjuna had died, Brenton and I had talked every day on the phone. Even if it was my day off or I'd gone to a stunt job, we still spoke—mostly to liaise about Arjuna. But after I went home from Park Road, I didn't call Brenton and I didn't have any calls from him either. I was angry and hurt.

Sled was surprised by my abrupt change of plans, because he knew that I was a ferociously loyal employee and didn't just 'drop' jobs. In LA, he picked me up from the airport in his Chevy, as he always did. As soon as I climbed in he said, 'So, what the hell is going on?' and I told him the whole story.

I told him that Craig had shown an interest in me and I had said, 'No way.' Since then Brenton was acting irrationally, and

Freda, me, Mum and Julie, 1973.

At the age of six, with my first dog Snoopy #1, 1976.

At the age of ten, on my first pony Candy, 1980.

Me, Julie and Freda. Freda's hens night, 1988.

Julie, me, Kate, Cloud, Freda. Freda and Bert's wedding, 1988.

The last time I saw my dad. Hayley, Freda, Dad, me, Cloud and Kate, 1991.

With Graham, 1993.

Graham teaching me about fire stunts, 1994.

With Mazena Godecki on the set of *Ocean Girl*, 1993.

Learning to work with young big cats at Sled's, 1995.

With Snoopy and Angel when life was going to plan, 1994.

Stunt-doubling for Kate Winslet on
*Holy Smoke*, 1998.

With Arjuna, 2000.

Performing a 'Hippodrome' on Bullet at Equitanna, 2002.

Stunt-doubling for Terri Irwin on *The Crocodile Hunter*, with Sui (Steve Irwin's faithful dog), 2002.

With Craig, Austin Powers the pony and Lucy the zebra on the set of *Racing Stripes*, 2003.

With Mum in Africa, 2003.

With Mum, having cuddles with Kota (the puma I found just after Arjuna died), 2003.

With Mum and Cleo the lion cub, 2003.

I didn't know what the hell was wrong with him. I was just pissed off with everyone.

He said, 'Oooh! You got a mess goin' on back there.'

No sooner had I finished telling him my story than his cellphone rang. He looked at its display screen and said, 'Whaddaya know—it's your boss.' Then he gave it to me and told me to answer it.

I said, 'No, no,' but Sled grabbed the phone, pushed 'accept' and handed it back to me.

I said, 'Hello. Gentle Jungle, Australian Division,' as an awkward joke and there was a silence. I repeated, 'Hello?' and Brenton said, 'Oh, hello—I'm looking for Sled Reynolds.'

'Hi, Brenton—it's Zelie.'

Silence. And then he said, 'Right, so that's where you've got to then—thought you might have gone there. Is Sled there? I'd like to talk to him.'

'Sure.' I handed the phone over. They talked briefly, Sled in short, cryptic sentences and then hung up.

I asked what he wanted and Sled said, 'To find out where you were.'

'He wouldn't do that.'

Sled replied, 'Reeeally.' Sled was always saying I was naive.

'No, he wouldn't do that,' I repeated.

Sled said slowly, like I was an imbecile, 'Zelie, he just rang to tell me there is a big tiger movie going this year in Australia, and would I be interested in coming out. I told him, "Yes, Brenton, that would be great," and we hung up. Do you think that's a coincidence?'

Anyway, it was awful. I felt confused and angry and just wanted to work, to forget about Arjuna, forget about Brenton, forget about Craig. I stayed with Sled for four weeks. As usual, I was well looked after and had a good time working with the animals. However, when pre-production had finished and filming was about to commence on *Scorpion King*, I received a phone call from Lawrence Woodward asking if I could come back to Australia to work on a new IMAX project called *Horses: The Story of Equus*. I decided to head home as I also wanted to see if Brenton had changed his mind and would let me raise those cubs.

I arrived back from the US and called to ask Brenton how the cubs were going. He told me that they'd grown strong and he needed to collect them from the vet's; yet he still wouldn't let me go to Park Road to raise them. He told me to wait until *BeastMaster* started up again. But I didn't wait, because in the meantime Lydia called from France. She'd now been there for two months, and she told me they needed an extra person for the season. I said, 'Book me on the next plane.'

# CHAPTER 24

# Working for royalty

I ran away to France—from Craig, from Brenton and from the memory of Arjuna—and went to work as a polo groom for Mark Boyden, husband of Princess Zahra Aga Khan. Zahra's father, His Highness Prince Karim Aga Khan IV, is the forty-ninth and current Imam of Nizari Ismailism, a denomination within Shia Islam, and is thought by his followers to be a direct descendent of the Prophet Muhammad. Lydia met me at the airport and we went out to the car park, where a driver was waiting for us. We were driven to the Aga Khan's estate, an hour outside of Paris, and I met Mark and Zahra in their beautiful home.

'Mini Mont', where Mark, Zahra and their baby Sara lived, was a warm and friendly home that they affectionately referred to as 'The Cottage', situated within the walled compound of the enormous Aiglemont estate. It was just amazing. At 'Mini Mont' there was a large lobby and entrance area, which was dominated by dog beds and bowls.

A year earlier, Zahra had rescued two strays, a male and a female, who had since had four puppies, now almost grown. Zahra wanted to keep the family together so she'd kept all four puppies, and the six of them now lived in the house. She told us that before the puppies had been born the two adult dogs had obeyed commands, but now all six of them ran together as a pack and they could be hard to control. She asked if Lydia and I could help a bit with the dogs while we were there, and I suggested that we first needed to defuse their pack mentality.

Lydia and I began by separating the dogs whenever we could; we would take them out and work with them individually. We taught them the basics—come, sit, stay and listen. Once they'd learnt to obey, we took them out two at a time and repeated the process; then again with three dogs, and finally with all six. I think we helped a little bit. But we said to Zahra that the training would have to be ongoing or they would probably slip back into their old habits, if they did not have time apart every now and then.

Mark and Zahra were very nice to both of us. We had a room each in the quarters inside the main compound, where Zahra's father, the Aga Khan, housed his jockeys and stablehands. Mark had thirteen polo ponies, which we had to prepare and get fit for the upcoming season which started in May. Zahra was warm and welcoming. At different times other horse professionals would move into the quarters as well. Because our quarters only consisted of a bathroom and bedrooms, we either ate with Zahra and Mark or meals were delivered to us from the main kitchen. We ate like kings, and we were spoilt rotten. Zahra had a lot of contacts and as a result we got to do lots of fun things, like going to shows or to the races; on one occasion we had a blast when she organised for us to go to a U2 concert (that particularly meant a lot to me, as U2 were one of my sister Julie's favourite bands). We were very grateful.

Meeting Zahra was inspirational for me. She was incredibly beautiful, with a fantastic figure—even though she'd just had a baby—and she was also one of the kindest people you could have the pleasure of meeting. She worked for her father in an office on the estate, overseeing the family's support for a number of humanitarian and charitable causes, which was very fitting because she was such a compassionate person. With us, she was casual and friendly—there were no airs and graces—while in public, for example at the races, she was regal and dignified.

On my first night there, we were asked up to The Cottage for dinner. Zahra asked about my family, and while I was telling her about them I mentioned that I had once heard that my father was born in England to a French mother during World War II. She told me that meant I could get an English passport and thus work anywhere in Europe.

She asked someone in her office to get the application forms I needed and then organised an interview for me for British immigration; within a fortnight I had an English passport to add to my Australian one. I said a silent thank you to Dad. I could now open a bank account in France and I didn't have the visa limitations that someone with only an Australian passport has.

Lydia and I were given the use of a Range Rover to drive around in, and on our days off we had a whole lot of fun exploring the countryside. One day we went out to lunch and found a cute little restaurant. We couldn't understand anything on the menu, and no one there spoke English. So we ordered what we thought was beef salad, because we thought we recognised two words, *boeuf* and *salade*. We were presented with what looked like raw beef brains on lettuce, and promptly laughed.

We didn't know what to think—surely they didn't actually eat that stuff? Maybe it was a joke they played on unsuspecting Aussies. Needless to say, we went hungry that day!

Another time we called into a pub. We attempted, with our few pathetic words of French, to order a sandwich. All we could come up with was *fromage* for cheese and *pain* for bread, and we performed an exaggerated charade of making a sandwich. The woman behind the bar did not look amused. She frowned and asked in rapid French, 'Are you sure? Are you sure? Bread and cheese?' Eventually out came a foot-and-a-half-long baguette, with chunks of camembert randomly poked into it and absolutely nothing else. We took one look, said a brief thanks, walked outside and burst out laughing. It was probably a good thing the Aga Khan was feeding us, or we would have starved in those early days.

Within days of being there, I told Zahra and Mark how much I wanted to meet Mario Luraschi, an Italian-born, French-based, equestrian whom Connie and Tad had worked with in Las Vegas. I knew he was very well known, not only in the film industry but also as an accomplished horseman and *voltige* rider (the European version of trick riding). He lived only about forty minutes from Aiglemont. I couldn't believe it—France is a big place, and yet he was just down the road.

Zahra found me his number and I spoke to him on the phone, which was difficult because, although he thinks he's fantastic at all languages, he speaks English with a heavy accent. Eventually, though, we were able to understand each other, and I organised to go to meet him at his home.

# CHAPTER 25

# In the forests of Ermenonville

Mario's place is very impressive. Located in the middle of Ermenonville Forest, it has lovely open paddocks and numerous stables with cobbled floors and walkways. As well as an outside arena, he has a beautiful indoor arena (called a *ménage*), complete with mirrors and old-style equestrian murals lining the walls. On the floors above the *ménage* is Mario's magnificent home.

Mario was quite athletic for a man in his fifties, he had a lovely warm smile and was very charming. He said I could sit a riding test with him and, if he thought I was good enough, he would let me stay and work there on a two-year apprenticeship. What he offered was a deal similar to that found in some training facilities in America: you are paid a basic wage for two years and, if you are used on camera or as a wrangler or a groom on a movie, he takes half of your fee. If you stick out the two years, you then become one of his stunt people, in which case you no longer receive a wage but you get to keep any money you make from films and live shows, and you aren't necessarily expected to turn up each day to do the chores.

I explained that I couldn't start an apprenticeship straight-away, as I was presently working as a polo groom. Mario said that was fine but I should still come back and do the test; if I was successful, I could start after the polo season finished. So I organised a date to sit the test.

I was a bit nervous before the test as I really had no idea what I was about to be put through. When I arrived, everybody stopped working and came to watch. Fadila, Mario's secretary, came out of the office with her assistant; her toddler was running around the place. Two of Mario's top riders, Leslie and Joelle, had come to watch with some friends of theirs who happened to be visiting. All the grooms and some of the stuntmen had come in for the day because they had heard that some girl from Australia was having a riding test. There were around twenty people along the edge of the *ménage*.

One of the grooms brought out a beautiful white Andalusian horse and Mario told me to ride it. As I rode his horse around him, he started telling me in his strong accent to do various things. I could barely understand a word and kept saying, 'Pardon?'

He became visibly upset, and started to shout. 'Oh, you can't hear me! You can't hear me? You stupid or something?'

I couldn't understand what had happened. He had been so charming before the test and now he was like a different person.

'I said, "Trot." You know the trot—you go up and down, up and down.'

I was thinking 'Shit! What have I done?' But I trotted the horse.

'Can you hear me?' he shouted. 'I said, "Canter"—you know, faster than a trot.'

When I rode towards him, I was almost too scared to look in his eyes. My heart was pounding and I tried not to look at all the people watching as he screamed at me, humiliating me.

I was starting to wonder if this was some sort of sick joke. Then I stopped the horse in front of him and he asked me to fall his horse. Again I said, 'Pardon?' I had never fallen a horse before. I had lain horses down, but not fallen one from the saddle. To fall a horse is when the rider, from the saddle, asks the horse to drop to the ground and lie on its side. It is one of the most common advance horse stunts used in performances, film and TV.

'Can you fall a horse, or not?' he demanded.

'No, I've never done that.'

'You a stuntwoman, yes? You a stuntwoman, and what you do on a horse—you jump off it?' He was becoming increasingly aggressive. 'Get off my horse before you break it.'

I dismounted, nearly in tears.

'You are not strong enough for here, are you?' he snapped.

'I think I am.'

'You look upset.'

I was almost too scared to say anything, but managed to get out, 'I don't know why you're yelling at me.'

'Because you can't ride for shit. You have a good seat, but that is all, you cannot ride. You ride like a stupid American cowboy rider.' He then yelled in French to one of the girls. I asked him what he would like me to do, and he said for me to wait while they got another horse.

Another beautiful horse arrived, a bay this time, and Mario told me to get on and do what I was told.

Following his instructions as best I could, I trotted the horse, cantered the horse, warmed it up, then stopped it in front of him when he finally asked me to.

'Right. Now lean down, grab the rein, pull and the horse will fall down. When he starts to fall, position yourself so you don't get caught under.'

I made a hesitant attempt and the horse didn't go down. Mario yelled at me, saying the horse didn't understand what I wanted—do it properly! I made about three more attempts with Mario screaming at me, and then the horse finally responded and went down onto the ground. I thought, 'OK, that was different.'

Mario looked at me. 'You have something I can work with,' he said. 'Yes, you can come, but you are shit.' And with that, he walked away and the tryout was over.

I left Mario's that day not really knowing how to feel about the whole experience. When I told Mark, Zahra and Lydia about it that night, I concluded, 'It's a very strange place.'

For the next few weeks, Lydia and I worked together to get Mark's polo ponies ready for the season. But during the first game he played, a warm-up match, Mark's horse slipped and fell over and Mark broke his collarbone. While he went off to hospital, Lydia and I were left wondering what was going to happen to our jobs.

The next day, Mark called us into his office and said that he now didn't have enough work for both of us, but that he wanted one of us to stay to look after the horses through spring and summer. Mark is very non-confrontational; he suggested we have a think about it and work out between ourselves who would stay and who would go.

I said to Lydia that obviously she should stay, because it was her job in the first place, but she said, 'He's going to want you.' I asked if she wanted to stay, but she wasn't sure. I wanted to go to Mario's to learn more, so for that reason I really wanted to stay on.

So I said to Lyd, 'I would like to stay,' and she said, 'Fine, I knew you'd want to.'

Then she said, 'Mum's coming and we're going to tour Europe.'

'Wow, that's cool,' I enthused. 'I want to do that.'

'Well, you're not—you're staying and working horses,' she retorted. So she got her own back, and thankfully we stayed friends.

# CHAPTER 26

# Mario

I was wildly excited about working with Mario, but I was worried about the rumours I was hearing about him expecting female staff to sleep with him, so before I started working there I asked to meet with him to discuss it face to face. We met at his stables and he suggested we go for a ride together in the forest while we finalised my working arrangements.

One of the grooms saddled two horses and we rode off side by side; he beckoned me over so that our horses were almost touching. He reached across and put his hand on my leg. I looked at him, wondering how I was going to say this. All of our communications to date had been difficult. He had such a strong accent and he could be difficult and rude. I knew I needed to be very clear and blunt.

'Mario, I need to talk to you about something,' I said slowly and carefully. 'Please excuse me if you find this rude, but there is an issue that is bothering me and I need to clarify it before I start to work with you. I have heard that if any woman wants to work at your farm, then you expect to have sex with them.'

He laughed; he said he thought that rumour was very funny.

'I need you to know that I am not here for sex,' I continued.

He laughed again in a teasing way and asked, 'How do you know?'

'Because I know.' I laughed, feeling slightly embarrassed.

'How can you say what's going to happen in the future? Why put limitations on your future?' he demanded.

'I want to know if I can still work here if I do not sleep with you,' I said awkwardly.

'Of course,' he said, with what seemed an exaggerated French accent. He looked at me intently. 'Are you gay? A lesbian?'

'No, Mario, I'm not.'

'Are you married?'

'No.'

'In a relationship?'

'No, Mario—I'm just not interested in having sex with you.'

Still laughing, he told me there was something wrong with me.

After that discussion I naively thought I was safe. He began to introduce me to people as 'Zelie No Sex'. They would all laugh and I'd be a little embarrassed, but I also felt quite proud as well. It would be very clear to the entire yard that I was not sleeping with Mario.

I got along very well with all the team and moved into a beautiful empty castle where Mark and Zahra were now accommodating me, and Mark's polo ponies were being spelled. I had a fridge and a bed, and Zahra brought me a stray kitten from the vet's to keep me company. I checked Mark's horses every day and still drove their car. Mark's horses were turned out in the paddocks around the castle, but I was having terrible trouble with the flies, which were so bad that some horses were losing weight as a result of the constant irritation, so I had to treat the horses each day with an insecticide and make sure they were comfortable.

The very first day I worked for Mario, he insisted I have dinner at his home that night, a celebratory dinner to welcome me. Above the *ménage* was one big open room, with a large kitchen area and an enormous central fireplace surrounded by a circular lounge draped in gorgeous fabrics and cushions. There was a huge dining table that sat twelve, and a steep staircase that rose above the kitchen and led up to a spacious bedroom. He proudly showed me everything, including the bedroom; he wanted me to go in there, but I made sure I only looked in from the top of the stairs.

All four of his *femmes* were present at our dinner. Mario was not legally married to any of them and I found the dynamics incredible. Three of his women lived on the estate. Joelle, who was his number one lady, was an incredible horse rider and stuntwoman; she lived above the stables in beautiful accommodation, kept warm by the heat rising from the horses stabled underneath. Leslie appeared to be the number two; she was very friendly and helpful to me, and was also an accomplished horsewoman and performer; she lived in a beautiful place at the end of the stables. Fadila, the secretary, seemed to be his third woman. A fourth girlfriend, Kathy, lived off the premises.

I found it a bit confronting, but the women themselves seemed more than comfortable with the situation. When I arrived, all four of them were preparing dinner for him, cleaning, having a glass of wine and chatting. When we sat down at the table, Mario sat at the head, with Joelle on his right; Leslie sat on his left, with Kathy on her other side. Fadila sat next to Joelle, and I was seated beside Fadila.

Mario was amused by my obvious shock, and lapped it up. He proclaimed, 'I am a king! I am a king, no?' The women were laughing and rolling their eyes and going along with it. He was saying, 'I have what every man wants—happiness, beautiful horses, beautiful women, freedom, money, fame. Those who say they don't want this are liars—they are too scared to admit the truth.'

I asked him, 'Do you mean every man wants more than one woman?' and he said 'Yes, of course.' And he laughed.

I never knew what was going on at Mario's place from one day to the next. I would turn up at work sometimes and think I must be late, because there were horses saddled up everywhere. The stuntmen would be helping prepare the horses, grooming them, painting their hooves with hoof oil, plaiting up the manes and tails elaborately and putting costumes on themselves and the horses. I'd find someone who could speak English and ask them what was happening. They would explain that Mario had some producers coming that day, which would happen regularly, and it would be a show-and-tell—rehearsing for a job, performing some jousting or a battle scene, or giving a dressage demonstration, or maybe one of the producers wanted to ride on one of Mario's magnificent stallions.

His estate was located in the most beautiful setting. Sometimes we would exercise the horses in the forest; it was an amazing experience to be out in that beautiful forest with all of those superb horses. I usually couldn't understand a word anyone was saying, but I didn't care—I just felt lucky to be there.

Thursday was the biggest day of the week, because it was stable cleaning day. First of all, the horse was led out. Three people were needed to clean out each stable, each person using a pitchfork to drag out the wet, sour, stinking straw. The alleyways of the stable complexes were wide enough to take a tractor with its trailer. Each stable was cleaned out and lime was then sprinkled over the floor; finally a deep bed of fresh straw would be laid over it, of which the horses promptly ate half when they were returned. Each day fresh straw was spread over the top of the old, but all of it was removed every Thursday—seven days' worth. The cobblestone floors outside gave the stables a wonderful old-fashioned look, but were a lot of extra work for the grooms to sweep by hand. All in all, keeping the place clean was a very big job and we all worked hard.

In July Mario sent me away to work on a medieval film for four days with Joelle and a couple of the stuntmen. When we weren't busy I would go and talk to her. She told me that Mario had high hopes for me, and that he had been waiting many years for someone like me to come along. This not only meant a lot to me, but it explained why he was putting more time into my training than that of the other girls. Mario gave me a lesson every day, unless he was too busy with meetings or entertaining producers or directors. I learnt more from him about classical dressage than I had learnt from anyone else. But I felt a bit of resentment from a couple of the female grooms who had been there longer than me but who weren't getting the lessons that I was. They were fine with me socially, but at work I started to feel tension. And even though I kept him at arm's length, Mario continued to flirt with me. I thought he was just having fun.

## CHAPTER 27

# Journey to Switzerland

One day in early August, Mario came up to me and said,
'Tomorrow, when you come into work, you bring enough
clothes for three days—I'm taking you to Switzerland for a job.'
I was very excited and asked what the job was. All he said was,
'You must fall off Emilio,' referring to a beautiful chestnut stunt
horse.

When I arrived at work the following day, my bags packed,
Chino—Mario's right-hand man, who was always very good
to me—started revving me up by saying how fantastic it was
for me to be doing my first solo stunt job with Mario. He told
me Emilio had gone ahead in a trailer with a couple of grooms
the day before; Mario and I were going to Switzerland on the
fast train, a five-hour trip.

Mario and I drove in his car to the enormous Gare de l'Est
train station in Paris. Just walking from the car park to the
platform we were stopped three times by people asking for

Mario's autograph. Up until then I hadn't realised how famous he was in France. He was very blasé about it—he just signed the autographs and had photos taken with people, and then we moved on.

When we boarded the train, I found we were alone in a first-class compartment. As the train pulled away, Mario was already trying to flirt with me; then he openly started trying to touch me and, when that didn't work, he then tried to pin me against the window to kiss me. Initially I ignored his flirting, but eventually I felt embarrassed and had to say, 'Mario, nothing is going to happen here.'

Then he became playful. 'Come on, my darling,' he said seductively.

I said firmly, 'Mario, please, I don't like this situation. Can you leave me alone.' I knew I had to be blunt and I felt awkward.

'Fine.' He got out his newspaper and sat with his legs stretched out across the doorway so I couldn't get out without walking over him.

While he read his newspaper, I sat looking out the window and thought, 'Oh goodness me—the things you get yourself into, Zelie.'

I was very excited as we crossed into Switzerland. I had grown up listening to Mum's stories about how beautiful Switzerland was and about her schooling there as a teenager. From the train window I saw storybook farmhouses with steep roofs matching the steep mountains rising up behind them against deep blue skies, a truly beautiful scene. The only thing missing from my

Mum's description of her childhood was the snow. I immersed myself in this picturesque landscape, escaping from the recent scene with Mario, finding a way to still thoroughly enjoy the moment.

Because the job had come up at such short notice I hadn't told anyone in Australia where I was going, but I couldn't wait to tell Mum where I had been.

A driver collected us from the station and took us to our hotel. A bunch of people, including the director, were waiting in the foyer to meet us. Nobody spoke English and I had no idea what they were talking about. They offered me a glass of wine, which I politely refused, and they seemed to talk for a very long time. I was tired and just wanted to go to my room, wherever that was. Eventually Mario gave me my room key and said I could go to my room if I liked.

Once there, I didn't know what to do, so I waited in my room in case I was summoned. I couldn't get the TV to work and had nothing to do, so I started writing on the hotel stationery about what had happened to me throughout the day as a sort of impromptu diary. At about nine o'clock, I had a shower. I didn't know whether to go to bed or not, or whether I'd be needed for a meeting later on, because the people Mario mixed with all tended to stay up late and then sleep in. I still didn't know where I had to be in the morning, or at what hour—it was very unsettling.

At about ten thirty, I finally got into my pyjamas. And then my room phone rang. It was Mario. He simply said, 'Come to my room.'

'OK, what number is it?'

It was the room next to mine. I felt I had no choice but to go, because I still had no idea what was happening the next day. I put on a hotel dressing-gown and walked out into the hall.

His door was ajar and I knocked. 'Come in!' he called out.

I said, 'No, it's OK.' I didn't feel comfortable going into his bedroom late at night.

He said, 'Ohhh, come in!'

I didn't know what else to do so I pushed the door open and walked in. I made a point of leaving the door ajar behind me. I walked down the small hallway past the ensuite into the room, then stopped in shock. Mario was sprawled out on the bed like some kind of *Cleo* centrefold model, in just a pair of jocks.

I tried to act natural and asked, 'So, how did the meeting go?'

'Ohhh, come here—come here and sit,' he replied as he patted the bed.

'No, I'm fine, Mario.'

'Don't be like that. Come and *sit*.' So I sat on the very edge of the bed, as far away from him as possible. Then he leant forward and grabbed me by the arm, smiling as he pulled me up next to him.

I got up quickly and said, 'Don't do that!'

His mood changed. 'What is wrong with you? When will you relax?'

I said, 'I'm quite relaxed when I'm not with you.'

'Well, relax with me—you being such a stupid bitch.'

'What is wrong with you?' I yelled.

'You are the most stupid person I have ever met in my life,' he said furiously. 'You could have everything you want in life if you could just relax.'

'You have no idea what I want in life,' I said. I was so irate and upset that I started to cry.

It was like a switch had gone off inside him. Suddenly he was conciliatory. He said, 'Calm down, let's talk.'

'Mario, I am so hurt by you,' I said. 'You have been nasty to me the whole time, even though you originally told me I could work with you and not sleep with you. You have tried it on a couple of times and I am not interested. I don't have to tell you the reason, but, if you must know, it's because I'm not attracted to you.' I felt I had to be blunt to get my point across. 'Where I come from, people don't sleep with their bosses.'

He said, 'OK, I understand that.' He now seemed sympathetic. The atmosphere changed again and I felt relaxed enough to sit back down on the edge of the bed and try to compose myself while he explained himself to me.

'Of course you don't *have* to sleep with me to work with me,' he said, 'but my horses are my love and my life. If you want to share my life and my love, then you *share* my love and my life. You don't just take what you want—my horses—without giving anything back.'

I had seen for myself how passionate he was about his horses—he loves them, and they are his world. He sometimes went down to the stable alone late at night and gave them treats over the stable door, kissing them and talking to them quietly. He told me now, 'You're sharing this with me, and yet you don't want to give me any love back—you don't want to give me any gratitude?'

I knew what he was saying. He wasn't saying, 'Lie down so I can have sex with you,' he meant that he wanted to make love and share.

I was still upset when I left him that night. Before I left his room, I asked him what time I was needed in the morning, but he didn't know. He dismissively told me I would be collected at some stage.

I woke early, dressed and looked out the window. I was too scared to go outside in case I missed the driver or whoever was going to collect me. I hadn't eaten breakfast, and I didn't know what to do. I just sat there on my hotel room floor and ran through my stretching routines over and over until there was a knock at the door. A man spoke in French and beckoned me to come with him. I took all of my belongings, because I didn't know what was going on or whether I'd be coming back to the hotel or not.

He took me onto the set. I could see Mario talking with the crew, but he didn't acknowledge me. A few of the stunt guys from Mario's were there as grooms, preparing Emilio, but I didn't know them terribly well.

I went over and gave Emilio a pat and said hi to the guys. I was whisked off by an assistant director to do hair, make-up and wardrobe, which took a couple of hours. Nobody spoke English and I was still none the wiser about the job.

When I came out of hair and make-up, Mario said the crew were waiting, so we had to do the stunt straightaway. I got onto Emilio, and Mario gave me my instructions. 'Okay, you must trot there, canter there and then I will stop Emilio. You must not look like you are stopping him. And then you fall off over the jump.'

We rehearsed the shot just once. It always gets harder in a situation like that, because the horse knows it's going to be stopped at a certain point and it tries to stop earlier each time. So with the camera rolling I would have to push Emilio on and then Mario would stop him off-camera, and I'd throw myself over the jump while making it look like an accident.

Mario didn't say anything between takes—he gave me no feedback at all—and we just did the same scene over a few times. At the end of it, we did some more shots of me cantering around and jumping another couple of jumps, and then Mario left and I was taken off to get changed.

I found a seat and again waited for some instruction. I was taken to a tent for lunch, which was a three-course sit-down meal as is normal on a film set in France. I saw Mario in the tent networking, but I didn't know anyone else, and no one spoke to me. The grooms had already left with Emilio.

The driver picked me up again and took me to the station. I was thinking, 'Shit, I hope I don't have to catch a train by myself. Fortunately, Mario met me at the station and we got on the train together.

Other than telling me what to do for the stunt, he hadn't said another word to me that day. He didn't talk to me again—not during the five hours on the train, nor when we got into his car and drove back to his place. Finally, we got out of the car and each grabbed our own bags. I said goodbye and he didn't answer. I began walking to my car and he walked towards the stairway to his home above the *ménage*.

I stopped, turned and asked, 'Do I still come back here to work tomorrow?'

He turned and said, 'Of course!' seeming surprised that I had asked.

It was late at night as I drove back home. I cried all the way, thinking, 'I'm never going back again.' I wondered whether my quest for knowledge and experience was worth the emotional torment. I had a very restless night and I woke up late and thought, 'Shit, I'm late for work'; then, 'It's not my work, I'm not going back there.' At that point every cell in my body cried out, 'Yes you are!'

I got up. I cried all the way in but, as soon as I got there, I put on a hard-arse face. I didn't know what to expect. I still felt uncertain about my future there, despite Mario's answer the night before. Had I lost my job? Did I even want the bloody job?

I arrived at work late. There was stuff going on, and so I went and started work.

## CHAPTER 28

# Ridicule and recognition

Two months passed; Mario gave me a lesson every day, but his manner towards me was rude and dismissive. I kept thinking, 'I hate you, I hate you—I hate every bit of you.'

I continued going to jobs during this time, doing some on-camera riding, but I never worked with Mario on set again. I worked with Chino mostly, and that suited me.

Whenever producers or other important guests came to Mario's, all the staff would line up to be introduced; Mario would introduce everyone else by name, but he always skipped me. Humiliated, I would look at the floor while he passed me by as though I didn't exist.

One day when a producer was visiting I decided I wouldn't line up. I didn't want to go through the humiliation again. So I stood behind a horse truck parked in the courtyard. But then Mario saw me standing there and motioned me over, pointing to where he wanted me to stand. I felt as though he was saying,

'You need to be here, so I can ignore you in front of all these people.' I felt I had no choice but to join the others. I knew the experiences I was having at Mario's were invaluable, broadening my knowledge of horses and my riding skills. I had had no prior experience with classical dressage and falling stunt horses. I told myself to tough it out.

One day we were told that five stuntwomen were coming from all around France to try out with Mario for a film that was being shot in a few months. I was quite sore that morning because I'd been shot off a horse for a film a few days before and I was still a bit bruised which can be normal after a stunt. I helped the other grooms to saddle and prepare five of the falling horses.

Everyone gathered around the outside arena to watch as the stuntwomen warmed up the horses. I could see that two of the girls could ride OK, but the other three weren't riding very well at all. Then Mario arrived and gave them their instructions. By then I had picked up enough French to understand what he was asking—they had to trot in a figure of eight, then canter one circle and fall the horse at his mark.

One by one the girls attempted to follow his instructions, but not one of them could put their horse down on the ground. By the time the fifth girl had tried and failed, Mario was swearing; when he got into that mood, everyone went quiet. One girl got off the horse, got into her car and left immediately; three others sat on their horses looking embarrassed. The fifth girl had fallen off her horse in her attempt to make it fall and was getting back on.

'Zelie, get on this horse!' Mario called out to me. I got onto the riderless horse and he said, 'Allez!' meaning Go!

I did the figure of eight, cantered the circle and fell the horse.

'Get off! Get on that horse,' he barked, making the other girls get off.

I did the same routine on every one of the five horses. Some of them I hadn't ridden before. I believe Mario's intention was to humiliate the stuntwomen for failing to meet his standards. When I'd finished he told them that was all and dismissed them.

Chino later told me that I was to do the job. The producers needed a horse and rider to be hit by a train. The stunt would be done in stages and then compiled as a complete take in editing.

From that day on, Mario began talking to me again. Now I noticed that he treated me like one of the men. With the men, he never made a fuss, just said, *'Bonjour'* every morning and got on with things. Whenever he had been away on a job, on his return he would invariably kiss everyone in the stables, both girls and guys, as the French do. He began to include me in that little ritual again. He was never especially nice to me, but he treated me like one of his staff again. I liked it, and I was relieved that I could stay on and continue to learn from him.

While I was waiting for the new film job that Chino had told me about, Freda called me one morning and told me Mum had been diagnosed with breast cancer. I think it was a Sunday, because there weren't many people around. Still, for privacy I walked around the side of a horse truck, sat down on the ground with my back against the tyre, and began to cry.

Fred had told me the situation wasn't critical and I didn't have to come home. But I knew I wanted to go home. I was thinking, 'What if Mum dies?'

Then I heard someone coming. Mario walked briskly past me. He looked at me briefly and kept going, then slowed, turned around and said, 'Ça va? Are you OK?'

'*Oui, ça va,*' I said, but he saw straight through me.

'Noooo.' And this man, who had treated me so coldly and rudely for so long, came and sat down next to me on the cobblestones. 'Tell me what's happened.'

Reluctantly, I told him about Freda's phone call.

'Ahh, my darling.' He held me to his chest and I cried and cried.

'Come! Come, get up!' he said at last.

We both stood up and he held my hands. 'Now, medicine is very good,' he said, trying to reassure me. 'Breast cancer is nothing—they chop the boob off, everything fine. I will pay for your flight home.'

'I have a return ticket for my flight home—Mark has already paid for it.'

'Fine, you come to the office now and I will explain to Fadila. She book your flight. You go. When you want—tomorrow?'

'Yes, please. But sorry—what about the job with the train?'

'Oooh, leave it—it's just a movie. It is not important like your mother. I just get one of the men and put boobs on—don't worry about it.'

He was so kind; you could not have asked for more. Once Fadila had booked my flight, Mario told me, 'When your mother is all better, you come back. It is coming into the winter now—it is cold, it snows, there are not many movies coming up. After winter, you come back and finish your apprenticeship. When you want to return, you just call and we pay for you to come back.'

I felt so much lighter, so relieved—it was as if an angel had just picked me up. I was no longer alone.

I called in to see Mark Boyden and told him what was happening and he said, 'Go, just go! We can look after the horses, no problem.'

The hardest thing for me was leaving my kitten, but Mark assured me he would get one of the grooms to look after him. That night I packed my bags, and the next morning one of the stuntmen, Cedric, drove me to the airport and I was gone. It was as quick as that. As things turned out, I didn't see Mario again for many years.

Working with Mario is fantastic for the experience, but you need to have skin like rhino hide! I learnt a lot in the six months I was there—not just from Mario, but from all the very talented people who work with him. It was an amazing experience, one I am very grateful for. I will never forget it.

CHAPTER 29

# Family

When I returned to Australia in November 2001, I landed at Sydney airport, where I needed to catch a connecting flight to Brisbane. Getting off the plane, I was excited to be almost home, knowing that I would soon see Mum.

I made my way through immigration and customs, and came out into arrivals, planning to go straight to the domestic terminal. People were being greeted all around me. Then I saw this cute guy walking towards me. I looked past him and then looked at him again, because he seemed to be walking boldly in my direction. I thought, 'He's quite cute,' and then I realised he was looking straight at me with a cheeky smile.

I had never before seen Craig showered and clean, or dressed in trendy clothes. Thank goodness my memory clicked just before he said hello.

Quick as a flash, I said, 'Craig? What a coincidence—what are you doing here?' I thought he must be there to meet someone else.

He said, 'I heard a little rumour that you were at Sydney airport for three hours between flights.'

I was astonished. 'How did you know that?' He just smiled.

While I had been in France, Craig had taken to calling me about once a month. Though in Australia I'd been uncomfortable about his interest in me, I always loved hearing from him, and it felt safe talking to him when I was far away in France meeting new people, having new experiences. He was really considerate, and never put any pressure on me. If I was in the middle of something and couldn't talk, he would understand.

One of the times Craig called me out of the blue, he had broken down on the side of the Hume Highway at South Gundagai. He had been driving to a friend's farm near the Victorian border to get a load of hay for the elephants and was now stuck there waiting for a part to arrive for his semi-trailer. When he called me and told me where he was, I said, 'My sister lives in Gundagai. Why don't you call her?'

I wasn't all that serious, but clearly he was quite bored and he had to wait in his truck until the following day, so he said he might call her. I gave him her number, but I warned him she might be picking up her kids from school. When we said goodbye, I wished him luck with his truck, and that was the last I heard of it.

He hadn't mentioned to me that from then on he had continued to call in to visit Fred and Bert whenever he was passing that way to get another load of hay. Freda would sometimes tell him what I'd been up to.

I remember Fred had called me after she met him and said, 'He's great, and he really likes you.'

I reminded her that one of the reasons I was in France was

to get away from Craig. I didn't want to feel attracted to him because he was older, and it was complicated.

Of course, because I was unaware that Craig and Freda were friends, it was only much later that I twigged it must have been she who told him I was coming back to Australia and would be passing through Sydney airport with three hours to spare.

He took me to a coffee shop in the terminal and I told him about the last six months. In my carry-on luggage, I had all of my precious photos, because I didn't want to risk them getting lost in transit anywhere, so I showed them to him and shared my adventures.

When my flight was called, he walked me to my departure gate. Suddenly I didn't want to leave him—I wanted him to come to Queensland with me. I had no idea what I was going home to. I didn't want to be saying goodbye; it was bordering on separation anxiety. For the last thirty-eight hours, ever since I'd found out about Mum, I'd been feeling so scared but being around him had made me feel safe and comfortable.

I just wanted to get off the plane, and go back to him and talk some more. Then I reminded myself how great it was going to be to see Mum and to be with my animals and friends again.

When I arrived in Brisbane, Lydia, who was now back in Australia, met me at the airport. As we turned to leave the terminal I still felt this urge to get back on a plane and fly back to Craig. My heart had begun to pound whenever I thought of him and I thought, 'Well, six months in France didn't really fix that feeling!'

It was so bad that when I arrived home I made up some stupid reason to call him just so I could hear his voice. We talked for a little while that day, and on the following days he continued to call me, which of course I loved. I couldn't help it—I just craved any interaction with him.

Mum had her surgery, but she didn't really tell us what was going on. She kept saying she didn't want us to worry. During this time I wanted to be as close to her as possible, both to support her and to comfort me. So that she didn't feel responsible for my return to Australia, I told her that I had been ready to come home.

After I had settled back at Maudsland Road and caught up with everyone, I made my way down to the Movie World studios to visit Brenton and his new assistant, Donna Wilson. I wasn't sure how Donna would feel about me as Brenton's former assistant, but she was so warm and friendly towards me that I could tell we were going to be friends, which was really nice.

She had done a fantastic job at raising the cubs, Indira, Shamarna and Koda. She was clearly very knowledgeable and passionate, to have spent all of those hours with them, and she is such a genuine, down-to-earth person.

In December 2001 I went to work on Steve Irwin's movie *The Crocodile Hunter* to double his wife Terri. I wasn't yet ready to head back to Mario's and all of the associated stress that his place entailed, but I did plan to return there after Christmas, provided Mum's health was OK.

We soon got the good news: the doctors were happy with the surgery; the cancer cells, which thankfully weren't aggressive and hadn't entered her bloodstream. Mum has been cancer-free ever since.

# CHAPTER 30

# Stafford

During one of our telephone conversations while I was in France, Craig had mentioned that his dad, Stafford, had been diagnosed with Alzheimer's. His condition declined and he died in November, not long after my return. I had only met him a few times—when he brought the macaque monkeys and baboons up to the set of *BeastMaster*, and during the few times I had visited Park Road.

The first time I met him, I wasn't allowed into the house without giving him a kiss first—'All ladies who come to my house must give me a kiss,' he informed me. I laughed and said, 'Of course,' and gave him a peck on the cheek. On that visit I also met his wife, Cleo. We all dined on one of Cleo's sensational meals and were thoroughly entertained by Stafford's stories of days gone by.

Walking around their house, I caught sight of a large photograph on the wall of Peggy, one of their elephants who had died several years earlier. Stafford came up behind me and said in a quiet voice, 'She was a good elephant that.' I asked him some questions about her and as he told me stories his eyes never left her picture. A tear rolled down his cheek as he said, 'We will never have another one like her.'

Everyone who knew Peggy raves about that elephant—they told me she was one of a kind, closer than a family dog. At that time I didn't know anything about elephants—how long they lived and how personable they can be, or how they relate with people—but I thought she must have been quite something, to move an old man to tears in front of a virtual stranger. It was a very touching experience. I was intrigued and wanted to know more about the family and their history with their animals.

At that point, all I knew was that they were a nice family who had a big property and lots of amazing animals. All four of the children—Mark, Sonya, Brenton and Craig—were involved with the animals. They grew up with them. I thought it was wonderful that the family still had many of the animals that they had kept during the decades of Bullen's Circus and then running the African Lion Safari Parks, all of which had closed down many years before. Clearly there was enough work for both Brenton and Craig to remain in the industry.

When Stafford died, both Craig and Brenton called me. I decided to go to the funeral. The family had been good to me, and I felt honoured to have met Stafford. There was something about him, a certain grandeur, and he had worked his whole life with animals. Meeting him had felt a bit like meeting a mentor I hadn't previously known about. I also wanted to be one more supportive person for the family, because I know how it feels to have support from others at a time of loss.

I expected to spend the day pretty much by myself, because I didn't know many people there, but people were friendly and came up to talk to me. As it turned out, I met many of those people again in the years ahead. Craig hung around a bit, but I told him not to worry about me. I still didn't know him very well and I thought surely there were others he needed to talk to.

There had been no physical contact between Craig and I at this stage, but there was obviously a strong chemistry between us that seemed to be getting stronger. I told him we were not going to happen—I liked him and clearly he liked me, but my reasons for not wanting to get involved remained. I wanted to stay friends with all of his family, and I was unimpressed by the fact that he had left his partner and their two children. I recalled the pain my father had caused by walking out of our lives.

Craig told me he would never walk out of his children's lives. He pointed out that he was still deeply involved in his children's lives, and his intention had never been to walk away from them. He was supporting them financially and saw them regularly as they were living at his house while he was living at his parents' house, both of which were at Park Road. He told me he wanted to be the best dad he could be and that, if he was an angry, sad person he was not going to be the best. He told me, 'I don't want to stay in a relationship just because my children are there. That way, I would surely have unhappy children.'

In spite of these discussions, I told him yet again—we were just not going to happen.

# CHAPTER 31

# Of course you can stay

But, of course, it did happen. In December two of the stuntmen I'd worked with at Mario's—gorgeous Cedric and *voltige* rider Eric—came for a visit. I spent Christmas with them and the Nicholls clan at Fred and Bert's, and during that time Craig came down from Sydney. We all had an enjoyable few days riding horses around the Gundagai hills, and the French boys got to experience an Aussie summer in the bush. After Christmas, Eric, Cedric and I drove back to the Gold Coast.

While I was in France, Fred and Bert had been looking after my two mares. I mentioned to Craig that I wanted to bring them back home, and rather than put them on a transporter for the thirteen-hundred-kilometre trip he suggested that he would drive back down to Gundagai, borrow Fred's float and bring them up. I thanked him for his offer, but told him not to put himself out. He argued that he was owed a longer holiday and said that he had a mate on the Gold Coast he wanted to catch up with, and finally that he would like to stay on and see how Brenton was doing with the third series of *BeastMaster*. In the end, I gave in. It certainly would be good to have the horses back at my place, and it would be nice to see him, but I told him emphatically, 'Don't think anything is going to happen.'

He drove up from Gundagai on a hot summer's day, and his LandCruiser ute kept overheating. Each time it broke down he'd call me and explain that he was waiting for it to cool down and they would be delayed. I am fairly sure the trip took him seventeen and a half hours; certainly, by the time he got to my house, I was more than impressed. I thought, 'This guy has stamina!' He had had to wait with his ute on the side of the road several times, but he'd looked after the horses and kept on coming.

There was a bunch of people at Maudsland Road when he arrived—Cedric and Eric, Lydia, and two other friends staying from overseas. We unloaded the horses, and they ran out across the paddock, bucking and squealing with their mates. I always love that part.

It was just on dusk, and everyone was making their way back to the house. Craig casually put his arm around me as we turned to go. He asked, 'Is it alright if I go get my swag and stay here tonight?'

Without even thinking, I said 'Of course you can stay here— you can stay in my bed.'

Shocked at myself, I stood with my eyebrows raised, just staring up at him. I thought, 'What the hell?' I must've sounded like such a tart!

He smiled, looked into my eyes and said, 'Really?'

I said, 'I feel like such an idiot,' and he laughed.

He said, 'Well, things are getting better.' And that was the start of our relationship.

As it turned out, this was also the beginning of our working life together. For a year we would both travel back and forth between each other's places, but I spent far more time in Sydney than he did on the Gold Coast because of his commitments to the family business, his children and his animals.

Craig and I both worked with animals, but our backgrounds were very different. Craig had spent years working and touring with the elephants. He liked travelling with the circus, moving from town to town around Australia doing 'one-nighters in the mud', as he called them.

He described the circus life for me. You pull into a town and set up the housing for the animals; then, rain, hail or shine you put up the tent (or 'the show', as they call it), and put on a performance. That same night, everything is pulled down and packed away into trucks, except the animals, who are loaded the following morning, when everyone moves on.

The Bullens had always had elephants, and in the 1960s Stafford had imported four Thai elephants into Australia to join the rest of the Bullen elephant herd. Bimbo, Siam, Sabu and Burma had arrived when Craig was a toddler, so they are about the same age as Craig and have been a huge part of his life.

At first Stafford and his brother Ken looked after the elephants, but as the kids grew up, Mark became one of the key elephant handlers, and then Craig, who is ten years younger, followed in his footsteps. When Craig was fourteen he and Mark used to present them in the ring and care for them. Sometimes they had to go find the elephants, because they'd broken out of their paddock and made their way into someone's award-winning garden or a sugar-cane field. It was a lot of responsibility for a teenager.

Craig's high-school years were dominated by his work with his father and the animals. He was only fifteen years old when he fought off their only aggressive elephant, Burma, when she attacked and almost killed Mark. A few years later the Bullens gave Burma to Taronga Zoo, and she currently lives at Taronga Western Plains Zoo at Dubbo with two other retired elephants. All that experience matured Craig significantly. When I asked him about working with elephants, he told me that a massive part of their training is simply building mutual respect. Obviously, because of their size, if they won't listen to you, you're in trouble.

Eventually, Mark and Sonya moved on from the family business, for different reasons. At the age of twelve, Mark had started breeding Welsh mountain ponies and he is now one of the world's most successful breeders. Sonya had worked with all the animals, especially the ponies and baboons, and had hand-raised the family's pet chimpanzee. She then married Rick and had two kids, and she is now settled on the Gold Coast. By the time I met the Bullens, it was only Craig and Brenton who had continued to work with the family's animals, taking on all the responsibilities that entailed.

When I first saw Craig around animals, I could see straight-away that he was very experienced and knowledgeable. As good and professional as Craig was, however, I felt that something was missing. I wasn't convinced he really enjoyed being around the animals, and yet he told me he did. I remember thinking to myself, 'If I can't see it, how can he feel it?' We talked about this a couple of times, but I'm sure he dismissed me as one of those bloody 'horse-whisperer' types.

Working with the animals had been his life and his job—along with fixing the water trough, repairing a fence, building a new trailer, changing an axle, repairing the plumbing or whatever else had to be done to keep the show on the road. There had been no time for stopping and smelling the roses or getting enjoyment from what he was doing.

I felt the animals were innocent victims in all of that. I used to say to him, 'Wait, wait—let's watch and see how the animals behave together,' and he'd say, 'What do you want to watch that for? We haven't got time to do that.'

He did like being around the animals. He much preferred that to fixing vehicles or building a fence; but he rarely got to enjoy the experience, because he was always in a hurry to get back to the neverending list of jobs to do. Consequently, I don't think they enjoyed him all that much. Yet the elephants loved him—he had probably travelled with the elephants enough to enjoy their company and for them to enjoy his.

I remember one day that was quite a turning point in our relationship. I was staying at Park Road with Craig, and we were drenching some young camels that had rarely been touched by people before then. They were friendly, but they hadn't been handled very much. They were being kept in a temporary holding yard, and before they were trucked to the old lion park they needed to be wormed.

Most of them we caught and wormed without much fuss. However, one runty young camel was being difficult. She kicked Craig when he tried to catch her; then they wrestled and she dragged him around. Finally she went quiet and he said, 'Quick, bring the drench.'

I took the drench over to him. He treated the camel and was about to let her go, but I said, 'Wait! What are you doing?'

'It's drenched, we can let her go,' he said, looking at me in bemusement.

'Didn't you tell me this was a fairly unhandled camel?' I said. 'Just wait. Let's be nice to her now—it doesn't have to be just a big scary experience for her.' Craig didn't say anything, but we led her around for a bit, patted her, gave her some grain and then we let her go.

At that point we both realised that I was someone who was born to lie on the floor and roll around with a dog and cuddle my pony, while Craig was born and raised to work animals, and then to get on with it—there were always plenty of other things that still needed to be done.

I knew that this was just the way he had been brought up, but I also know you can do so much more with animals when you connect with them on an emotional level.

Those early days were an amazing time in both of our lives. I hadn't been with Craig very long at all before I felt that I could marry him, and that scared me. I told him how I felt because I wanted him to know what an impact he was having on me, and I felt safe saying it because I knew he wasn't the marrying type—he had never married before. He agreed that he didn't like the thought of marriage.

Being around him I had also started to think I wanted to have kids. There was something about him that was making me rethink all the strict promises I'd made to myself after Grahame died, about not getting attached or having children. Craig was flattered when I told him, but at the time neither of us took these changes in me too seriously.

CHAPTER 32

# Ned Kelly

In February 2002, Mark Eady contacted me. He had the entertainment contract to organise and choreograph a performance of the story of Ned Kelly at the Royal Easter Show in Sydney and he asked if I would work with him as a liberty horse trainer. To train a horse at liberty is to teach it to respond to verbal or visual cues without any direct contact, and it requires a lot of trust and respect between trainer and animal. I had trained liberty horses with both Sled and Bobby, and I jumped at the chance.

I was excited about the opportunity, but despite the adequate eight-week preparation time I soon became apprehensive. It would be the first time that I would be solely responsible for how a horse performed. I voiced my concerns about committing to the job to Sled; he said that he and his new girlfriend, Tamara, would come out from America for a couple of weeks to help. I was surprised and relieved by his offer.

I would need two white horses for the performance. I already owned a beautiful white Andalusian mare, J'adore, and I bought another white gelding out of my own funds. Split—so named because he had a split at the top of one of his ears, from an old injury—was trained for both riding and harness work (pulling a carriage). He had a lovely soft nature and was to be my back-up horse.

In early March Sled and Tamara turned up as promised. With his trademark sense of humour, Sled told me I was ready for this job, that I'd be fine and that I should look on the bright side—I could stuff it up as effectively as the next person! He spent most of the two weeks he was there laughing at me for being so stressed. He told me I would be alright—and I was.

The script called for the white horse to gallop unassisted through gunfire to the actor who was playing Ned, who would be standing in the middle of the show ring, a football arena which had been constructed for the 2000 Sydney Olympics.

The show ended with the boy who played the young Ned Kelly riding J'adore bareback into the centre of the ring, where he slid off. J'adore then lay down. The boy lay down next to her and the spotlight went out.

Each night there would be a hush, and then the crowd would erupt into applause. I was so proud of my two talented horses, but especially my kind-hearted J'adore.

My first independent liberty act, with my own beautiful horses, was a success.

# CHAPTER 33

# Travelling with elephants

The Bullens' elephants were booked to go to Burtons Circus in Adelaide for the April school holidays and Craig invited me to go along. This was to be my first experience helping him with them in a circus environment.

Before we left, I learnt the basics of how to handle them, how to deal with the inter-elephant politics—who was fed where, who was loaded onto the truck first, all the important basics. I had been around the elephants a little bit before then but I hadn't been responsible for getting them to do anything. Those elephants normally perform like clockwork, but they can still behave like naughty little kids if they think they'll get away with it. You could almost see them thinking, 'Aha, you're new—I might just casually lift my back foot and lean it out towards you, or maybe swish you with my tail.' Of course, I'd be thinking, 'Is this elephant going to kick me?'

Whenever I felt uneasy I would ask Craig what I should do,

but he was so used to being around them that it was difficult for him to understand my uncertainty. I remember thinking to myself: 'Not everybody grew up with elephants.'

He had taught me a few commands, such as 'Toi!' In Thai, this means 'Back up' or 'Back off'. One day I had to say this to Siam, but she just looked at me and didn't budge.

I looked at Craig and he said, 'Tell her again.'

I said, 'Toi . . . Please?' Of course she ignored me.

At that, Craig came over and growled, 'Siam,' and she obeyed straightaway. It was as though Dad had arrived home from work and was disciplining a naughty kid. She backed up immediately and then she looked at me, as though she was thinking, 'I saw that you had to call him over.' So that's how it was for a time. I was totally in love with Bimbo, though, because Bimbo never tested me. She would come when she was called and would do anything I asked.

I told Craig I would never ask an elephant to do something if I knew that they didn't respect me. I was too scared of what they might do. He didn't think much of that. 'I don't know what your problem is,' he said. 'If they don't do what you ask, you growl at them and they behave themselves.'

I thought, 'I don't want to growl at an elephant.'

But even though it was difficult at times, it was an amazing experience and I knew how lucky I was to be having it. I was delighted when the elephants finally accepted me and let me into their group. It was an honour to be around those gigantic pachyderms that the whole world seems to love.

Their life at Park Road was like a big holiday for them—they had huge paddocks with dams to swim in and endless supplies of grass and hay, plus a giant shed to sleep in at night. But you

With Zoey the zebra foal and Ben Hur the pony while working on *Racing Stripes*, 2003.

Trick riding on Lobo during pre-production of *The Legend of Zorro*, 2004.

On Lobo in Mexico working on *The Legend of Zorro*, 2004.

With Antonio Banderas, 2004.

I get a kiss from Wonkey with Chakeeta standing by in Mexico, 2004.

Working on interspecies bonding with Billy the chimp and Wallace the lion, 2005.

With Craig, Jamie and Jim Stockley working Sasha and Azarro the cheetahs on the set of *Elephant Tales*, 2005.

With Craig and Jerry the giraffe during pre-production on *Elephant Tales*, 2005.

Working with Billy the chimp, 2005.

Working Percy with Craig on the set of *Charlotte's Web*, 2005.

With Craig on J'adore on our wedding day, 2005.

The horse girls at our wedding. Lydia, Heidi, Tamzin, me, Freda, Melody, Brit—The Magnificent Seven, 2005.

With Craig and Colt, helping him down from Tai the elephant, 2009.

Colt having cat cuddles, 2009.

Trick riding on Mozart, pictured here in a full fender layout (a trick-riding position I was in when Mozart's front hooves slipped in the damp clay and he fell on me, breaking my left ankle and leg), 2009.

With Nelson, Craig, Colt and Columbia and Princess the leopard in 2009.

Cueing Abraham to rear when he is captured by the German soldiers on the set of *War Horse*, 2010.

Cueing Abraham to rear when he is cornered by the tank on the set of *War Horse*, 2010.

Working Abraham from within the chalked circle (to stay out of the shots of three cameras) on the set of *War Horse*, 2010.

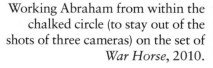

Waiting with Abraham for the cameras to roll, with Steven Spielberg on *War Horse*; 2010.

With Freda, Kate and Cloud, Christmas 2011.

With Colt on Traveller, 2012 (El Hogan Photography).

could see how much they loved travelling. As soon as they heard the elephant truck start up, they would come running across their paddock, trumpeting and hustling to be let through the gate to load up.

The time for our departure came about quite quickly, and all of a sudden we were getting ready to leave. The elephants were being transported by Craig in the semi-trailer, and I was to drive on my own in the support truck, which carried all of the hay and equipment and also towed the ten-metre caravan. I hadn't towed anything like that before, let alone over a distance of fourteen hundred kilometres.

A few years back I'd got my truck licence and I had limited experience driving a truck. One time I was driving one of Wayne's horse trucks and he said, 'You don't really have a truck licence, do you?' That's how good I wasn't.

There were too many things to organise before we left for me to get any practice in the truck, but Craig had showed me some of its little idiosyncrasies. He said 'When you change gears, you have to pump the clutch twice, and it's sticky in third gear.' It had a double H pattern gearbox in reverse, and I knew that was a little bit funky. I hadn't said a thing to him, for fear of sounding incompetent, but, as we drove out from Park Road, I think I was shaking. I told myself sternly, 'Zelie, it's a truck—how hard can it be?'

We set off at four in the morning. I followed Craig out of Park Road and away we went. We had a fair bit of stopping and starting at the traffic lights through Sydney before we reached the freeway, but we went pretty well. At the first fuel stop, Craig asked me how I was going in the truck and I said, 'OK. I think I've got the hang of it.' He sort of smiled and gave me a hug.

He didn't say anything else to me about it at the time, but for years afterwards he told people how impressed he was that I had got into this great big truck with a gigantic caravan on the back and driven to Adelaide. I was so glad I didn't say what I was thinking, which was, 'What do you think you're doing to me? You think I can just get in and drive that truck?!' Instead I had fallen back on the words I had told myself many times growing up: 'I can do it, I can do it.' And thankfully, it all worked out fine.

# CHAPTER 34

# Education and welfare

*'It requires very little knowledge to care
passionately about animals. It requires a great deal
of understanding to care properly for them.'*

John Webster, Emeritus Professor, Bristol University UK

Craig and I loved what we were doing; the elephants loved what they were doing; and so did the public who came to see the elephants—to stand near them and just watch for hours as these big gentle giants moved around, grazing and socialising. It was wonderful to see how everyone, from children to the elderly, responded to them. Sometimes people came up to us to say they remembered seeing the elephants with Craig's dad or grandfather.

I am always more than happy to answer questions anyone has about the animals. Soon after I began working with the elephants I started to carry around a little photo album with photos of them at Park Road—in their lush grassy paddocks, playing in the dam and rolling in the mud, and rubbing against the big trees, their own personal scratching posts.

When the elephants are working and travelling we pull up every night at a designated circus ground allotted by the local councils or at friends' country properties. Depending on where we stop for the night, the elephants can wander among the trees, have a dust bath, or swim in a lake or a dam. Although they love performing and the attention they receive from the public, their life is not simply being in the ring and then back in the truck. I explain to people that they love their life.

On one trip, we called into Fred and Bert's farm and let the elephants out in the front paddock which is heavily timbered and has a shallow dam. We laughed as the locals pulled over in amazement and came to see what was happening, including a team of shearers who had finished work for the day and who already had a couple of beers under their belt. One of them exclaimed that he'd heard about seeing pink elephants, but this was ridiculous.

I got a lot of pleasure out of educating people about the elephants. Sometimes they would say things like, 'They don't look happy' or 'I don't know how I feel about this'. Then I would tell them how I felt and what I knew; and, most importantly, what to observe in the elephants and how to read their emotions.

Craig, who had put up with inexperienced people's comments all of his life, would make me simultaneously laugh and cringe sometimes when he heard some concerned person say to me, 'Those elephants don't look happy.' Craig would shout out, 'Oh really? What do your elephants look like when they're happy?' In other words, if you don't know elephant expressions and body language, then don't pass judgement.

The downside to being with the elephants was experiencing the animal rights extremists. It was a very steep learning curve. I had always thought, 'Fair call—these are people who are concerned about animals and who are voicing their opinion.' But when I saw first-hand how violent and abusive these people could be, I was astonished. Some of them weren't interested in the truth or what more experienced people had to say about working with animals.

If I got into a debate with them, I would sometimes say, 'Yes, of course animals have emotions. But do you have a dog?' And they'd come out with something like, 'No, I don't have a dog. Dogs should be running free—I don't even think blind people should exploit dogs.' When I heard that sort of thing, I thought 'What planet are you from?'

Circus carries with it an unjustified stigma, thanks to a mixture of bad publicity and a few bad eggs. While travelling overseas I have sometimes seen farm animals, performing animals and even pets living in inhumane conditions, and it's broken my heart; I've wanted nothing more than to get those animals away from the people who are mistreating them or not providing adequate care, but I also know often the situations are complicated. In countries with low socio-economic status, many animals suffer from starvation, and/or lack of medical treatment. I know that not everyone in the world is innocent, but I sure know that the people who are innocent don't deserve what they get from animal activisits!

Many of the animal rights activists don't have a real working relationship with animals; they appear to be more interested in causing economic damage, sensational headlines and misery than actually understanding the true relationship existing between humans and their animals. If animal rights activists truly cared about animals, I believe they would focus on things like the cruelty to dogs in countries where they are beaten before being eaten, but they seem to be more interested in causing problems in industries where the animals are productive and happy.

Through my work I know many people who own animals as companions or who depend on animals for their income; the vast majority of them put the welfare of their animals above their own. They will risk their lives in fires and floods to save their animals; they go without sleep to look after sick animals; they spend huge amounts of money to give their animals the best vet care—sometimes, even when they can't afford to take proper care of themselves. All the farmers and horse breeders I know are dedicated to the welfare of their animals, because they get the best results from happy, contented animals. And because they care.

Of course, there are animal rights activists and then there are animal welfare supporters. It was only relatively recently that I learnt the very important difference between 'animal welfare' and 'animal rights'. People who love, care for and work with animals care deeply about animal welfare. Craig and I are animal welfare supporters, as are most people who love and adore their animals—they want their animals to live in fantastic conditions, they want their animals to be happy, they want them to look good. They won't look good if they are badly treated.

If you have a dog, you'll know how excited it gets when you get home from work or school. To see that same excitement in an elephant is to me just the utmost pleasure, because of their grandeur and intelligence.

The first time we came back to Park Road after being away for several months, the reception Craig received from the elephants made me cry. He didn't think anything of it—he just said, 'Hey there, girls,' and hugged them, with his arm around one trunk and around another's leg, while they were all 'peeping' (a noise they make through the end of their trunk, expressing comfort and happiness). It always amazes me how gentle they can be with their trunks; here they were caressing, encircling and smelling Craig with joy. It is just a beautiful thing. I am really grateful to have that knowledge of elephant behaviour, and how much they love their human family.

CHAPTER 35

# The Man from Snowy River

After the trip to Adelaide, we took the elephants back to Park Road for a well-deserved break. That was when Tony Jablonski got in touch with me. He was putting together a live show that was to tour around Australia; he wanted to know if I could train a liberty horse to rear for him and if I would trick ride in the show. I jumped at the chance.

At the time, Craig wasn't happy at Park Road. He had lived and worked out of that place all of his life. The more I got to know Craig, the more confused and frustrated I realised he was. Since Stafford had died his sons were trying to run the business and things had become messy. Brenton and Craig fought a lot. Craig had a lot of difficulty expressing his frustration. When he tried to communicate with any of his family, but particularly with Brenton, the conversation seemed to deteriorate into personal attacks on each other. I thought they were both beautiful people, and was really upset to see them so divided. Brenton was trying to be the man who organised the jobs and Craig felt like he was being treated as Brenton's employee. When I took up Tony's job offer, Craig decided to come with me.

*The Man from Snowy River Arena Spectacular* took us all over Australia. Instead of camping and travelling with caravans as we had with the circus, we were accommodated in motel rooms and had the option of being flown between cities. Craig and I drove from place to place and stayed with our horses, the way I always like it.

I had previously travelled in Craig's domain, but now he was in somebody else's travelling tour, and I was blown away by how handy he was. He drove trucks when others got tired; he had horses rugged and feeds ready by the time we'd changed out of our costumes; he would put his hand to anything, from helping backstage to being out front to giving constructive criticism. As always, he became indispensable and I loved him seeing me perform. I couldn't have been happier to have had him by my side.

He was the most impressive person I had ever been around, and I know that I wouldn't be where I am today without Craig. You know the old saying, 'Behind every good man there is a good woman'; well, with us the roles are reversed—he is the person who has helped me achieve everything I have in the last ten years. He is so quiet and unassuming, but I wish he could get more credit—and yet he doesn't seem to crave that. I think he appreciates it when he is recognised, but he doesn't seek it out.

We worked with some great people on that show. In particular, it was terrific to catch up with Lee Kernaghan again. He is a lovely, unaffected person who exudes happiness. He is also a very talented and well-respected man, and has done lots of fantastic things for the music industry, giving pleasure to many through his music. Even though by now he had become a very successful country and western singer, he was still the same humble fun man I remembered from Movie World. His wife, Robyn, was pregnant at the time, and she still performed on keyboard and sang all the way through the Arena spectacular with Lee and the rest of the band.

He composed a song for the show, about a guy who rescues a damsel in distress by jumping off his horse onto a team of runaway horses. The sequence was performed by the buckboard drivers (a buckboard is a long open carriage) and trick riding. The song was called 'Snowy Mountains Buck Jump', and we rode our horses back to front and stood in our saddles as he performed it.

It was a load of fun to have such a fantastic guy on the team with us and to rekindle our old friendship.

When we finished touring with Tony, Craig and I returned to Park Road and took the elephants on a run up the north coast of New South Wales with another circus for the school holidays. For the first time we had Craig's two gorgeous kids with us. Nelson was six and Columbia was three, and they appeared to love being on tour as much as we did. They even performed as part of a whip-cracking act. Columbia was so adorable—she'd tell her dad to hurry up when he was getting ready for a show or she would be late for her performance.

I loved traipsing around like a gypsy; I still love it. I love that you can set up somewhere and create a little township with the people you have been travelling with; and then soon you are all back on the road and setting up somewhere else, where there is a whole new world of people to entertain, who bring their own excitement and energy with them. Obviously there are times when it is difficult—for example in thunderstorms or hot, dry, dusty conditions, or when you're not feeling like being on show. For plenty of people we know, their home is their truck or caravan and they wouldn't have it any other way. For me, personally, I eventually like going back to my home, to the peace and privacy.

When you're working on a show, you don't tend to watch the entire thing. Once the kids had finished performing and the elephant act was over, Craig would put the elephants away and the kids and I would go back to the caravan, which was parked alongside the tent.

On one particularly wild and windy night, we were all back in the van and Nelson was looking out the window, because it was raining and blowing a gale. Then he suddenly called out, 'Dad, the tent's falling down!'

Several of the Bullens had previously tried to explain to me the amount of pressure and responsibility you bear when you are the 'tent boss', meaning that you're in charge of all the seating that has to be erected and the temporary structure that is raised over the top of it. If the seating or the tent were to collapse, many lives would be in peril. I hadn't fully understood this responsibility until that night, when I witnessed a 'blow-down' on a sandy lot in a torrential gale.

Hearing Nelson's words, Craig and I rushed to the window and watched as part of the tent collapsed, and the other half flew up and exposed seating and people. Fortunately, before the collapse happened, the ringmaster had seen it starting to come away and calmly asked over the PA system for everyone to leave the tent as quickly as possible. No one was hurt.

When we'd left the tent earlier, I'd seen one of the performers, a talented Moroccan tumbler and dog trainer, waiting backstage to perform an act with his dogs. Now, as the tent came down and the rain washed over them, I could hear him calling for his favourite kelpie cross. He loved that dog, and he kept screaming her name out into the storm; he had found all of the others, but she was still missing.

Craig told me to keep the kids with me as he ran out to help unhook the canvas and to get it all back under control. They eventually found Mohammad's dog, who was patiently waiting under a pile of canvas, but the memory of that poor man shrieking out for his dog still gives me goose bumps.

CHAPTER 36

# Jim and Silvana

Sled had contacted me about an animal movie possibly coming up in South Africa; however I didn't want to get my hopes up, so I had put it out of my mind—sometimes movies come off and sometimes they don't.

Then, in May 2003, I received a call from Genevieve Hofmeyr, who was working as production manager with Lloyd Phillips, the producer, whom I had previously worked with in Namibia. She told me that Sled was off the movie, because of a disagreement between him and production, but was I still able to do the picture?

I told her I'd have to think about it. I didn't want to be disloyal to Sled, so I called him, but he was on a downer and wouldn't come to the phone. Instead I spoke to him via Tamara, and let him know that I'd been approached to do the film. I heard him in the background telling her that I might as well go ahead. As a result, I took the job, but I now know he didn't mean it and that he felt betrayed when I went. He hasn't spoken to me since, and I miss him—I miss his fun.

Sled had originally been planning to use Craig as a zebra trainer, and I asked Genevieve if they still wanted that to happen. She said that would be up to the man now in charge of the zebra department, and Craig had to submit a résumé. Fortunately, his application was successful.

We arrived in South Africa in June 2003 to work on *Racing Stripes*, which was a very big animal movie. The animal department was extremely well treated, and we met many lovely people. We were given one or two days off every week, and on the weekends we went to game parks. We did a lot of travelling in a short space of time and met many animal people at the different game parks.

Among the first people we met were Jim and Silvana Stockley, based in KwaZulu-Natal. Craig knew of the Stockley family because Jim's father had been friends with Stafford (in fact, it was during one of Stafford's overseas trips that he met Jim's family and was inspired to open his own drive-through safari parks in Australia and New Zealand), and also because Craig had worked for Jim's cousins at Chipperfield's Circus in New Zealand several years before. Craig and Jim had led almost parallel lives in different countries. They both came from circus families, had raised and trained various exotic animals, and as a result they basically understand each other without having to speak. They got along very well.

Jim is a little older than Craig, and is extremely articulate and very well educated. To this day, I turn to him for advice on many issues. For example, I had always thought it strange that the Bullens didn't get along better, but Jim explained that that's often the way with circus families as can happen in any family business.

Silvana also fascinated me—she was so youthful, always immaculately dressed, and full of energy. I love her attitude to life and enjoy her stories, her experiences, her humour and her company. She too had been raised in a circus family, and I found it so helpful to talk to them both. I knew I adored Craig and yet there were still things I didn't understand about him. Jim and Silvana helped me by explaining, and they continue to help me understand many complicated situations at different times.

Jim and Silvana, along with Jim's sister Jane and her husband Brian Boswell, run a zoo on their private property; but they also have a circus that travels throughout Africa, plus an animal-training facility, a large studio for filming bluescreen, a game ranch and a drive-through lion park.

For an outside film company, it makes sense to go and shoot films on the Stockley property, and many do. The Stockleys have the facilities, generations of animal knowledge, and animals on site that have been hand-raised, handled, trained and loved. Every time we go there, there is something new happening that we can be involved with, whether it's getting slobbered on by a baby giraffe, looking after a range of big cat cubs, hand-raising young monkeys or a rhino, or taking a look at a new circus act in training. It's a pretty unique set-up.

Their property also provides winter quarters for Jane and Brian's circus. Jane is a delight to be around and her brother Jim is monumental in animal work throughout Africa and the world.

Working in South Africa was a totally different experience for me, compared to the last film I had been on in Africa. *Running Free* had been shot entirely in a secluded location in Namibia, whereas *Racing Stripes* was set on a farm near Durban and security there was very tight.

Before this job, I had no idea how dangerous South Africa was. The intensity and frequency of crime was shocking. Many of the South African tribes are still strongly influenced by witch doctors, some of whom are pretty shonky. It wasn't unusual to read in the local newspaper about various barbaric practices, such as a witch doctor who had boiled up a child's head for medicine. One potent belief in some of the communities is that you can be cured of AIDS if you sleep with a virgin, so rates of child rape are high and sometimes even babies are victims.

I adore South Africa. Although, I would not recommend it as a backpacker destination, I would highly recommend it for a well-planned holiday with a reputable travel and tourist company. On our days off, we used to rent a car and just set off with a map, heading towards a game park. On the way we sometimes had to stop and get petrol, and we usually had no idea what that petrol station would be like. We could easily find ourselves in a very hostile environment, wondering if we were going to be able to get out. Many of the people around us were clearly very poor, and you could often feel the hostility. At times we needed to act very carefully to be able to get out of those situations.

We were very lucky in a couple of instances. On one occasion, Craig, two American trainers and myself had got lost in

Pietermaritzburg. We turned left instead of right at a particular intersection and the American boys began to freak out. We were in this very rundown area and they were yelling, 'Wind up your windows! Let's get out of here—look at how they're looking at us.' Craig was driving and even he was obviously uncomfortable, but at the time I just thought they were being dramatic.

When I told Jim that story, he looked at me and said, 'Zelie, you need to learn about Africa—you need to develop a local antenna. If you are the only tourists in an area and you feel hostility, that is because you are in the wrong place and you may be in real danger.'

South Africa is potentially a very dangerous place, but it is also a place of beauty and magnificence, opportunity and adventure.

# CHAPTER 37

# *Racing Stripes*

Jim Stockley supplied some of the zebras used in *Racing Stripes*. Along with the rest of the zebra crew, Craig had a series of complicated situations to work out, often with the smaller barnyard animals. My job was to train the three brown miniature ponies who played 'Tucker', one of the main characters; they all had to be liberty trained. Often the horse and zebra departments had to pull together to achieve the sequences.

I was very grateful to Bobby Lovgren and Bill Lawrence, two of the horse trainers, for their continuous guidance. In Namibia in 1997 I had been Bobby's assistant; I hadn't seen or worked with him since, but he realised that I had continued to practise what I had originally learnt from him and that I had a 'feel' for it. Since *Running Free*, Bobby's reputation as a liberty horse trainer had escalated, and he was now considered to be one of the best in the world. In the seven months we worked together in South Africa he took my training skills to another level.

Bill is an American Indian who was born and raised on the White Swan reservation in northern United States. He has generations of horsemanship behind him and has raised, handled and educated thousands of wild horses in his lifetime. I know it is not unusual for him to muster in thirty wild horses, and break them in on the reservation all at once. He has an innate well-tuned response to reading a horse, he is a natural.

I was on set with my ponies most days, often all day. It was right up my alley, although I have to say that my knees have never been the same since. When I first started training the ponies, I had been wondering what was wrong with them and why they didn't obey my cues, but then I realised they couldn't see me or my cues! I quickly learnt to lower my cues and spent much of my time kneeling or crouching and it was hard going on my knees and ankles.

It soon became apparent to me that I needed an assistant to help me with training the ponies. At the same time, the woman in charge of the barnyard department had become very bossy and demanding. She had told me not to do any training sessions with the ponies unless she was there, because she wanted to learn how I did it. I wasn't comfortable with that, so I would shut the barn door and continue to train on my own, but then she would come in and tell me off.

In my career I've been lucky enough to have been shown a lot of training techniques and methods by various people, and also how to handle various situations, but it was never because I'd demanded that they show me their secrets! Professional trainers are generally private about showing their techniques to strangers—they first need to know the person's capabilities. Chris Anderson taught me, very early on, that in the film industry attitude is ninety per cent of how good you will get. I learnt that, when I arrived on someone else's turf, 'rolling over and showing your belly'—never being presumptuous, and never pretending to know more than I did—resulted in almost everyone I met being very generous to me with their knowledge and experiences.

I went to talk to Bobby. He had predominantly trained me and he didn't want his knowledge passed on willy-nilly, so he sorted it out with the producer, Lloyd Phillips. Bobby also knew that I needed an assistant but there wasn't enough time to train anyone. Then I had a thought. I told him I knew of a horse girl from Australia I'd worked with before—maybe she could be my assistant. I spoke with Lloyd, and then I called Brit.

I'd heard of Brit Sooby for years before I actually met her. She and Tamzin had been best friends at school, and Tamzin had told me all about her. When Tamzin got married, Brit and I were both her bridesmaids; I got to know her a bit then and thought she was really sweet.

Later, Brit had moved east to become a stunt performer. I had welcomed her into my home and introduced her to people and stunt coordinators whom I felt would help her, and away she went. She is a lovely girl and we'd quickly become friends.

After Craig and I had left for South Africa, she'd had a very emotional breakup with her first serious long-time boyfriend. She called to talk to me; she was devastated and didn't know what to do. Her world had been tipped upside down and she was thinking of travelling, so I suggested she might like Africa.

In August, Craig and I picked her up from Durban and we asked how her flight was. 'I hate those long economy flights,' she replied. 'Is there anywhere we can get a soy latte?' Craig and I looked at each other and thought 'Uh-oh.' We were in Africa; someone could well kill all three of us and take our money and steal our clothes—and she was after a soy latte?

She looked at our faces and asked, 'Is that a bad question?'

But as it turned out Brit's easygoing personality meant she fitted in with the crew, and she adapted to South Africa quickly. As my assistant, she was a huge help.

One of the sad things for me on *Racing Stripes* was learning that I couldn't help every single person that I came into contact with.

There was a bit of theft going on within the animal department, and one of the stable staff was sacked to be made an example of. People had been stealing bread and other things and this particular guy was sacked because he had used some shoe polish. A trainer had asked him to darken some rope with the polish so it didn't look brand new, and then he'd used some of it to polish his own shoes. I really rebelled against that, saying that I didn't think it was fair, but I was told repeatedly to stay out of it and that I didn't know how things worked in South Africa.

The guy who got the sack hung around for weeks, begging for his job back; then he started to work for free, wanting to pay for the shoe polish he'd used—anything to rectify what he had done. Even when we moved locations, he continued to turn up, but he wasn't allowed to return. In situations where many people are poor, if you steal or do something wrong, there is always someone there to fill your shoes. Whatever he had earned wasn't much, but it was important to him.

He seemed like such a lovely guy. His English was poor, but he always smiled when I said good morning to him, unlike a lot of the local workers, who would look down at the ground. Understandably, some of them were hostile towards white people, while for others it is part of their culture not to look a woman in the eye—they think it is disrespectful. Or they might feel that you are trying to pity them, which is an insult to them also.

There were all sorts of cultural issues and problems. I didn't fully understand it. Seeing people be treated unfairly was very hard. I used to spend some of my living-away-from-home allowance at the store on things for the staff, such as chocolate and locally made jewellery, until I was asked to slow down with that as well. I learnt there were several reasons for that: I could be taken advantage of; I would be seen as weaker than the others, so I would get pestered and hassled; or I was making myself different from everyone else, more vulnerable. Some of the local people told me that I was setting myself up to be stolen from as I would be identified as having money. I just had to make myself back off, and that was hard.

We were working in a well-guarded compound provided with vehicles, drivers and security guards. As a result, we had a false sense of security. Craig, Brit and I used to go jogging along our road. The Van Gessels, the lovely people who owned the B&B where we were staying, said that it was fine to do so as long as we were back before dusk. 'Don't stop and talk to anyone,' they advised us, 'and if a car slows down, don't look at the car—just keep jogging.' It all seemed a bit over-protective, I thought.

It was a lovely little road and we had been jogging along it for months, but then Craig read in the paper that a man had been found there eating another human being. Boiling in a pot next to him were parts of the person he had been eating—right where we went running. I thought, 'We're fine jogging along here? When the people are eating each other on the side of the road?'

We worked long hours on *Racing Stripes*, but we were well looked after and we had a lot of fun. It was the first time Craig had been to any part of Africa and he loved it, as I did.

At the end of production, the hardest thing for me was leaving behind those ponies I had trained. My career is a childhood dream come true, but there is one major setback. When I work with an animal for any period, I usually end up falling totally in love with it. I go in knowing it's not my animal, but when I form a relationship with that animal, I feel obliged to ensure that it continues to have a good life. That animal has learnt to trust me. Just because production has packed up and gone home doesn't mean that I can leave it until I feel comfortable about the sort of life it will go on leading. Saying goodbye to that animal at the end of the job can be completely devastating for me, but my sadness is eased somewhat when I know that the animal is going to a loving, knowledgeable home.

Two of the ponies, Mini-Me and Austin Powers, were returned to their owner in South Africa, who had a great home. However, we didn't know where the third pony, Ben Hur, was going to go. Although I would have loved to bring him home with me, we couldn't import him into Australia because of quarantine restrictions against African horse sickness, a deadly virus spread by insects that has no known treatment.

I was delighted when Jane and Brian Boswell bought him for their circus. Once I showed Jane all of Ben's cues, he fitted into circus life very quickly. He still loves the attention he draws when he performs in front of a large crowd, and Jane has a team of six miniature ponies who have become Ben Hur's family.

CHAPTER 38

# Fort Worth and Las Vegas

We enjoyed being with the Stockleys so much that, when filming finished on *Racing Stripes*, we didn't leave Africa straightaway but instead took the opportunity to explore other countries nearby, Zambia, Botswana and Zimbabwe, before returning to the Stockleys' for Christmas.

During the filming of *Racing Stripes*, Tad Griffith had called and asked if I wanted to be part of an international trick-riding act he was putting together for the Fort Worth Stock Show and Rodeo in Texas at the end of January. I didn't need to be asked twice; I was very excited by the prospect, but also nervous. I am never at my fittest when I'm shooting a film and working long hours, not to mention eating a lot of great catering food. On the other hand, I couldn't believe my luck: although I felt unfit, I had with me in South Africa our very own personal trainer—Brit! Utilising her expertise and experience, Craig and I both got into shape before the end of filming.

After Christmas we left South Africa and went home for a couple of days, repacked for a northern hemisphere winter and flew to the US then headed to Tad and Wendy's. There we met up with the one of the other trick riders, Tonia Forsberg.

Tad worked with Tonia and me, rehearsing for two solid weeks. The pressure was on, and I loved it. It was going to be the first time Tad had performed at his old stomping ground, Fort Worth, since his mum had passed away, and I was honoured to be involved.

We hauled Tad's horses the 2200 kilometres down to Texas in a gooseneck trailer with Tad, Wendy and their two little boys. Tonia had left a day or two before us in her own truck and trailer; it was a long way to go by herself. When we arrived, we met the third woman of our team, Niki Cammaert, who came down from Canada.

We were in the opening parade and then we had a twelve-minute act; during our trick-riding act we each had individual tricks that Tad had chosen for us to perform. When we became too sore from doing a particular trick we would swap them round. On my first night, just as I was about to go into that amazing arena, I remembered being up there in the audience with Heidi all those years ago and thinking what an amazing trick-riding arena it was—and now I was about to ride into it. It was the most exhilarating moment.

In the buzz of the live-show environment, Tad was in his element—managing us and each of his horses, looking after costuming, rehearsing, performing and socialising. We rehearsed each day before performing.

Craig and Wendy were invaluable as the ground crew, both of them again proving themselves completely dependable and wonderful. As had happened with Jim, Craig also became very close friends with Tad; it was as though they were family, in a way. Of course, Tad also came from a live-show background. He knew exactly what it was like: you travel, you pick up the animal poo, you perform and give it everything you have; then you get in your truck and do it all again in a new town. I could see a lot of similarities between Craig and Tad, and I think Wendy and I are alike in some ways too. Like us, they tend to 'live in the moment', and they obtain a lot of joy from their lives and from the people around them.

Tad and Craig both knew lots of the same characters from their parents' generation and the legends from each other's countries. For example, John Brady—Australia's best-ever rope spinner and also an awesome whip-cracker, sharpshooter and trick rider—had worked with both their fathers on different shows. There was lots of crossover.

I've always loved Wendy and Tad, and I was stoked that they embraced Craig like one of their own. Craig was impressed at what great people they were too.

Despite all of Craig's previous travelling, he had never been to Las Vegas. So, after the Fort Worth show finished, we decided to hire a car and go and see some shows. We didn't book any accommodation; we just turned up. We didn't want to spend too much money either: I said to Craig that I didn't care about luxury—as long as there were clean sheets and a clean toilet I'd be happy. When you are uncertain when your next job is coming you need to be careful with money.

When we arrived in Las Vegas we found this dive of a place that we will call the Joyous Inn. It was an older-style two-storey motel complex, painted pink, and it was surrounded by vacant land, almost as though someone had bought all of the land around it and was waiting for the owners to sell out so they could develop the block.

I ran into reception to see if I could look at a room. There was an undesirable-looking woman behind the counter and some trampy man standing there eyeballing me in a dirty trench coat. The place smelled of mould and cigarette smoke. But I knew we couldn't afford to be fussy.

I asked first if they had any vacancies (naturally they did) and then if I could have a look at a room. The woman took me upstairs and opened a door. I didn't want to touch anything inside—there was a mirror on the ceiling and it was so sleazy. But I pulled back the sheets and, yep—clean. I went into the bathroom and looked at the toilet; both the toilet and shower were old but clean. For twenty-one dollars per night we decided to stay, but we felt like we'd walked straight onto the set of a B-grade movie.

That night we went to see some shows and then wandered through the casinos sightseeing, as you do in Vegas. We arrived back at the motel in the early hours of the morning, and went to bed.

At some ungodly hour there was a knock at the door. It wasn't a normal knock—it was a frantic, frenzied bashing at the door. We both sat bolt upright.

A man was yelling, 'Let me in, open the door!'

Craig got up, stark naked, went to the door and asked, 'Who is it?'

The bloke shouted, 'There's a water leak downstairs—I need to get in!'

Craig turned, pointed at me and said, 'Get your clothes on; I've seen this in a movie. He's going to burst in here, shoot me and rape you.' I started to laugh, but he was dead serious and I began to wonder if he was right. We both started to get dressed; I kept tripping over my clothes, and even though I was scared I couldn't stop giggling.

By now this man was almost smashing the door down. 'Let me in! What are you doing?'

Craig asked for some proof of who he was, some ID, and the man started swearing. I thought then and there that this couldn't be someone who worked at the hotel. Craig then said that, if he wanted us to open the door, he'd have to go downstairs to reception and get them to ring and verify that there was actually a leak. The man left and next thing we know the phone rang.

We looked at each other and Craig answered the phone. He told them that he had checked and there was no water leak in our room, but they insisted that they needed to get into the room and make sure.

The guy came back to the door and moved over to the window alongside, where Craig pulled back the curtain. The bloke had about two teeth in his head and they were both rotten; he was wearing a dirty trench coat. Maybe it was the staff uniform. He held up his ID and it's like it is out of a cartoon with illegible writing and a fuzzy photo. Craig told him, 'That's not real ID, mate,' and he said, 'Yeah, it's my ticket.'

We ended up letting him in. He burst in, quickly looked in the bathroom and then said, 'There's no leak here.' At that, he stormed back out.

Craig and I lay back down on the bed, unable to sleep, and asked each other if that had really happened. We eventually laughed and then suggested to each other that maybe next time we pay a little more than $21 per night for accommodation!

CHAPTER 39

# Wonkey

After our eventful travels in the US, Craig and I went home to Maudsland Road in March. I was there, working horses and doing some trick-riding training, when I received a phone call from Bobby. He said that he was on a job and asked if I was available in the near future to go to Mexico. He didn't give me much information, other than that I would be training a donkey.

'How cute,' I said.

'Yeah,' he said. 'Bill and I aren't touching the friggin' donkey. It'll be right up your alley!'

He called back a few days later. 'OK, you're training a donkey and a pig. We need you to leave in ten days' time for six to eight weeks' training pre-production.' He explained that they might also be able to keep me on once production started, when I would be working alongside them in the horse department.

Woo-hoo! I was heading to Mexico, to work on *The Legend of Zorro*.

It was the first time I would be away from Craig since the *Man From Snowy River* show in 2002, and I found it hard to think about being away from him. On the upside though, it was one of the first times I had been confident that my animals would be well looked after while I was away.

I asked Craig if he would come over and visit while I was there; he said he would love to, but it was an expensive flight. He suggested we first see what I would be earning. Craig is cautious when it comes to finances, but I had stopped putting much thought into any type of planning when Grahame died.

When I arrived in Mexico in May 2004, they had all been in pre-production a couple of weeks already. Bobby was the liberty horse trainer, Bill was both Bobby's assistant and a second horse trainer, and I was there to train a pig and a donkey.

In fact, I needed to train two donkeys (you always need at least one animal in reserve), for a scene with Zorro's son. Two white donkeys had been chosen for the job. When I first went to look at them, I thought it must be some kind of a joke. One was a cheeky young donkey, but the other looked as though he had been beaten all of his life—he stood with his head lowered and his ears flopped to the side, looking like he just wished the whole world would go away.

I named him Wonkey, because just before I left for Mexico Craig's little girl Columbia had told me that all white donkeys are called 'wonkeys'. At the beginning I could not persuade, manipulate or coax that donkey to move one foot. No matter what I did, he just stood there and hoped that I would vanish. I literally sat in his pen with him for days before he even looked at me or dropped his big ears towards me. Most of the time, he would turn away from me and pretend I wasn't there. But by the end of the shoot, that donkey had become a wonderful little liberty donkey, and I adored him.

Funnily enough, at the beginning of his sequence for the movie Wonkey's role involved not moving. Zorro's son gets on him with a makeshift bridle and no saddle, goes, 'Yah, yah,' and tries to get the donkey to chase after his father, but instead of running off the donkey just stands there. Then the boy says something to the donkey in Spanish, and the donkey trots off out of shot (when cued by me off screen). My initial reaction to my stubborn little donkey was: 'Well, at least you've mastered the first bit.'

Much of what I saw in everyday life in Mexico was shocking. Seeing how some of the people treated their animals, through either ignorance or poverty, was difficult for me to accept. Of course, many of these people struggle to feed their own children, let alone giving the little donkey who works for them all day enough feed, or medical care when it needs it.

Many families care for their working animal to the best of their ability; it's not uncommon to see young kids out grazing the family donkey in the late afternoon so it can get enough to eat. But we also saw some shocking things. I had a flashback to a time when I was working in Jakarta and we came across a working donkey with a bridle grown into the side of its head because it was never taken off. In Mexico we saw skinny little knock-kneed donkeys banging their hocks with each stride, pulling a wagon loaded high with who-knows-what, and the entire family sitting on top of it all. You could see the animals' ribs and hips poking out; they had their heads down, with their ears flopped to the side, and it was all they could do to put one foot in front of the other. It was difficult to walk past and not get involved.

As I've mentioned, it seems completely ridiculous to me that, in developed countries such as Australia, England and America, there is so much animosity from animal activists towards professional animal people when it is the animals in third world countries who really need their help and care. I wish that all of the concerned people in the western world who feel strongly about making things better for animals could focus some of their energy towards animals who really do suffer, day in, day out, in hostile environments where people either don't know better or can't find a way to make it better. That is where they need to be directing their energy.

That was the world little Wonkey had come from, and it had obviously had a severe impact on him. He had been very poorly treated at some stage. Normally we like to immerse our animals in the pre-production environment, so they get accustomed to the film set. But with Wonkey we had a problem. Because of his past experience, I couldn't get him to walk through any group that contained locals. He would walk right past a bunch of *gringos* (non-Mexicans) happily enough, but if local Mexican people were there, he would try to turn around and head back to the animal compound.

I knew we were in trouble because, when he came to do his scene, there would be many locals involved. He would be off lead, at liberty, and I thought he would either take off or just stand still with his ears flopped to one side and refuse to do anything. It was so bad that I had to embarrassingly explain to the lovely first assistant director, Bruce Moriarty, that in pre-production I hadn't been able to get Wonkey accustomed to working among the local people.

Bruce said, 'What are you telling me? I have to clear the set of Mexicans?' Of course, most of the crew were Mexican.

'I don't know what to tell you,' I said.

'Oh Jeez, alright I'll just ask those standing around if they could leave.' Bruce said.

He didn't discriminate, of course, but he asked everyone who wasn't essential to leave.

Wonkey happily did the scene after that. He did well, but it didn't make the film—in the end, it was cut in editing.

# CHAPTER 40

# Antonio, Mexico's hero

Once I was in Mexico, one thing led to another, and because of some staff changes, Lloyd Phillips and Bobby decided I could stay for the whole shoot, to help Bobby and Bill in the horse department.

I learnt a lot on *Zorro*, particularly from Bobby. We all shared a house, lived in each other's pockets, and saw good and bad things about each other's work ethic and private lives. They both saw how much I was pining for Craig, until one day Bobby said, 'For goodness' sake, if it will cheer you up a bit, get Craig over here. He is good to have around anyway, and we could do with another capable person.' Seeing Craig again was exciting; I felt like a teenager when I saw him after the weeks we'd been apart. He arrived and due to the staff changes we were both kept on as animal trainers.

We worked with such a beautiful team of local people— hard-working, honest and proud. They felt important; they had a great self-image and a sense of grandeur, but they weren't big-headed. Some of them had next to nothing, but they were always happy and vibrant and they supported and looked after each other. Their family and team spirit was amazing.

There were some great horsemen there who worked as wranglers. They were very kind and warm towards me and I was happy to be accepted as part of their family. They introduced us to their families—to these gorgeous vibrant happy kids, who could all ride before they could walk. When I started to work in South Africa, it was a culture shock, but I found Mexico incredibly warm and welcoming.

I made a big effort to try to speak Spanish with the wranglers and they thought that was hilarious—I made a fool of myself regularly. The head wrangler, Chico Hernandez, was a highly respected, 'don't mess with me' sort of man. He had an impressive array of equipment and horses, and had done some big movies over time. I got along very well with him, and continue to keep in touch.

I also loved working with Antonio Banderas. He is, to this day, the nicest actor I have ever met. He is warm, kind, considerate and compassionate, and amazingly enough, he seemed to have an endless supply of energy for the countless extras and fans who all wanted a piece of him.

On our first day on set we were filming a scene with about four hundred extras. Not surprisingly, many of them had never been on a movie set before, and when Antonio arrived they could barely contain themselves. He is a hero in Mexico and they adore him because he often portrays courageous Mexican characters on film.

On that first day, Antonio stood up on a section of the set and spoke to everyone in Spanish, and then in English. He said he appreciated them all coming and getting dressed up and being a part of the movie; he made everyone feel like they were important actors alongside him. I hadn't really seen anything like that before. I had never seen anybody with his degree of fame give so much time to so many.

After his speech, he then proceeded to sign autographs for a very long time. I thought he had started something that would be impossible to finish, because there were so many people lining up, but he just stayed and stayed and stayed. The extras talked about it for days afterwards on the set. I'd be getting a horse ready, and I'd hear them saying things like, 'I can't believe he shook my hand,' 'He smiled at me,' 'He looked into my eyes.' I thought, 'What a gift he has given to all those people.'

Even though Antonio's riding was already very good, Bobby had been doing quite a lot of work with him in pre-production. The horses do a lot of rearing in the *Zorro* movies and, wherever possible, the director, Martin Campbell wanted to use Antonio himself because he is athletic and coordinated. An inexperienced rider can easily off-balance a horse when it rears, and can even pull the horse over backwards if they use the reins to 'hold on', but Antonio is a good rider and he listens.

I think he is incredibly professional, but also has an admirable character. Before Craig came into my life, I had felt a bit sour about the film industry. I'd gone sour on the stunt industry too, because I'd seen too much stuff that I thought was immoral. Sometimes, I found myself in situations where, if I had wanted to cheat, to lie, to be nasty or to backstab, then I too could have climbed higher up the ladder. It could be very bitchy and cliquey, with people using power and position to get their own way. I didn't want to be a part of it, I didn't feel I needed to manipulate people or make demands to get my own way, I wanted my work to speak for itself and continue to work in the industry and enjoy the spontaneous lifestyle that comes with it.

Meeting Antonio, and seeing that it was possible for someone to reach his level in the film industry and remain such a lovely person, was sufficient to give me new courage and inspiration to continue in this sometimes tainted industry, knowing that I could still be true to myself and that I didn't have to join in with the nastiness in order to survive.

# CHAPTER 41

# Zorro in action

As well as all the rearing, for *The Legend of Zorro* we prepared some fun liberty sequences, plus a bucking horse, a lot of riding horses and carriage horses. We also had to get horses to tolerate trick riding.

In the 1998 film *The Mask of Zorro*, my trainer and mentor Tad Griffith had performed an amazing and famous trick-riding sequence, which he was working on when I first met him. It was so cool—so how could it be topped? It was the best trick-riding sequence that I know of in modern film.

The production company had initially talked to Tad about working on the sequel too, and he had some fantastic new ideas. But, the situation changed and the scheduled trick-riding sequence was replaced by a wagon chase at the beginning of the film.

I was excited by all of the training challenges. One scene required Zorro to stand on the saddle of a horse galloping alongside a train; then he had to punch his fist through a window and grab a bad guy.

Bobby, Bill and I had a blast training the horses for that scene, and it was my first experience of trick riding on a Friesian. Friesians are a powerful, compact breed with elevated movement. I had ridden them in Namibia with Bobby and Sled and I remembered them as being big cumbersome horses, but was surprised at how smooth these horses in Mexico rode. It was a fantastic experience, galloping alongside a moving train and then slipping down the side of the horse into a 'forward fender' (sitting alongside the horse at belly level with one foot in the stirrup) and finally hopping up into a 'slick stand' (standing upright on top of the saddle).

We had regular use of the locomotive department for practice and it was great fun galloping along beside moving trains. When we couldn't rehearse with the train and its crew, we would go out and rehearse the big black Friesian horses on vast stretches of open land nearby. Bobby would park his horse at one end, Bill at the other, and I'd gallop the Friesian, Lobo, who was my favourite, from Bobby to Bill and back again, teaching it to gallop fast and straight while accommodating trick riding.

Bill and Bobby did the rearing horse work, and some great gag stuff. They had a horse pretending to smoke a pipe, and another leaning against a wall cross-legged and acting drunk.

In the climactic horse sequence, Zorro jumps his horse off a rocky outcrop onto the top of a moving train. Then he looks up to see a tunnel fast approaching, so he turns his horse a hundred and eighty degrees and spurs him on, jumping from carriage to carriage. Finally the horse jumps down through a large skylight into the caboose at the end of the train, just before they reach the tunnel. Zorro now hears some bad guys heading in his direction, so he jumps onto the rump of his horse, stands up and cues the horse to buck him up through the skylight again. After a back somersault, he lands on the caboose roof, ready to fend off the baddies.

That sequence was filmed using green screen. The horse was ridden across stationary simulated train carriages. At the end of each 'carriage' were small jumps for the horse to jump over; these were removed during editing so it looked like the horse was jumping from carriage to carriage.

Bobby's father had been a South African show-jumping coach, and Bobby himself is very experienced in show jumping, so he was invaluable in that entire sequence. The 'train' stood about a metre and a half off the ground; although it obviously wasn't as hazardous as doing the sequence on the roof of a real moving train, it was still a difficult and dangerous sequence to shoot and it took a lot of planning and safety measures to keep both horse and rider as safe as possible.

The stunt and horse departments normally work together in pre-production to practise any hazardous horse action. Gary Powell was the stunt coordinator on this movie; he was great to work with, as he was very respectful of the horse department's knowledge and opinions. However, the stunt guys had a very hectic schedule and, although they intended to rehearse the back somersault for the final sequence, my suspicion is that they probably thought it would be pretty simple, not too technical. I don't think they considered the complication the weight of a grown man pushing down on a horse's rump in high-heeled cowboy boots would have for a horse trying to buck. The person would have to know how to stand, how to distribute their weight, so they're not making it uncomfortable for the horse.

While we were training the horse for this part of the sequence I had been the guinea pig. Bobby had trained the horse to buck and kick up as high as he could, and I would stand on the horse's rump in a harness underneath a scaffold that the stunt department had rigged up for us. This enabled us to take the weight off the horse's rump at just the right moment. Craig was on the other end of the rope; when the horse bucked on Bobby's cue, Craig would work the rigging and haul me up off the horse's back at the moment he felt me move, making it look as though the horse's movement is flinging Zorro onto the roof. It was my job to time it so as to get my weight off the horse as he bucked, to make it as comfortable for him as possible.

Directors are extremely busy during pre-production, so it's common practice for the different departments to send video footage of rehearsals to the director to update him on how they are progressing. Bobby sent a video to Martin Campbell's trailer of the shot he wanted, filmed from the angle he'd requested, of me being bucked off the horse. It was successful and looked good—everyone seemed pleased with it.

Antonio Banderas had six stunt doubles on *The Legend of Zorro*, if I remember correctly. We arrived on set the day we were to film the bucking shot and Antonio's main acrobatic double had the rigging fitted and climbed up on the horse's rump. But the horse was visibly uncomfortable; he wouldn't stand still, let alone be cued to buck.

So Bobby discretely said, 'Zelie, get over there and tell the stunt guy how to stand, or this is never going to work.'

I tried to explain to the stuntman what he needed to do. At first he was receptive and appreciated my help; but, after a while, when it still wasn't working, he became frustrated and made it clear that he felt the horse hadn't been well trained.

The problem was that the way he was standing in those cowboy boots was uncomfortable for the horse. We made several more attempts, but even when the horse agreed to buck and the winch was pulled at the same time, it didn't look realistic at all. Worse still, the horse was getting to the stage where he didn't trust the system we'd set up in training—he didn't know when he was going to get a poke in the bum from those heels or why.

The director was understandably getting very irritated and wanted to know why it wasn't working. The horse department didn't want to blame the stunt department and the stunt department didn't want to blame us, but in fact each side thought the other was to blame. It is a difficult situation when something like that happens on set.

Finally the director said, 'OK, I've seen footage of this working in rehearsal—what's the problem today?'

To the stunt department's credit, they accepted some of the responsibility. The director said, 'Put Zelie in the costume. That's what she does, that's her job—to stand on horses.'

So they did. They put me in the boots and the costume, and hid my hair under a little black wig. Antonio thought me doubling him was funny.

I doubled Antonio to do that stunt. I didn't do the acrobatics; I only did the lift. They filmed it in short sequences: they needed to show Zorro standing on the horse, the horse bucking, Zorro being shot up through the roof. Then they cut to the top of the train—the stuntman, using a mini trampoline inside the carriage, did a back somersault out onto the back of the carriage.

A lot of people said I did such an amazing back somersault out of the train and I still find myself explaining that, no, it wasn't me. All I had to do was be bucked off a horse. It worked well, and it looks great in the movie.

CHAPTER 42

# Moriarty to the rescue

I was so pleased to be able to meet and work with Jack Lilley on *Zorro*. Jack has been working in movies since the 1950s; he is one of those old-time legends who did the crash-and-burn horse work in the early westerns, and he has fantastic stories to tell. He was great fun and he spent a lot of time sitting in a chair in the animal compound, telling people what to do.

One day Jack was barking orders at someone when his mobile phone rang. He talks loudly at the best of times but he's even louder on the phone. While he was having this conversation, I was busy training a pig for a scene where she licks Antonio's face.

This particular pig had been picked for her looks, not her temperament, and when she arrived she was totally feral. She was a grown sow who had just had her piglets weaned off her, so she was hormonal, with big saggy boobs, and she would squeal at me when I went near her.

I taught her about kindness and restraint. She learnt 'looks' (to turn her head a certain way), to 'mark' (to go to a spot marked on the ground) and to 'target' (to look at and hold her gaze on a particular object, for example a tennis ball on a stick, to achieve specific eye lines). But, above all, I taught her to trust me, which was perhaps the most important ingredient in our relationship if I was ever to get her gentle enough to lick Antonio's face. It was Jack who had suggested we call her Stella, after Antonio and Melanie Griffiths' daughter, who really liked her and would come to visit her in the animal compound. Jack had seen the progress I was making and seemed to be impressed with my work, but I figured most of what he was saying was just encouragement.

Anyhow, I wasn't really listening to his phone conversation, but after a while I heard him say, 'She's the best little pig trainer I've ever seen. Yeah, take her, take her. When does it go?' I realised that he was talking about me and was instantly curious.

He got off the phone and said to me, 'I've just been telling my nephew, Larry, about you. He's doing a pig movie in Australia, and he wants you on board.'

'When's that?' I asked.

'Next month.'

Pre-production began on the pig movie *Charlotte's Web* while *Zorro* was still being filmed. Craig was able to be replaced. I was in deep, so I stayed in Mexico until the film ended. Craig flew home early, picked up our dogs, drove down to Melbourne, rented a house for us and got everything set up, so I was able to just waltz in and start work when I arrived back from Mexico. But before I left, there was something I had to sort out.

I had become very attached to both of the donkeys I worked with in pre-production. Once filming was over, the younger donkey was going back to his home, a little Mexican farm where he had been well looked after before the film. I was happy seeing him go back there because, unlike Wonkey, he hadn't arrived traumatised—he was a happy, healthy little donkey.

Wonkey was also supposed to go back to where he had come from, and I was heartbroken. I had spoken with Craig extensively about bringing Wonkey home with me to Australia. Craig at first said I was being ridiculous. Did I know what the quarantine procedures would be for donkeys coming from Mexico to Australia? Not only the cost, but what Wonkey would have to go through?

I said, 'I can't do it, Craig—I can't leave him here to this life.'

Then I had an idea. I called Tad and asked, if I paid for the shipping and quarantine, which would not have been as arduous for Wonkey as coming to Australia, whether he and Wendy would house the donkey in California for the rest of its life. Tad and Wendy said, 'Yes, of course.' So that was the plan. It was still an expensive option—it would have swallowed up a good portion of what I earned on the film—but I felt I had little choice.

I ended up telling Bobby and Bill. I'd expected them to ridicule me, but they actually thought it was pretty cool: the donkey had been good, they had seen in what condition he arrived, and they saw how he had developed. Every day when I arrived at the compound, he would call out to me when he saw me—*Heehaaaawww*—and carry on until I'd answer him in the same seesaw tone: *Wooooonkeey*. It was just beautiful—I loved him and he loved me.

One day I was telling Bruce Moriarty how much I was going to miss Wonkey and about Tad and Wendy taking him for me. I told him that I thought the world of Craig for supporting me in this. I was about to spend a lot of the money I had just made in the last six months in order to get that donkey to Los Angeles, where the Griffith family now lived.

Bruce said, 'That's a pretty big deal.' Then he thought about it and said, 'You know what? I might just talk to my wife.'

He made a phone call and came back. He told me that he and his wife Jill had a lot of coyotes around their horse ranch. In the past they had lost foals to coyotes, before they started keeping a mule in with the weanlings to protect them. 'We lost our mule last year,' he explained, 'and we've been thinking about getting another mule or a little donkey to run with the weanlings, to keep them calm and safe.' He had explained the situation to Jill and she had said, 'Oh, for goodness' sake, save that donkey.' I thanked Bruce and cried. Then I went and privately cuddled Wonkey, and cried some more!

They bought him from his local owners and paid for him to go to their ranch in the US, where they have ten foot of snow every year! The donkey and weanlings are stabled at night; they get well fed and cared for. He certainly landed on his feet, that little Wonkey. He is their family pet; the Moriarty children apparently love him.

Bruce is one of those incredibly busy men in the film industry, but he still finds time every now and then to send me an update photo of Wonkey, being cuddled by a kid, playing in the snow or snuggled up in his stable. It makes me feel so happy.

# CHAPTER 43

# Tita and Flaca

Jack Lilley's nephew, Larry Madrid, is one of Hollywood's most successful animal trainers, and he was the head animal coordinator on *Charlotte's Web*. So, in November, off we went to work for Larry.

The main animal character in *Charlotte's Web* is, of course, Wilbur the pig. There were five full-time pig trainers on that film, but every trainer at some stage or another ended up training at least one pig or two extra, to help keep the number of pigs up to the amount we required.

Piglets grow fast and we used sixty-four pigs in total, divided between the trainers, with tiny new piglets arriving approximately every six weeks. Craig's background makes him incredibly versatile, so he was a floating trainer, helping everyone. On *Charlotte's Web* he trained pigs, cows, geese and ducks. But it was while we were working on *Charlotte's Web* that we found out Craig had developed an allergy to ducks. This big strong man, who handles and trains big cats and elephants, can't handle a few ducks! He kept breaking out in a rash. I found the whole thing pretty funny and told him he was such a wuss.

One of the challenges in the movie was that the pigs had to all look the same, so as to successfully play the same character. In different weather, pigs grow different amounts of hair, and individual pigs at different ages grow different thicknesses of hair, so not only were we washing piglets all of the time to keep them clean, we were also running horse clippers over them regularly to trim each piglet's hair to exactly the same length. As a result, we had to buy industrial-size heaters to keep them warm all of the time without their winter coat. It was quite comical seeing the trainers trying to keep sixty-four different-sized piglets still, while giving them a quick trim with the clippers—until the piglets got used to it they would wriggle all over the place.

The very first piglet that I was allocated and fell in love with I called Tita, after a lovely young Mexican girl who had worked in the horse department on *Zorro* (and who would come back into our lives a few years later). Tita was a great little working pig but she developed black spots between her shoulder blades and we couldn't use her as she no longer matched the other piglets. Jodie McKeone, one of the other trainers on the job, found her a beautiful home, where she was going to grow to be a big fat sow.

My next favourite piglet was Flaca. *Flaca* is a Spanish word that means 'skinny girl', and a couple of the Mexican wranglers who couldn't remember my name would call out to me, 'Ay, *flaca*.' It's usually intended as a compliment in a rough friendly sort of way, like a wolf whistle.

On *Charlotte's Web*, we had different trainers working together using different methods. We all needed to pull together and work as a team to make different shots work, but there was a little bit of rivalry between the American and the Australian trainers at times. I remember feeling amused by some of the American trainers—at how surprised they were by my lack of technical training knowledge and my poor ability to put into words exactly what my training plan was or whose technique I was using.

Typically, pigs respond predominantly to food reward. But, knowing that pigs have a hierarchy within their social group, as many animals do, I choose to train pigs with a degree of pressure. I'm comfortable using pressure as one of my training techniques, because animals naturally put pressure on each other within their natural hierarchy. However, this technique differentiated me from the other pig trainers.

In training, we use an animal's natural instincts as much as possible. For example, horses are a herd animal, and we sometimes use the presence of a horse off camera to get a desired look or attitude from the horse working on camera. An example of using pressure as a training technique is when teaching a horse to move off; if you want a horse to walk forward, pressure is applied behind the ears by the halter and the horse walks forward to release that pressure. Eventually the horse will move forward without the pressure, whenever the trainer provides the appropriate cue.

One of the misunderstood issues concerning animal trainers is the use of pressure during training. People sometimes think using pressure is cruel, and it certainly can be if you're not a good enough trainer to be able to read the animal, and to know how much pressure to apply and exactly when to stop. It is the trainer's responsibility to make the animal feel as safe as possible, so it trusts that you are not putting it in danger; then the animal can do what is asked confidently. I don't see it as being any different to asking and reinforcing, like teaching (training) a child to brush their teeth daily.

During filming, any one of a number of things can prevent the animals and their trainers successfully completing the desired shot. Where an animal's training is entirely based around food rewards, once it is full there's no chance it will continue working. But because Flaca was accustomed to working under pressure and could happily perform even when she didn't feel very hungry, she was often brought in when the other pigs wouldn't comply.

When Craig and I watch *Charlotte's Web*, we can see that Flaca is in a substantial part of it. In the story Wilbur grows up, and so, as our little piglets grew, we were sometimes able to use them in different scenes. The older pigs were easier to work with, because they'd had the most handling—some of them up to six months of training. It was during the training and filming of the youngest piglets that I believe Flaca made me look good. She trained up very fast. She was the smallest pig that could lie down, and she was the only pig that was trained to look up. Pigs find it quite hard to look up, because of the structure of their neck and body, and in the movie the pig was required to look up a lot, to talk to the spider.

One American trainer in particular seemed incredulous and wanted to know the name of the method I had used. My methods are a complicated mix of many things learnt from many people, as well as from my own trial and error, and this was the first time I had really thought about how I train. I eventually told her that I simply tried whatever I thought would work to get them to understand what I wanted them to do.

We laughed about the fact that I didn't have a specific method, but I had some very successful pigs and I know I held my own.

Craig and I also trained a very large boar for *Charlotte's Web*, which was a change from the multitudes of sweet little piglets. His name was Percy; he was three or four years old and weighed over three hundred kilos and was over a metre and a half in length. He was a very big pig and therefore potentially dangerous. Because pigs are so food orientated and because he was like a bottomless pit, with Percy food training became our main method.

The problem was that we needed him hungry enough to want to work, but not hungry enough to become pushy. It took a bit of trial and error to work out what foods worked best. We found out from his owners that he absolutely loved chocolate Nougat Honey Logs, and they knew someone who worked at Cadbury who could get chaff bags full of off-cuts. Percy loved them: it didn't matter if he was almost full, he could always squeeze in another little Nougat Honey Log, a bit like Flaca with a cream bun.

Percy was a full-grown stud-breeding boar; but, fortunately for us, he was a good-natured animal who had clearly been treated well by his owners. Still, we respected the fact that he was a potentially dangerous animal, so one of our first priorities was leash-training him to ensure he was safe around the crew.

Pigs can be very vocal and training Percy to tie up was a very noisy experience. One of the first lessons a horse learns is to accept a halter, to be led by a lead rope and then to be tied to a post or rail and to wait patiently. It is an important lesson for both the horse and the owner's safety, and we teach it to all domesticated animals. This was Percy's first lesson from Craig and I as his new trainers.

Larry came and watched that first lesson as we got Percy accustomed to wearing a harness, to being led around and finally to being tied to a rail. The three of us stood by and reassured him as he pulled back and loudly told the rope off. Percy was lovely and, other than being vocal, he handled everything very well.

In the film, Percy had to lie down and 'talk' to the piglet. We taught him to lie down on cue, to look left and right, and to get up on cue. One of the problems we faced was how to squeeze his gigantic bulk into the relatively small stable on the set. It wasn't practical to lie Percy down and then set up the cameras around him, because then he would have to lie down for too long, so he had to learn to lie down exactly in the right spot, once the cameras were already in place. Considering his age and his size, we were all happy with the degree of accuracy that we got with that kind-hearted animal.

At the end of filming, even though I knew all the animals would go to a good home, I wanted to keep Flaca. She had been the runt of her litter, just like Wilbur in the movie, and she was also one of the ugliest. In the movie she's definitely not one of the cutest piglets—she has pointy ears and her eyes are quite close together, and she has a long pointy snout. We didn't know how big she was going to grow, and we didn't care; I really loved her and wanted to look after her for the rest of her life. Each day when we got to work and the pigs would be squealing and running around anticipating their breakfast, I couldn't wait to get to Flaca for a cuddle.

We brought her back to the Gold Coast with us and she still lives with us today. I attempted to keep a few others too, but Craig gently reminded me how much more attention she would receive being our only pig. So we only kept Flaca, safe in the knowledge that production had found the rest of the piglets good homes. The producers had paid transport and labour costs to ensure that the properties were checked out before the animals were delivered, and the new owners had to sign affidavits saying their pig would live out its natural life. My sort of happy ending.

# CHAPTER 44

# Bittersweet

*Charlotte's Web* holds bittersweet memories for me. We had lots of fun and met some lovely people and animals, but right towards the end Snoopy was put down. He was nearly seventeen.

Snoopy had been there through Julie's death, through Dad and Grahame and so many other testing times. When I walked away from Creekside Court after Grahame's death, during that really ugly time in my life, I felt as though Snoopy and I were the only ones to get out alive.

When Snoopy was about fifteen, he had been run over and ever since the lower half of his body had been partially paralysed. It was a Sunday afternoon and we had taken some rubbish to the tip. I fully blame myself for the accident; I had let him off the ute, and wasn't protective enough with my beautiful ageing mate, who had gone deaf. The man who hit him was not necessarily at fault. He was reversing slowly when he bumped

Snoopy. As I looked up and saw the car heading for Snoopy, I called out to him to move but he didn't hear me or the car. His foot went under the back wheel and then slowly the car rolled over his pelvis. That poor man—Snoopy was screaming and I was a mess.

Craig and I rushed Snoopy to the only twenty-four-hour vet service available at that time, which was an hour away in Brisbane. They said it didn't look very good. I asked if there was something we could do. Could we perhaps make a trolley for him to move around on? I told them I couldn't lose that dog.

The vet said he would give him a day or two, but he wasn't positive about the outcome because Snoopy's back half wasn't responding to nerve tests. That didn't surprise me because, when I had picked him up at the tip and placed him in the passenger foot well of the ute, I could see he didn't even know what his back end was doing. And he was in a lot of pain—it was just awful.

I went up to visit him at the vet's each day. They had given him medication to take away the pain, but he would look at me pleadingly when I left, wanting to know why I was going away without him. I was traumatised to be leaving without knowing if I would see him alive the next day.

The vet told me he could operate, but the success rate was very slim and he asked whether I really wanted to put Snoopy through that. I was trying to figure out what to do. All the tests showed he had no coordination, no feeling whatsoever, in his tail and back legs.

I have prayed a lot in my life, even though I don't know who to. In my younger days I'd say, 'Please, God, if it is you I'm supposed to pray to,' but during that time I simply focused on Snoopy; I virtually meditated over his healing, as much as I could. I spent so much time thinking about that dog, saying, 'Please get better, please, please'—he was everything to me. I knew he was getting old, his sight wasn't good, he had gone deaf, but I really felt it wasn't his time to go, not like that.

After three days the vet said we could possibly give him one more night, but he wasn't very optimistic because Snoopy hadn't improved since I brought him in. They were looking for any sign of feeling, but he had reacted negatively to every test for several days. The vet staff had to carry him outside to go to the loo; he was very unhappy and the vet asked me how long I wanted him to go on like that. He said, 'It's your dog, your decision.' I asked them to just give him one more night before I made a decision, and they agreed.

When I called the following morning to see how he was, the vet nurse said, 'Well, you wouldn't believe it, but he's standing up.'

I was trying not to get too excited. 'Did you stand him up, and then he stood by himself?' I asked.

'No, we came into work this morning and he was standing up in his cage. He managed to get up by himself.'

Craig and I brought him home. His tail never worked again, and his back legs wasted away, but somehow his nerves had repaired enough for him to stand up. If he was feeling particularly cocky, he could sort of trot and shuffle around. That was how he got around in the last two years of his life.

By then Aura had come into our lives, and they ended up having two litters of puppies together, and he continued to have a very full life with us. I didn't care how much I had to lift him up or down from places, or carry him when he became tired, he was still with us and enjoying life.

When we were in Melbourne working on *Charlotte's Web*, his kidneys had begun to fail. Twenty-four hours before we put him down, he unmistakably told me that it was time for him to go. It was a Sunday and he looked pleadingly into my eyes, all day, and as painful as it was for me to recognise this, I knew it was time. The vet came out to the house that we were renting and helped him go to sleep in my arms, rather than in the sterile veterinary surgery.

We gave him a little going-away dinner. I lay on the floor with him. I held him and kissed him. I stroked his silky soft ears. I cried and looked into his smiley eyes and I thanked him over and over. It was Snoopy's time.

One cloudy morning we were driving to the set of *Charlotte's Web*, when Craig turned to me and told me he'd had the coolest dream the night before. He told me it had included us getting married on top of Beechmont Hill in our friends' paddock overlooking the Gold Coast and the ocean at sunrise.

After he had finished describing his dream, we were both silent for a moment. And then he asked, 'So, do you want to do that?'

'What? Get married?' I replied.

'Yeah.'

'OK.'

That was pretty much the extent of his proposal. I gave him a hard time about it later: of all the beautiful places we had been to around the world, he had chosen to propose to me while driving to work through Melbourne's grey pre-dawn suburbia!

The friends whose place he'd seen in the dream were Bill and Laurie Bird. Together with their hard-working mum, Sylvia, the Birds run a dairy farm in Maudsland, one kilometre down the road from my place. I had ridden past their place one morning not long after I'd bought my home in Maudsland Road, just as they were taking the dairy cows back to their paddock. I had stopped and I asked if I could muster my young horses with them, as it would be a terrific experience for them. They agreed, and that was the start of a beautiful friendship. The Birds are true Queensland farmers, living in the heart of the tinselled fantasia that is the Gold Coast; they built the impressive post-and-rail fence around my property and I loved spending time with them.

When Craig and I got to work on that grey day, I told another Aussie trainer, Joanne Kostiuk, about Craig's proposal. She and I had become good friends. She looked at me and asked, 'So you're getting married?' and I said, 'I'm not sure.' When I thought back to our conversation, Craig hadn't actually asked me formally—he'd just asked whether it was something I wanted to do.

'Well you should probably find out,' she laughed.

I went to Craig later in the day and said, 'Well, are we doing that or not?'

And he looked at me and asked, 'Do you want to?'

'OK.'

'Well, yes, we will then,' he said and went back to work.

I went back to Joanne and said, 'Yes, we're getting married.'

'Can I tell everyone?'

'I don't know,' I replied. But of course she did.

Well, you know what people are like—especially in a closed community like a film crew. One person told another, and it spread so quickly that soon people were coming up and congratulating us.

Craig was probably thinking, 'How did that happen? I just said I had a dream . . .'

# CHAPTER 45

# *Elephant Tales*

Towards the end of production for *Charlotte's Web*, Jim Stockley rang and asked if we could go to South Africa to work on an animal film called *Elephant Tales*, written and directed by Mario Andreacchio. The job would start in June.

Before we went to South Africa, we set a date in October for the wedding, spoke with Bill and Laurie Bird about using their paddock, and found a terrific venue at a friend's picturesque polo complex for the reception. I sent off the wedding invitations, hoping we would be finished on *Elephant Tales* and back from South Africa with enough time to finalise the wedding plans when we returned.

*Elephant Tales* was being filmed at the Stockleys' property as well as at a few extra locations in a nearby game park called Tala. It's a kids' movie about two elephant brothers, Tutu and Zef, who go in search of their mother, who has been taken by poachers; along the way they have adventures and befriend some baby animals. For us as trainers it meant a lot of time sitting on the grass, letting the various young animals bond. We had a cheetah, giraffe, chimp and warthog, plus lion cubs, baboons, and of course the four young elephants, most of them owned by Jim Stockley and Brian Boswell.

It was a wonderfully relaxed film to work on, largely because Mario was so accommodating with the animals. When the script called for the baby chimp to sit on top of the giraffe's head so as to get a better view, we explained that neither of the animals would be particularly happy with that situation, and Mario quickly changed it so the baby chimp climbs up a tree next to the giraffe.

Jim was the head trainer; his son Jamie, Craig and I were additional animal trainers. Craig and Jim concentrated mostly on the elephants, but helped with all of the animals.

On one occasion when we were in the wildlife reserve, someone on the crew shouted, 'Rhino!' A nearby wild rhino had smelled the elephants and come over to investigate. The entire crew was so professional: there was no unnecessary screaming or running. A rhino can attack baby elephants and of course people. Everyone calmly got out of the rhino's way and climbed into the vehicles, while Jim and Craig took the elephants behind one of the trucks so the rhino couldn't see them. Thankfully, rhinos have extremely poor eyesight and he wandered off after not finding anything of interest.

The Stockleys once again made us feel like part of the family, and while we were working on the film Jamie started going out with his now wife Dana, who was working as the director's personal assistant. It was a dream job, to work in that environment with those animals and people, and we are all patiently waiting for Mario to ring with the green light for *Elephant Tales Two*! It's a perfect example of why we feel guilty calling our job 'work'.

After we'd finished work on *Elephant Tales*, we flew Craig's mother Cleo over to South Africa for a holiday so she could meet the Stockleys. She had always wanted to meet them because she knew Stafford had known Jim's dad. She adored them and, naturally, they adored her. They knew how to make her feel like a queen of the circus world and, like everybody else, they were amazed at how witty, savvy, capable and independent she was for a woman of eighty years.

To show her what we had grown to love in that country we took her to some beautiful game parks. We spent her last few nights in South Africa at a gorgeous game park and then we drove her to the airport to fly back to Australia.

On the way to the airport she said she felt sick, so we stopped the car. Thinking she might be car sick, we suggested she sit in the front seat. However, by the time we arrived at the airport I was feeling a bit sick as well, so we thought that the prawns Cleo and I had eaten the night before may not have been as fresh as they should have been. Craig hadn't eaten them and he was fine.

I was sick for a couple of days, but it wasn't really bad food poisoning. However, Cleo was very ill. The airline's ground crew took her into the airport lounge before the flight; she deteriorated further on the flight, and the flight crew almost took her off the plane in Singapore, to hospitalise her, but she hung in there and kept on going to Australia.

She didn't recover from that for over a month and she never fully regained her appetite again. She kept saying the food poisoning had knocked her around, but I kept worrying that it was something else, especially when she started losing weight.

# CHAPTER 46

# A night wedding, is it?

While we were in Africa I kept getting emails saying, 'I'm sorry, I think there's a typo on your wedding invitation. It says 6 am—shouldn't it be 6 pm? A night wedding, is it?' And I would have to reply, 'Ah, no, it is at 6 am.' Some people rang saying, 'That's so typical of you— why would you do that?' Others said, 'What a fantastic idea—that's so you and Craig.' We wanted to get married early in the morning because that's how it was in Craig's dream, and because it happens to be our favourite time of day. In Queensland in October, sunrise is soon after four, and Craig had originally been keen to get married then, but I said, 'No, I think we need to draw the line somewhere—the light will still be beautiful at six.' I had already received so much grief about the whole thing, particularly from Cleo, that I thought we should compromise. The feeling would still be there at six in the morning.

On the morning itself I don't think anyone thought it was a good idea, except Craig and me. It was cold and windy, and the view wasn't as good as we'd hoped, because of the sea mist. But it was still a beautiful feeling when everyone came up there to share it with us.

Craig had asked me what I wanted to arrive in for the wedding. We had recently bought a Silverado Chevy ute, which had always been a dream car for both of us, and I knew he would want to arrive in that. From the beginning I knew that I wouldn't be arriving in a horse-drawn wagon but on horseback. I wanted to keep it a surprise for Craig, though, so I told him I would ask Wayne if we could borrow his big Ford F250 for me to arrive in.

Craig wanted his son, Nelson, to be his best man. Together with his good mate Darryl 'Woodsie' Woods, the three of them were going to arrive at the wedding in our Chev. As far as Craig was aware, Wayne's F250 would bring Columbia, who was to be the flower girl, together with Mum, Tamz, Fred and me.

At first I'd thought that just my two matrons of honour, Tamzin and Freda, would arrive with me on horseback. They can both ride and we have nice quiet horses. But then I got more ambitious and thought, 'I wish all of our horses could come.' Finally, it dawned on me that there were so many beautiful ladies who had been really important and significant in my life, and who all rode. So as well as Tamzin and Freda, whom Craig knew about, I secretly phoned Heidi, Lydia, Brit and Melody, a close friend from my pony club days. It all took a bit of organising, but so many people helped put it together. In the pre-dawn, the seven horses were secretly loaded and driven up Beechmont Hill, where they were saddled by my cowboy friend Martie Addy and some other friends and stood ready for our arrival. I rode J'dore, our beautiful white Andalusian mare, Tamzin rode Bosito, Freda rode Bullet, Heidi rode Nakota, the horse Wayne and I had bred, Brit rode Cassity, Lydia rode her black thoroughbred Abby, and Melody rode a horse of Marty's.

After Craig had 'proposed', I'd gone bridal dress shopping in Melbourne. Dressed in jeans and a T-shirt, I felt like Julia Roberts in the scene from *Pretty Woman* when she was rejected by the shop staff. It was awful! I went alone and the staff were rude to me; the dresses they showed me had huge meringue skirts or that clingy body-hugging look. I didn't like either style very much, so decided to design my own.

Once I'd decided that I would ride my beautiful Andalusian mare, J'adore, to the wedding, I thought that instead of a traditional white gown I'd like to wear a flowing Spanish-style cowgirl dress in bright red raw silk. Tamz and Fred organised their outfits from either side of the country, with Tamzin's clever aunts making matching riding outfits, complete with a giant wrap that flowed over the rump of their horses in gold raw silk. It was anything but traditional.

I wanted Mum to be part of the arrival party, too, so I asked Donny Ross, a film friend of ours who supplies harness horses and wagons, if he could bring Mum, Columbia and Aura in on one of his old-style country buckboards. I also wanted to involve Tamzin's and Freda's kids, and there was room enough to seat them on the hay bales Donny had put in the back of the wagon.

When Mum arrived on the wagon, I was stunned at how beautiful she looked—it blew me away. Mum is a beautiful person inside and out, and on this day she was truly radiant. Her clothes looked beautiful on her, the girls had done a great job with her hair and makeup, and she was oozing with happiness.

Before the wedding, I'd asked Wayne if he would stand at the gate in his pyjamas with champagne and orange juice to hand out to people as they came in. The idea was to take the mickey out of ourselves, because we had pulled everyone out of bed so early. He'd laughed and said, 'I don't know if I can do that—I might be a bit embarrassed.'

'No way! You be embarrassed? You can wear your cowboy boots if you want,' I said, trying to talk him into it.

He said, 'Schultzie's here. I'll see if he'll do it.'

Les Schultz is an absolute riot of a character. He's from the Northern Territory and is as full-on Aussie outback as you can get. Schultzie agreed to do it, but he didn't own any pyjamas so on the day he was dressed in a pair of borrowed flannelette pyjamas from Wayne's wife, Rona, who also gave him a little waistcoat to throw on over the top; he put on his beat-up bushie hat and cowboy boots, and handed out glasses to the guests as they arrived. He was only too happy to be the life of the party—he was perfect.

So, soon after six o'clock, my six friends and I jogged past a smiling Schultzie on our horses, and headed on through the paddock to where everyone was waiting. Because I can be a show-off, I thought I'd lay my horse J'adore down to dismount. Then Mum came and took my hand, and we walked towards Craig together.

Our arrival had the tremendous dramatic impact I had wanted, and it brought tears to Craig's eyes. Afterwards I think he went and punched Martie on the arm and threatened Donny Ross, saying, 'I can't believe you kept that a secret from me!'

In between having a manicure before the wedding and having to wash seven horses with the girls, I couldn't have done it without all their help. Everybody was involved, everyone pulled together, and it was so much fun.

We held the wedding reception at a stunning renovated two-storey Queenslander at the polo club. A band played, and we had a continental stand-up breakfast for everyone, supplied by movie caterer friends. So many people were involved to make our wedding the special day it was, with many only charging us at cost price or not charging at all.

On the night of the wedding, Craig and I decided I would go off the pill. We had been umming and ahhing about having a child for a while. Before Craig I had been terrified, but he made me feel safe; he finally convinced me by saying he knew the joy of having children and he didn't want me to miss out on that.

CHAPTER 47

# Colt, with no regrets

We arrived back from our honeymoon and not long after that I began to suspect I was pregnant. My boobs were swollen, and when I realised I'd missed a period I called Tamzin. I wanted her with me when I took the pregnancy test. I still had mixed emotions about getting pregnant and my old issues revolving around fear and loss had re-emerged.

Yet again Tamzin came to my side, leaving her husband and two kids in Perth. I met her at the airport and we stopped at a chemist on our way home. Back at Maudsland Road, I went into the loo, peed on the stick and came out to show it to Tamz. She smiled her beautiful soft smile and said, 'Congratulations.'

Oh my God, really? A baby? I couldn't believe it.

All through my pregnancy I talked to the baby all the time; whenever I started to get frightened about it dying, I just thought, 'Zelie, you cannot control it,' which helped to disperse the fear.

Tamz had very kindly said she would be at the birth with me. She had trained and worked as a nurse and then as a midwife in Perth after leaving school, and had later worked at the Gold Coast Hospital as a midwife. I was comfortable booking in there and she arrived the day before my due date. But then she had to hang around for a while, as we ended up being fourteen days overdue.

I had been getting Braxton Hicks contractions for about two weeks, and Cleo had been taking the mickey out of me, saying, 'That's not a contraction, love—you wait!' And she would laugh. She was very excited about another baby coming into the Bullen family. She kept saying, 'It's a boy! It's a boy!' A very large part of me also hoped the baby was a boy, because I knew I could cope with a boy. I don't know much about make-up, nail polish and clothes shopping.

When Tamzin arrived we talked about various birth plans and ways it could go. I was adamant I didn't want drugs—I didn't want to be out of it when my baby was born. Tamzin had also explained to me about the impact of drugs on the baby. I just wanted to do it naturally, with no intervention if that was possible. I was a little apprehensive, but then I reminded myself that women in third world countries give birth without intervention all the time.

When I was coming up to two weeks overdue, Tamzin held my hand and said, 'The doctors will now start to pressure you to be induced. It's your right to say no—you're a free woman, you can do what you like.' She talked me through what it's like to be induced, the pros and cons.

I did get a lot of pressure from the maternity staff and I continued to say no. I know if I hadn't had Tamz there, I would have listened to them out of fear, because they were the experts.

I now understand why Tamzin is the best at what she does. I think anyone lucky enough to have her guide them through that experience should count their lucky stars. She is very calm and informative, and she instils confidence. I went into labour at home and Craig and Tamzin drove me to the Gold Coast hospital, and were both a wonderful support to me when I was in labour.

During the birth, I remember standing in the shower at the hospital as contractions hit and I was letting the water run over me. Tamz came in to check on me and I asked her, 'How much longer do you think I'll have to endure this?'

She smiled, slowly shook her head and said, 'I don't know.'

And I said, 'Wrong answer!' But it wasn't much longer after that that he was born.

I hadn't planned to do this, but during the labour I imagined I was pushing our horse truck up the hill behind our house! And then Colt Stafford Bullen was born. It was a really beautiful birth—as beautiful as it could be with that much agony. It was certainly very peaceful and calm, and ninety per cent of the credit for that goes to Tamzin. She gave us so much useful information during the pregnancy, and she has such extensive experience and knowledge. I love the fact that Colt was born at five minutes past six in the morning and we were going home by midday that day. Tamzin stayed with us for another two days. I had such a feeling of panic when I realised that she wasn't going to be there the following day, even though Mum was there and Craig and Cleo. She told me I'd be fine with their help, and pointed out they'd all done it before.

Tamzin sacrificed her own life and family to be with us at that time. I remember her being on the phone to her kids on the verge of tears at night, explaining to them she'd be home soon. She is my hero.

Colt was born in July 2006. At the time the ABC was filming the Bullen family for their *Dynasty* program and they wanted to film Colt's birth. But Tamzin had said, 'Zelie, I think that's a really bad idea. You'll have so much to do in there that you won't want a camera there as well.' Thankfully, Tamzin put a stop to it; but they did film Cleo meeting Colt for the first time, which was really lovely. Cleo kindly didn't tell me until after he was born how desperately she had hoped for a boy. I'm glad she didn't tell me—I might have felt guilty if we'd had a girl. She said, 'Finally I get to see the Bullen name live on.' He is the only Bullen boy in his generation to carry the name. In this day and age it may be considered an old-fashioned notion, but it was still an important one to Cleo.

'Not a bloody lot to ask,' she said. 'I had four kids—three sons. You'd think one of them would have a Bullen boy.' Even among Craig's cousins' children there isn't a boy who carries the Bullen name, so Colt was the only one in the fourth generation, as Craig's son Nelson has his mum's surname.

'I wonder if he'll like animals,' I said to Cleo one day.

'Of course he'll bloody like animals!' she confidently told me. 'He will—he'll carry it on.' I was proud and happy for her, but it was mixed with protective emotions—not wanting to burden our newborn son with expectations. I needn't have worried; Colt himself would show us soon enough how he felt about animals and performing.

# CHAPTER 48

# Times a-changing

While I was pregnant, Aura died. Losing her within a year of losing Snoopy was heartbreaking. She was run over on Maudsland Road, which was always very busy.

When I'd gone to the loo in the middle of the night, I let her out for a wee. I went back to bed straight afterwards; I didn't know where Aura was and I was tired, so I thought she could stay outside.

When I got up the next morning she wasn't waiting on the doormat like she normally would, and straightaway I had a horrible feeling. Craig found her body on the side of the road while I was searching and calling for her across the paddocks; I thought maybe she had been bitten by a snake. Craig yelled out, 'Babe, babe, I've found her,' and my heart just sank, simply from the way he said it.

I called back, 'Is she dead?' and he said, 'Yeah, she is.'

The neighbours from across the road had just got two new

dogs, and Aura had seen them from the back of the ute when we'd pulled into the driveway the day before. She had such blue heeler loyalty that she didn't normally go up to the road, but we think she must have gone to introduce herself to the new dogs in the middle of the night, and was hit and killed.

Aura was only six years old and she was taken far too early. She was my dream dog. Snoopy was my best friend, but Aura was that protective loyal dog I had always wanted on the back of the ute. I felt totally ripped off to have lost that dog.

Looking after Colt was all-consuming for a while. I wasn't prepared for how much time a newborn baby takes out of your day. The lawns were left unmown, and while my horses were fed and healthy they weren't washed or checked as regularly as I normally liked.

Colt's birth was such a life-changing event for me. I had been quite arrogant about motherhood, imagining that it would be a piece of cake for me, but in fact I found it shocking at first. My world as I had known it suddenly came to an abrupt end, and for a while I felt angry at others for not warning me. Of course, many of them had, and they reminded me of that later; but I had been too arrogant to listen. I just thought I would take everything in my stride—that, as always, I would cope. In that respect, having a child was a very humbling experience. I could easily have become depressed, even though it was joyful and beautiful at the same time.

When Colt was eight weeks old, I felt ready to take on my first horse job since his birth.

It was only a few days' work, for Jonathan Shiff, and we used my liberty and riding horses—Bullet, Avatar and Nakota. Mum came along to help with Colt. I have a photo of her sitting on a chair reading a book, just off set and happier than a pig in poo, next to a pram with a little baby Colt asleep in it, with his little baby toes sticking out of the sheet. But even with Mum's help I don't think I was really ready to go back to work when I did that job. When it was finished I was glad to go home with Colt again.

And then I lost J'adore. I hadn't seen her for a day. The five other horses in the paddock were happily grazing within sight of the house, but not J'adore. I said to Craig that I would climb the hill at the top of the paddock to look for her, so he stayed with Colt and I headed off. I found her dead in a gully, having died from a freak paddock accident, every horse owner's nightmare. I sat down and cried and cried.

I cried for the loss of that beautiful animal; I cried out of guilt, because I felt I had put my newborn child's needs above my duty to check on my animals more regularly; I cried out of hormonal imbalance. I cried, thinking my heart would break.

Then I called Evanne Chesson, a friend in Melbourne who breeds horses, including Andalusians and Friesians, and whom I have always admired because of her strength and capabilities. I asked her if she had any Andalusians for sale. She said no, but she did have some Friesian mares that she should probably move on. So we packed Colt up in the Chevy and drove the eighteen hours to Melbourne, then drove back again with five new horses. By now Colt was about six months old.

Not long after that, we were asked to do some liberty work on *The Ruins*, a film being produced by Steven Spielberg's company DreamWorks. We used the new Friesian mares we had bought from Evanne. I had only recently broken them in at that stage, but we were very careful not to overload any one of them and they did well. It felt good to be back working my horses, and once again Mum came down from Cairns to look after Colt while we were on set.

It was very healing for me to put my time into the animals again. However, I was still struggling to adjust, because I was then tortured with guilt about not being with Colt for two or three hours at a time. It was a difficult process, and it still can be. I still get that sense that I need and want to be with him and have to fight the urge to down tools and go and hang with him for a while. Often I will do just that; nothing is as important as these years when he is growing every day.

The mares in *The Ruins* were ridden bareback by actors and stunt doubles, and Julie, one of our Friesian mares, had to learn to rear on cue. Evanne gives all her horses human names and I am very opposed to that. We always laugh about it, she says I give our animals freaky made-up or foreign names. In the case of Julie, though, I wanted to keep the name—I wanted it to be in our lives again. Somehow it seemed right—Colt was just born, J'adore had died, and I had a beautiful new horse with a beautiful name. Julie quickly became a nice little liberty horse.

When Colt was about eight months old I was offered a position as the assistant horsemaster on Baz Luhrmann's movie *Australia*. I knew it was going to be a much larger job than those I had been involved with in the last six months and that it would be with people I didn't know. I always strive to do my best at work and I knew that, if I accepted, I would be putting all my energy into this job and there would be stress involved. I was worried about not spending time with Colt. I had a big talk to Bobby on the telephone about it all and he said, 'Walk away, Zelie, walk away.' So I turned it down, which was a difficult thing to do; but I felt it was the right thing to do at the time.

Craig agreed. In the end, it worked out well because Evanne Chesson asked Craig to work with her in her background horse department, so he went and worked on the film, while I stayed home with our baby.

One of the fun jobs that came up at this time was another Australian movie, *The Black Balloon*. It was fun because I managed to get Nelson and Columbia involved. I had wanted to include them in as many family things as possible, especially after Colt was born. I was concerned that they might feel insecure about Colt coming into their dad's life and I wanted them to be able to get to know their little brother, and he them.

The three of us drove down and met Nelson and Columbia in Sydney for the job. I played a mum driving down the road; I had to brake to avoid hitting an actor as he crossed the road, and then yell out the window at him. There were to be a couple of kids in the back of the car, played by Nelson and Columbia.

Craig looked after Colt off set while Nelson, Columbia and I went to work. They got to be movie stars for a day: we went to make-up, then wardrobe; we shot the scene and they earned a little money for their day's work. When they went back to school they could tell their friends they had just been in a movie.

When the movie came out, they were excited when they saw themselves on the big screen. Columbia said, 'It was so quick!' after seeing herself on the screen for a brief minute, and we told her, 'Welcome to the movies!'

One day in August 2007, Cleo rang and spoke to Craig. 'Well, son,' she said, 'I've just been given my death sentence. There's nothing they can do, I just have to sit it out now.' She had been diagnosed with liver cancer. She was shocked and upset, but stoic to the end.

She had been so happy and energetic when Colt was born. We'd noticed that she'd lost weight, but there was still so much life in her and we thought she had another ten years or more in front of her. When she got sick, though, she went downhill very fast.

Tamzin had explained to me that liver cancer is one of the fastest progressing of the cancers. Once your liver shuts down, it's all over. And that's what happened: Cleo barely ate anymore—sometimes she would try to eat, and other times not.

We spent quite a bit of her last months with her. We would go down to Sydney and stay a week with her, and it would turn into two weeks; we would find ourselves thinking, 'We'll stay a few more days.' Before Colt went to bed at night, I would take him in to say goodnight to Cleo. She was in pain and miserable, but he would give her a hug and she loved it, opening her arms and saying, 'Goodnight, my boy.'

During that time, I got to know Craig's eldest brother, Mark. Before that, our relationship had been quite superficial, but as Cleo got progressively worse, Mark was there more and more—he was like an angel to her. I would stay up talking to him for hours on end—I found him interesting and fun, and I loved getting to know him.

Cleo wasn't sick for very long before she went into a hospice and then passed away. From her diagnosis to her death was only four months. Naturally I was very sad seeing Cleo die. I was, of course, even sadder for Craig losing his mum, and for Colt, who now had only one living grandparent, my mother. I had always thought Cleo would be around to tell Colt circus stories and to play a large and influential part in his life.

Just after we buried Cleo, we took Colt to Africa for the first time. Jamie and Dana had asked Colt to be the ring bearer for their upcoming wedding. At around the same time Jim was doing a film called *Mr Bones*, so it was great to be able to help him on that also. It was really nice finally introducing Colt to our African family, the Stockleys, and all the lovely things their place has to offer, like feeding giraffes and lion cubs. It was a comfort to be back with the Stockleys and to experience a happy ceremony after such a tragic one as Cleo's funeral.

# CHAPTER 49

# Running away with the circus

In October 2007, more and more work started to come in. Thankfully, the lovely Beverley Bryan came into our lives at this point to help us out. Craig had known Beverley for most of his life; she had grown up in the circus, spending most of her childhood and teenage years with Ashton's Circus. She helped us when we worked at home, living in a caravan and looked after our place and the animals when we travelled away. At times she would come away to jobs with us, so she could look after Colt while we were working.

I recall the first time I was apart from Colt for the whole day, working horses in the hot sun while Colt and Beverley played in the cooler shade off set. It almost killed me being separated from my boy all day; I found it difficult to fully focus on work.

In November, we began to train three circus acts for Frank Gasser, founder of Circus Royale and Circus Olympia. Then we literally ran away with the circus and travelled with them for four months, settling the animals in. Frank encouraged us to stay as long as we liked. It was a beautiful few months. Colt had just turned two and was able to be involved in almost every part of our work. He played with the gorgeous little girls Savannah and Isabella, whose parents also worked in the show.

Craig and I trained a mixed miniature-animals act, a single pony act with a beautiful pony called Belle, and a duck act. For the latter we raised and trained ten Indian Runner ducklings; Colt helped me handle, feed and clean them. More than that, he guided the ducklings along in their training and then worked with them in the circus ring. Craig had taught our two-year-old to bow on exiting each of his acts, which of course always caused the audience to erupt in 'ooohs and ahhhhs'.

For the first two years of his life, Colt had been a shy little boy, not wanting to leave my side; but when he went into that circus ring, his life changed. I also thought it was wonderfully fitting to see him, a fourth-generation Bullen, performing in Frank Gasser's circus: as a young man Frank had been brought out to Australia by Colt's grandfather, Stafford, to work in Bullen's Circus.

Frank and his cousin Rene were both very good performers and there isn't much Frank hasn't had a go at over the years. Even though I hadn't known Stafford very well, I knew Cleo well in her later years and her relationship with Frank Gasser was very special. I was touched deep in my soul that Colt's debut in the ring was under Frank Gasser's name. The cycle felt complete—now the youngest Bullen was being nurtured by one of the warmest men in the business, who owed his start in Australia to Colt's remarkable grandfather. Both Frank and his wife, Manuela, were so warm to us all, and I knew Craig loved being back with Frank and back in the circus environment.

Once we were satisfied that the animals were happy and settled, we then went to work with Frank's nephew, Sonny Gasser, and his wife, Barbara, on their travelling horse show, *The Horseman from Snowy River*. On this tour, there were eighteen beautiful horses, including Andalusians, Lipizzaners, four Friesians, one Clydesdale, one miniature, four Arabs, and one Quarter Horse—all stallions or geldings. I love how passionate Sonny is about working with animals, and horses in particular.

Sonny and Barbara had asked me to trick ride on the show, and help train their daughter Katherina ('Gigi'), who was eleven years old at the time. We readily agreed. I was really enthusiastic to trick ride again, and was excited to meet and work with a Russian Cossack rider, Jamal Charepov. Soon after we'd first met, Craig had told me about Jamal, who had come to Australia with the Moscow Circus in the 1980s, and I loved fulfilling another dream—to meet and ride with this talented Cossack rider.

Trick riding in a circle was a whole new experience for me. Normally trick riding is performed fast in a straight line or around a large arena. It was fun—I didn't have to focus as much on what the horse was doing, because Sonny worked the horse from the centre of the ring and I could concentrate purely on what I was doing.

We met a gorgeous young girl on the show, Julia Burey, who had just finished an equine course in the Hunter Valley and had joined Sonny and Barbara as a stablehand for her first job. I enjoyed helping Julia, who had started trick riding with Sonny and Jamal.

Not long after we arrived, Barbara asked if I knew of a schoolteacher who might be suited to the travelling life to help tutor the kids on the show, so I suggested a fun, vivacious girl, Maggie Ashley, who lived just down the road from our home in Queensland. We had recently met Maggie and she had worked as a groom for us a little at home and on *The Ruins*. She was just finishing her teaching degree and I knew she was ready for a change. She happily came to join the show as we travelled around the country.

I really loved that Colt was being raised in a lifestyle that was in between home life and movie work. It felt like an extended family environment, and he had other kids to play with.

# CHAPTER 50

# Grace

The show took a break over Christmas, and Craig and I decided it was the perfect time to visit Tad and Wendy, who had had their fourth baby by then and still hadn't met Colt. For three years we'd been wanting to get back and see them and it just hadn't happened.

Nothing could have prepared me for how wonderful it was seeing Colt with their children. I had always thought their boys were beautiful and well mannered, but they treated Colt just like one of them. Gattlin, Callder, Arrden and Garrison are very well-rounded kids, and are very much part of a team. They look after each other and support one another, and have vibrant personalities. All of them are incredibly talented; although they're not even teenagers yet, the two oldest, Gattlin and Callder are doing very well in the film industry as up-and-coming actors and stuntmen.

The boys are fourth-generation trick riders and have ridden

at some of the biggest shows in America. Gattlin and Callder can perform full-grown men's tricks, and there is nothing cuter than seeing little Arrden going into one of his routines on his little Shetland pony as it flies around the ring.

We love being with the Griffiths. Every time we go there and spend time with them, the family is bigger and better and more fun—it's like being at home, but with even more stuff happening all the time! They are yet another family we wished lived across the road from us, so we could spend more time with them. I would like nothing better than for Colt to be around the boys all the time; he loves them and they call him their Australian brother, and we refer to the Griffith boys as his American brothers.

At that time there were only three rules in the Griffith house: don't lie, be nice to each other, and be nice to the animals. When we came home, they became Colt's three rules too.

Another thing we brought back from that trip was saying grace. We had been home a couple of days when Colt, now three, asked why we hadn't said grace. It was a ritual the Griffiths followed before each evening meal, and Colt liked it, so now we do it too. We don't have a set prayer; we often start out by saying, 'Thank you for this food,' and then we progress to recalling whatever has happened during the day. If we know someone who's sick we'll express the hope that they get better. Sometimes we simply say thank you for the banana skin being yellow. We don't necessarily thank God in our grace. I don't have any education in that department, so I don't thank God as such or ask Colt to specifically thank God. Our grace is just a general 'thank you' to the universe for everything we have or hope for.

I feel that there is an amazing energy source inside all of us. I have had access to it a couple of times and gone, 'Wow.' It's a natural high that I have felt as an adult and remember feeling as a child. I am not sure how to connect with it properly, but I wish I could 'plug in' whenever I felt like it. For me it feels like love, peace, unlimited unconditional freedom, wisdom and power.

I know there are people who think God exists in each of us, and I understand what they are talking about, though personally I don't call it God. I believe we can all find confidence in ourselves. And, once you find it, it is like a vortex of unlimited possibilities.

In January we returned to Australia and went back to work with Sonny and Barbara. Like most travelling shows, when it's time for a performance it's all hands on deck. This time Craig was also on a horse and he went into the ring to perform in an Akubra and Driza-Bone at the beginning of each show. When Craig and I were performing in the show's opening troop drill, the older kids would supervise Colt backstage. He was always very good; he understood how important it was not to leave whoever was looking after him when Mum and Dad were busy. Once the troop drill was over, Craig would get off his horse and take Colt to the caravan for a bath and dinner, or they'd sit and watch the rest of the show.

I suggested to Sonny that he invite Mark Eady to have a look at the show, and Mark came on board as an outside director. He gave some great input, with fresh new ideas and ways to improve the flow of the show; he also managed to work Colt into the show with the miniature pony.

With Frank's show we had seen how Colt liked being involved, but it was on Sonny's show that we truly realised how much Colt loves to perform. Craig was particularly thrilled that Colt displayed such natural showmanship skills; he carries on the family tradition from Craig's father and grandfather. We all wished that Stafford and Cleo were there to enjoy it with us.

CHAPTER 51

# My toes are facing
# the wrong way!

We had been with Sonny and Barbara for over a year, and away from home for a year and a half, when I had my accident.

I was trick riding on Sonny's beautiful horse Mozart, a gorgeous Andalusian stallion I loved to ride. We were showing in the New South Wales city of Wagga Wagga and there had been a terrible storm only hours before the show commenced. The ground was waterlogged, but the arena where we performed, which was always in the centre of the tent and covered in sand, seemed unaffected. However, as is often the case, the tent had been erected on a slight slope, although the surface appeared to be dry, the stormwater had in fact soaked into the back corner of the arena, under the sand. The trick-riding act always finished the show so, as usual, the surface had been churned up when we rode out to perform, exposing some of the wet clay base beneath.

One of the most popular trick-riding moves is the 'full fender'. In this trick I turn my head and torso to the right and continue to pivot in that direction as I slide down the left side of the horse and finish up facing the ground; but then I turn my head to face forward again, sitting down low on the left side of the horse. My left foot/ankle is firmly in the left stirrup, my right foot and calf are tucked under the horse's body along the girth to brace myself, with my body jutting out perpendicular to the side of the horse. Holding your legs in tight and bracing the right-hand side of your torso holds you in the trick and, as you get more confident, you can drop further towards the ground and drag your hands and hair in the sand. It can be a spectacular-looking trick.

On this wet night in Wagga, it was when I dropped down into the full fender that Mozart slipped on the moist ground and fell on top of me, stabbing my left foot and ankle into the ground under his weight. Along with the thud of the impact, I heard a loud crack.

I was pleased to see that Mozart was uninjured; he got up straightaway. Craig and Sonny's brother-in-law, Michael, were beside me in an instant. As I spat out the sand, I looked down at my left ankle. It was twisted backwards, facing the wrong way. My left toes were pointing towards the heel of my right foot and I remember thinking, 'That doesn't look good!'

They carried me off-stage while the rest of the performers and crew did their best to ease the tension among the shocked crowd. Craig took me straight to the emergency department at Wagga Base Hospital, while I consoled a very shocked and upset Colt on my lap and struggled to ignore the pain. I forced myself to act composed for our son, and I was amazed when I later realised that I hadn't shed one tear.

Freda and Bert drove over from Gundagai and were in the hospital room the following morning when the surgeon gave us his verdict. He said it was a particularly bad break, the worst he'd seen of that type. I had a grade-three fracture of my talus bone, meaning that the bone had broken into several pieces, which had been distributed through the soft tissue of my ankle. The only grade higher is a grade-four break, when part of the talus bone breaks away and penetrates the skin, so it was fairly bad. A grade three was almost unheard of until the early 1900s, when air force pilots would present with them after crash landings. It is a very rare break and is mostly seen in people who have survived high-speed car accidents or bad parachute landings or, I guess, when a horse has fallen on them when they are balancing underneath the girth!

Interestingly enough, I had thought about that trick many, many times over the last few months, thinking that I didn't feel a hundred per cent right doing it on a tight circle. But everyone loved that trick, especially on a circle at speed, when you can get really close to the ground, so I'd kept performing it.

Tad, of course, told me off later. 'Well, what have you learnt from that? Listen to yourself! There are plenty of other tricks to please the crowd.' He went on, 'What have I told you before is the most important thing about trick riding? Footing, footing, footing. If your footing is slippery, rocky or uneven, do not trick ride.'

Poor Craig felt so guilty about not checking the surface before I came on—it was something he almost always did without me even knowing. He said to me afterwards that he should have warned me to watch that back corner—it was just a feeling he had.

I hadn't noticed the surface. I should have, but I didn't. It was silly of me—you should always prepare thoroughly for a dangerous performance and I'm not proud of how complacent I had clearly become. You should always do your own checks and, as Tad said, you should always know the footing is safe.

The surgeon went on to explain that the talus is one of the most important bones in the ankle joint, linking the leg and the foot. It not only articulates with the bones of the lower leg at the ankle joint, it also connects the ankle to the mid-foot. One of the worst complications that can happen with this sort of break is that the blood supply gets permanently cut off to the talus, effectively killing it and not allowing it to heal. Unfortunately the blood supply to my damaged talus had been interrupted. I had also broken off the bottom of my fibula, one of the two lower leg bones connecting to the talus, and dislocated the ankle joint.

The surgeon told me that I would probably always walk with a limp, and I wouldn't be able to run again. He said the ankle probably wouldn't work like it used to—it wouldn't roll or rotate properly, and I wouldn't have full flexion. But, more importantly, I wouldn't get sufficient strength back to be able to spring off it.

Finally, he said that I had less than a five per cent chance of ever having a functioning ankle again, and I should start to think about a change in career.

# CHAPTER 52

# Five per cent

I cried for about five or ten minutes at the hospital, once Fred and Bert had left. Then and there, I wanted to speak to Tad and tell him what the surgeon had said; he was the only person I really wanted to talk to.

Craig said to me, 'I'll get him on the phone, but you need to remember that that doctor has no idea of who you are, what you are capable of and what you want to do with your life. He is used to dealing with people who aren't motivated, people who listen to statistics, who don't focus on their health or their attitude.'

It was exactly the right thing to say to me but, although I appreciated hearing those words, I doubted them. I was still very shocked by the surgeon's stark prognosis and I thought that Craig was just doing the husbandly thing and trying to support me. I wanted to believe him, but I wasn't sure if he was right.

Craig called Tad on his mobile. As I lay on the hospital bed trying to compose myself, I could hear him in the corridor explaining what had happened. Then he came back into the ward and passed the phone to me. I heard Tad say, 'Hi, sweetie,' and I could barely stop crying.

'Tad, they said I'll never trick ride again.'

He was kind but stern. 'Well, why would you listen to them? What would they know about you?' Then he repeated, almost word for word, what Craig had just told me. For a moment I thought it must be a conspiracy between Craig and Tad, but then I realised that I'd just heard their entire brief conversation so there was no way Craig could have prompted him. The knowledge that these two very important men in my life believe in me so unconditionally still brings me to tears.

'Big deal—it's only your talus bone,' said Tad. 'I've broken my talus bone.'

'You did? They told me it won't heal.'

'What would they know? They're just used to dealing with people who don't take care of themselves.'

Sonny and Barbara came in to visit not long after my conversation with Tad, and I told them what the surgeon had said. And Sonny said, 'Oh, Zelie, don't you listen to him. I broke my talus bone. I don't have the same power I had in that ankle, but I don't need the two per cent extra I had before the break—I'm doing just fine.'

I thought, 'Well, there you go, doctor!' I was so happy. Hallelujah, I actually knew some of the five per cent who had made it through this injury. From then on, I never had an ounce of doubt that I would get back strength and movement in my ankle.

On the second day after my emergency operation, I was surprised when Barbara asked if we would be staying on with the show once I got out of hospital. She said there were always plenty of things to do, which of course was true. I could still organise and fulfil several of the stable manager duties; there was promotion work, and I could sell tickets. As far as she was concerned, we still had something to offer the show.

I had had a bad reaction to the anaesthetic and Craig put his foot down and said, 'No, we're going home.' He told me I wouldn't rest properly if we were still working on the show; it was a serious situation and I had a mighty healing job ahead of me that I needed to focus on. I knew he was right, but I was very sad to be leaving.

As it turned out, the healing process was an amazing journey; it was a beautiful time. I was confined to a very limited physical existence. Before then, I had always been able to get out and do what I wanted to do. Even after Colt was born and I had to deal with the constant demands of a beautiful newborn baby, I was still able to carry him around with me as I did things. But suddenly I wasn't allowed to put any weight on the ankle. I spent those two months sorting out photos, catching up with things in the office and, most importantly, spending quality time with my little boy, something I had unwittingly been pining for.

Of course, saying I had a nice healing journey is a bit like saying I had a nice birth! There was pain and suffering involved, but I was really proud of my accomplishments. I got on the internet; I researched; I saw naturopaths; I asked questions, speaking to every person who I thought could assist with my healing to find out what knits bones back together and what stimulates capillary growth.

I did reiki; I did a lot of visualising; I consumed every vitamin and mineral supplement that claimed to improve circulation and bone strength. Sometimes I wanted to lie on my bed and cry, but I would tell myself that the crying wasn't helping the healing, so instead I would meditate and visualise my ankle healing.

I had a lot of fun visualising—I became quite creative, trying to maintain my interest and enthusiasm. I imagined different colours oozing around my ankle, in both gaseous and liquid forms; I would close my eyes and imagine noble good guys on horseback, dressed up in suits of armour and tribal warrior costumes, clearing the way for the capillaries to grow and multiply and heal the broken bone. I visualised a lot of crazy stuff, but I believe it was all positive energy going into my ankle at every moment.

Sometimes while I was visualising these things my ankle would tingle and get hot, and I'd feel it start to throb. Perhaps that was a normal physiological response and I only happened to notice it because I was focusing on my ankle, but I felt that, by pouring in all of that positive energy, I was actually stimulating a response. All I know is that I focused very hard and I willed it to heal.

Every morning I'd get up and go to the loo, either hopping or slowly hobbling on my crutches, and occasionally I crawled all the way. On my first morning at home, I had looked out of the toilet window at a staghorn fern that was growing on a little tree just outside and it had a tiny little bud growing on it. I thought, 'How cool, it's growing a new leaf!' I looked at that leaf every single day, and I watched it getting bigger and bigger, and I would imagine my capillaries spreading out through my ankle like the growth of that strong healthy little leaf. By the time I could walk on my ankle again, that leaf was as big and healthy as all of the others.

When we arrived home from Sonny's show, just days after the accident, we had my ankle assessed again by a different doctor. Lydia did some research for me and she found the best ankle and foot surgeon in Brisbane, Dr Greg Sterling. Craig and I liked him as soon as we met him. He looked at my leg and the x-rays and said, 'Hmm, that's a very bad break,' and 'I haven't seen one like this before.' (Maybe he needs more trick-riding patients!)

He told me I was lucky because my surgeon at Wagga Base Hospital had done a very good job. He could see where the break was, but at every angle on all the x-rays, the surgeon had lined up the bone perfectly.

I told Dr Sterling about the doom-and-gloom report the surgeon had given me—that if the bone died, they would have to fuse my ankle in one position—and he said, Doctors like to give people the statistics and tell you probable outcomes so you have some sort of idea.'

'I intend to get better,' I said.

'Well, good for you,' Dr Sterling said. He was very supportive, but he also said that I needed to understand the severity of the situation. I knew how bad it was, but I was still utterly determined to heal myself. So he said, 'Well, you do that— knock 'em dead then.'

The surgeon in Wagga Wagga had told me that I definitely couldn't walk on my ankle for three months and that I shouldn't really put my full weight on it for six months; he had said I would have to rely on crutches and then move on to a walking stick. But after two months, Dr Sterling said he was happy for me to start to put weight on my ankle as it was healing very well. When he looked at the new x-rays, he was amazed to see that the blood supply had recovered and was now nourishing my healing ankle. He said, 'This is looking good. I can't promise you anything—sections of that bone may still die, but we won't be able to determine that until further down the track.'

I smiled when he told me this and thought that maybe it had healed because I'd been looking at that plant outside my toilet window. I said, 'No, I think we're going to be right.'

Then he looked at me, smiled, and said again, 'Well, good for you.'

When I went back one year later, after returning from working in Europe, I had more x-rays done and Dr Sterling was again shocked. He said he could barely see where the break had been and there appeared to be full blood supply back to the bone.

I said, 'I told you,' and he said, 'Yes you did.' He asked me to show him some stretches and then to hop up on the examination table. He manipulated my ankle and was amazed at how much flexion and stability I had got back. When he told me that I should be very proud of myself and that he had never seen anything like it I got the biggest buzz and I hugged him. He was a bit surprised, and then he and Craig laughed. It was a very emotional moment. He asked for my permission to duplicate my notes, as he wanted to use it as an inspirational story, and I said go for it. I felt proud, and incredibly grateful that Craig and Tad had been right.

CHAPTER 53

# Working for Spielberg

About three months after the accident, we were called by a
man we had worked with on *Zorro*, who wanted to talk
to us about a movie coming up in England called *War Horse*. It
was based on a children's novel by Michael Morpurgo and he
said it had a big budget; it was a Steven Spielberg production.
He said that they wanted to hire me as the liberty horse trainer,
and that there would also be a team of stunt horse trainers from
Spain.

I thought, 'Woo-hoo! What fun!' I had worked on Steven
Spielberg films before; but he only directs a few of his films
himself, and at this stage I was not told that he was directing.
The discussion on the phone was just about the bare basics of
the job and it sounded good. I explained that I was recovering
from a broken ankle, though I had just been told I could bear
weight on my injured leg again and didn't have to rely solely
on crutches anymore. He wasn't worried about my injury and

281

asked if we could get there as soon as possible. He also asked how many liberty horses I could train, and I told him I could train four full-time; I also requested two for Craig to work with, in between assisting me.

When I requested that a script be sent to me there was a short pause at the other end of the phone. Then he said, 'That won't be happening. The script is under lock and key—it has to be signed out and then back in.' He told me that even the heads of department had to go into the production office to read it and then leave it there when they left. He suggested that I read the book it was based on to get an idea of the story.

My friend and former neighbour at Maudsland Road, Tanya Bangay immediately bought the book for me online. By the time it arrived in the post, I didn't have much time and so I had to read it overnight two days before we were due to fly out to England. My heart pounded while I was reading it realising what the horse role would involve, but I also wondered why I was the only liberty horse trainer they were planning on getting, because I could tell that four liberty horses wouldn't be able to cope with the workload of this demanding story.

At our next phone call I asked him how many liberty trainers there would be—surely there would be more than just me? When he confirmed that I was to be the only one, I voiced my very strong opinion that we would need more. He said, 'Just get over here and we'll sort out any issues when you arrive.' During our conversation he made it very clear that he wasn't prepared to discuss the matter any further from a distance. My questions were causing doubts within the English horse department and he didn't want to feel like a fool for having recommended me.

As frustrated as I was at not being able to discuss it further right away, I felt the best thing to do was to get over there and read the script. The day before we flew out, we learnt that Steven Spielberg was to be the director; while I was very excited to hear this, I also knew his expectations would be high.

Craig and I packed up in the usual rush, making sure everything was organised at home for the next six to eight months. Then, in May 2010 together with Colt, we hopped on a plane bound for England.

*War Horse* was to be filmed in Devon, in the south of England, and various locations around London. Craig and I had opted to live in a caravan on site so we could work the horses for longer each day without worrying about commuting. Most importantly, it meant we could spend the maximum amount of time possible with Colt. However, we knew he would need someone to look after him while we were working. Maggie Ashley had agreed to leave Sonny and Barbara's show in a few weeks' time and come over as Colt's nanny, but we also needed someone to be there during pre-production.

Marianna Monroy was a young local Mexican girl who had been brought on to assist with the horse make-up when we were working on *Zorro*, back in 2004. Horses, like actors, have make-up applied so they resemble a character, or if more than one horse is playing the same character, so they are identical. It turned out that Marianna had never been around a horse before, but we didn't know that until about three weeks into her working with us. I had seen her squat down right behind the horses' hocks, which was dangerous, so I went over to her and suggested she stay to the side of the horse, and she thanked me. I then said, 'What have you done with horses previously?' and she said she had never been around them before. I was amazed. She was so peaceful around them—relaxed and calm. She happily led the horses around and tied them up. She was just doing her thing.

I grew to love beautiful Marianna—or 'Tita', meaning 'little', the nickname her family called her—and now we flew her from Mexico to meet us in England. We knew she would do a great job of looking after Colt before Maggie arrived. With Tita's help, he could hang out with us—playing Tonka trucks in the sand, drawing with crayons, or playing games with Tita. He could be right there with us and then retreat to the caravan for rest times or in bad weather.

He had celebrated his third birthday in a circus tent and now he was turning four in England on a film set. I was so happy when Mum came over to share his birthday; she stayed with us for six weeks before returning home, and then she rejoined us for the last month of the shoot.

*War Horse* was a physically and emotionally demanding film. It was very politically orientated, but the hardest thing for me was having to spend more hours away from Colt than I ever had before, mostly during filming. There were days when Craig and I would get out of bed and go to work hours before Colt woke, and return at night-time when he was already asleep.

That caused me a lot of suffering. I don't think Colt suffered— he was doing alright. Mum was there a lot of the time and he had Tita, whose patience and energy seemed unlimited. Our love for Tita and our trust in her proved totally justified. When Colt began to speak some Spanish, it melted our hearts—it sounded so adorable. In a relatively short time Colt had learnt to love her as much as we did. Eventually we asked her to stay on until the end of the movie, and we were so relieved when she agreed to. It was a great opportunity for her, and we simply altered Maggie's role from nanny to my assistant.

About four weeks into pre-production, Julia Burey called me. She said it wasn't the same on the show since we had left, and she was unhappy. Julia, I felt, looked upon Craig and me as her second parents. I told her to get out of there, to gather up her courage and do something else—go travelling, go home. Anything. I told her she was welcome to use us as a first base if she wanted to. If she came over and there was no job on the film, she would have the opportunity to meet a hundred and fifty horse people all at once—there would surely be a horse job somewhere. In fact, by the time she got on the plane, a job had become available for her on the movie as a floating assistant.

Maggie and Julia suffered through the mud and the long hours, the weather and the usual film politics, but they both had an amazing experience on *War Horse*. They knew they were very fortunate to get their first break on a film by Steven Spielberg. I told them they were getting spoilt, starting at the top.

# CHAPTER 54

# Politics and war

When we first arrived in England, I quickly read the script and realised that my early concerns were more than justified. I was really worried when I read through all the intense scenes, particularly those where the horse runs riderless through a battle scene and also when he gets entangled in razor wire.

The script was also very descriptive when it came to the horse's expressions and emotions. Of course, the more descriptive a script is of the animal's emotions, the better the actor that animal will have to be. I tried in vain to get that simple message through to the horse department who had employed me. Liberty horse action is not their specialty and they didn't understand how demanding it is for a horse to work at liberty for extended periods of time. The more trained horses you have to rotate, the more chance you have of being able to get the exact shot the director needs.

What they did know was that this job was the biggest project I had ever done, and they felt that I was being nervous and overly cautious in wanting to bring in more trainers. I tried to explain to them that I was only nervous because I knew that to do the film properly we needed several trained horses, which of course meant we needed more trainers. Much to my frustration, I couldn't get that through to them. The people who believed me were not in a position to help, and the people who were in a position to help didn't act.

Originally I was told we had twelve weeks' pre-production; but, by the time we arrived in the UK, we had just over ten weeks before filming was to begin.

A major problem when we first arrived was that only four adult horses had been supplied to play the main horse character, Joey (the 'war horse' of the title), plus one two-year-old horse to play the young Joey, a yearling, and an older mare to play his mother. When I asked about a foal, which we needed to depict Joey as a baby and growing up, I was told they'd get one later. It then truly dawned on me how much they didn't know. All of the horses needed a lot of training to perform as liberty horses at the calibre required for a Steven Spielberg production, and we needed more horses! As well as the liberty horses, we also needed additional horses to be trained for harness work and to be ridden in other scenes by actors, and stuntmen, but the horse department had assumed that the same four horses could be used for all this work.

I was completely shocked. They didn't realise the level of training and concentration a liberty horse needs.

Craig and I worked for three weeks training the horses we had, all the while trying to get our point across. We were under pressure and stressed, working hideously long hours; the daylight in England at that time of the year was allowing us to work up to twenty hours a day, which we did trying to get it all done. What I should have said, simply and clearly at the very beginning, was: 'You cannot do this movie with only one horse trainer and four horses—that's too big an ask.'

I eventually said to the guy who had called me originally: 'Don't you remember? You were on *Zorro*—we had nine horses playing Zorro's horse, Tornado. And Tornado wasn't even the lead character—Antonio Banderas was. Antonio had six stunt doubles. *War Horse* is a big movie, about a horse, and we need more than four to play it!'

We now had two months to go; of the four horses we had, two were proving unsuitable as liberty horses. But we continued to train them, thinking we just had to go ahead with what we had. In the end, those two horses ended up working in other departments—one became a stunt horse, and one became a harness horse. We were eventually able to replace them with other liberty horses, but of course then these two new horses had to begin their training from scratch.

As well as assisting me, Craig was working with the two young horses—the yearling and the two-year-old. I tried to explain to the horse department that we couldn't have just one young horse of each age—what would we do if something happened after we had spent three months training it?

'Like what?' they asked.

'Like it bangs its knee walking out of a stable,' I said. 'I don't know—anything.'

When I finally got my message across, I was heavily repri-manded by the producers in an emergency meeting. They asked why it had taken me three weeks to bring this to anyone's attention. It was then that the truth was revealed—that I had already been speaking out, but in hindsight, too passively.

The producers were scathing towards the men who had hired me. 'So, OK, you guys don't know about liberty training and you bring a liberty trainer from Australia. She arrives here and then you don't listen to her?'

After that crisis meeting some lovely people were involved in trying to make it work, and some quick decisions were made. During that meeting, the producers asked me exactly what was needed and I told them we required three more trainers. After that it all virtually happened overnight. Craig was immediately officially bumped up from my assistant trainer to a second horse trainer. He had already been working as a horse trainer anyway, because we knew how much work was ahead of us and how much trouble we were in.

I then contacted Bobby Lovgren and Bill Lawrence, the two best liberty horse trainers I knew, and asked if they could come and join us. We were down to only seven weeks of pre-production by the time they arrived. Bobby brought with him from America his exceptional bay thoroughbred liberty horse, Finder, knowing he would be invaluable on such a movie. We were also supplied with some more horses to play Joey, which meant we had thirteen in all, including two younger horses and a couple of two-year-olds for the young Joey scenes.

We were a long way behind and it was tough going, but at least we now had a shot at producing the incredibly demanding sequences required for this film. We all pulled together and began intensive training.

# CHAPTER 55

# War horses

All of the horses on that movie—not just those playing Joey—had to be prepped before filming started. We trained them to be war horses, without of course the hardship that they would have had to deal with in a real war. They had to get used to alien things that would usually make them feel frightened, such as smoke, and the sound of bombs and gunfire.

The liberty horses playing Joey and the other main character horse, Topthorn, needed to feel secure while these things were going on around them—both for the welfare of those horses, and in order for them to be able to perform. Training animals to get used to those sorts of things is a gradual process. Some of the horses accept it quickly, especially the horses who already have experience on other movie sets.

We often trained the horses at night. We would lay them down in sand mixed with dark soil to resemble mud. It needed to look real but, just as importantly, we needed the horses to be comfortable and feel as safe as possible. They would not lie down and stay down if it was unpleasant, and we wouldn't want them to. We didn't subject them to anything louder than necessary—the loud noises can be added in post-production, once filming is complete.

They were trained in groups, so they had company, which helped them feel secure due to their herd instinct. We would put the quietest horses at the front and the most nervous or fidgety horses at the back, so the calm would radiate like a ripple effect through the mob.

We began the training for the war scenes with the help of the special effects department, who set up small puffs of air along the ground, so the horses became used to the noise and effect without becoming alarmed. They could then be moved closer to the animals at the trainer's discretion. As the horses began to feel comfortable and realised they were not in danger, the special effects department then laid down small mortars, which consisted of a canister of compressed air covered by pieces of foam and garden peat.

When the small explosions were first let off, some of the horses took fright, jumping and snorting. But as they accepted there was no danger, we increased the size of the mortars and, when we felt they were ready for it, moved the horses closer to the explosions. We continued with this gradual process until the horses became completely desensitised—until they were yawning, resting a back leg and dozing off in spite of the noises, even with smoke surrounding them and peat and foam falling all about them. Once they know it doesn't hurt and they're not in danger, they are comfortable.

When you have a lot of horses galloping, or action among the bombs going off, the horses need to focus on what the trainer or rider is asking them to do. If it is a stunt horse and it's galloping with two hundred other horses in a battle scene with bombs going off, the horses aren't scared of the bombs—they are more focused on where all of the other horses are going and what is happening, which is normal herd instinct.

The scene in *War Horse* that people most often talk about is when Joey is trapped in the barbed wire. Of course, in reality he wasn't. We had three horses trained to perform in that sequence, but we only ended up using two of them. One of the horses was the talented Finder, Bobby's thoroughbred. Finder is the best liberty horse I have ever encountered, and it is his loyalty to Bobby—along with his supreme athleticism—that makes him unique. The other horse was a beautiful trusting Andalusian, Sueno, who was owned and well trained by the awesome Spanish stunt horse team.

For that scene, the special effects department made a plastic breakaway 'barbed wire' that looked real and yet had a very low breaking strain. It had perforated joins every metre so it would pull apart easily if the horse should ever resist or stand on it.

Preparing the animals for that sequence involved training them to kneel and lie down, and then getting them to look as though they were struggling. We would ask them to lie down and then to get up, but before they were completely up we would ask them to lie back down again, so it looked like they couldn't get up. That entire heart-wrenching scene was trained behaviour.

People often ask how we make the animals act out emotions, for example the wide-eyed 'scared' look Finder has during the barbed-wire scene. This is where the trainer–animal bond is particularly critical. We had trained the horses to be comfortable with the 'bombs' and other war elements while they were on their feet, and we had also trained the Joey horses to appear to struggle to get up, but we saved putting the two elements together until the cameras rolled. When the horse was lying down he naturally felt more vulnerable, so he was aware of the sounds in a way he wasn't when he was on his feet. This is another reason why we need to have so many liberty horses to play one character. If we ever feel a horse is starting to leave its comfort zone, then we can change to a different animal and remove, reassure, rest and relax the one who has just performed.

Because Finder trusted Bobby so much, he continued to work with him through all of those elements—the dark, the bombs, the noise, the mud, the harness and the fake barbed wire— knowing he could get up whenever he wanted to.

*War Horse* is one of the most challenging jobs I've ever done. It couldn't have been accomplished without all of the trainers pulling together. At many times Bobby, Bill, Craig and I worked closely with the four Spanish stunt horse trainers—Ricardo Cruz, Hernan Ortiz Redondo, Eugenio 'Salmon' Alonso and Ricardo Cruz junior—who did a fantastic job with the stunt horses, the harness joeys, and the joeys who carried the actors. They are some of the best stunt trainers and horsemen that I have had the pleasure of working with.

Abraham was one of the first four horses we were given to train in England. A solid-boned, large-framed Warmblood from Holland, he had a real 'leave me alone' attitude and was the most difficult horse I have ever started to train at liberty. Although I could tell he was very intelligent, I found him obstinate and difficult to communicate with for the first few weeks of our time together.

His sensitivity and aloof attitude forced me to constantly reassess my approach to his training. Every day I had to draw on several different training techniques and past experiences, and once again I was so thankful to have Bobby by my side to offer his opinion and advice.

As time went on, Abraham began to soften, his walls dropped and trust developed. With a careful mix of kindness, patience and assertive boundaries, I was able to get through his tough exterior, and he began to express what a sweet gentle soul he is. I loved this animal and felt grateful to him for what he was able to teach me. He became affectionate towards me and we developed a real connection.

Time and time again, I called on Abraham to work closely with the actors. He was gentle with them and I was able to get a performance out of him that surprised me. Although there were times when I didn't trust his thoughts or the look in his eye, he proceeded to prove to me just how kind he is.

One of the toughest sequences we had to film was a scene where Joey's friend, Topthorn, who is lame, is being led up to replace a horse that had been trying to pull a huge cannon up a steep hill and had died of exhaustion. Joey knows Topthorn is injured and isn't up to it, so he volunteers to take his place. This was all to be conveyed by a horse, so there was no dialogue of course—just his acting performance at liberty. Joey volunteers by breaking away from the soldier holding him and gallops up the steep incline; he rears, to get the attention of the soldiers and to show that he is healthy and able, and then he positions himself in the traces and waits patiently while he is harnessed up, before looking back down the hill as Topthorn is led away past the gun, back into the ranks of the horses following behind.

When we were filming, Abraham, playing Joey, couldn't see me from his starting position at the base of the hill, so I had to call him up to me. He broke away from the soldier and galloped up a very steep muddy incline past the massive gun that the horses were pulling up the hill. He had to pull into position just before Topthorn was placed there. He could now see me and he stood and reared on command; then, as they harnessed him, I asked him to 'look away' as they led the lame horse back. We did all of that in one shot at liberty.

There were eighty horses in the background and it was a massive set-up. There were three cameras on that sequence, and they could see 'the world', as we call it on set—meaning they can shoot nearly everywhere. I had to position myself between two cameras and there was very little training space to work in. When we work the liberty horses, it can often be likened to a dance—we are using our body language to ask them to do one, or a series of things. So being in a confined position can inhibit the message you are trying to get through to the horse.

We began to film and then we had to cut, because I had stepped into frame—into B camera's view. We filmed a second time and then I was told I was in A camera's view. The third camera was filming tightly on Joey. It was frustrating as I wasn't sure what my boundaries were, so the camera department drew a circle with some powdered chalk and, once they'd looked at the edge of shot for all of the cameras, drew a circle to show where I was allowed to be. When I looked at the circle they had drawn, I was pretty concerned, because it was less than a metre in diameter and I had a lot to convey to Abraham. But he did it and I was pleased to see that that particular sequence in the film looks great and accurately depicts the scene as described in the book. I was very proud of Abraham for working under those conditions.

When we were first contacted to work on *War Horse* I negotiated our wages at a slightly lower rate with the stipulation that, if Craig and I opted to, we could bring home up to two horses of our choice at the end of the job. I knew how attached I can get to the animals I work with and I knew in advance how much work and love goes into them during such intense times, when you can be spending every waking hour with them for extended periods.

It wasn't until we began filming, when we'd been in the UK for about three months, that I began to know that Abraham would be coming home with us. It was a big decision—an expensive exercise with very real risks. Craig and I discussed it extensively—the fact that he was a gelding and therefore not suitable for breeding; the fact that he was a Warmblood, which is usually not my style of horse; the fact that he was too hot-headed for actors to ride, should we ever want to use him for future work at home. None of those valid reasons stopped my heart and poor Craig knew it. But in the end, it was not to be. As filming drew to a close, the man who owned Abraham refused to let him be a part of that agreement.

# CHAPTER 56

# Recipe for success

**W**ar Horse was a lot of mud, sleepless nights, cold and rain. All of that lovely rolling green English countryside is green for a reason—it rains. A lot. I have never owned wet weather clothing like I bought in England!

Working with Steven Spielberg is essentially like working for any director—you want to do the best job you can. Part of his recipe for success is sticking to the schedule. When we first saw the schedule, we had a bit of a chuckle to ourselves. We thought, 'We'll see. Wonder how long this shoot will run over.' But I don't think it went even one week over schedule. It was amazing how true to that schedule they stuck, and for that full credit goes to the first assistant director and co-producer Adam Somner.

Although we always want to do a good job and always want the director to be satisfied, as the animals' custodians, trainers have the responsibility to protect the animals and to always ensure their working conditions are comfortable.

On film sets, situations often arise that are not ideal for animals. These situations can pop up at the last minute for any number of reasons, but largely because every department has its own complex series of jobs to do and, more often than not, most of the crew are not animal savvy. When problems arise, the professional thing for us to do is to approach the assistant director's department and highlight any undesirable conditions or requests.

There are also times when we are asked to get a performance from an animal that is not practicable—for example, where the wind and smoke machines have been set up too close to the animals' working area, or the electrical cables have been rolled out without leaving room for the horses to be brought onto set. When working on a high-demand set like one of Spielberg's, the atmosphere can be tense, depending on what the demands are at any particular moment. It's during these times that we feel the need to speak up. Sometimes we need to be able to suggest or offer an alternative animal behaviour or a different method of obtaining what we think the director wants.

Spielberg is a very personable man, though very tough. He and his team work quickly and efficiently. He is quietly spoken, and a man of few words, which at times made it difficult to understand exactly what it was he wanted. He sets a fast pace and is always very focused on what is going on in his mind, so there are limited opportunities to seek more information. Also, he was always surrounded by an entourage. As a professional, you don't want to barge in, but I found that, when I needed to discuss something important with him, he was very approachable. They would be just about to roll and we would have to say, 'I'm sorry, I just need some more clarification,' or 'Before we roll, can you please specify where you want the horse to look?', and he was never irritated by the interruption or made us feel like idiots for asking.

When he thanked me at the end of the movie, he made me feel like solid gold. At the time, Craig and I were being sent off with Abraham and a second unit crew to another location, to take some photos and to film a live version of the *War Horse* paperback book cover. Abraham needed to look alert and majestic, with his mane blowing in the wind and the sun setting behind him, as the camera dollied in towards him. Now, every time I see that shot, on book covers or on movie posters, I miss Abraham and remember the last time I saw him.

It was the final day of shooting; the main unit was setting up for another shot. Knowing I might not see him again, I walked over to say goodbye and thank you to Adam Somner; it had been a pleasure and an honour to work with him. He insisted that we wait while they called Steven from his trailer.

When Steven arrived, Adam said, 'Zelie has been waiting to say goodbye to you—she's being sent off with the second unit.'

Spielberg said, 'Zelie,' and hugged me. He said in his soft gentle voice, 'Thank you for all of your hard work. All of the love that you have put into your animals is on screen. It's on my screen, and it will be there forever.'

It was a very special moment for me, a definite highlight of my career.

## CHAPTER 57

# Grand circus tour

*War Horse* was such an exhausting and emotional haul for me that I didn't want to come straight home afterwards. I needed to go somewhere else for a while to wind down. I was completely drained from the politics and the stress; Craig and I both felt depleted.

As we were already in Europe, we decided to go on a tour. Mum was still with us in England then too, and I had always loved the idea of spending some time in Europe with her. I wanted to share her love for these countries, and I thought it would mean a lot to her if we all had this adventure together, especially now she had two generations to enjoy it with. The place I most wanted to go with Mum was Holland; she had told me so many things about this country she had come to love.

From the moment we left English soil, I felt relief. We bought a little car, loaded it up and set off on the ferry to Calais. We drove to Holland and caught up with an old friend we had met in South Africa when we were working there on *Racing Stripes*. The Van Gessel B&B had been our home away from home for six months; since then Jerry Van Gessel had moved back to Holland, and we loved staying with him again.

One day we caught the fast train in to Amsterdam to look around. It was winter and we were all jacketed up against the weather. When we walked through the red-light district, the scantily clad women were sitting in their windows as usual and Colt kept asking, 'Why aren't those girls cold?' I assured him they probably had very good heaters in their rooms.

Naturally we wanted to see lots of European circuses. Among those we visited was one of the famous Medrano circuses. One was in France, where we caught up with an old friend of Craig's, Marcel Peters. Marcel specialises in training big cats and was presenting the animal acts for Medrano when we visited, doing one-day stands in the snow and ice. Another show was way down in the south of Spain, one of the Mondial circuses. We drove that long road trip in order to catch up with some of its best performers, the Messoudis. Craig knew Heidi Messoudi from their childhood, a beautiful performer, who married a talented Moroccan tumbler, Siad. Together with their three skilled sons, Yassin, Soffien and Karim, they have become well known in the European circus world as one of the most talented hand balancing and juggling family troupes. They are all beautiful people who were a big inspiration for Colt.

Before we left Paris we also saw the Cirque d'Hiver Bouglione, which has been running since 1852. It is a non-travelling circus that shows in a permanent building year in and year out, and I was in awe of each of the acts and the regal atmosphere—in fact, the entire production.

With its extensive history, European circus culture is very different to the culture of Australian circus. The old circus families in Europe are one step down from royalty. There are sometimes four or five generations of family working in the same show and the lifestyle is heavily ingrained into each generation. In many places, being in circus is considered very prestigious. By contrast, when Craig's grandfather, Perc, started Bullen's Circus in the early 1920s and then worked through the Great Depression, nobody had any money. There was no background or history; he literally headed off with one truck, a pony and a monkey.

When people go to watch a circus in Europe, they dress up. It reminded me of how beautifully dressed and presented Cleo always was. Craig tells stories of Stafford and Perc putting up tents in their three-piece suits, because so many of the townsfolk would come to watch the big top go up.

On our way to Spain, Craig, Colt and I called into Mario Luraschi's, unannounced.

All those years ago, I had phoned him after Mum was given the all-clear from breast cancer. He had asked how Mum was, and I told him he had been right—it hadn't been life-threatening and she had made a full recovery. He'd then asked when I was coming back; I told him I would like to one day, but not yet. I then explained that I had fallen in love with Craig, at which he had laughed and said, 'Oh, love, love—what you know of love? OK, we wait. When your love finished, you come back.'

Visiting him now, after so many years, it was great fun to see my old friends again. Mario asked if we were staying. I said, 'No. I just needed to show you that my love had not finished.' He laughed and seemed happy for me.

We also wanted to spend some time with the Spanish stunt team from *War Horse*, so together with Mum we travelled down through Spain to meet their families and their horses. When we arrived at Ricardo Cruz's homestead, I experienced all over again the same amazement I'd felt when I first arrived at Mario's—how can one person have so many wonderful horses in one place? Imagine the most magnificent Andalusian stallion you have ever seen—every stable at Ricardo's has one. Truly impressive.

After some time with the 'Stunt Cruz' team, Mum flew home and Craig, Colt and I hopped on a plane from Madrid to Johannesburg, to make a surprise visit to the Stockleys. We had been threatening to turn up on their doorstep for a while. It was just what we needed to complete the post-*War Horse* wind-down. During that stay we decided to join them all for a white Christmas back in France close to the German border, where Silvana's lovely sister and her family run a delightful B&B. We were incredibly grateful, being so well looked after by loving people. We all made it a Christmas to remember!

A couple of years earlier, when Colt was eighteen months old, we had visited South Africa and went to Boswell Circus. There I saw Ben Hur, the little pony I had left with Jane and Brian four years before. I asked Ben to sit and, although he hadn't performed that particular trick since I last saw him, he did it willingly. We brought Colt in and took a photo of the two of them.

When we went back to South Africa in 2010 to visit the Stockleys and the Boswells, Jane could see how much Colt, now four years old, loved being in the circus ring and how much he wanted to be a part of it, so she said he could lead a pony or a pig into the ring during a show, or we could even see if he was brave enough to do a small routine with Ben Hur. I ran through a couple of things with Ben, and he was still right on cue even after all these years.

Colt and Ben did a little act together and it was one of the strangest and yet most beautiful experiences I've had since Colt came into our life. The crowd loved it and Colt loved it and he tells everyone about his pony in Africa, and I love that he knows who Ben is.

Our travelling life has some disadvantages—predominantly having loved ones scattered around the world, whom we all miss terribly—but it has far more positives. When we are happily at home, Colt talks about missing Jamie and Dana Stockley's daughter Shaye in South Africa, or the four Griffith boys in America; and when we are working overseas or interstate, he pines for his gorgeous Aussie friends.

# CHAPTER 58

# Safe

In early 2011 we returned at last and settled back into life in Australia with our own animals. It's always so nice to return to our piece of paradise on the Gold Coast, to enjoy time together catching up with our home life and loved ones.

One of the other negatives of our lifestyle is that over the years I have missed out on some very special events as a result of working away. I have missed friends' weddings, the births of their babies and many other occasions, including my youngest sister Kate's twenty-first. If I have any regrets in life, it's that.

Fortunately, this time we made it home in time for the birth of Lydia's baby girl and for my sister Cloud's wedding. She married her long-term partner Gavin and became pregnant soon after, and in October Craig and I found out that we too were expecting another baby. I was delighted that the cousins would be so close in age, and completely thrilled to be able to give Colt another sibling. With impeccable timing he had just started asking for a baby sister.

Yet once again, fear crept into my thoughts, though I pushed it aside with the overwhelmingly joyful expectation of having another little person coming into our lives.

But our delight soon turned to despair: after a pregnancy of only ten weeks, our little one no longer had a heartbeat. I was soon booked into the Gold Coast Hospital for an operation to remove the incomplete pregnancy.

I was emotional as Craig dropped me off and took Colt away for the day to explore some of the local parks. Craig gave his mobile number to the nursing staff and we warned them that, the last time I had come out of general anaesthetic (after breaking my ankle) I'd had a bad reaction to the drugs. We had decided that, if I was taking a while to recover from the anaesthetic, Craig would keep Colt away until I was ready to leave, rather than letting him see me in that state or trying to keep him entertained in the hospital's corridors.

All went to plan at the hospital, but when I tried to call Craig while I was in recovery he didn't answer his phone. Over the next three hours, grief and fear engulfed me. I called Tamzin, who now lives on the Gold Coast with her family, and she immediately came to my side—yet again. The nursing staff continued to call Craig's phone, but still he didn't answer.

I was trying to remain calm as I called Jan, Kate and several others to see if they knew where the boys were. I was asking everybody the same question: Why isn't he answering his phone? No one could give me a convincing explanation and all of my past fears of loss came back.

In the end, Tamzin and I drove around the Gold Coast

looking for our Chevy pick-up, then filed a missing persons report at the police station. As the hours went by, I became frantic. I was terrified that something had happened to my boys. I just kept saying, 'Please, please, please.'

Finally, Craig and Colt arrived back at the hospital. The staff told them how concerned we all were and about the state I had left the hospital in. Craig called me immediately. I was already nauseous; but when Craig's name came up on my phone I felt as if I was going to pass out.

Tamzin drove me back there as fast as she could. When she pulled up at the hospital entrance and I saw them, I simply fell out of the car onto them and hugged and hugged them, crying. All I could say for hours afterwards was, 'Thank you, thank you, thank you!'—Craig and Colt were safe.

Something had gone wrong with Craig's phone. It had seemed to be working and looked like it was on, so it was only when he thought it strange that he hadn't heard from the hospital at all for several hours and he tried to ring me that he realised it wasn't working.

Although I felt grief for the baby who didn't live to join our world, it was suppressed by my overwhelming gratitude that my boys were safe.

# Epilogue

One day, quite early in my relationship with Craig, I was looking out the window and I saw him arriving home. As he walked down the hill, Snoopy and Aura ran up to him. Up to that time I had often pointed out to him that he very rarely patted the dogs. I knew he liked to be with animals, that he was good with animals, and that he understood them, but I didn't see a whole lot of lovin' going on. And that was—and still is—my world: enjoying and loving animals.

On this magic day I realised that he had learnt to relax and enjoy the dogs. As they came up to greet him, he said, 'Hey dogs!' and then he squatted down on the grass and they rolled around on him. He gave them a cuddle, and I thought, 'Look at him enjoying the animals.' It was really fun for me and I didn't half tease him about it afterwards.

Only as recently as when we were working on *War Horse*, I reminded him to take his time despite the intense workload. As I've said, the individual relationship an animal has with his or her trainer is crucial. If an animal doesn't like you, if there isn't yet a relationship or the bond isn't strong, you are not going to get the same results as if you and the animal have an appreciation and mutual respect for one another. We were both under pressure on *War Horse*—there was a lot we had to get through each day—but there were times when I'd suggest he take a horse for a walk, let it pick out some fresh grass and just hang out with it for a while.

That's what I like doing. Training is great fun, but I am still just as happy to be hanging out with the animals.

As far as I'm concerned, there are two very important aspects of becoming a good trainer and I don't think either one of them can be taught beyond a certain point. The first aspect is timing, the second a sense of 'feel'. Craig's timing is impeccable. His ability to read an animal is better than that of most people I know, and yet I think in the last ten years his sense of 'feel' has reached an entirely new level.

I have learnt a lot from him about wild and exotic animals, and I think he has learnt something from me about horses, particularly the wide range of personalities that horses can have. He spent his early life around horses and circus ponies, but he seemed to treat them all in the same way. I have shown him that's not a good idea with horses.

Of course, experience is the third most important factor in becoming a great trainer but, without the natural timing and feel, your ability to learn from experience is limited.

Different people have different priorities. Some people want money, some fame; others want a large family, job satisfaction or a high-rolling career. Me? I want to be happy.

I quite simply believe that the most important thing in life is to be happy.

I don't have any solid theories about the meaning of life or what the universe is all about—to be honest, I give those topics very little thought. I choose to live simply and to follow the dreams that bring me happiness. I have lived through some of life's hardships, as many people have, and as hard and disturbing as those times have been, they have only made me stronger in the long run.

I know what it's like to be sad, depressed, nervous, anxious, jealous, guilty, embarrassed and resentful; and I choose instead to walk the paths that make me feel excited, alive, vibrant, enriched, enlightened, empowered, loved—in short, I choose to be happy.

I have seen people try to satisfy some desire or hunger inside them with superficial things, and the hunger only grows and they always feel they have to get the next thing—the nice car or house. It is like a band-aid treatment, a short-term fix. Instead the 'hunger' needs to be tackled with a holistic approach—find what it is that will make you feel better. Not just a temporary satisfaction, but internal peace.

I think the best way to find internal peace is to stimulate your passion and follow your dreams. One of the ways I do that is by helping others. I like there to be happiness around me: I get an internal reward when others find happiness. I love helping others find happiness in themselves. That help can be as simple as saying to someone that they look nice today, or telling them,

'You know what you are really good at . . .' Quite simply, it feels good when those I care about feel good.

Feeling beautiful inside—loving who I am, who I have become and who I am continuing to become with each passing year—gives me a sense of pride that is enveloped in love. And it brings immense satisfaction.

I have very vivid memories of being a young girl who loved animals, growing up on the outskirts of Perth. I had an abundance of love, and experienced wonderful opportunities, but I know I saw more ugliness than the average kid. I was well nurtured and yet I also recall a lot of insecurity. I was exposed to various situations, opinions and lifestyles that sometimes brought me confusion, disappointment and anger.

I didn't know or appreciate until much later in my life how tough it must have been for my amazing mum back then, or how much she struggled to make ends meet on her own as she tried to provide her three little girls with everything we needed. I have only realised fairly recently, with the help of ABC-TV's *Australian Story* producer Kristine Taylor, that back then I must have turned to animals for relief, for freedom and for an escape. Back then, I thought that, if I wanted to have a job with animals, I would have to be a veterinarian. Training animals in the movie business and Hollywood were a universe away.

I sit here now on the wooden veranda of our beautiful dream home, nestled on our luscious fifty-acre property in South East Queensland, while my adorable five-year-old boy naps in the warm autumn afternoon sun. My amazing husband is feeding the animals and I have the immediate company of our lovely fourteen-year-old cat Cougar. I sit here drafting these closing words for a book that my incredible sister Freda helped me write about my life. I feel humbled that we were approached to write it, not by one publishing company but by three, soon after the *Australian Story* program featured my life.

I don't have that sense of 'I've made it to the top!'; nor do I want to say to you, 'Listen to me, I'll tell you how it's done.' But I am honoured that I have been able to provide inspiration to so many. I certainly do not claim to have all the answers in life, nor do I know why some people seem to have to endure more pain than others, but I can tell you what has worked for me to date and what I have observed throughout my life. It has taken a lot of heartache and suffering for me to learn to think the way that I do.

Before my beautiful sister Julie died, I too used to be one of the majority who has a basic plan mapped out for their life. All I can tell you is that the more I held onto that plan and the need to control my destiny, the more heartache came my way. The more I 'let go', the easier and happier my life became.

I continue to be amazed at how many people I meet who seem to lack happiness and confidence, and who say they feel 'stuck' in some form of job, relationship or lifestyle. I try to encourage them to think about what they'd rather be doing or how they'd rather be living. Many have placed limitations on the way they see their life. They don't seem to realise that their rigid restrictions prevent them from being where they want to be, or from doing what they want to do, or from being with whom they want. I find myself hoping in my heart that they can learn to 'let go' of all their perceived barriers, and that they can start to dream wildly and follow their passions.

The largest and most common mistake that individuals seem to make is to put happiness as their goal, their finishing line. I have also made this same mistake myself in the past, but those days feel like a long time ago now. In the past I have said, 'I will be happy when I have the team of horses that I want,' or 'I will be happy when I don't have to deal with that issue anymore.' It's far easier, more rewarding and a lot healthier to simply find happiness along the way.

I think it's all largely related to your ability to see that the glass is half full rather than half empty. That is a valuable skill; it is well worth investing time to learn how to master it. As I showed myself when I healed my smashed ankle, positive outcomes are produced by positive energy. That's such a simple way to create more of what I want. I truly believe you get what you think about.

As lucky as I feel in my life, there are still things that I want. I hope I never lose that. It's the journey of achieving my dreams that is the fun part—having the experiences and feeling the emotions along the way. If I undertook no more journeys, I might stagnate from sitting here in my bliss for too long! I crave adventure and love and I have become pretty good at either finding it or creating it along the way, whichever way I go.

And for those of you who tell me you don't know what to do with your life, I'll repeat to you what a lovely man, Alex Kuzelicki, once said to me: 'If you do what you love for long enough, you will be successful.'

If I can offer anyone advice at all, it is to stop and smell the roses, to self-assess and invest time into developing your own personal dreams. To follow your passion, to believe in yourself, to have faith in a very simple fact, that 'like attracts like'. When you feel good, you attract good.

Enjoy!

# Zelie's acknowledgements

As I have already mentioned in this book, I believe everyone is largely responsible for the world they create around themselves. Having said that, I have a strong desire to express my gratitude for all of the influences that have obviously been out of my control. I am mostly referring to having been lucky enough to have been born in Australia and into the family that became known as mine. Regardless of whether I have drawn them into my life or not, I also acknowledge the countless opportunities that have come my way and the innumerable doors that have swung open for me in the last forty-two years. More importantly for me at this point in time, is a great feeling of relief at being able to thank all of the people I want to in this segment of the book, including several people who were written into the first draft and who were taken out by our lovely publishers and editors for various reasons. Sometimes the reasons were as simple as needing to cut down our final word count or educating me as a writer when I was told that a 'roll call' of names becomes confusing to the reader. I have found writing these acknowledgements overwhelming. It has been an emotional process thinking about so many loved ones from so many walks of my life and remembering all they have done for me throughout the years. It has been difficult to simplify it all, to put all of my gratitude into only a couple of pages, but here goes.

Thank you to my husband Craig and to my son Colt for sharing this world with me, for providing me with more stability than I have ever had, and for allowing me to feel love at a level that I was sure I had banned myself from. I feel such childlike safety when I'm with you both. Your efforts, achievements, good days and bad days are an honour to share. Craig, you are my best friend; I can no longer imagine a life without you. Colt, I am often fascinated by how my mind revolves around what is best for you and how everything else takes second place in priority to firstly creating happiness for you. I joke now that you will always be my little boy, but I can already feel you becoming the man I know you will one day be. I am proud of both of you and consider myself the luckiest person alive because you are my family.

Thank you to Mum for the happiness, the variety of experiences and the learning you provided through my wonderful childhood. Thanks for the intense, endless love that you have for your three children and our families, for always giving your best to us and for the sacrifices you have made for us along the way. I am thankful that you join us around the world to share parts of our lives and I always feel that words are not enough to express the immense gratitude I have that Colt has you as a grandmother.

Although over the years I have already thanked one person more than any other in my life, I feel a strong desire to acknowledge her again now. My big sister, Julianna Esme Thompson, you were my rock, my mentor and my friend. Julie acted as my second mother and I still find it difficult to believe that I have lived longer in this life without her physical presence by my side. Over the years I have pined and mourned for her; the intensity has come and gone in waves but the longing ache I have for her increased dramatically six years ago when Colt was born. How I craved her being here to share him with us.

Thank you to Bertie, Hayley, Charlotte and Sam Nicholls, as well as Adrian, Hannah and Liam Mondy for all of your love, fun and support and for being so selfless and understanding through so many of the times in my life when I have taken up your wives' and mothers' time. Thanks to Nelson and Columbia for being such great kids and for being beautiful siblings to Colt.

I would like to thank my stepmother Jan and my two younger sisters Cloud and Kate for being such a massive part of my world, particularly in the last twenty-one years. Sometimes I struggle amid our busy lives to think of ways to show you three ladies just how important you are to me.

Thanks to all of the people from my childhood, especially my maternal grandma and grandpa for the stability they provided 'in the background' and to my uncles and aunties and cousins who continue to offer support and friendship. Thanks to all of the Bullens and to each of the Trasks, to Kenny Rodgers, Inese Dzenis, Donna Wilson and Mandy Grey for your involvement in our lives and for your heartfelt support over the years as our relatives.

To the families who, at some point in time, were an extension of my own little family in my mind. Thanks to the Hollands, the Hubers, the Gardners, the Wearmouths, the Lloyds, the Goughs, the Lemanns and Hendersons, the Bushes and Lenkeits, the Stanleys and the Van Nuses.

Thank you, Lance Holt, for your incentive, energy and ability that developed the wonderful alternative schools which were loving learning environments for us kids.

Thanks to Warwick Newton and Naomi Howell for my first lessons in friendship. Thanks to Vanessa (Ness) Holland for being like a sister to Julie and I. Thanks to Peter Holland, Bobby Juniper, Henry Hall and Phillip Lloyd for being what I considered father figures to me. Thanks to my childhood horse-riding buddies, namely Anne Gardner, Jean Wearmouth, Felicity Lloyd and Melody Semmler; you guys were my best friends. A special thanks to you, Mel; despite our long-distance relationship, the love and support continue into my present life. Thanks to Elena Jenson for years of love and fun and for teaching me much about life, the power of the mind and about courage and determination from a young age. Thanks to Danny Murray for your sensitivity. Thanks to Paul Stanley for being my first true love and for taking such good care of me for so long. Thanks to Paul Pernechele for continuing to be my friend. Thanks for the memories to so many of my schoolfriends and 'Hills' friends and also to many of Julie's close mates, who looked out for me and treated me like their very own little sister, particularly when we lost Jules. Thanks to Collette Howard for your love, our laughs and for helping me through some difficult days.

My time at Warner Brothers Movie World was a monumental

stepping stone for my soul, my personal development and also for my career. Thank you to everyone who was a part of that and of my younger stunt-training days; I have so many fond memories and so much gratitude for that time in my life. Thank you, Grahame O'Connell; you remain in my heart.

Thank you to Heidi Mackey, Lydia Emery, Brit Sooby, Wayne Glennie, Mark Eady, and, of course, Tamzin Mondy and my beautiful sister Freda Nicholls. You are the people I've turned to the most. Each of you gives me strength in different ways and I treasure all of you and your families.

Thanks to Tanya, Chris, Audrey, Lulu and Minni Bangay, Corrina Duke, Mark Bonner, Alan and Val Morris, Julia Burey and Maggie Ashley for coming into our lives and for being the type of neighbours and friends of whom one can only dream.

I am extremely grateful for the teachers of my career, namely Tad Griffith, Sled Reynolds, Bobby Lovgren and Bill Lawrence. I have learnt that to have knowledge passed on to you is an honour not a right and it is something that I hold very close to my heart. A sincere thankyou to each of you.

I have met a massive amount of wonderful and talented people in both the film industry and the live show industry, many of whom I am lucky enough to call friends. There are too many to list but I would like to say a thankyou to each of you for your involvement in, and impact on, my life.

I want to thank all of my friends and acquaintances in the circus industry for welcoming me, a 'josser', an outsider, into your wonderful world. I knew nothing of your world or your lifestyle when I met the Bullen family, nor of your culture, your history, devotion and pride and yet I have been warmly welcomed by some of the world's most incredible people.

I want to thank Silvana Stockley for your insight into my life and for inspiring me in several ways, specifically in being as direct as I've always wanted to be. Jim Stockley, how do I thank you for *everything*? For your extensive knowledge and experience, your much-appreciated advice, your direct approach combined with your finely developed skill in managing my emotions, for your wit, for continuing to be my sounding board, but mostly I want to thank you for your time and effort that has resulted in the unique friendship we share.

I would like to thank Richard Walsh at Allen & Unwin for his persuasive techniques in getting me to agree to having a biography written in the hope that it may help and inspire other people. Thanks for your sensitivity and at times brutal honesty; it has been great to completely trust you with my stories. A big thankyou to your caring team of professionals at Allen & Unwin.

If I have left anyone out of these acknowledgements, it is due to a busy schedule and an ever-changing lifestyle; it has not been done out of disrespect.

Lastly, I am not sure how to thank my big sister Freda enough, for all she has done for me in my life, for her completely committed love and support and for often making me wonder if I am truly worthy of her admiration! Together we have laughed and cried our way through this book. I had completely underestimated how difficult and time-consuming the bio-graphical process would be and if it weren't for Freda's skilled and experienced way of dealing with my time management amid both of our busy lives it would never have been finished, of that I have no doubt! For that reason and due to her deep understanding of many of the emotional issues, I know that she is the only author who could have created this book to be the finished product it has become. Congratulations and thank *you*, Freda Marnie Nicholls, xxx.

# Freda's acknowledgements

What a journey! When Zelie first asked me to write her story, I must admit, I felt a little daunted. I had written plenty of articles, but I knew a book would be different, in size if nothing else.

There is an array of people I need to thank and acknowledge, and I will start with Maggie Hamilton, for the early encouragement as we embarked on this project; to Jim Stockley for providing such sage advice at the perfect time; Eloise Hogan, who took the beautiful cover photos of Zelie and her family; Professor John Webster for allowing us to use his quote; Leanne Owen for her input in the animal education and welfare section of the book; and a very big thankyou to my dear friend Nikki Miller, who read my first draft and offered such heartfelt feedback. To my mum, my stepmother, my beautiful sisters Cloud and Kate, and to all of my extended family and beautiful friends, thank you for being there.

To Craig and Colt for letting me take Zelie away to work on the book, whether it be on the phone, computer or in person, thank you boys.

Extra thanks to one important person who came into my life because of this book: Richard Walsh, thank you for all of your understanding, advice and sharing of boundless experience. Your edit of the first draft was truly considerate and educational. I continue to feel humbled by your feedback and lucky to be able to consider you a friend.

Publishing is a remarkable process, carried out by an array of dedicated people, who ultimately provide us with wonderful books to savour. I would like to thank all of the staff at Allen & Unwin, especially our senior editor Siobhán Cantrill and publisher Claire Kingston, both of whom have helped in so many ways, and are an absolute delight to work with. A huge thankyou to the beautiful Clara Finlay, who did a stupendous job at copy-editing; both Zelie and I loved how you polished the story until it shone. Thank you ladies, and thank you everyone who played a part, no matter how big or small, in getting this book published.

My sister Zelie, I thought I already knew your life; it was an amazing experience to see it entirely through your eyes. Thank you for that privilege and for telling me about your life with such raw emotion. You remind me to look at my glass as being half full not half empty, thank you.

To my kids, Hayley, Charlotte and Sam, thank you for bringing such joy into my life. To my hard-working husband Bert, thank you for asking me to share your life with you all those years ago; you have made my life whole. I love you, 'mountains even'.

And thank YOU for reading Zelie's remarkable story. If you have ever considered writing a family memoir, I thoroughly recommend it. It is a wonderful record of a life and an amazing opportunity to talk and listen that we rarely give each other. Everyone has a story, and I hope you have truly enjoyed Zelie's.

# Sign up for the 1001 Dark Nights Newsletter
and be entered to win a Tiffany Key necklace.
There's a contest every month!

Go to www.1001DarkNights.com to subscribe.

As a bonus, all subscribers will receive a free
1001 Dark Nights story on 1/1/15.
*The First Night*
by Shayla Black, Lexi Blake & M.J. Rose

# One Thousand and One Dark Nights

*Once upon a time, in the future…*

*I was a student fascinated with stories and learning.
I studied philosophy, poetry, history, the occult, and
the art and science of love and magic. I had a vast
library at my father's home and collected thousands
of volumes of fantastic tales.*

*I learned all about ancient races and bygone
times. About myths and legends and dreams of all
people through the millennium. And the more I read
the stronger my imagination grew until I discovered
that I was able to travel into the stories… to actually
become part of them.*

*I wish I could say that I listened to my teacher
and respected my gift, as I ought to have. If I had, I
would not be telling you this tale now.
But I was foolhardy and confused, showing off
with bravery.*

*One afternoon, curious about the myth of the
Arabian Nights, I traveled back to ancient Persia to
see for myself if it was true that every day Shahryar
(Persian: شهریار, "king") married a new virgin, and then
sent yesterday's wife to be beheaded. It was written
and I had read, that by the time he met Scheherazade,
the vizier's daughter, he'd killed one thousand
women.*

*Something went wrong with my efforts. I arrived
in the midst of the story and somehow exchanged
places with Scheherazade – a phenomena that had
never occurred before and that still to this day, I
cannot explain.*

*Now I am trapped in that ancient past. I have
taken on Scheherazade's life and the only way I can
protect myself and stay alive is to do what she did to
protect herself and stay alive.*

*Every night the King calls for me and listens as I spin tales.
And when the evening ends and dawn breaks, I stop at a
point that leaves him breathless and yearning for more.
And so the King spares my life for one more day, so that
he might hear the rest of my dark tale.*

*As soon as I finish a story... I begin a new
one... like the one that you, dear reader, have before
you now.*

# Glossary

*Fallen Angel*—Believed to be evil by most humans, fallen angels can be grouped into two categories: True Fallen and Unfallen. Unfallen angels have been cast from Heaven and are earthbound and wingless, living a life in which they are neither truly good nor truly evil. In this state, they can, rarely, earn their way back into Heaven. Or they can choose to enter Sheoul, the demon realm, in order to complete their fall, grow new wings, and become True Fallens, taking their places as demons at Satan's side.

*Harrowgate*—Vertical portals, invisible to humans, which demons use to travel between locations on Earth and Sheoul. A very few beings can summon their own personal Harrowgates.

*Memitim*—Earthbound angels assigned to protect important humans called Primori. Memitim remain earthbound until they complete their duties, at which time they Ascend, earning their wings and entry into Heaven. See: Primori

*Primori*—Humans and demons whose lives are fated to affect the world in some crucial way.

*Radiant*—The most powerful class of Heavenly angel in existence, save Metatron. Unlike other angels, Radiants can wield unlimited power in all realms and can travel freely through Sheoul, with very few exceptions. The designation is awarded to only one angel at a time. Two can never exist simultaneously, and they cannot be destroyed except by God or Satan. The fallen angel equivalent is called a Shadow Angel. See: Shadow Angel

*Shadow Angel*—The most powerful class of fallen angel in existence, save Satan and Lucifer. Unlike other fallen angels, Shadow Angels can wield unlimited power in all realms, and they possess the ability to gain entrance into Heaven. The designation is awarded to only one angel at a time, and they can never exist without their equivalent, a Radiant. Shadow Angels cannot be destroyed except by God or Satan. The Heavenly angel equivalent is called a Radiant. See: Radiant.

*Sheoul*—Demon realm. Located on its own plane deep in the bowels of the Earth, accessible to most only by Harrowgates and hellmouths.

*Sheoul-gra*—A holding tank for demon souls. A realm that exists independently of Sheoul, it is overseen by Azagoth, also known as the Grim Reaper. Within Sheoul-gra is the Inner Sanctum, where demon souls go to be kept in torturous limbo until they can be reborn.

*Sheoulic*—Universal demon language spoken by all, although many species also speak their own language.

*Shrowd*—When angels travel through time, they exist within an impenetrable bubble known as a shrowd. While in the shrowd, angels are invisible and cannot interact with anyone—human, demon, or angel—outside the shrowd. Breaking out of the shrowd is a serious transgression that can, and has, resulted in execution.

*Ter'taceo*—Demons who can pass as human, either because their species is naturally human in appearance, or because they can shapeshift into human form.

*Watchers*—Individuals assigned to keep an eye on the Four Horsemen. As part of the agreement forged during the original negotiations between angels and demons that led to Ares, Reseph, Limos, and Thanatos being cursed to spearhead the Apocalypse, one Watcher is an angel, the other is a fallen angel. Neither Watcher may directly assist any Horseman's efforts to either start or stop Armageddon, but they can lend a hand behind the scenes. Doing so, however, may have them walking a fine line that, to cross, could prove worse than fatal.

# Chapter One

*You can be a king or a street sweeper, but everybody dances
with the Grim Reaper.
-- Robert Alton Harris*

"There's very little that frightens me more than the Grim
Reaper when he's horny."

From his desk chair, Azagoth snarled at the fallen angel
standing in his office doorway. "I'm not horny." He frowned.
"Okay, maybe a little." Or a lot. For six months he'd refused to bed
the females Heaven had sent his way, but those halo-pushers didn't
give up, because apparently, there was another angel outside waiting
to get some hot Grim Reaper action. "But I'm not backing down.
I'm sick of being used to create Heaven's little army of hybrid
angels."

That was true enough, but there was far more to it than being
tired of being used like a prize stallion. Satan himself had threatened
Azagoth with an ultimatum, and while Azagoth and his realm were
untouchable, his children were not. And no one fucked with his
children. Not even the Prince of Darkness.

"My lord," Zhubaal said cautiously, "your deal with Heaven—"

"Deal?" Azagoth snorted as he reached across his desk for the
expensive-ass bottle of Black Tot rum that Limos, one of the Four
Horsemen of the Apocalypse, had brought him earlier. "It wasn't a
*deal*. I volunteered to fall from grace to run this horror show of a
demon graveyard. *They* changed the rules. *After* I gave up my life."

Yep, just a few decades after he'd been expelled from Heaven in order to create Sheoul-gra, a unique realm designed specifically as a holding tank for demon souls, Heaven changed the game. The archangels suddenly decided they needed a special class of angel to watch over anyone living in the human realm who was important to the fate of the world, and they insisted that Azagoth should father those angels.

And he had. For thousands of years he'd taken the angels they sent into his bed and created lots and lots of earthbound, hybrid angel children known as Memitim. But now he was done. Aside from Satan's threat hanging over his head, Azagoth was tired of screwing females who looked down their noses at him or who just laid there like sacrifices until he was done.

Oh, sure, there were the curious ones who at least made an attempt to participate, and there were the lusty few who figured they'd enjoy doing a bad boy. But for the most part, he might as well have been banging blow-up dolls.

Yeah, it was awesome.

Archangels were asshats.

"But sir, you need to do something. You're...testy."

Testy? Zhubaal hadn't seen testy yet. *Testy* had gotten Azagoth's last assistant disintegrated.

"Send the female back, and have her tell her superiors that...no, wait. Send her in." Kicking his booted feet up on the desk, he broke the seal on the alcohol bottle with a vicious twist. "I'll give her my message personally."

"As you wish."

Zhubaal gave a deep bow and left, returning within seconds with a tall, stately brunette in white and ruby robes, and Azagoth groaned. This wasn't an angel who had come for a roll in the hay. Mariella was a Heavenly messenger who swept in the way she always did, as if she owned the place, her head held high, her long strides sure and brisk.

"Azagoth," she said, all snooty and shit, "it's time to stop whatever game you're playing and get back to work."

He raked his gaze over her in a blatant show of sizing her up for sex. She wouldn't lower herself to screw him, but he got a measure of amusement out of screwing with *her.*

"So you're volunteering to spread your legs for me?"

She cringed at his crudeness as he knew she would. Most angels were *so* uptight. "I'm a liaison, not a bedmate. I'm here to convince you to stop being a fool."

"Ah." Keeping his gaze on the angel, he put the bottle to his lips and took a deep, long pull, savoring the sweet burn of the liquid pouring down his throat. He drank until Mariella's pinched, judgmental expression threatened to make her skin crack, and with exaggerated relish, he smacked his lips and wiped his mouth with the back of his hand. "Well, here's the deal. I'm not doing your bidding anymore."

"Yes, you are."

Carefully placing the bottle on a pad of paper, he pushed to his feet and moved around to the front of the desk, noting how she managed to keep that pinchy expression even as her copper eyes assessed him from head to toe. She liked his black slacks and turtleneck...and the way she went taut said she despised the fact that she liked anything about him. Man, he loved messing with angels' heads.

"Or?"

"Or," she said, her tone pitching low with gloom and doom, "we replace you."

He barked out a laugh. "Good. Replace me. I've been stuck in this realm for thousands of years, dealing with nothing but demons, evil humans, and the angels Heaven sends for me to service. Someone else can have this shitty job."

"I don't think you understand," she said silkily. "*Replace* is a nice word for destroy."

Azagoth's pulse kicked up a notch. It was fun when someone threatened him. *Game on.* "And I don't think *you* understand. You can't destroy me. I've put safeguards in place."

Her eyes narrowed into slits. "What kinds of safeguards?"

He gave a dramatic pause, partly to irritate the angel, and partly because he totally got off on dragging out the win. Finally, he steepled his fingers together like a cheesy cartoon villain and said, "The kind that will release all demon souls from Sheoul-gra upon my death."

She gasped in outrage. Because sure, it was okay for her to threaten him, but turnabout was clearly *not* fair play. "And Hades allowed this?"

Hades, who ran Sheoul-gra's Inner Sanctum where demon souls were kept, had little say in what Azagoth did, but they'd long ago hammered out a working relationship that gave the fallen angel independent authority over the Inner Sanctum. Azagoth could overrule him if needed, but in general, he left Hades alone.

"Actually," Azagoth said as he casually propped his hip on the desk, "it was Hades who suggested it."

"That blue-haired bastard."

He'd give her that one. Hades was a world-class dick. Azagoth liked that in a fallen angel. "Now," he said, "you get to listen to my demands."

"Which are?" she said through gritted teeth.

"I want a female."

She shot him an exasperated look. "What do you think we've been sending you? You keep turning them down."

"I don't want a female to fuck," he said, still being as raunchy as possible. It drove angels nuts, and sure enough, her lips puckered as if she'd sucked a lemon. "I want one to keep."

Outrage mottled her perfect, ivory skin. "You want an angel to *keep*? As what? A pet?"

"As a mate."

"Oh, that's precious." She laughed, and the blood that usually ran cold in his veins started to steam. "You want a mate? *You? Why?*"

*Because I'm lonely.* That was only part of it, but it was a big part. He could have simply told Heaven to stop sending him females because Satan had threatened to start killing Memitim if even one more was born, but he didn't want to spend the rest of eternity alone. He'd seen one of his daughters, Idess, willingly sacrifice so much for the male she loved, and she'd risked her life on more than one occasion to make sure other couples were happy. The depths to which people felt love had stunned him, and deep inside, it had sparked a desire to have that for himself.

That was assuming he *could* love. He hadn't felt anything but anger and amusement in thousands of years, and even those emotions rarely reached a level beyond what he'd consider mild.

"My reasons are my own," he said. "Send me a female to keep."

"I'm sure this female you want will be so happy to be constantly pregnant," she drawled.

"Oh, did I give you the impression that I'd keep making Memitim angels for you?" He pushed off the desk and moved toward her, enjoying the way her eyes sparked with anger and superiority even as she inched backward. "Well, newsflash, you Heavenly puke; no children that come of the union with my mate will ever be handed over to you."

She flared her cinnamon wings in annoyance, but he kept his own wings tucked away. When he took his out, it usually meant he was on the verge of killing.

He wasn't there yet, but he had no doubt this angel could push him to it.

Not that it took much.

"I'll inform my bosses, but don't expect an answer you'll like."

Even now, after he'd made clear that he held all the cards—or the souls, as it were—she continued to think she had the better hand. Amusing. *Mildly* amusing, of course.

"You're still not getting it, are you? I'll get what I want. There's no other choice." He halted in front of her, so close she was forced to look up at him. "And tell them that the next angel they send better be prepared to stay, because I'm keeping her."

"How nice," she said snottily. "Are you going to keep her in chains? Rape her if she refuses to bed you?"

Suddenly, his hand was clamped around her throat, almost of its own volition. Angels did that to him, made his body parts act independently of his brain. He felt her reach for her angelic ability to strike at him, but this was his realm, and here *he* controlled the use of power.

"Send someone willing." He bared his fangs, giving the angel an up-close-and-personal look at one of the things that made them so very different despite their angelic origins. "I'm warning you. Because the next angel who steps through that doorway won't be leaving. Ever."

# Chapter Two

Lilliana scurried through the pristine white halls of the massive Archangel Complex, her heart beating like a hummingbird's. She'd only been here once, several hundred years ago, and it had merely been to deliver a message from her superiors in the Time Travel Operations Department.

This time, she was here because she'd been summoned, and that could only be bad news. Her direct supervisor, an angel humans would describe as nerdy and shy, had warned her that after her latest screw-up, she might earn more than just a suspension from TTO.

She broke out in a sweat at the thought. Her work was her life. The only connection she had with her dead mother. If the archangels took that away from her...she shuddered. Sure, she'd committed a grievous offense, but there had been extenuating circumstances. She'd been kidnapped, held captive, and forced to do things she hadn't wanted to do. Her nerdy supervisor understood...but he didn't think the head honchos would. Besides, rules were rules, and Heaven's tolerance for rule breakers was notoriously nonexistent.

Stomach churning, she entered the garishly maroon and gold offices of Raphael. *The* Raphael. She might vomit on his robes.

A petite, flaxen-haired female looked up from her crystal tablet, a device that was the human equivalent of an electronic tablet device...if human tablets had advanced by about ten billion years. She gave Lilliana a bored once-over, pausing to wrinkle her nose at Lilliana's unfashionably loose brown hair. Lilliana could change it with a mere thought, maybe piling it on top of her head like a giant ostrich egg the way the other female wore it, but she'd never cared about current fashion. She did, however, care about looking stupid.

"To your left." Egghead went back to tapping on her tablet.

Lilliana turned down the hall, which ended inside a room with walls that seemed to be made of white smoke. A marble fountain, an extinct palm tree, bronze statues...the room was filled with the most eclectic mix of objects from different time periods.

An angel appeared before her from out of nowhere, and although she'd never seen Raphael before, she knew him instantly. He stood a full foot above her five foot eleven inches, and his golden hair fell in a shiny curtain around broad shoulders draped by a lush, purple velvet mantle. Jewel-encrusted rings circled every finger, and a gold sun-shaped pendant hung halfway down his chest, standing out starkly against his snowy white suit.

If she had to describe the style of his outfit, she'd go with royal-retro-pimp.

"You're late." His deep, dark voice rumbled through her, jangling her already unsteady nerves. "Late to a meeting with an archangel."

She was most certainly *not* late, but it didn't seem like a good idea to argue. "Ah...I got lost—"

He cut her off with a savage sweep of his bejeweled hand. "Your excuses don't interest me. I have a proposition for you."

Wow. What everyone said about archangels was true.

They were giant douchebags. With terrible fashion sense and taste in decor.

"What kind of proposition?"

"I understand that you're curious about the underworld."

Her pulse picked up a notch. Most angels nursed a deep hatred for anything related to demons and their realm, Sheoul, and one never knew how much trouble you could get into by being too inquisitive. Plus, too much curiosity threw up a red flag for those who watched for signs of potential defection to Satan's camp.

"I wouldn't say I'm overly curious," she said, choosing her words carefully, "but I do find it interesting that many ancient human structures are replicated in Sheoul and vice versa, and I'd love to study the links between them."

"What if I said I could give you that opportunity?"

She cocked an eyebrow. "I'd say...what's the catch?"

"The catch is a big one." He gave an ominous pause she

suspected was calculated to make her lungs seize. It worked. "You'll have to take a mate."

What little air she had in her lungs whooshed out in a rush. "A mate?" she choked out. "Why?"

"Because this particular male wants a mate, and we need him, so he gets what he wants."

In other words, this particular male, clearly a standup guy, was using blackmail to get what he wanted. She licked her dry lips, buying herself time to speak without sounding as if she'd run a marathon. "And what about what I want?"

The archangel regarded her with disdain, as if what she wanted was of no consequence. "How about we go over all of the terms of this deal before you decide what you want."

"Of course," she said tightly. She had a feeling the terms were going to be pretty one-sided, and that side wouldn't be hers. "Who is he?"

"Azagoth, collector of souls."

Her heart stopped. Just quit beating. "The Forgotten One? The Grim Reaper?" Holy shit. He had to be kidding. "Is this some kind of joke?"

"I have no sense of humor."

She'd heard that about Raphael. About most of the archangels, actually. "But you want me to *mate* Azagoth?"

Raphael inclined his head in an impatient, curt nod, as if this wasn't something to get all worked up about. How could he be so calm?

*Because it's not* his *head on the chopping block, that's how.*

The ex-angel, sometimes known by those in Heaven as The Forgotten One, was occasionally spoken about with respect, but most often, contempt. He'd been a hero in Heaven, the person who first identified Satan as a rotten apple who was planning a coup against his angelic brethren. Because of Azagoth, Satan had been stripped of his wings and cast out of Heaven to create his own realm known as Sheoul, where he'd set up shop breeding evil minions.

Too late Heaven realized they should have put Satan down when they had the chance, because centuries later, his demonic creations began to die, and with nowhere to go, their disembodied souls wreaked havoc on the Earth. Azagoth volunteered to create Sheoul-gra, a holding tank for the souls, but *why* he volunteered was the topic of hot debates and wild conspiracy theories.

The only thing anyone agreed on was that he'd been corrupted by evil and was one of the most dangerous and powerful beings outside of Heaven. Fortunately, he was contained inside his own realm...but his reach extended far beyond it, and that had always been a concern for The Powers That Be in Heaven.

Raphael let her stew in her thoughts for a moment before adding, "And full disclosure; you can never leave his realm once you get there."

Her jaw dropped. Closed. Dropped again. Unable to leave Sheoul-gra? She'd be trapped. Imprisoned, just like she'd been when she was kidnapped by a crazy angel bent on getting revenge on an archangel, a situation that had gotten her into this mess in the first place.

Finally, she managed a squeaky, "Never?"

"Not...in the traditional sense." Raphael produced a cup of nectar from out of thin air and held it out to her, but she refused. She doubted her stomach could hold anything down right now. Plus, refusing something offered by an archangel gave her a sinful feeling of satisfaction. "But according to my intel, he possesses a *chronoglass*."

Surprise flew through her. "I thought we had the only two in existence."

"Apparently not."

"So he can time travel?"

Raphael shook his head. "He wasn't born with the ability. We believe he uses it to view current events in the human and demon realms."

What a waste. Angels with the ability to time travel could do so only under limited circumstances and with the assistance of a handful of very rare objects. *Chronoglasses* were the most versatile and powerful of all the time travel objects, and Azagoth's would be invaluable to Heaven.

"Wait...you said he can view the events of the demon realm too? How?"

"His *chronoglass*, unlike ours, is double-sided. One side allows a view of the human realm, and the other shows the demon realm." Raphael sipped the nectar she'd refused. "With his *chronoglass*, you can escape his realm once per day for an hour. But you will be restricted to the past, and as always, contact with anyone you know is not permitted, and so is any manipulation of events that could change history." He angled his body closer, putting on the pressure without saying a word. "So. What say you?"

*I say you're insane.* "As, ah...generous...as this offer is, I'm going to have to refuse. I have a job here."

He casually took a drink of the nectar, and she got the feeling that he was stringing a noose. "Do you."

She swallowed. Which wasn't easy, given the invisible rope tightening inexorably around her neck. "Excuse me?"

"Did you think we could let your recent transgressions slide?" He waved his hand, and one of the smoky walls became solid ivory.

Against the white backdrop, in perfect, high-def 3-D, a movie started up. A movie that showed her, three months ago, as she traveled through time to various locations to gather objects.

An angel named Reaver had asked for some special gifts for his five-thousand-year-old children, items from their childhoods. It was against the rules to bring objects back from the past, but he'd pulled her butt out of trouble once, and she'd owed him.

But holy crap, had she paid for what she'd done. Fifty years of time travel with supervision only, plus a hundred years of listening in on human prayers, sorting them, and presenting the most urgent ones to the Prayer Fulfillment Department.

So. Freaking. Boring. Humans could pray for really selfish, stupid stuff.

The movie jumped ahead, and she watched herself handing the items to Reaver. "I've already been punished for that."

"And clearly, you didn't learn your lesson," he snapped, suddenly and inexplicably irritated. "Because not a month later, you broke one of the most important time travel laws and caused an imbalance in Heaven that we're still trying to correct."

"I had no choice! If you'd just listen—"

"Silence!" He hadn't raised his voice, but the echo of his command circled the room a dozen times before fading away. "You say you had no choice, so now I'm giving you one. You can go through the dissection trials to have your ability removed. You will then be assigned to menial labor for the rest of your existence, or you can mate Azagoth and be able to time travel once a day. Which is it?"

She shook with a combination of rage that the circumstances of her crime were being disregarded, and terror that both punishments were not only horrible, but permanent. Losing her freedom was her greatest nightmare, and now she was facing it in a lose/lose situation.

"I need time to think about it." Even her voice trembled.

"I'm not giving you time," he said. "But I'm in a generous mood, so I'll tell you what. Go now to Sheoul-gra, and you'll have thirty Earth days to change your mind. At the end of the thirty days, the realm's exit will be sealed to you, and you will never again be allowed to leave except for an hour a day when you use the *chronoglass.*"

Her belly twisted, and again, she was glad she'd refused the nectar. "Will I lose my wings?"

"No. You'll be like Azagoth...a fallen angel, but...not. He is like his realm; unique."

This could not be happening. She searched Raphael's handsome face for any kind of sign that despite his claim of having no sense of humor this was just a big joke, but the archangel's expression was all business.

"What about the Memitim? Will you still be sending angels to him to...breed with?"

She could hardly get the last part out. Azagoth was the father of all Memitim, and she seriously doubted Heaven would just let him stop producing little baby Reapers. Or maybe he wouldn't want to stop. Maybe he was like her father, donating baby batter for the greater good and not giving a shit about his offspring.

"He won't be creating any more Memitim. We're reversing their sterility and changing Memitim from a class of angel to an ability any angel can be born with."

How easy it all sounded. She wondered how the Memitim felt about the fact that their inability to reproduce was by design and could have been reversed at any time.

She closed her eyes and considered her options, crappy as they were.

The removal of an angel's time travel ability was brutal. Agonizing. And in some instances, fatal. Even if one survived, the process and the loss were traumatic, and the angel was never the same. Lilliana had encountered two angels who had undergone the process, and their empty eyes haunted her to this day.

As if having her ability taken away wasn't bad enough, she'd then be stuck doing menial tasks for the rest of her life...but on the bright side, maybe she'd be so lobotomized from the time-travelectomy that she wouldn't care.

And didn't that sound like a wonderful life?

Her other choice was to become the mate of a depraved angel, a male who was the keeper of demon souls. A male who had volunteered to be booted from Heaven...or, if the rumors were true, he'd not so much "volunteered" as *been* volunteered.

Sort of like what was happening to her right now.

Except that after she mated the Grim Freaking Reaper, she'd be stuck in his realm, which, by all accounts, was a shadowy, dreary place that resembled Athens—if Athens was drenched in darkness, overrun by creepy demon things, and had been decorated via an unholy alliance between Guillermo del Toro and Anne Rice.

Really, though, there was a clear winner here. Between the choices of suck and suckier, suck won out.

Opening her eyes, she gave in to the inevitable. "I'll go to Sheoul-gra," she muttered. At least she had thirty days to change her mind once she got there.

"I'm happy to hear that. You leave immediately." Clapping his hand on her shoulder, he leaned in, his voice dropping to a conspiratorial murmur. "Now, if one were to somehow get out of Azagoth's realm with his *chronoglass* within that thirty days, one's past transgressions might be forgiven. Especially if one were also to destroy the spying stone we believe he's using to spy on us."

She nearly tripped over her own feet. He was giving her a way out of this crappy deal?

Raphael stepped back and finished his nectar. "Oh," he said, as he tossed the empty cup to the floor and strode toward the exit, "and good luck. Azagoth is an asshole."

# Chapter Three

Lilliana's skin crawled as she took in the massive palace before her. True to her intel and research, the building, and all those surrounding it, were fashioned after ancient Greek structures. Great pillars rose up from the ground to support walls that went on forever. But unlike the bone-white framework that typified Greek construction, everything here was blackened, as if polluted by centuries of smoke buildup. She wondered what would happen if she scraped her fingernail down a wall.

Everything here felt...wrong. Even the air buzzed with a low-level sinister energy, as if she were standing next to a leaking, demonic nuclear power plant. Instinctively, she reached for her angelic power, but it was as if she struck a barrier. She could feel her power inside her, but it was trapped somehow, and no matter how hard she tried, she couldn't reach it.

Raphael had warned her that her powers would be all but useless here, but she'd hoped that somehow he was wrong.

Not so much.

Shuddering, she inhaled the air that stank of decay and filth, and climbed the seemingly endless steps to a landing that was as sprawling as a football field. The doors before her, large enough to allow a pair of elephants inside, opened up as if by magic.

No one was standing at the threshold to greet her. She hadn't been sure what to expect, but silence and a warehouse-sized room filled with gruesome artwork and fountains that ran with blood wasn't it.

Lilliana walked inside, her pristine white gown dragging on the polished obsidian floor. She hated the stupid dress, but it was what

Raphael had insisted she wear, as if she were some sort of child bride being offered up to a sleazeball who'd paid for her.

Which probably wasn't far from the truth.

At the far side of the room, a lone figure appeared through another set of double doors. Male. Tall. Blond. Handsome. Evil.

Fallen angel.

He gestured for her to approach, and although she'd been conditioned since birth to despise fallen angels, she obeyed. What choice did she have, after all?

"I am Zhubaal," he said, when she was a few yards away.

Up close, he was obscenely good-looking in his black leather pants and wife-beater that revealed a massive, muscular upper body, but the malevolence in his gaze made her shiver. Relief that he wasn't Azagoth was tempered with fear that her soon-to-be mate would be hideous...or that his eyes would be filled with something much worse than cruelty.

"I'm Lilliana," she replied as steadily as she could, but she cursed the slight tremor in her voice.

"I know." Zhubaal smiled, and if she'd thought his gaze was fiendish, his smile was a hundred times worse. This was not a male she'd want to piss off. "Tell me, do you feel like a sacrificial lamb?"

Fallen angels were assholes. "I was given more of a choice than any lamb."

He snorted and started down a long, twisty hallway. "Keep telling yourself that."

She amended her last thought. Fallen angels were *major* assholes.

They arrived at an arched doorway that seemed to be carved out of a solid piece of bone. A slab of thick wood studded with iron squeaked open at Zhubaal's shove.

Warm orange light spilled from the opening, illuminating a room that was chilly despite flames that stretched a full six feet in height inside the fireplace on the far wall. In front of the fire, there was a claw-footed oak desk scattered with papers, pens, and tiny jade animals.

And standing next to the monstrosity was an impossibly beautiful dark-haired male with eyes the color of vibrant emeralds. His expression could have been carved from a solid block of ice, and the blade-sharp lines of his jaw and cheekbones only emphasized the hardness of his appearance. The fang tips glinting between his full lips were the icing on the *oh-shit-what-did-I-get-into* cake.

"Hello." His deep voice turned her marrow to pudding even as a wave of heat licked her skin. "I'm Azagoth."

Dear...God. He was both magnificent and frightening. "I'm Lilliana," she said, somehow keeping her tone even, her words sure.

He strode toward her, his black slacks defining long legs, his European-style leather shoes tapping against the ebony floor, his rich gray dress shirt rolled at the sleeves to reveal powerfully muscled forearms. Lilliana resided in Heaven, where all male angels were perfect specimens of masculinity, but something about Azagoth made every last one of them seem average. Hell, even Raphael, with his jewels and furs, couldn't touch Azagoth's simple elegance and raw sexuality.

Or his deadliness.

He halted a couple of feet away. "Why are you here?"

She blinked, not understanding the question. Surely he understood the deal that had been struck between him and the archangels.

"Ah...I'm here for you."

He looked at her as if she were completely daft. "I know. But why *you?*"

"I don't know why," she answered honestly. This was a punishment, yes, but the archangels could have chosen anyone to toss up as a sacrifice, so why her specifically? She'd wondered, but in the end it didn't matter, she supposed.

Azagoth's remarkable eyes narrowed. "Then why did you agree to mate me?"

She wasn't sure she was ready to tell him. She could think of little more humiliating or insulting than trying to explain that being here was the least distasteful of two horrific options. "First, why don't you tell me why you wanted this?"

If she'd thought his gaze was cold before, now it glazed over with ice. "Obviously, I desire a mate."

"But why?"

He smiled, but it was as frostbitten as his eyes. "How old are you?" he asked, ignoring her question.

"I'm coming up on my four hundred and thirty-sixth birthday."

He made a sound of disgust. "So pathetically young." His gaze took a long, appraising tour of her body, and she bristled. "And you're wearing white. Your idea? Or did the archangels send you to me looking like a virgin ready for the volcano?"

He'd hit *that* nail on the head. "It wasn't my idea."

"But *are* you a virgin?" he asked, and wow, he had balls, didn't he. No, she wasn't a virgin—at least, not in one sense of the word, but the hell if she was going to give him the satisfaction of an answer. When she remained silent, he cursed. "You are, aren't you?"

"You say it like you might ask if I'm a cockroach. The sneer was a nice touch."

"A *virgin* cockroach." His mouth twitched in amusement. What a strange sense of humor. He returned to his desk and pulled a parcel out of a drawer. Lush gold silk surrounded the package, which was tied with a red satin bow. He handed it to her. "You will wear this."

She had no idea what was inside the package, but she'd had it with his attitude. "I have my own clothes, but thank you."

"Your shipment from Heaven is being delayed," he said, and she had a sneaky suspicion he had something to do with that. "So no, you don't have clothes. You will wear what I give you."

Okay, then. The question now wasn't whether or not she needed the full thirty days to decide if she was staying. The question was how long it would be before she could get out of here. At this rate, she'd be out the door in an hour. Screw the *chronoglass*. Dissection was looking better and better.

"Tell you what," she snapped. "I'll wear whatever is in this package if you start using the words 'please' and 'thank you.' And if you stop being a dick."

One dark eyebrow shot up. "The innocent little angel has teeth," he mused. "I like it."

She clenched said teeth. "Good. Now maybe you can show me to my room?"

"*Our* room," he said with way too much relish. "From this day on, we share a bed. We share *everything*."

* * * *

Azagoth wasn't sure what to think of the striking angel who had shown up on his doorstep, but he *was* sure she wasn't here of her own volition. He'd bet his pearly-white fangs that she'd been forced into mating him, and he'd bet the deal had been couched inside a "choice."

*You can do what we "suggest," or your life will be a living hell.*

The words, spoken to him by the archangel Gabriel, rang in his ears as if it were yesterday. Yeah, what the archangels called a "choice" was more like a prod with a lightning bolt in the direction they wanted you to go.

As he waited for Lilliana's reaction to his announcement, he gave her a good once-over. Okay, maybe a twice-over, because damn, she was *fine*.

Unlike most of the angels who came to him, Lilliana was in no way petite or delicate. She looked like the type of female who could hold her own against him in physical combat, and then melt into a puddle of ecstasy when the battle was over and he was between her legs. He admired that in a female.

Of course, there was a lot to admire about her.

Long, sable lashes framed eyes the color of the purest amber, and sturdy, angular features defined her ageless face. This angel was tall, solidly built, with only the slightest of curves in all the right places and muscles that gave her an Amazonian warrior aura. Her chestnut hair flowed over slender but powerful shoulders, and he wondered if it was as silky as it looked.

"The same bed, huh?"

Her question was rhetorical, so he crossed his arms over his chest and waited for a genuine reaction from her. In reality, he'd had another room prepared for her, but he wanted to see how she handled him. He wasn't easy to deal with, and any female who fell apart within minutes of meeting him wasn't going to last.

Despite what he'd said to Mariella yesterday, he wouldn't force anyone to stay. He was a cold, heartless bastard, but even he didn't want to spend eternity with someone who couldn't hold their own against him. He could deal with hatred, but he couldn't deal with fear.

A crying, cowering female in his bed just didn't do it for him. On the other hand, angry sex could be fucking hot as shit.

So which way would Lilliana go? Fight or flight? Hate or fear? The stubborn glint in her eyes told him that meek acceptance wouldn't be an option. Good. He didn't want a doormat for a mate, either.

She lifted her chin and looked down her nose at him in that

infuriating way most angels did. As if he was so beneath them, what with his own realm, servants, and more influence than most archangels could claim.

"I was hoping we'd have time to get to know each other," she said crisply, "but I'll deal. Touch me without my consent, however, and you'll lose an arm."

So, fight over flight. And probably a touch of hate. He liked her spirit. She needed to work on her threats, however.

"Never threaten someone with losing a limb when you can go gorier. Try this next time: *Touch me without my consent and I'll gut you with my teeth and then strangle you with your own intestines.*" He imagined her saying that, and his pants grew uncomfortably tight. "See how much better that sounds?"

She glared. "If you'll give me paper and a pen, I'll take notes."

He was starting to like this chick.

"I'm assuming the angels have sealed the portal behind you so you can't leave unless I expel you?" At her clipped nod, he waved for her to follow him. "Come on. I'll show you to our room." He led her to the grand double doors at the rear of his office, and with a mere thought, they whispered open.

Lilliana stood in the doorway, gaping at his bedroom-slash-playroom. "Oh. My. Gaudy," she breathed. "Please tell me I can redecorate."

Zhubaal had warned him that females didn't appreciate man-cave decor. Or torture-room decor. Turned out he was right. "Sure. But nothing nautical. Or American Southwest."

She didn't miss a beat. "I was thinking more along the lines of screw-you minimalist. First thing that goes is the spanking bench."

Damn, he was liking her more and more. Too bad he'd have to break her little haloed heart.

"No furniture goes until you've tried it first. But the rest...meh." He gestured to the walls covered in rich tapestries, priceless artwork by famous human and demon painters, and giant mirrors framed in pure gold. "The color scheme was popular a thousand years ago. It's time for an update, I suppose."

She sniffed haughtily, which was *such* an angel thing to do, and stalked inside. And wow, nice ass. Perfectly packaged in the satin dress, it was a little less full than he liked, but there was still plenty of padding in that heart-shaped bottom. He could picture her bent over the spanking bench as he gripped her hips and thrust against her, her skin flushed with ecstasy and pink from sensual lashes.

"The bed can stay," she announced.

Of course it could. It was big enough to sleep six, which meant she could put a lot of space between them. She could try, anyway.

"The bathroom is through the doorway to your right," he said. "The hallway straight ahead leads to a kitchen, dining room, and TV room. I get pretty much every TV station in the world."

She frowned. "How?"

"Same way Heaven gets it. Demon technicians can warp and tune any manmade signal into something usable down here." He gestured to a huge oak cabinet. "The wardrobe on the left is yours. There are clothes already inside. I'll leave you to it."

She turned to him, that ridiculous gown sweeping across the floor. "Where are you going?"

"I have a job to do. Places to go, people to kill, and those demon souls don't admit themselves into Sheoul-gra, you know." He started toward the door. "Join me after you change, and I'll show you around your new home."

"Wait." She started after him, but as he swung back around to her, she checked up like she'd hit a wall, as if realizing that being alone would be better than being with him. "What about my powers?"

"What about them?"

"I have none." She hugged herself, no doubt feeling naked and exposed without them. "How am I supposed to defend myself in this place?"

"There's nothing here that can harm you. Except me." He glanced at his watch. He probably had time to usher in a few souls, show Lillian around, and check in with his *griminions* before his next appointment arrived. Looking up again, he caught her gaze. "But I can't think of any reason I should harm you...can you?"

She gave a forced smile. "Of course not."

"Good. Let's keep it that way." He headed toward the door again, pausing at the threshold to say softly, "I'm not a cruel person, Lilliana. But I'm not a forgiving one, either. Betray me and you'll see exactly how unforgiving I can be. There are no second chances."

He left her alone, closing the door behind him.

# Chapter Four

Lilliana waited until Azagoth shut the door to stick out her tongue at him.

"Join me after you change," she mimicked. "I'll show you around your new home. Betray me and you'll see exactly how unforgiving I can be."

Yeah, real mature. But the guy was infuriating. And obnoxious. And handsome. She couldn't forget handsome. The image of him standing next to his desk lingered in her mind, the way he'd been so casual, and yet, there was a coiled intensity about him, as if he could snap her neck with one hand while chugging rum from the bottle on his desk with the other.

Why in the hell did she find that sexy? She was an angel, for Heaven's sake. She was supposed to be sweet and pure, and...that was a load of crap.

Angels were, in truth, ruthless warriors who fought for the side of good, often with stunning brutality. They fought dirty and didn't always follow the rules. Then there were the politics—many angels had their own agendas, and those agendas often didn't mesh with what was best for either the Earthly realm or the Heavenly one.

So, okay, she wasn't sweet and pure, but she probably shouldn't think Azagoth's lethal aura was sexy.

Tossing the package he'd given her onto the black satin bedspread, she looked around the room, and this time, she didn't bother to hide her shock. When she and Azagoth had first entered, she'd schooled her expression into calm nonchalance, but inside she had been hyperventilating.

She'd seen a lot in her centuries of life—demons and humans

were extremely creative when it came to sex—but she'd never thought she'd be expected to participate in anything kinky. Heck, her ex, Hutriel, a high-ranking member of the angelic Eradicator Force who hunted the illegal offspring of angels and fallen angels, had despised the kind of messy sex humans and demons enjoyed so much. Angel intimacy, especially among the hardcore conservative old guard, was polite and clean, more of a merging of souls than bodies. Hutriel had *definitely* been old guard. He would have hated Azagoth's lair.

She wrinkled her nose at the huge wood and padded leather St. Andrew's Cross in the corner. It was much nicer than the one some sex toy salesman tried to get her to "try" when she'd walked past his store while hunting a demon once. And Azagoth's leather-wrapped restraints were a far cry from the sales guy's metal handcuffs.

Oh, but not to fear, Azagoth also had handcuffs hanging from a wooden rack next to the spanking bench. All sorts of restraints, whips, paddles, gags, and items she couldn't identify kept those cuffs company, and she shivered.

And yet...curiosity, and maybe a *screw-you* aimed in Hutriel's direction, nudged her over to the rack, and she found herself running her fingers over the surprisingly supple leather strands on the floggers and testing the fabric of the blindfolds. What would it feel like to be blindfolded and bound, completely at the mercy of someone like Azagoth?

Again she shivered, but this time, it was accompanied by desire curling in her gut and spiraling outward until even her skin flushed with pleasant tingles. Maybe she should be appalled by Azagoth's collection and her reaction to it, but she'd always been adventurous and eager to try new things. With the right male, she'd give this stuff a go.

But Azagoth wasn't the right male. So far, he'd proved to be an arrogant prick, and in any case, as soon as she found his *chronoglass*, she was out of here.

She moved over to the huge oak wardrobe and held her breath as she opened it. To her relief, there was nothing too weird hanging on the rack or sitting neatly on the shelves. But black wasn't her color, and leather wasn't her material. She was definitely a slacks and blouse kind of gal, so the midnight satin corset and metal-studded leather miniskirt got shoved to the back of the stack.

She finally chose a pair of plain black leggings, a maroon long-sleeved, fitted crop top with a turtleneck collar, and knee-high boots with four sets of buckles down the shaft. She checked herself out in the mirror, was surprised that the outfit wasn't completely horrible and actually flattered her athletic figure.

She'd always compensated for her lack of feminine features and curves by wearing her hair loose and long, and her clothes were always on the conservative, lacier side. But somehow, these form-fitting garments enhanced her femininity even more than the flowing, delicate gown she'd been forced to wear. Huh.

Sinking down on the massive bed, she opened the package Azagoth had given her. Inside was a simple but elegant Tiffany key pendant on a delicate silver chain. It was beautiful, but why would he want her to wear it?

She wasn't going to. Already she realized she had very little power down here, and one thing Azagoth wasn't going to take away was her ability to choose. Very carefully, she put away the chain and left the box on the mattress.

The mattress she was going to have to share with Azagoth.

Unbidden, an image of him naked and lying next to her as that deep voice whispered raw, naughty things, made her skin flush and her breasts tingle. Was that what the angels sent here for him to service felt like when they were standing in this room?

The thought was enough to knock her halo back on straight. There would be no sex, because she was leaving.

Taking a deep, bracing breath, she opened the door to Azagoth's office. The wall directly across from her had opened up, revealing a green-glowing cross-sectioned tunnel. A parade of demons shuffled through from left to right, each one escorted by a three-foot tall *griminion* shrouded completely in black. As she entered the room, the parade stopped, and Azagoth swung around. His expression remained neutral, but she swore his eyes darkened as he raked her with his gaze.

"Better," he rumbled.

"Flattery isn't your strong suit, is it?"

"And taking direction isn't yours."

So he'd noticed the missing necklace. Tough shit. She ignored him and glanced over at the tunnel. "What's going on?"

"These are souls of dead demons and evil humans. My *griminions* are escorting them into the lower Sheoul-gra levels known as the Inner Sanctum."

"Where Hades lives?"

He inclined his head. "Hades keeps them contained and suitably miserable until they're reincarnated."

She eyed the demon souls, which appeared to be as solid as they had been when they were alive. "I'm assuming demon souls are like those of humans? Non-corporeal while on Earth and in Sheoul, but solid in Sheoul-gra and Heaven?"

"It's exactly the same. Human and demon souls appear as ghosts on the Earthly plane, but are fully realized in Heaven and Sheoul-gra."

If only humans understood that their bodies on Earth were shadowy versions of what they would become after they died and returned to the Heavenly plane where they'd been created. They'd be much happier, not worrying so much about defiling themselves or even injuring their bodies. Their short human lives were but a thin thread in the fabric of their true existences, a drop in the ocean of their lifespans.

Azagoth made a sweeping motion with his hand, and the wall slid closed.

"So you just sit around all day and watch souls walk through a tunnel?"

A faint smile twitched on his lips. "That's just one of my duties. Come on. I'll show you around."

He took her down several winding hallways, pointing out various rooms that led to quarters for his *griminions*.

"What, exactly, are *griminions*?" She watched one of the troll-like creatures scurry through a doorway and disappear into the darkness.

"During the negotiations between Heaven and Sheoul over the creation of Sheoul-gra, it was agreed that I would be allowed to create a species of demon that could assist with the retrieval of souls."

"And you made creepy little skittery things?"

"Not...exactly. My design used imps and gentle Huldrefox demons as a base, combined with a species of demon that can see ghosts. Satan took out the Huldrefox and threw in extra imp. Now I have a bunch of Oompa Loompas with the intelligence of doorknobs." He shrugged as if trying to dismiss the almost undetectable fond note in his voice. "They're loyal little guys, though."

He kept walking, but she slowed him down several times to ogle the priceless weapons and art on his walls. He had tapestries and paintings believed lost to the ages, and weapons wielded by legends and kings. She wasn't sure how long it took them to get to the huge antechamber she'd walked through when she'd first entered the building, but as he explained some of the demon artwork, she only half-listened as she kept her eyes peeled for his *chronoglass*.

Disappointed that it was nowhere in the room, she followed him outside, with its blackened landscape and gray sky.

He looked out at the buildings surrounding his giant manor. "You can explore those at your leisure. Most of them are empty shells."

She eyed a pulsing vine hanging off one of the rooftops and made a note to avoid the native flora. She'd battled a lot of demons in her life, but she'd never spent enough time in Sheoul to get to know how creepy—or lethal—the vegetation was.

"Why are the buildings here, if they're unused?" she asked him.

A shadow darkened the emerald light in his eyes before disappearing a heartbeat later. "As humans built up their cities, I added buildings to match."

Okay, so that wasn't really an explanation, but she got the sense that if she asked for more, he wouldn't give it to her. "Why is everything here so...filthy?"

He dragged a fingernail down the surface of a pillar, leaving behind a thin line of white stone. "Sheoul-gra's soul is tied to mine. As I succumb to the malevolence that seeps out of Hell, so do the buildings."

So this was what thousands of years of demon-grade sewer leakage would do to a realm. No wonder there were angels employed full time to patch cracks between the human and demon realms. She could only wonder about the extent to which miniscule doses affected humans. But Azagoth had been exposed for thousands of years.

"When you first built this place, everything was white?"

He nodded. "And green. There used to be grass here. Trees. Flowers. Animals. Everything died over time."

She studied his profile, looking for any hint of emotion, but his face might as well have been carved from the same stone used to erect the buildings.

"I'm sorry," she said. "It must have been hard to see the realm you created waste away like that."

His expression hardened even more. "I made my choice." He spun on his heel and headed back inside.

Making a mental note that his realm's demise was a sore subject, she caught up to him as he strode inside the most amazing room yet.

It was a huge, cozy library with floor-to-ceiling shelves of books. A grand fire burned against one wall, and in front of it, a weathered leather sofa was angled so a person could lounge against the pillows and read by the light of the flames. In the center of the room was a recliner, and next to the chair was the object she'd been looking for.

She tried not to stare, but she'd never seen a double-sided version before.

"It's a *chronoglass*," Azagoth said, and she decided to keep the truth of what she knew close to the vest.

"It's amazing," she said truthfully. Framed by a gold rim, the pane of smoky mirrored glass stood at least ten feet tall and four feet wide, easily a third larger than either of the *chronoglasses* in Heaven. "Can you time travel?" Raphael had indicated that he couldn't, but she'd rather hear it from Azagoth himself.

"No."

"Then what do you do with it?"

"I use it to see what's going on in the world." In three graceful strides he moved in front of it. Instantly, the smoky color gave way to a clear view of the bustling streets of Paris.

Evidence of the recent near-apocalypse was visible in the scorch and pock marks on the sides of buildings and on the sidewalks, as well as the broken windows and twisted metal streetlamps and bike racks. But the signs of recovery were there too, in the open shop doors, speeding cars, and even a few tourists.

"But how do you choose the time period you want to see?" she asked.

"I can't." He reached out, a wistful smile playing on his lips as he traced a finger over a street sign. "I can only see what's current. Only those with time travel ability can choose to see events from the past."

"Can you at least choose the location?"

"That," he said, "I can do." He gestured to an odd black ball sitting on top of a stone stand. "It's sort of a mystical remote control."

She moved toward the ball, fascinated by this new discovery. She'd never heard of anyone using a *chronoglass* for anything but traveling through time. "How did you get all of this?"

"I made a deal with a fallen angel named Harvester. This was the first half of what she owes me."

Harvester, daughter of Satan? Wow. Her name had become household in the last few months. As the only fallen angel in history who had not only been restored to full angel status, but who had mated the most powerful angel in existence to become stepmother to the Four Horsemen of the Apocalypse, she was a rock star in Heaven. It was rumored that she still had to fight evil impulses, but according to most, that only made her an even better choice to be the Horsemen's Heavenly Watcher.

She skimmed her fingers over the *chronoglass's* shiny surface. "You do know that Harvester is a fully restored angel now, right?"

He tilted his chin in acknowledgement. "I'm aware."

Of course he was. For being trapped in isolation, he seemed to be well connected. "Were you also aware that she's mated to an angel named Reaver, who was recently promoted to Radiant status?"

His wry smile said he knew even more than that. "Of course. Were you aware that Reaver has an evil twin named Revenant, who was also raised to the Sheoulic equivalent of a Radiant?"

"He's a Shadow Angel?" she asked, stunned at the news. She'd known that Revenant was the Horsemen's evil Watcher, but she had no idea he was Reaver's brother—or that he was so damned powerful.

"Yes," he said. "It's been thousands of years since either Heaven or Sheoul had seen angels of their status." His smile turned malevolent. "Which means something big is about to happen. Just wait. It's coming."

At a tap on the door, they both looked up to see Zhubaal enter. "You have a visitor, my lord."

"Show him to my office," Azagoth said. As the fallen angel slipped away, Azagoth turned to her. "Feel free to explore my realm. No sentient being will harm you, but be wary of the plant life."

"It would be helpful if I had powers," she muttered.

In a surprising move that took her breath away, he was suddenly in front of her. Towering. Menacing. His aura practically dripped with a dark, magnetic energy that tugged her toward him. She actually took a teetering step forward.

His hand came up to cup her cheek in an astonishingly tender touch. Her pulse pounded in an erratic rattle through her veins, and desire spiked. How he could do that to her, she had no idea. She should have been immune to the charms of an arrogant, bossy male, given her experience with Hutriel.

Quickly, she banished her ex's name from her mind. He wasn't welcome here. She had enough to deal with already.

"In time, I'll allow you some access to your powers." His expression was still doing an imitation of the marble effigy on his desk, but his green eyes smoldered with intense heat. "But not until I'm sure you want to be here."

"I'm here, aren't I?" She sounded breathless and wanton, as if he'd been talking about sex, not getting her powers returned. *Idiot.*

He dropped his hand, and she felt the loss as a sudden chill on her skin. "Not the same thing."

No, she supposed not. "Is there any place that's off limits to me?"

"As my mate, what's mine is yours. You can go anywhere except the Inner Sanctum, where the souls are kept. It's a dangerous place for anyone, especially an angel."

"Gotcha." Sheoul-gra's Inner Sanctum didn't sound like a place she'd like to see anyway. Ever.

"Good." He glanced at his watch. "I have to go, but I'll catch up to you soon. I think we might have a lot to talk about."

She nodded, watched him leave, and then wondered what he'd meant by that. She didn't want to talk. Didn't want to be here.

Worst of all, she didn't want to be attracted to him.

Sadly, it was too late.

＊ ＊ ＊ ＊

The cloaked, hooded figure waiting inside Azagoth's office turned as he entered. The male angel, whose features were concealed by shadow, bowed his head in greeting.

"I hope you have some information for me, Jim Bob," Azagoth said, using the code name he'd given the angel over a century ago when Jim Bob had agreed to be Azagoth's spy in Heaven.

One of his spies, anyway. Azagoth had several, each useful in different ways. Some, like Jim Bob, came to him of their own free will, their reasons ranging from wanting the best for the Heavenly realm to having some secret, personal agenda. Others were unwillingly recruited thanks to intel Azagoth gained from the souls who came through Sheoul-gra. Azagoth didn't give a shit how his spies came to him, as long as they didn't screw him over.

Jim Bob, whose real name Azagoth didn't know, inclined his head again. "I was able to ferret out some background on your mate." He gathered the plain brown cloak more tightly around him, as if his jeans and German flag T-shirt would reveal his true identity. The paranoid moron.

Azagoth didn't give a shit who the guy was in Heaven. Mighty archangel or lowly desk-jockey Seraphim, it didn't matter. Still, Azagoth would bet his right wing that Jim Bob was a high-ranking motherfucker, maybe of the order of Virtues or Principalities. The male radiated impressive power even here, where all power but Azagoth's was diminished.

"Lilliana is of the order of Thrones." Jim Bob's gravelly baritone took on a disdainful note, and the fact that he looked down on Thrones confirmed Azagoth's suspicion that the guy was very high-level, since Thrones weren't exactly serfs. "When she was an infant, her mother died in a time travel incident. Her father refused to take her in, and she was sent to the battle angel academy to be raised until it could be determined whether or not she possessed the time travel ability."

Interesting. The ability to travel through time was so rare as to be almost nonexistent. "And?"

"She tested positive." Jim Bob began to pace, his long strides carrying him across the room in a dozen steps. His heavy-ass work boots didn't make a sound. "At the age of fifty, she was taken out of battle angel rotation and sent to Time Travel Operations, where she worked for almost four centuries. She had a clean, if unremarkable, record of service until recently, when she was punished for stealing items from the past. Shortly after that, she went AWOL and didn't show up for work for months. No one could find her until she broke out of the *shrowd* in medieval England."

Azagoth was rarely taken by surprise, but that news did it. When angels traveled to the past, they did so within an impenetrable bubble known as a *shrowd*. The *shrowd* rendered them invisible and limited their ability to interact with the residents of the era. One of the most important and heavily enforced rules for time travelers was that they never leave the *shrowd*.

Maybe her infraction was what got her sent here. But why had she done it in the first place? Had she been running from something? He knew it was possible for angels to leave the *shrowd* in order to reside—or hide—in the past, but he didn't know how they avoided getting caught. Apparently, Lilliana didn't know either.

"Why did she break out of the *shrowd*?"

"No idea."

Disappointing. "What about lovers?" he asked. "Does she have any? Did she have to leave a male in Heaven to come here?"

*Please say no.* Not that he personally gave a hellrat's ass, but if he was going to have to put up with a crying, broken-hearted female for all eternity, he'd like a heads up and a lot more rum.

Jim Bob shrugged. "If so, she kept it quiet. The only relationship I found was with a male named Hutriel, but that ended decades ago."

Excellent. Azagoth stared into the fire as he contemplated everything he'd learned. When he looked back over at Jim Bob, the angel stopped pacing. "You look puzzled," Jim Bob mused.

"I'm just wondering why she wasn't destroyed for breaking out of the *shrowd*. Was mating me her punishment?"

"Perhaps."

How not helpful. Azagoth ground his molars in frustration. "Can you at least tell me if her ability to time travel was removed before she was sent here?"

"It was not."

Well, wasn't this all unexpected. He recalled how Lilliana had seemed so amazed by his *chronoglass*, so clueless about what it was and what he did with it, all the while knowing she possessed an ability that could activate the device.

It seemed as if his new mate had been keeping important information from him. Time to find out why.

And, perhaps, remind her that he dealt in death. Not forgiveness.

# Chapter Five

Lilliana had no idea how she was going to get that giant *chronoglass* out of Sheoul-gra. For a few minutes after Azagoth left her alone, she'd tried to lift the thing, but it soon became clear that without her powers, she was going to have to drag it out. Which was going to take time and was going to make a lot of noise.

She'd have to plan this heist well.

She always thought best when she was walking, so she'd gone out to explore the buildings Azagoth had said were empty.

And they were...of people. Hellrats and other strange little demonic critters scurried around, and the pulsing, maggoty-pale vines had climbed walls and penetrated windows and doorways. As she wandered through structure after structure, she found evidence of what must have, at one point, been a bustling community.

One entire building had been dedicated to living quarters complete with private bedrooms. In another building, she found several long-empty community baths. There was even a huge hall filled with long tables and chairs. Wooden and stone food trenchers still sat at some of the seats, as if waiting to be filled.

Who had lived here? And why had they left?

It was all so eerie, and that was *before* she reached the Roman-style colosseum, its sandy basin littered with demon bones. Ancient weapons, none newer than about two hundred years old, hung from racks on the walls.

The soft thud of footsteps echoed through the structure, and it took all her years of training not to make a run for the nearest scythe. Panic in a strange place never ended in anything but death. In a controlled spin, she whirled around, breathing a sigh of relief when she saw Azagoth, his long strides eating up the distance between them with effortless grace.

But her sense of relief was short lived. His mouth was a grim slash, and his glacial, calculating gaze left her feeling trapped, as if he was a gladiator and she was a declawed, defanged lion. For a split-second, she reconsidered grabbing a weapon. Instead, she squared her stance and met him head on.

"I've been exploring your buildings," she said, going on the offensive. "Seems you left some information out."

"Your righteous anger falls flat, given that you withheld shit from me too."

"I don't know what you're talking about—" Suddenly, they were no longer standing in the arena. They were back in Azagoth's library, and as he gestured to the *chronoglass*, her gut twisted.

"You failed to mention that you can time travel."

*Oh, shit.* "It wasn't a secret." Not...really. The truth just complicated things. Things like trying to steal a *chronoglass*. "But out of curiosity, how did you find out?"

"A lot of people owe me a lot of favors," he bit out impatiently. "Now, why did you keep this news away from me?"

She swallowed. She'd always been a horrible liar. Every angel had to go through espionage ability screening as a youth, and she'd gotten a record low score. Nothing like being notorious for being *the worst* at something.

"Answer me," he demanded. "Is it because you thought you could run away? Breaking news, Angelcake, it won't work. This device only works for an hour at a time...unless you break out of the shrowd." He smiled, enjoying her discomfort. "Which is something you seem to be okay with."

She inhaled sharply. "What do you know about that?"

"Does it matter? If it makes you feel any better, I don't give a shit what crimes you committed in the past. But let's be clear on one thing; down here, you don't fuck with me. So tell me, are you planning to escape using the *chronoglass*?"

"That would be stupid. I'd be bringing Enforcers down on my head. I'd spend every minute looking over my shoulder for them. Eventually they'd find me and kill me." She folded her arms over her chest and glared. "And don't call me Angelcake."

"Enforcers won't find you if you cut off your wings." He ran his tongue over his teeth as if savoring the uncomfortable pause.

"Angelcake."

Asshole. But the asshole was right. Any angel who cut off his or her wings became instantly undetectable to angelic senses. Any angel who would normally "feel" another angel's presence under certain variable circumstances wouldn't register her at all. Even face to face, an unobservant angel could very well believe the wingless angel was human.

"I'm not cutting off my wings," she assured him. "I hate pain, and seriously, why is this such a big deal anyway?"

"It's a big deal because you kept it from me for a reason. I want to know the reason. I don't tolerate deception. I'd tell you to ask my last assistant about my low tolerance, but his soul is busy being tortured and buttfucked in the Inner Sanctum." He laughed. "Buttfucked in the Sanctum. Get it?"

Apparently, the males of all species remained children no matter how old they got. "I get it. Sanctum sounds like rectum." She rolled her eyes. "So clever."

His smile remained, but his eyes were shards of ice. "Now, the truth. Why did you act like you barely knew what a *chronoglass* was while failing to tell me you could use it?" He snapped his fingers imperiously. "Let's hear it. My patience is wearing thin."

If he snapped his fingers again, she was going to break them. "Maybe I just wanted something for myself," she said. "I'm in a strange place, expected to mate with a strange male, and I have nothing of my own. Not even clothes, because *somehow* they've been delayed. So maybe I wanted an hour to myself now and then, outside of here." She glared. "Jackass."

Even though she'd called him a jackass, the shards of ice in his gaze melted a little, just enough to dull the sharp edges. "I can...understand that."

Holy shit, he'd bought it? Then again, it was the truth. If there had been no hope of getting out of this deal by stealing the mirror, she'd have felt exactly as she'd just said.

He stepped forward so suddenly she jumped. "Take me someplace."

"Excuse me?"

He stepped closer, but if he thought he could intimidate her with his height, he was an idiot. She'd gone through battle training with males far taller and bigger than he was.

None of those males, however, could hold a candle to

Azagoth's lethal elegance and oozing sensuality. It was as if he had been born for killing and sex. The battle angel in her could appreciate the former. The female in her definitely appreciated the latter. And the thing that sucked was that she shouldn't be appreciating anything about him. He wasn't exactly an enemy, but neither was he someone she could afford to get attached to.

"Take me someplace," he repeated.

She tipped her head back to meet his gaze. "Ask nicely."

"Take me someplace...please."

"You could have at least made an *attempt* to make it not sound like an order."

Clenching his teeth, he ground out, "Will you please take me someplace."

Well, it wasn't quite what she was hoping for, but she doubted it would get any better. Besides, she was ready to get out of here for a while. "Fine," she said. "But you should know that I'll have full use of my powers once I'm outside your realm."

One corner of his mouth twitched. "Should I consider that a warning?"

"Just don't be surprised if you find yourself riding a bolt of lightning if you piss me off."

"I'm into kinky shit, so that works."

He gripped her palm, and she sucked in a sharp breath at the shock of awareness that shot up her arm. She stole a glance at Azagoth, but apparently he hadn't felt a thing, because he was as snarly-faced as ever.

Well...good. They didn't need to be having any kind of mutual "moments."

Although, really, it was a little insulting that he didn't react. At all.

Shoving aside her irrational annoyance, she reached deep inside for what angels in her field called the Triple T...the time travel tingle. Independent of her other, currently unusable, angelic powers, it started deep in her pelvis and spread outward, until it was as if she could actually feel time and space inside each and every cell. Now all she had to do was think of a specific time period...then a location...and there it was.

Instead of reflecting their images, the *chronoglass's* surface became a window, beyond which was an ocean of drifting desert sands.

"Ready?" At Azagoth's nod, she squeezed his hand tight and led him into the mirror.

Instantly, dry heat blasted them as their feet sank into the hot sand. Releasing Azagoth, she glanced around at the scenery. It was exactly as she'd known it would be.

Utterly desolate.

She'd dropped them in the middle of the Egyptian desert, where there was nothing but rolling dunes of sand. Only the cloudless azure sky added color to an otherwise monotonous field of beige.

*Take that, Azagoth.* He'd wanted to go somewhere outside of Sheoul-gra, so she'd brought him to the most boring, featureless environment she could think of.

Feeling smug, she pivoted around so she could soak in his disappointment.

Turned out, she was the one in for a letdown. Azagoth's eyes were closed, his face tilted toward the sun.

"Egypt," he sighed. "Damn, I miss the desert." Inhaling deeply, he smiled.

She gaped. "Seriously? You *like* this?"

"I miss...warmth." Gripping his collar, he yanked, ripping his shirt and popping buttons with such force that one pinged her in the forehead. "And the breeze...ah, damn, I miss the breeze."

He flung his ruined shirt to the ground, and good Lord, he was ripped. Muscles flexed under smooth, bronzed skin and made the multitude of incredibly lifelike tattoos plastered on his chest dance. She let her gaze rove hungrily over him, committing his body to memory, because she had a feeling no male would ever match Azagoth's savage beauty again.

He came off as detached and calm, but his ruthlessness as one of Heaven's most decorated and successful Interrogators was well documented. Humans, demons, and fellow angels alike died at his hand, but not before they endured a lot of pain.

Azagoth's skill with his hands extended to females as well, but instead of agony, they felt pleasure. His bedroom exploits were legendary, and now all Lilliana could do was wonder how many females had let their fingers play along the lines of the serpent tattoo that curled around his left pec. How many had dragged their tongues down the hilt of the sword on his breastbone, all the way beyond where the blade disappeared under his waistband. And how could Lilliana possibly touch him in ways no one else had?

Not that there would be any touching.

He kicked off his shoes and socks, tossing them aside without any care at all. Which made her wonder where he got his clothes. She hadn't noticed a bustling shopping mall in any of Sheoul-gra's outer buildings.

"What year is it?" he asked as he walked in circles, his gaze now transfixed on his toes sifting through the sand.

"I don't know exactly." She watched him bend over to scoop up some sand, and her mouth went as dry as the desert air at the way his slacks hugged his fine ass. Swallowing against the dryness, she continued. "I haven't been doing this long enough to aim for specific dates, or even specific years. I can usually get myself within a decade of my goal, though."

"A decade?" He straightened. "How long have you been doing this?"

She smiled wryly. "Why don't you tell me, since you know so much about me." When he said nothing, just looked up at the sky like he'd never seen it before, she went ahead and humored him. "Almost four hundred years."

Pivoting around, he looked her up and down the way a prospective buyer would examine a horse. "Sounds like a long time to still be off by ten years. Are you a slow learner?"

She stared, speechless for a second. "Am I a slow learner?" she practically sputtered. "I'm far ahead of most time travelers by this age, you arrogant ass."

"Huh. If your accuracy is that bad now, I'd hate to have seen you when you first started. You want to see the Battle of Gettysburg but find yourself running from dinosaurs. That would suck."

"It happens," she snapped. Because something *similar* had happened to her. But instead of the Battle of Gettysburg and dinosaurs, it had been the Battle of Almansa and saber-toothed cats. The worst part of it was that animals often could see angels inside the *shrowd*.

And it turned out that saber-toothed cats were freaking *mean*.

He laughed and slogged through the sand, his elation putting a severe damper on her exasperation. "Come on." He made a *follow me* gesture. "Let's walk."

"Are you kidding me?" She threw her hands up in the air.

"There's nowhere to walk to. The nearest human settlement is a hundred miles away."

"So? Would you rather just stand here?"

She glanced longingly over her shoulder at Azagoth's library, visible through the rectangle portal that would allow them to go back at any time.

"Fine," she muttered as she jogged to catch up.

She supposed she could understand why Azagoth would want to stay in this giant cat litter box, given that he'd been shrouded in darkness for thousands of years. And really, it said something about him that he wasn't angry that the first place she'd brought him was the middle of nowhere. If anything, he was excited.

Even now, he was walking with his face to the sun, his arms outstretched, as if he was giving the desert a big hug. His hair, which had been perfectly combed before, was mussed by the breeze, and a hint of a smile gave him an irresistibly boyish appeal.

He looked over at her when she caught up, and his smile turned downright dangerous. Oh, not dangerous in the deadly sense. Dangerous in the, *I want to be flat on my back on a mattress with you*, sense.

Abruptly, he came to a halt.

Startled, she did the same. "What's wrong—"

Azagoth spun her, silencing her with his mouth on hers. Stunned, she stood there like a dolt, her heart pounding so hard she felt her heartbeat in her lips where they were mashed against his. One big hand came around to tangle in her hair as Azagoth deepened the kiss, swiping his tongue along the seam of her mouth, tasting and testing until she felt her body sway against him.

Yes, definitely dangerous...

"Thank you," he murmured against her lips.

And then he was walking again, leaving her standing in the sand, knees weak and her insides quaking with the kind of arousal she hadn't felt in...well, ever. And he was sauntering away as if that kiss, brief as it was, hadn't affected him at all.

Muttering obscenities to herself...on the loud side, so he'd hear, she tagged along as he tread lightly across the endless expanse of desert, stopping every once in a while to just look up at the sky or gaze out over the sand.

It seemed like they'd only been wandering for a few minutes when the telltale pressure started in her chest. Their hour was coming up.

"It's time," she said.

Azagoth cranked his head around to peg her with his intense gaze. "For what?"

A gust of wind blasted sand in her face, and she had to spit out the grit before she could speak. "To go."

The light that had been sparkling in his eyes snuffed out. "So soon?"

"Soon? I don't know about you, but I could use a glass of something very wet and icy."

"I could go for something wet," he drawled, and oh, damn, the places her mind took that.

Pretending she hadn't heard a word, she reached for him. "I think the *chronoglass* will automatically suck both of us back into it, but to be safe, give me your hand."

For just a second, he hesitated, as if he wouldn't mind being stuck here, but in the end, he reluctantly took her hand. Instantly, the same warm awareness as earlier shot through her body, and just like before, Azagoth showed no hint that he felt anything at all.

Closing her eyes, she let her senses drift as the time travel pull made every cell in her body vibrate. The buzz grew more intense, until it felt as if she was being torn apart...and a moment later, they were back where they started, standing in front of the mirror, staring at their own reflections.

Azagoth looked at the shimmering surface, and she wondered if he saw the same sadness in his eyes that she did.

"Azagoth?" she said quietly. "What's wrong?"

All around her, the air crackled with a coming storm. "I have to go." His voice was little more than an inhuman drawl, steeped in rage and pain and a few other emotions she couldn't identify.

And then he was bolting out of the library, leaving her confused and alone.

The strange thing—besides his behavior—was that she was used to being alone. She was okay with it, had learned at an early age to rely only on herself and to be okay with her own company.

But for the first time in her life, she didn't like her own company.

And there was no way in hell that she wanted to analyze the reasons for that.

# Chapter Six

Azagoth got the fuck out of the room. Away from Lilliana. Away from the female who had given him the gift of stepping outside of his realm for the first time in thousands of years. Who set his blood on fire when he'd taken her hand. And when he'd kissed her. Holy hellfire, today had been the best day he'd had in eons. Maybe in...ever.

He could still feel the sand on his feet and between his toes as he hauled ass to his office. The halls were empty, which was good, because right now he didn't trust himself not to disintegrate anyone who got in his way.

He hit the door at a dead run and slammed it closed behind him. With a thought, he shut down the soul tunnel and went straight to the fireplace.

The flames licked at his bare skin, but as usual, he felt nothing. How odd, given that the Egyptian sun had engulfed him in warmth.

Trembling all over, he gripped the mantel so firmly that the stone beneath his fingers gave way. He'd leave one hell of a set of handprints once he got himself under control.

But *could* he get himself under control? What the hell was happening to him? The moment he'd stepped from his library out into the desert and breathed the hot, dry air, something inside him had broken open, releasing a trickle of sensation he hadn't been able to identify. It had been familiar, and yet foreign, maybe what humans called déjà vu. Whatever it was, it had been pure and pleasant, a kind of joy that wasn't dependent on evil or violence or death.

But the moment he'd rematerialized inside his library, the

sensation had morphed into something much less pleasant, as if the river of emotion seeping out of the fissure had become polluted. Tainted in the way only malevolence could do.

Hatred and pain and the desire to destroy something had overwhelmed him. He hadn't been prepared for the onslaught of feelings, and now his body was shaking and cramping like he'd overdosed on some human designer drug.

Closing his eyes, he made a futile attempt to corral his runaway emotions, to gather them up and stuff them back inside the icy tomb where they'd been interred for so long. He'd been such a fool to want to feel something again. How could he have forgotten that emotions were bad, bad things?

He growled at the sound of a tap on the door. "Go away."

The door whispered open, and he gripped the mantel even harder as his wings writhed beneath his skin. His true form, the one that literally frightened the piss out of most demons, was itching to break out and rip something—or some*one*—apart.

Soft footsteps padded inside, and he got a whiff of the warm citrus fragrance that was unique to Lilliana.

Instant, embarrassing hard-on.

Okay, so he couldn't rip her to shreds, but dammit, he wasn't ready to talk to anyone, let alone the female who had just drawn something from him he hadn't felt in forever.

*This is your own damned fault. You wanted a mate, an angel who would warm you from the outside.*

Yeah, well, he hadn't expected to be warmed from the *inside* too.

"Do you not understand the words, *go away*?"

He heard her drawn-out inhale, as if she was gathering her own temper. "You seemed upset. I wanted to make sure you were okay."

"I'm Azagoth, the Grim Fucking Reaper, king of my domain. Of course I'm okay."

"What, so the Great Azagoth doesn't have feelings?" She made a noise that sounded suspiciously like a stomp of her foot. "Is the Great Azagoth also so rude that he can't talk to someone face to face?"

Irritated now, he rounded on her. "I told you not to come in."

She stiffened, but instead of defending her actions as he expected, she inclined her head. "You're right. I shouldn't have barged in and demanded something of you when you clearly want to be alone." Pivoting crisply, she started for the doorway.

"Wait," he blurted, his mouth operating independently from his brain. "I didn't mean to be a bastard."

The words came out stilted and unfamiliar to his own ears. How long had it been since he'd apologized to anyone? Thousands of years, probably. No wonder he was so rusty.

Lilliana turned around slowly. "What happened? You seemed so relaxed and happy when we were in the desert, like you were a normal person and not the Grim Reaper. Now you're extra...reapy." She cleared her throat. "Also, you've sprouted horns."

Of course he had.

She eyed him like he was a rabid hellhound, and when her gaze dropped to his feet, he barked, "What are you doing?"

"Checking for hooves."

He was pretty sure his horns grew larger. So did his dick.

Irritation that he couldn't control his own body, let alone his emotions, pissed him off even more. Made him...as she put it, *extra reapy*. Then she was walking toward him, her long, fluid strides kicking her slim hips out with each strut. The bare expanse of her belly became a focal point as she came closer, and suddenly, all the writhing, shifting feelings inside him narrowed into a single stream of lust.

Much, much better. Fury, joy, sadness, guilt...those were things he couldn't deal with. Lust, though...*that* he could handle, and handle very well.

"Look," she said as she halted in front of him. "It wasn't my fault that we had to come back. We used up the entire hour—"

A tap on the doorjamb cut her off, and they both looked over to the open doorway where Zhubaal stood, outfitted in leather and weapons.

Not a good sign.

"My lord, I had a meal sent to your dining room." He gestured down the hall. "And...you have another visitor."

"Send them away. I'm done for the day."

Zhubaal shifted his weight in an uncharacteristic display of unease. "Sir...it's Methicore."

Instant alarm shot up Azagoth's spine, and he instinctively stepped in front of Lilliana. "Is he alone?"

"Aye." Zhubaal's tone was grim. "I shackled him with Bracken Cuffs."

The cuffs, designed to neutralize supernatural abilities, weren't necessary, not when Azagoth was the most powerful being in his own realm, but with Methicore's history, it was a wise precaution. Plus, being shackled was humiliating, and Methicore deserved it. And worse.

"Send the bastard in."

Zhubaal bowed deeply and left. As soon as the door closed, Lilliana stepped closer. "Who is Methicore?"

"He's a vile excuse for an angel," he growled. "A pox upon his kind."

She frowned. "How do you know him?"

Azagoth inhaled deeply, doing his best to keep the monster throbbing inside him at bay. "I know him," he said thickly, "because he's my son."

\* \* \* \*

*Bastard. A vile excuse for an angel. A pox upon his kind.*

Azagoth's words about his own son completely obliterated any warm fuzzies Lilliana had begun to feel for him. It was too reminiscent of her own father's rejection of her. She'd been the product of breeding for a purpose, and when she'd approached him a quarter of a century ago in an attempt to get to know him, he'd made it very clear that he wanted nothing to do with her.

*"I have a mate and sons now, and I don't need you barging into our lives and ruining everything."*

In other words, his family didn't know about her. He'd kicked her out of his grand residence with instructions to stay away from him and his family.

Looked like Azagoth was no better than dear old dad. She should have known.

As Zhubaal escorted Methicore inside, anger at the way he was chained boiled up. She'd been shackled the same way only a few weeks ago, and the memory of being rendered helpless and at another's mercy closed in on her in a claustrophobic wave.

Methicore stopped a few feet inside the doorway, but Zhubaal remained outside, his hand hovering over a blade at his hip. Was this male truly such a threat? Or had Azagoth taken a page from her father's playbook? The moment her father had realized who she was, he'd summoned two underlings to flank her, as if she'd come to murder him instead of beg for acceptance.

"Father," Methicore drawled. "Did you take out your horns on my account? How special." He resembled his sire in height and coloring, but he was slimmer, and where Azagoth's eyes had glazed over with icy indifference, Methicore's burned with hatred.

She wasn't sure which was worse.

"Why are you here?" Azagoth's expression gave nothing away, as usual. "I told you to never return."

Oh, gee, Lilliana thought sourly. That sounded familiar. Azagoth and her father should get together for drinks and bond over woeful tales of their inconvenient bastard offspring.

"I wanted to tell you the news in person," Methicore practically spat.

Azagoth might as well have yawned, he looked so bored. Even his horns had disappeared. And he was still hoofless. "What news?"

"The kind that makes you fucking irrelevant." Methicore smiled darkly, the resemblance to his father becoming uncanny. "All Memitim are Ascending to full angel status as of today...and we've been given the ability to reproduce. You're done, asshole. No longer needed."

Surprise flickered in Azagoth's eyes, but it quickly snuffed out. "Is that all?"

"No." Methicore's grin widened. "Also as of today, *as of the second I leave*, access to your realm will forever be cut off to Memitim." He tapped his chest with pride. "My doing, of course. You'll never see any of your sons or daughters again."

Lilliana gasped in horror, but there was absolutely no reaction from Azagoth. Did he not care about his children at all? Slowly, as if this was all just so very ho-hum to him, he turned his back on his son and stared into the fire.

"I have no use for you," he said softly. "Begone."

Lilliana's heart crumpled like aluminum foil as a flicker of hurt flashed across Methicore's face. It was quickly smothered by a triumphant smirk, but she wasn't sure what he had to feel good about. Revenge was far more poisonous to the giver than the receiver. Besides, Azagoth didn't seem to be disturbed by the fact that he'd never see his offspring again, so Methicore's victory was hollow. She actually felt sorry for him.

Methicore shot Azagoth the bird and moved toward the door, pausing at the threshold. "Female." His eyes locked on her, and the calculation in them left her feeling more exposed than anything Azagoth had done so far. "You'll get nothing from him but a cock that's as frozen as his heart. Come with me, and I'll give you what he can't."

"Have a care, son." Azagoth's quiet voice held an ominous edge that seemed to make even the flames in the hearth shrink back. "For some species devour their young."

Methicore swept out of the office with a snarl. The moment the door slammed shut, Lilliana rounded on Azagoth.

"You *bastard*." She spat out the word with all the contempt she could muster. "How can you be so cruel to your own son?"

"Me? Cruel?" His hands formed fists at his sides. "I'm not the one cutting off access to my children."

"As if you give a shit."

"Do not," he growled, "presume to know me after a few hours of prancing around my realm."

Prancing? She'd never pranced in her life. "I don't have to know you to know your kind."

He swung around, his jaw tight and unforgiving. "My kind?"

"A breeder." The very word pissed her off. "A stud for hire who doesn't give a damn about the lives he creates."

He jerked as if she'd shot him with an arrow. She'd struck a nerve, hadn't she? "Shut. Up."

"Fuck you," she shot back. She hated being so crude, but something about this male and this realm brought out her bitchy side.

"Shut up," he ground out, "or I'll make you shut up."

He clearly had no idea how stubborn she was, something that had driven her kidnapper nuts. "You can't make me do anything."

He came at her, his gait loose yet predatory. "I can make you do *everything*."

Unbelievable. "Are you aware on any level whatsoever how arrogant you are?"

"This is my realm, angel. I *am* this realm. My reach extends beyond Sheoul-gra's boundaries to the deepest pits of Hell and the highest levels of Heaven. So yes, I'm aware of my self-confidence, and when I tell you that I can make you do something, I mean it."

*You can't make me stay here.* Oh, she couldn't wait to get out of this depressing place. "What will you do? Beat me into compliance? Torture me?"

He stopped in front of her, his gaze roving boldly over her, lingering on her breasts and bare skin of her belly. "Only a fool and a coward would harm his mate, especially if they have to co-exist for eternity." He bared his teeth in what she assumed was a smile. "I have other ways of getting what I want."

"Well, I hate to break it to you, but short of torture, you can't make me do anything."

His smile became downright wicked. "I can make you beg for the mere whisper of my breath on your skin. I can do things with my tongue that will make you scream with the exquisite intensity of it. And I can make you come so hard, for so long, that you'll pass out from pleasure."

"Sex," she said bitterly. "Typical male, thinking that's all females want." Never mind that she *did* want it. Lord help her, to experience an orgasm like that...oh, yes, please.

"Sex," he said huskily, "is only the beginning. I can make you a queen. I can give you an entire realm."

She snorted. "You mean this?" She made an encompassing sweep of her arm. "This cold, dreary realm full of death and *griminions* and fallen angels? Yeah, it's what every girl dreams of."

A tense black silence hung like a pall in the air, and she had a feeling she'd pushed him too far. Despite what he'd said about not harming his mate, she braced herself for a blow.

And one blow was all he'd get. Her power was muted down here, but she'd fight him until her last breath. Or she'd get the hell out of here and happily submit to the dissection team that would extract her time traveling ability.

But Azagoth didn't raise a finger. Instead, he dematerialized, leaving her alone. Again.

# Chapter Seven

Azagoth materialized in his library, wishing he could scream in fury and agony. But all the emotion that had nearly crippled him earlier had found its way back into the desolate, frozen wasteland he called a soul. Although he supposed his soul had been sucked out of him a long time ago.

Snarling, he swiped a soda-bottle sized crystal chess piece off his desk and crushed it under his boot. Methicore had given it to him, a reminder that Azagoth was a king, and the world was his chess board.

Methicore should have remembered that.

Azagoth ground the heel of his boot on top of the piece, relishing the sound of destruction.

His son had betrayed him yet again. Not only betrayed, but destroyed every relationship Azagoth had forged with his sons and daughters. Not that he'd ever had much in the way of relationships, but at least he'd been able to visit with some of his offspring now and then. The ones who hadn't abandoned him when Methicore led the rebellion against him, anyway.

Funny how Azagoth had seen Satan's insurrection coming from a mile away, but he'd been utterly blind to Methicore's machinations. Then again, by the time his son had risen up against him, Azagoth's ability to sense deception had been dulled like a blade that had sawed too much bone.

And then there was Lilliana and her unwelcome observation about him. Calling him a breeder. *A stud for hire who doesn't give a damn about the lives he creates.*

The real pisser was that she was right. But not about all of it.

He did give a damn about his offspring. He might not be able to feel true love for anyone or anything, but he *did* care.

He cared *too* much, and Satan had exploited that fact in order to get what he wanted from Azagoth.

The demon had never forgotten Azagoth's role in his expulsion from Heaven. Talk about holding a grudge. What a big, whiny baby. So Satan hadn't succeeded in taking over Heaven. He was King Shit of his own domain now. Who else could say that?

Oh, right—Azagoth could. Not that Lilliana gave a crap.

She'd given him the greatest gift of his life by taking him to the desert, but when he'd offered a gift of his own, the key to Sheoul-gra, she'd mocked him and flung it right back in his face.

*This cold, dreary realm full of death and griminions and fallen angels? Yeah, it's what every girl dreams of.*

How dare she, he thought, as he flashed himself outside his manor. How dare she reject anything that he, the Grim Reaper, offered? Females creamed themselves over him. They'd come to him by the thousands, begging for any scraps he'd throw their way. Granted, they were demons, but they'd been high-ranking, influential females from every species. Before her recent demise, even Lilith herself had approached him on multiple occasions to try to convince him that a union between the two of them would make them the most powerful couple in existence.

No thanks. He'd already been screwed by her. In more ways than one.

Frustrated, he kicked at the oily soil beneath his feet. It felt nothing like the sand in the desert. He looked into the distance at the dozens of buildings and beyond, to what used to be a forest filled with life, rivers, and lakes. Now there was nothing but gnarled tree trunks and stumps, dry creek beds, and one lake so stagnant that its toxic stench sometimes crossed the barrier between Sheoul and Sheoul-gra. Denizens of Sheoul's Horun region had affectionately named the affected area The Grim Reaper's Asshole.

*It's what every girl dreams of.*

Azagoth's heart went dead in his chest. Holy shit, Lilliana was right. Demons might think of Sheoul-gra as a treasure, but no one else, especially not an angel, would think that any of this was a gift.

What a fool he'd been. What a fucking dumbass.

He had nothing to offer Lilliana. Sure, he could give her great sex. Better than great. But beyond that? Nothing. His realm, which had once been teeming with activity and life, was dead.

The only thing for her to do down here was what Azagoth did; meet each evil soul as it came through the tunnel, and then decide its fate before sending it to the various levels of the Inner Sanctum to await reincarnation. Assignment to hard labor? A stint in Hades's dungeon? Maybe roasting in the Eternal Field of Flames or swimming in the Acid Pools of Agony?

And really, he should *not* have let Hades name shit in the Inner Sanctum. Azagoth wanted to beat the fallen angel every time he was forced to say, or even think, of the miserable area known as Feces-palooza.

*Oh, hey, Lilliana, let me take you on a tour of your wedding gift. Yep, check out Disembowling Beach. We can honeymoon in Feces-palooza. And just wait until I take you to Boiling Piss Pond and the Fetid Razor Swamp.*

Fuck.

Scrubbing his hand over his face, he decided he needed to rethink his strategy. If Lilliana was truly here because she was given no choice, eternity with him would, literally, be hell for her. He was a bastard who traded in death and pain, and while he liked to tell himself that he'd been corrupted by thousands of years of life in Hell, the truth was that even as an angel he'd been in the business.

Interrogators weren't exactly nice people.

Okay, so where did he go from here? First, he supposed, it might help to know why, exactly, Lilliana had agreed to mate him. Jim Bob had indicated that this was a punishment, but Azagoth wanted to hear it from Lilliana herself. Had she been given any choice in the matter at all? And if so, why had she agreed?

He couldn't do anything about Methicore and his idea of revenge...at least, not in the immediate future. But he could take care of what was happening right now in his home.

Home. What a joke. Home was a horror show of a necrotic realm. Dream stuff, there.

As he contemplated his next move with Lilliana, he headed back inside and straight for the bedroom. He expected her to be waiting for him, but to his surprise, she'd climbed into bed, her chestnut hair spilling over the black satin pillowcase in a shiny wave. The clothes she'd been wearing were laid neatly on the recliner next to her wardrobe and, he noted, the sapphire silk baby-doll nightie was missing from the hanger.

Man, he wished he hadn't missed her putting that on. He could imagine her hard body loosely covered in luxurious material meant to caress her smooth skin, and when he added himself to the picture, the nightie became a shredded pile on the floor.

Mouth watering, but not for food, he made a quick detour to the kitchen to see if she'd eaten, and he was pleased to see that she'd made a huge dent in the Italian food Zhubaal had scored from one of Azagoth's favorite restaurants. Azagoth could cook, but one of his few pleasures was eating the best foods in the world, and Zhubaal had a knack for knowing exactly what Azagoth was in the mood for.

Too bad his mood for Italian had passed, because the three pasta dishes, steamed mussels, and tomato bisque looked amazing. What was left of it, anyway. Apparently, his angel had a hearty appetite.

The thought made him practically purr inside. He loved a female who could eat.

Returning to the bedroom, he eyed his erotic furniture, wondering if she'd show as much enthusiasm for sex.

*How could she? She doesn't want to be here.*

He shook off the thought. He'd make her want to be there. Sure, he didn't have a plan, but he had the power to bring anything she wanted into his realm. He could keep her content. Happy, even.

*Keep telling yourself that, jackass.*

With a growl of frustration, he stripped naked and climbed between the crisp sheets. She was lying as close to the edge of the mattress as possible, her back to him and the covers tucked under her chin. He closed the gap between them, easing himself close to her, but just short of touching. He didn't trust himself. If he touched her, he'd need to keep touching, and he wanted to give her time to adjust.

*How gentlemanly of you.* Yeah, well, his soul might be warped into something unrecognizable and his emotions all but dead, but his memories were fully intact and untainted by Sheoul's evil influence. He remembered his mother and how she'd been so timid and afraid of new experiences. It had hurt him to see, especially not knowing what had made her that way.

Those memories were what made him handle his nervous bedmates differently than he handled the others. While he might not actually *feel* sympathy for faint-hearted females, he knew he used to, before he came to Sheoul-gra. And despite the rumors, he had *never* taken a female by force or coercion.

He certainly wouldn't start with his mate.

"Lilliana?" he murmured. "I know you aren't asleep."

"What gave me away? The fact that my eyes are open?"

Apparently, the theme tonight was ornery. He could play that. "You have a sharp tongue, female." He caught a lock of hair in his fingers, and so much for not touching her. "May I suggest that you put it to better use?"

"May I suggest that you go to hell?"

"That insult has no bite, given that we're already here." Not technically, of course, since Azagoth's realm sat on a special plane between the human realm and the demon one, but the barrier between Sheoul and Sheoul-gra was extremely thin, allowing far too much leakage between them.

She sighed. "What do you want?"

Bracing himself on one elbow, he leaned in, inhaling the fresh rosemary mint of her shampoo. His cock stirred, and whaddya know, that scent was apparently an aphrodisiac.

"Tell me," he breathed into her ear. "Tell me why you're here."

"You really want to know?"

He inhaled again, this time catching the faint citrus spice of her skin along with the shampoo. She was a living, breathing dessert he couldn't wait to taste.

"I'm not in the habit of asking questions I don't want the answers to," he said, letting his lips brush the skin of her cheek.

She inhaled sharply, and the unmistakable aroma of arousal rose up all around her. His body responded with a primal surge of hunger, and his rapidly swelling cock went all *helllooo, baby* on her backside.

Another inhalation, this time a little ragged. "I...ah, I was given a choice between being demoted and stripped of my abilities or mating you."

Azagoth had known the answer, but hearing her say it felt like a punch to the nuts. *Buh-bye, baby.* "And how difficult was your decision?"

The mattress creaked as she turned over to face him. Light from the fire danced on her face, softening her features, but making her eyes glow with a defiant glint.

"I'm sensing that there's a right and a wrong answer here, so why don't you go ahead and tell me which one I should pick." She propped herself up, matching his pose. "And why does any of this matter? I'm here. Isn't that enough?"

No, it wasn't. Being here wasn't the same as *wanting* to be here. If he had any emotions left in him at all, he'd be happy if just once, someone—anyone—truly wanted to be with him.

"It doesn't matter." Impulsively, he kissed her on the forehead before rolling away to leave her alone on her side of the mattress.

Weird, but this was the first time his massive bed didn't feel big enough.

# Chapter Eight

Azagoth was gone when Lilliana got up the next morning. She experienced a fleeting twinge of disappointment, and then she buried her face in her pillow as she remembered feeling the press of Azagoth's erection against her butt. The velvety tip had nudged her solidly between her cheeks, spreading heat through her pelvis as her nerve endings sparked with awareness.

Everything about Azagoth and his realm might be polar-level cold, but his body was definitely in the triple digits.

How she'd been able to speak a single word, let alone entire coherent sentences after that was beyond her comprehension. Her heart had hammered so hard and erratically that she'd felt it in her spine, and her lungs hadn't been able to get enough air.

If things hadn't gone rapidly downhill right after that...nah. She'd have told him to roll over to his side of the bed and stay there.

While she lay on her side and stared at the spanking bench across from her.

Yawning, she started for the bathroom, slowing to give the bench a swat for keeping her awake for a good part of the night while she played out scenes in her head involving it and Azagoth. Inevitably, those scenes had turned ugly when she thought about the other females who had enjoyed a good spanking at his hand.

Sometimes, an imagination was a terrible thing.

His bathroom was the only truly light part of his manor that she'd found. Rough-cut white marble gave the room a masculine edge, but it was modern and elegant, and she could spend hours in the shower. Though she had to wonder why he needed five shower heads and two marble benches, but the heated floor tiles were a nice touch. How many females had he brought in here, anyway? She pictured him naked, water and suds sluicing over his muscular body, and suddenly the shower got a lot steamier.

*Stop it.*

Now he was on his knees, his tongue catching rivulets as they cascaded from her breasts to her abs.

*Stop it!*

In the next moment, she was bracing herself against the shower wall as he licked her sex, alternating quick flicks against her clit with long, firm strokes through her wet valley.

*Stop. It!*

Her blood quickened and her breaths came fast and hard as she drove her hand between her legs. In her mind, it was Azagoth's tongue circling her sensitive nub before thrusting inside her core, and when her climax took her a second later, it was Azagoth's name that whispered across her lips.

And damn, imaginary Azagoth was good. Her knees shook as she dried off, but the mouthwatering smell of bacon spurred her on. Once dried, she selected a pair of skinny jeans, boots, and a form-fitting violet sweater from the wardrobe, then followed the aroma of food to the kitchen.

Where she found a redheaded female in ripped-up jeans and a lacy fuchsia corset doing dishes.

"Breakfast is on the table," she said with a perky smile.

"And you are..?" She'd better not be one of Azagoth's bedmates. Not that Lilliana was jealous. Offended, yes. Jealous, hardly.

The female wiped suds off her cheek with the back of her hand. "I'm Cataclysm. Call me Cat."

"Azagoth failed to mention that he has a fallen angel for a cook."

"He hired me this morning. And I'm Unfallen, not True Fallen."

Meaning she'd been expelled from Heaven, but she wouldn't be evil to the point of no return until she entered Sheoul and became a True Fallen.

"So you're trying to earn your way back into Heaven, huh? I can think of better ways to do that than working for the Grim Reaper."

She shrugged as she shoved a cast iron pan under a stream of hot water. "Life in the human realm with no angelic powers is dangerous for Unfallen. Here I'm protected from demons and angels alike. It's a good gig. I wasn't about to turn it down. Especially because suddenly, everyone is working overtime to drag Unfallens into Sheoul. I was almost caught twice in the last week."

Lilliana found a towel to dry dishes and stepped up to the counter. "Why the urgency?"

Cat snatched the towel from Lilliana and pointed to the table, which was loaded with pancakes, bacon, some sort of egg casserole, and mixed fruit. It was enough to feed half a dozen humans, but Lilliana figured she could down most of it herself. She'd always had a healthy appetite, and food was a guilt-free pleasure.

"Sit," Cat said. "And I don't know what's up, but everyone's scared. Just six days ago, one of my friends was dragged into Hell. When I saw her yesterday..." She shuddered. "She tried to force me into Sheoul. So, here I am."

As far as fallen angels went, Cat didn't seem too bad. Besides, Lilliana didn't have any room to judge, given her own disgraced status.

"So," she said, as she filled a plate with food. "What did you do to get the boot?"

Cat bowed her head. "I fell into temptation."

"Sex with a demon?" Lilliana slathered butter and syrup on the pancakes.

"A demon?" Cat wrinkled her nose. "No. Gross. Although...have you ever met a Seminus demon? Because if there's a demon out there who can tempt an angel..."

She fanned her face, and Lilliana rolled her eyes. Yes, the sex demons were legendary lovers who, as a species, had gotten more than one female angel kicked out of Heaven, but was having a half-an-hour-long orgasm really worth the risk?

Okay, maybe.

"Anyway," Cat continued, "do you know the Four Horsemen's ex-Heavenly Watcher, Gethel?"

The bite of fruit in Lilliana's mouth soured. "The evil bitch who wanted to start the Apocalypse by slaughtering one of the Horsemen's children? And who is now carrying Satan's baby? That Gethel?"

"Yes," she said wryly. "I see you know who I'm talking about.

Anyway, I was her apprentice when she was still an angel. She made me do a lot of things that were questionable, but I did them anyway. Who was I to question the great Gethel, Heavenly Watcher to the Four Horsemen of the Apocalypse, you know? By the time I figured out that she was working for Team Evil, it was too late. I was in too deep."

"And you were punished by expulsion."

"Yep." She held up a pitcher of orange juice, but Lilliana shook her head. "So here I am. Thank you for giving me this chance. I was starting to get scared. It's very dangerous for my kind out there right now."

Footsteps signaled an approach, and a moment later Azagoth entered, looking scrumptious in black jeans, a forest green Henley, and Dr. Martens. His gaze traveled up and down her body, and her cheeks grew hot as her shower escapade roared back into her head.

"I see you've met your assistant," he drawled.

"Assistant?"

He swiped a grape from the fruit tray and popped it into his mouth. "Cataclysm is here to handle all your needs. Her chamber is down the hall."

"I...um...why?"

"Because Zhubaal has enough to do already." He went for a slice of apple next. "And you were right about my realm being no prize for someone like you. The least I can do is make this punishment of yours more tolerable. So for as long as you're here and you want her, Cat will be as well."

Okay, so now she felt like a piece of shit. Cat was here for her, so when Lilliana left with the *chronoglass*, Cat would be out of a job and a home, and she'd be vulnerable to anyone who wanted to hurt her or force her into Hell to complete her fall.

Dammit, she did not need this complication. She wanted to get out of here, and now she had Cat's future to consider.

"Well, thank you," she said as she pushed to her feet. "Did you come for breakfast? I'm just finishing up—"

"I came to ask if you'd take me someplace."

"Ask?" She snorted. "Is this going to be like last time?"

He swore, and yup, looked like they were in for a repeat of the drill sergeant routine. So she was shocked when he said, "Will you please take me someplace? I'd really like to get out of here for a little while."

"You're lucky I have nothing better to do," she said, only half-teasing.

She'd planned to spend the day in his library and wandering around his realm in search of anything that might help her get the *chronoglass* out. She doubted she'd find a moving dolly, but there were millions of items with the mystical power to render even the heaviest items much lighter. A lot of spells, too.

Azagoth led her out into the hall, where he started in the direction of the library. "We'll find something for you to do."

"Like what?" Walking next to him, she waited for a crude comeback like, "You can do me," but he didn't. He was serious.

"I don't know," he said. "But I was thinking of creating a new level in the Inner Sanctum, one appropriate for demons who aren't evil."

"All demons are evil. That's why they're demons."

He shook his head. "Just as there are angels and humans who are bad, there are demons who are good." He slowed to let a *griminion* scurry past. "There's good and bad in everyone, Lilliana. Some just have to work harder than others to overcome their nature."

She supposed that was true, but boy, did it ever fly in the face of everything she'd ever been taught in battle angel classes.

"What do you do with these 'good' demons now?"

"I send them to the first level, which is a vacation spot compared to the others," he said. "And I authorize their reincarnations first."

"Aw, look, there *is* some good in you," she teased.

He laughed. "Sending non-evil entities back into the world isn't out of the goodness of my heart. It floods Sheoul with neutrality, which means the truly evil demons will pay any price for me to authorize the reincarnation of evil souls." He winked. "I'm very open to bribes."

Charming.

"Why are you being so nice and talkative all of a sudden?"

"I wouldn't go so far as to say, *nice*, but you are my mate, and this is your realm now too. *Cold and dreary* as it is," he added. Ouch. He still had a bite, didn't he? "You need to have your own space and purpose."

Lilliana could just shake her head. How could someone who was so awful to his children be so thoughtful to someone he barely knew?

"People in Heaven think you're a monster, you know."

"I am." He pegged her with a dark stare. "Don't let my calm exterior fool you. There's a beast inside me that's capable of horrors you can't imagine."

She didn't doubt that.

They arrived at the library, where a fire was roaring in the hearth, but the temperature in the room was more akin to someone having left the freezer door open.

"Oh, and just FYI, something I forgot to mention last time." She shrugged like it was no big deal, but it kind of was. "There are a handful of fallen angels who can sense entries into the *shrowd*, and they make it their mission to destroy any angel who travels through time. It's rare that they find their target, but when they do..." She shuddered. She'd come up against them twice, and her mother had lost her life to the bastards.

"Any angel, fallen or not, who dares to challenge me will spend all eternity as artwork in my great hall."

She frowned, remembering all of the grotesque statues. The ones that looked like humans, demons, and...angels...in agony.

"Wait. So all of the sculptures in your..."

"Yes. Instead of sending their souls to Sheoul-gra, I bound them in statue. Some of them have been there for thousands of years. I'll bet they're quite insane by now."

"You can...you can even do that to angels? Even if they haven't turned evil? Their souls should automatically return to Heaven."

He shrugged. "I'm the Grim Fucking Reaper. This is my domain, and if I want to keep a soul, I can." He shot her a sideways glance. "I told you I'm a monster."

She'd be wise to remember that.

Because holy shit.

Inhaling the dusty tobacco scent of the library, she started toward the mirror, but something crunched under her feet. "I'm sorry." She sidestepped, cringing at whatever it was that she'd broken. It looked like a crystal chess piece.

"S'okay." He swiped the bits of crystal off the floor and tossed them into the trash. "It was broken before you stepped on it."

Realization dawned. "*You* broke it. Why?"

"It was a gift from Methicore," he said gruffly. "I want all reminders of him gone."

Her heart clenched. She'd sent a rare singing iris from Heaven's Covenant Mountain to her father once, hoping to open the lines of communication before their first meeting. When she'd finally met him face to face, he'd returned it to her.

Broken into three pieces.

"I don't understand how you can reject him so thoroughly." She searched his face for some sign of regret, but she saw nothing in his expression but disgust for his son. "What did he do to you?"

He looked startled that she'd ask. "Why do you want to know?"

"Weren't you just on the 'we're mates' trip a few minutes ago?" she reminded him. "Maybe we should, I don't know, talk?"

He swept some papers off his desk and into the trash can, covering up the broken chess piece. "Maybe I'll talk when you're ready to do the same."

"I've answered every question you've asked."

"Really?" Crossing his arms over his broad chest, he pegged her with a hard stare. "Then why don't you tell me why you're really here? Because something isn't adding up, Lilliana."

"I told you," she ground out. Was he never going to let this go? "I was given a choice between two evils. I picked this one."

"How sweet. But I know that. I want to know what made coming here more appealing than remaining in Heaven, even in the diminished capacity they offered you."

*Oh, I figured it would be easy to steal your property, get out of here, and be restored to grace.*

She probably shouldn't say that. She'd try another truth.

"Maybe I'm not ready to discuss my private humiliation with someone I just met."

A slow, bitter smile spread over his face. "Exactly."

"So your son is your private humiliation?" She probably shouldn't be pushing him on this when he'd made it clear he didn't want to talk, but dammit, she wanted to know what it took to make a father reject his own offspring.

"Private?" he laughed. "No, he's a very public humiliation." He gestured to the *chronoglass.* "Enough talk. I'm anxious to see where we're going. Somewhere warm, I hope."

"Sure," she said sweetly. "Let's go."

# Chapter Nine

They stepped out onto a frozen wasteland with nothing but ice and snow as far as the eye could see. Not even the sky could offer color or texture. Gray, featureless clouds had turned it into a blanket of blah.

Lilliana watched Azagoth carefully for signs of annoyance that she'd brought him to someplace so cold and barren, but just like when she'd dropped them into the Egyptian desert, his expression conveyed awe and excitement. He wasn't at all pissed off. If anything, he lit up like the Christmas tree in Times Square.

"This isn't someplace warm, but I forgive you." Grinning like a loon, he extended his hands and let a flurry of snowflakes sift between his fingers. "I hate the snow," he said, but she never would have guessed that with the way he was acting. He even stuck out his tongue and caught a flake on the very tip. She hated that there was something very appealing...and sensual...about that.

"For someone who doesn't like the snow, you seem pretty taken with it."

"Because I haven't seen it in eons." He scooped up a handful, and with a sly grin, he beaned her with it. Right in the forehead. "Gotcha."

Sputtering, she wiped snow out of her eyes. "Really? How old are you?"

Bam! Another one hit her in the chest, and then he was running away from her, his boots slipping on the ice, but he never fell. She wanted to be annoyed, but his blatant joy was infectious. Smiling in spite of herself, she hurled her own snowball at him, using just a touch of angel flair to control its trajectory. Damn, it was nice being away from his realm and being able to use her powers again.

It nailed him in the back of his head.

"Payback's a bitch, Azagoth!"

His laughter rang out in the still Arctic air as he skidded and whirled. And then, and as far as she could tell, he went down intentionally to roll in the snow.

"This is amazing!" he called out.

Yes, it really was. How many people could say that they'd witnessed the infamously grumpy ruler of the dead romping like a child on a school snow day? All he needed was an inner tube and a hill.

Abruptly, he leaped to his feet and lifted his face to the gray sky. "Clouds," he said. "What a strange thing to miss." He swung around to face her, his big body as relaxed and loose as she'd seen it. "Before I fell, I used to make clouds in Heaven sometimes, mainly for a change from the blue sky. I made them orange, just for fun."

How could this male be the same as the one renowned for his ruthlessness as an angel? The history books she'd read had left out a *lot*.

"I made rainbow clouds," she said, encouraged to have finally found something in common besides a father-child hate relationship. "It was back when I was young and we were learning how to control our ability to think things into existence." Channeling a trickle of power, she painted a swath of primary colors across the sky before letting the gray drab take over again. "My instructor got all pissy and changed them to white, like everyone else's."

"So your rebel nature extends beyond taking me to the crappiest places you can think of?"

*Busted.* "I suppose."

"Rebels aren't exactly tolerated in Heaven." He grinned, a heart-stopping, breathtaking grin that made her go hot right here in the middle of a deep freeze. "I like it."

Suddenly, another snowball came at her and popped her in the chest. She hadn't even seen him throw it.

"Oh, yeah?" With nothing more than a thought, she sent a huge wall of snow at him. His eyes flared, and for a moment she thought he'd flash himself out of the way, but instead he stood there, his expression almost blissful as it crashed over him like a giant wave.

As he shook snow out of his clothes and hair, he chuckled. And then, in a motion so fast she didn't see it, he was on top of her.

They went down in a tumble of limbs and snow, his body coming to a rest on top of hers as she sprawled on her back. She didn't feel the cold—not like most beings did, anyway. But she couldn't miss the stark contrast of the ice beneath her and the warmth of Azagoth's big frame above her.

"Did you really think you could get away with that?" He tweaked her nose, and she was momentarily speechless at the playfulness. This male with wild, windblown hair frosted with snow couldn't be the same guy who possessed the power to destroy souls. The same guy who had so coldly thrown his son out of his realm.

The same guy who had given her an assistant, free access to his realm, and pretty much the freedom to do whatever she wanted.

Maybe, just maybe, he wasn't all that bad.

Smiling up at him, she said, "Maybe I let you catch me."

One corner of his mouth twitched in an evil smile, and she knew she'd stepped into a trap of her own making. "Then you wanted to end up like this, did you?" Shifting, he settled more fully on top of her. His thigh slipped between hers, and she felt the blatant stab of an erection against her belly. "You wanted to feel my body against yours?"

*No. Yes.* Oh, dear Lord, she didn't know what she wanted. Not when he rocked his hips, driving that big bulge against her core. She sucked in a breath, and unbidden, her body arched upward to meet him. Her breasts pressed into his chest, and she wondered how they'd feel in his palms.

"I thought so," he purred. So arrogant. And really, so right. The bastard.

She bucked, but even she had to admit it was a half-hearted effort. Same as when she said, "Get off of me."

"I'll consider it." He dipped his head and nuzzled her throat.

The shock of his cold nose on her skin made her hiss, but a heartbeat later, his lips sliding along the curve of her neck made her moan. One of his hands tangled in her hair to hold her steady for his kisses, and the other came down lightly on her waist. His palm rubbed slow circles as it moved upward until his fingers brushed the underside of her breast, and a shock of desire shot straight to her groin.

It startled her how quickly need ignited her blood, and her heart beat so hard she could hear her pulse in her ears. Without thinking, she gripped his arms and drew him closer, until she could feel his nipples harden through his shirt. How long had it been since she'd given in to a male like this? Not since Hutriel, and even then, she'd never had the desire to bite every button off a shirt just to get to his powerful chest.

Then again, Hutriel had been all about "proper" lovemaking. And proper lovemaking meant an orderly removal of clothing, and afterward, there could be no lingering looks or touches. There was no penetration, just a tangling of bodies and limbs as you surrendered your soul to the merging. An instant, all-over body orgasm was the reward, an orgasm that could last for hours and leave you drained for a day.

Sure, it was awesome with a capital *A*. But for all the soul-melding, it wasn't especially intimate. Not on a physical level. And that was something she had desperately craved. Hell, she'd craved closeness of any kind after being denied it following her mother's death and her father's rejection.

Her father's *third* rejection.

Azagoth shifted, dropping his hand to her thigh and lifting her leg to his waist, putting her core in full contact with his erection. Ecstasy speared her, spreading through her sex and warming her so quickly that she might as well have been in a sauna, not in ten below Arctic temperatures.

Arching against her, he slid his hand beneath her shirt. Oh, damn, the skin-to-skin contact was decadent, but as he began to smooth his palm upward, she went taut. She shouldn't be doing this. Not when she was planning to leave. It wasn't fair to either of them.

*You're worrying about him? The male who serviced seventy-two angels a year, plus the devil-only-knew how many demon females?*

Yeah, she was kind of an idiot. But how could she feel such conflicting emotions all at once? How could she hate him but crave him? Want him but at the same time want to push him away?

The pull of the mirror rescued her from her own scrambled thoughts. She cleared her throat. "Are you still considering getting off of me?"

His voice was a silken whisper against her throat. "I'm

considering getting you off."

Heat flushed her body. "We're going back in a few minutes."

"It can't be time." His mouth trailed upward, along her jugular, and shivers of pleasure shot through her. "We just got here."

It felt that way to her, too, and truth be told, she felt a twinge of disappointment herself. She'd meant to take him to the most horrible, boring place she could, and he'd loved it. She'd ended up having fun.

Total fail.

"Sorry, but—" She broke off, sucking air as his lips captured her earlobe. How could such a small thing feel so good?

"But what?" He traced the shell of her ear with his tongue. So. Very. Good.

The tug of the mirror intensified, becoming a buzz that drowned out all the pleasant things Azagoth was doing to her.

"But we have to go."

His head came up, and his gaze bored into hers. "I don't want to go."

Crazily, neither did she.

But the *chronoglass* had other plans, and a moment later, they were back in Azagoth's office, lying on the carpet.

He was still on top of her.

And his hand had moved to her breast. But the look on his face said that he was anything but happy to be back. His eyes were wild, glinting with anger and what she thought might be confusion.

He'd freaked out last time when they'd come back, but she'd never found out why. She'd written it off as Azagoth being Azagoth, but twice now was too weird to ignore.

He looked down at her, fangs jutting from his upper jaw. Those things probably shouldn't be a turn-on, but then, she was rapidly discovering that there were a lot of things about Azagoth that shouldn't be sexy.

And *way* too many that should.

"Hey." She palmed his cheek, letting her thumb stroke the contour of his blade-sharp cheekbone. "What's wrong?"

"Not...used...to..." He broke off, panting, his lips peeled back in agony. "Emotion."

Emotion? How could he not be used to emotion? She'd seen him pissed as hell. She'd seen him smile. She'd seen him happy as a puppy in a meadow during their time travel jaunts.

But whatever was going on, it was clear he was in pain.

"Hey." She tilted his face down, forcing him to look at her. His gaze was glassy, tortured, and so very different from how it had been a moment ago. "I liked it better when you were kissing my neck." He groaned, his teeth clenched as if he was fighting with himself. Gently, she tapped on his cheek. "Focus. Come on, rein it in."

"Can't. Worse than...last time."

Shit. She'd seen something similar before, when she'd been a young angel in battle training. The male named Dreshone had been an empath with such strong abilities that it had been hard for him to function. He'd undergone a procedure to have his ability minimized, but the price had been a big one; his own emotions had been dulled, which had made him an extremely lethal warrior, but once per decade, he'd suffered a meltdown of uncontrollable emotion that had required lockup to prevent him from hurting anyone or himself.

But as far as she knew, Azagoth wasn't an empath, so what was going on?

"Azagoth, listen to me—" He snarled and started to push off of her, but she gripped his biceps hard and dragged him back down. "No. You aren't running again."

His deep growl rumbled through her body, reigniting the fire that had been burning her blood when they'd been lying in the snow. And wasn't it funny that his anger was turning her on as much as his lips had been.

"Don't...want to...hurt you."

Yeah, she didn't want that, either. "You won't. You've never hurt any of the angels Heaven sent to you over the centuries." News of that nature would have been the talk of the angelic airwaves.

"I never felt like...this."

Maybe time travel had an adverse effect on him. "Just focus," she said softly. "Focus on me."

His gaze locked with hers, and she saw the moment he went from furious to...well, furious *and* aroused. And she knew, in that moment, that no matter what happened next, nothing between them would be the same again.

# Chapter Ten

Azagoth concentrated on the female beneath him, his body a mass of writhing, twisting contradictions. Like the last time he'd come back from time travel, he was reeling from emotions he couldn't handle.

Now it was happening again, only on a grander scale. The fissure that had opened inside him last time had cracked open further, leaving him overwhelmed with feelings. Joy, sadness, anger, jealousy. He wasn't even sure what event or person each emotion was attached to. It was just all bubbling out, as if thousands of years' worth of denied feelings were breaking free of their bonds.

*This was what you wanted, asshole. You wanted to feel. Be careful what you wish for.*

True enough. He'd been so cold inside for so long. And now he was cold *and* insane.

Distantly, he heard Lilliana talking. Felt her fingers digging into his arms. Felt her thighs clamping around his hips to hold him still. Felt her core pressed firmly against his raging erection.

Focus. He tried gathering the maelstrom of emotions together and forcing them down, back into the fissure. *Focus.* Reaching deep, he tried to separate out each one and associate it with an event, a person, anything to understand why he'd be so angry or jealous, but each time an image started to form, it scattered to the wind and was replaced by a black hole of fury.

*Focus!*

The female beneath him shifted, tugging him closer, rubbing her sex against his. Whether or not it was intentional didn't matter. He instantly locked up as his body took command of his mind and did the focus thing.

Of course, the focus was all in his dick. Whatever. He'd roll with it.

Zeroing in on Lilliana, he panted through the gnawing tension that made him feel as if he could explode into violence and death to become the corrupted monster that legend—and a few firsthand accounts—had made him out to be.

As he dropped his mouth to hers, a thread of guilt wove its way through the messy tangle of emotions that were fading to the background. He was using her. Doing to her what all the females before her had done to him. He'd been a stud for hire for Heaven, and demon females only came to him for bragging rights. Oh, sure, he fucked them well, but ultimately, all they wanted from him was sex. For pleasure or for other reasons, he was nothing but a lay and a means to an end.

And now he was using Lilliana to bring him out of an emotional overload he couldn't handle.

Also...what the fuck. When had he started having regrets or caring about anyone but himself? There was a reason he'd volunteered for Grim Reaper duty, and it sure as hell wasn't so he could go all Dear Diary about shit like being used.

Lilliana's hands were stroking his arms now, her slow, light touch soothing his mood but stoking his lust.

*Focusfocusfocus...*

"Azagoth," she whispered against his mouth, bringing him right back to the place he needed to be.

He slid his hand under her shirt again, caressing her smooth, taut skin as he kissed her quiet. But this wasn't enough. Not nearly enough.

With a growl, he gripped her shirt and tore through it as if it were paper. And glory be, like most angels, she wasn't wearing a bra.

Her gorgeous eyes watched him with curiosity and desire as he lowered his head to take one berry-red nipple into his mouth. Licking and sucking eagerly, he cupped the other breast, filling his palm with her warm flesh as he settled more fully between her thighs. His cock was aching like a sonofabitch behind his fly, and he shifted again so he could reach between their bodies and unzip. While he was down there, he yanked open the buttons on her jeans and drove his hand inside.

Lilliana gasped as his fingers found her center and stroked the silk fabric of her underwear.

"How many lovers have you had, angel?" He kissed the swell of her breasts and worked his way down her belly.

"One," she breathed. "Just one. And I don't want to talk about him."

Neither did he. Partly because he didn't want any other male to be here right now, and partly because he'd just had the strangest urge to arrange for that male's painful death.

Eager to wipe the bastard from her memory, he reared back on his heels and yanked her boots off, followed by her jeans and underwear. It was all done in a matter of seconds, and then his clothes joined hers on the floor, torn and wadded.

Ah, damn, she was gorgeous, sprawling naked in front of him like a feast to be savored. Her hair fanned out in silky waves on the Persian rug, her kiss-swollen mouth parted for her panting breaths, and her thighs spread just enough to catch a glimpse of the bare, glistening female flesh between them.

Her gaze dropped to his groin, and at the sight of his thick sex, her eyes flared. Oh, yeah, she wanted it.

Smiling, he wrapped his hand around his cock and stroked. The tip of her tongue came out to swipe her bottom lip, and he groaned at the sudden image of those lips wrapped around his shaft, that tongue flicking and laving.

Releasing himself, he leaned forward and cupped her intimately. Fuck, she was burning hot down there, and he groaned again as he pushed a finger between her folds. Every cell in his body was vibrating as he dragged his fingertip through her wet heat to that swollen knot of nerves that made her gasp.

He stroked, lightly at first, avoiding the sensitive tip. In moments she was panting and grinding, arching into him and riding his hand as her taut body chased the pleasure he was giving her. Holy hell, she was a wild thing, gripping him so hard her nails dug into his skin. He had to taste her. It wasn't a desire; it was almost a biological imperative.

Jacking his body off of her, he reared back, hooked his hands under her hips, and dove between her luscious thighs. He buried his face against her sex, reveling in how slick her flesh was against his mouth. He spread her wide with his thumbs as he used the flat of his tongue to lick right up her center.

She cried out as the tip of his tongue clipped her clit. He did it again, and she cried louder, her body quivering, her fingers clamped on his scalp to hold him exactly where she needed him.

She tasted like sugar cane and passion fruit, clean grass and crystal water, all things he hadn't seen, felt, or tasted in eons.

"Azagoth," she gasped. "I'm going to...oh, *yes.*"

She bucked wildly, tossing her head back and forth, her body straining and her hips lifting off the floor as she came. *Beautiful*, he thought. So. Fucking. Beautiful.

Even before she came down, he mounted her, desperate to get inside and feel something besides the cold.

"Wait," she breathed, reaching for him. "Let me—"

Panting, crazy with need, he started to insert a finger to test her tightness...and froze.

Betrayal squeezed him like a vise, and all the emotions he'd managed to put away began to rise to the surface again.

"You lied," he croaked. "You're a virgin."

"No," she said firmly. "I've joined with a male in the way of angels."

Some might see the whole soul-sex thing as, well, sex, but even as an angel, he'd preferred the messy, downright dirty physical sex that humans had. So maybe she hadn't lied, but she hadn't been completely honest, either.

Sitting up, she palmed his chest, holding him with her gaze. "You're getting that crazy look again." She dragged her hand down, over his sternum, his abs, and finally, with a shaking hand, she grasped his cock.

"Shit," he gasped.

She had him now. He was hers for the taking, and as her hand began to move, so did his hips. He pumped into her closed fist, his hips pistoning back and forth as she worked him.

His head fell back, and he heard himself talking, swearing...he wasn't sure. All he knew was that stinging, molten heat was building in his balls and shaft, and when she squeezed him harder, sweat bloomed on his skin.

Sweat. He never sweated.

"Fuck," he breathed. "Oh, damn...Lilli..."

She sped up the pumping rhythm, and then her other hand joined the party, cupping his balls and rolling them in her palm.

"Tell me what to do," she whispered, but he didn't have the

breath to tell her a damned thing. What she was doing was just fine.

"Just...ah...yes."

His climax was a spiraling, hot coil of bliss that, for a single, glorious moment, shattered the ice that had encased his soul for so long. He convulsed with the intensity of it, the absolute joy of truly *feeling* a release.

Watching her as she watched him set him off again, and another searing orgasm blew his mind and body apart.

As it waned, he folded his hand over hers and helped her ease him down as his hyper-sensitive cock jerked reflexively in her palm.

"Wow," she breathed. "I've never done that before."

His hand shook as he reached for a tissue on his desk. "What, you've never made a guy come with your hand?"

"My ex thought physical sex was repulsive."

"Your ex was a dipshit." Gently, he wiped his seed off her skin and then lifted her off the floor and carried her to the sofa in front of the fire.

Climbing onto the cushions next to her, he gathered her against him and tugged a blanket down over them both. She stiffened at first, and he understood that. He couldn't remember the last time he'd lingered with a female after sex. They came here for one purpose, and it wasn't to be cuddled.

He'd never longed for any kind of connection after sex either, so this thing with Lilliana...it felt foreign. And yet, it felt right.

And as she rested her hand on his chest, directly over his heart, he *knew* it was right. Now he just had to figure out how to stop the emotional blowouts he kept having when they came back from time travel. Of course, if sex was the key to stopping them in their tracks, well, he supposed he could deal.

He just hoped Lilliana could, too.

# Chapter Eleven

Azagoth didn't know how long they laid on his couch, bodies tangled together as they caught their breath, but eventually, Lilliana, her head on his chest, began to trace lazy circles on his abs. The intimacy of it—of all of this—left him in a state of awe and, truth be told, anxiety. Somehow, she was drawing emotion out of him, and he couldn't help but wonder how damaging that could be.

"Azagoth?"

"Hmm?"

"Why did you volunteer for this job?" Postcoital drowsiness permeated her voice, and he experienced a flicker of male pride that he was responsible. "To lose your angelic status and live among demons?"

He shrugged, knocking one of the pillows off the sofa. "Someone had to do it."

"Bullshit." Her fingers skated over his rib cage in an almost playful sweep. "I might be young, but I know that no one sacrifices freedom without a good reason."

He tucked one arm behind his head and gazed up at the wood-beamed ceiling. "Didn't you read everything you could find about me before you decided to become my mate? Surely you had an entire term devoted to me in history class."

"Three terms, actually." She drew the number 3 on his sternum. "You're quite the historical figure. The first term was devoted to your life as an angel known as Azrael and the events leading up to your expulsion, and the second and third terms were devoted to your life as Azagoth."

"I got three terms?" He grinned. "Nice."

But damn, the name Azrael brought back memories. And how odd was it that he preferred the memories he'd made as Azagoth over those that went with his Heavenly name?

"Yes, well," she said, "the history I learned painted you as an entitled playboy who chose to lose his wings because he'd rather rule an empty kingdom than follow others in paradise."

It figured that historians would twist the facts to fit whatever agenda they had. Angels were no more scrupulous than humans when it came to molding the truth into fact-based fiction.

"Then what's the point of asking why I chose this life if you already know?"

"Because only a fool believes everything they read or are told." She dragged the backs of her fingers up his sternum, and pleasant tingles followed in their wake. "So what's the real story?"

He supposed he owed her the truth, given what she was committing to. It was just so strange to owe anyone. *He* was the one who usually held all the I.O.U.s.

"I did it because I was tired of feeling," he said simply, because that's what his long-ass story boiled down to in the end.

Pushing up onto one elbow, she frowned down at him. "Feeling what?"

"Everything." He kept his gaze glued to a rough-cut beam overhead. "Did your history classes teach you that I was an empath?"

Her brow shot up. "But you were an interrogator with the Internal Corruption Investigation unit. Empaths aren't allowed. How can you torture people if you can feel everything your subject feels?"

"At the time, no one knew I was an empath. And it wasn't all torture," he said, maybe a little defensively. "Most of what I did for the ICI was ask questions. Being an empath gave me an edge when it came to detecting lies."

"Which is why you were the most successful ICI interrogator in history," she mused. "It was you who uncovered Satan's plot. You were unstoppable. Until you mysteriously quit and disappeared for a few centuries before returning to volunteer for the Grim Reaper gig."

Those few centuries had been the worst years of his life, so full of loneliness and regret. Funny how when you had no one to talk to, you relived everything you ever said and did, and when most of it wasn't pretty, you learned to hate yourself real fast.

"I quit because I was a cocky, spoiled, arrogant playboy, just like you said. I kicked ass at my job and I knew it, and then one day I got it wrong. I was so sure of myself that I mistook a young angel's fear for a family member for fear he'd get caught lying. Long story short, he was innocent, and he lost his wings because of me." He glanced over at her, expecting to see disgust on her face, but all he saw was curiosity. "Naturally, at the time I didn't blame my bad judgment on my arrogance. I blamed it on the fact that I wasn't a powerful enough empath. You know, if only I'd been even more empathic, I wouldn't have screwed up. So I did something stupid, a mystical spell went wrong, and one day I was the most empathic angel the world had ever seen."

She cocked her head, and her hair tickled his chest. "So what happened? You don't seem to be all that empathic to me."

"No kidding." There was a crack in the ceiling beam. He should get that fixed. "What happened is that my world went to shit. I couldn't be within a mile of a human or I'd feel everything they were feeling. Being within a hundred yards of an angel would drive their emotions and thoughts into my head like a knife. So I left ICI and isolated myself for two hundred years. It wasn't until a call was put out for volunteers to oversee Sheoul-gra that I realized I could do something useful again. The benefit being that here in the demon realm, my empathic ability doesn't work."

"I'll say," she muttered.

"What I didn't anticipate," he continued, "was that I'd lose more than my ability to feel what others feel. I've lost my ability to feel almost everything."

"You're saying you don't feel pain? Or anger? Or joy?"

"Anger stirs, but barely and not often. Otherwise..." He shrugged. "I've even lost my ability to feel heat. Only the ever-present biting cold. If not for the fire, I think my flesh would turn to ice."

"That's why the fire doesn't produce heat, isn't it? Because you absorb it all."

"Yes." He closed his eyes. "What I wouldn't give to be warm. Even when you took me to the desert, I could barely feel the sun on my skin." He took her hand and dragged it to his right pec, directly over the skull engulfed in flames tattoo. "These tattoos were designed to contain pain and emotion. I took them from one of the Four Horsemen, Thanatos, in hopes that I could access the pain. And for a while, I did." He sighed. "It was...glorious."

"Pain was glorious?"

He took a strand of her hair between his fingers. It was so soft, so different from the hard, cold texture of the world he'd created around him.

"I was happy to feel something...anything." Bringing the curl of hair to his nose, he inhaled her fresh scent. "But it didn't take long to drain the tats. Now they're as empty as I am."

"I'm sorry, Azagoth." Her pity put an end to this party, and he sat up with a curse. "Oh, no," she said, grasping his wrist. "What's wrong?"

He didn't need—or want—her sympathy. He'd made his bed and he'd lie in it. With her, preferably. But he did want her to understand that it wasn't her job to make him happy. Nothing and no one could do that.

"What's wrong is that none of this is fair to you," he said, breaking her hold so he could swing his legs over the side of the sofa and stare into the fire. "I wanted a mate. I didn't expect complications."

"So I'm a complication?"

He winced. "Not...you. This situation. I'm not usually impulsive, but I asked for a mate before considering what life down here would be like for her. A dark, creepy realm and a mate who can't feel anything. What a catch I am."

Oh, look, the pity party had started up again. Rock on.

"You're wrong," she said fiercely. "You can feel. I watched you in the sand and the snow, and I promise that what I felt coming off of you was sheer happiness. You felt that. I saw you. I *felt* you."

"And trust me," he said, "those were the best two hours of my life. Then we came back." He caught a glimpse of the *chronoglass* out of the corner of his eye, and he swore the thing mocked him. "When I was with you in the desert and Arctic, it felt as if the chains holding my emotions at bay broke. But the moment we return, all that emotion shifts to pain, like my body can't handle it."

"Maybe it can't. Your emotions have been bottled up for a long time. Maybe they're starting to break free." She shifted on the sofa so she was sitting cross-legged and facing him, the blanket tugged up to cover her all the way to her breasts. Shame, that. "You're empathic, but not down here, right?"

"Right. Except..."

"Except what?" She poked him in the thigh, startling him with her playfulness. "Tell me. I can handle it."

He scrubbed his hand over his face, knowing it probably wasn't wise to talk about other females when you were with the one you just made come.

*Just spit it out.*

"The only time I feel anything is when I'm fucking," he blurted. "And it's not even my emotions I'm feeling. It's the female's. So imagine how awesome it is to be servicing an angel who doesn't even want to be here. Who loathes me or is terrified. Yeah, it's great. But you know what the worst part of it is? Some small part of me is grateful even to feel their disgust and fear, because at least it's *something*."

Damn, that was some nice babbling, wasn't it?

He risked a brief peek at her, expecting to see revulsion, but all he saw was more pity. Which was somehow worse.

"Okay," she breathed. "So you can't feel your own emotions. But you *used* to have them down here, right?"

"Yes, thanks for the recap."

She huffed. "What I'm trying to say is that maybe this is the beginning of you starting to feel again. It started happening after the first time travel session, right?" At his nod, she continued. "So the time travel must be triggering it. Was it worse the first time or today?"

He thought about it for a moment. "Today, but you were a good distraction."

A shy smile turned up one corner of her mouth. "You're welcome." The blanket had fallen to expose deep cleavage and the delicate swells of her breasts, but sadly, she tugged it up to her throat. "But I was afraid I was going to lose you again for a minute there."

"When?"

She turned as red as a Sora demon's ass. "When you, ah...when your finger discovered..." She cursed and blurted, "Why was my virginity such an issue for you?"

It was his turn to curse. He'd done so many stupid things in his life, and the virginity thing was one of them. She was going to think he was a serious idiot.

*That's because you're an idiot.*

"Remember I told you about how I did something stupid and became a stronger empath?" At her nod, he scrubbed his face again. If he had any emotions, he'd be embarrassed. "That something I did was a female. A succubus. A virgin succubus."

"Oh...shit." Angels weren't supposed to fornicate with humans, let alone demons, but of all the demons, succubi were the most forbidden. Virgin succubi were the worst of the worst, and if caught, the offending angel would pay dearly—perhaps even with his wings.

"*Shit* doesn't even begin to cover it," he said gruffly. "And I didn't know she was a demon at the time."

Lilliana smiled wryly. "Isn't that what they all say?"

Probably. But he'd prided himself on being too smart to fall for any demon tricks, especially those coming from succubi.

"I thought she was a human sorceress," he explained. "I'd made a few, let's say *shady*, inquiries through underground networks about a spell or a token that could increase empathic powers. She said she could help. She was the perfect mix of vixen and maiden, and I fell for it."

"Wait...if you were an empath, why didn't you sense the fact that she wasn't human?"

"Because most breeds of succubi can project false emotion and mask their true identities with aphrodisiac magic. Virgin succubi, in particular, are impossible to detect as demons."

Lilliana shifted, and the sound of the blanket rasping against her naked body made his sex stir again. Quickly, he swiped his pants off the floor and threw them on.

"A succubus's virginity is priceless," she said as she watched him dress. "The moment her barrier is broken, a massive wave of power is released. People pay outrageous sums to deflower a virgin succubus and reap the benefits of that power. So why would she just give it to you when you didn't even know what she was?"

He sank back down on the couch. "Because when an angel deflowers a virgin succubus, she absorbs a huge amount of his power in return. Now, picture a succubus who possesses abilities generally available to angels." At her expression of horror, he laughed bitterly. Yeah, she got the picture. "Thanatos once accused me of being the Horsemen's father. I played it off like he was way off base, but the truth is that I did fuck Lilith." He remembered how sweet she'd been. How delicate. How fucking good she was at deception. "It was Lilith who granted me my wish to be more empathic. She was the virgin."

Lilliana sat back hard against the back of the couch, as if her body would no longer support her.

"Oh...wow." Her hand clutched the blanket so tightly that her knuckles were white. "So that's how she became so powerful...powerful enough to trick Reaver into sleeping with her and fathering the Horsemen."

"Everything comes with a consequence. I took her virginity and got what I wanted, but I also set into motion the events that almost led to the Apocalypse. She absorbed many of my powers, turning her into the most powerful succubus to ever live. Then she seduced Reaver, and the Four Horsemen of the Apocalypse were born."

"Holy crap." Lilliana flopped onto her back, eyes wide and staring at the ceiling. "You know, my life has been very boring compared to yours."

Unexpectedly, he laughed, a flat-out, genuine laugh as he stretched out beside her once again.

It was then that he noticed it. His lungs seized and his body trembled, and it took forever for his brain to process the reality as he stared into the fire.

For the first time in thousands of years, he felt the warmth from the flames.

# Chapter Twelve

It turned out that when someone informed you that they had deflowered the most infamous succubus in history and set off what would become major apocalyptic events, you shut down. At least, Lilliana did.

She'd lain there with Azagoth in surprisingly comfortable silence, her mind spinning with more questions. But eventually, she dozed off, and when she woke, Azagoth was gone. But fresh clothes had been laid out on the table next to the sofa, and next to the clothes was a tray containing a turkey sandwich, a bowl of fruit, an assortment of cheeses and crackers, and two decadent desserts. She decided she'd eat the caramel cheesecake first, and save the fudge truffle cake for last.

Whoever brought the food and clothes had also set out a pitcher of ice water, a pitcher of pomegranate juice, a bottle each of red and white wine, three different types of beer, two cans of cola, and a can of Sprite. Apparently, Azagoth wanted her to float out of here.

She looked around for the clothes he'd stripped off her, but they were gone, and a blast of heat bloomed in her cheeks at the memory. He'd been intense. Primal. A male drowning in a need he couldn't satiate without a female.

The moment she'd seen him suffering in emotion he couldn't contain, all she could think about was making it better, and when the tension inside him had shifted from confusion and violence to sex, she hadn't hesitated. Not until the moment of truth, when it looked as if intercourse was imminent.

She'd panicked a little, not because she was a virgin, but

because somehow joining with him like that would make things real between them, and she wasn't ready to go there. Not when she was still planning on leaving.

So it was probably a good thing he'd freaked about the virginity thing, but criminy, the reason for his spaz attack had blown her mind. He'd been seduced by the most infamous succubus in history. He'd *deflowered* the most infamous succubus in history.

Holy shit.

His actions had kicked off pretty much everything that had happened in the human, demon, and angelic worlds up until now. No wonder he'd taken this job. Even without the empathic curse that had driven him here, she'd bet he'd have volunteered anyway, purely out of guilt.

The overload of events and information from today turned her brain foggy, so she gave it a rest while she dressed and ate. The fudge truffle cake turned out to be almost as decadent as the orgasm Azagoth gave her, and she decided she definitely needed another piece later.

*A piece of cake...or of Azagoth?* Maybe she could have her cake and Azagoth too.

The thought made her blush as she finished eating, and then she went through his books for something to help her get the *chronoglass* out of here.

For the second time, the thought screamed through her in a blast of remorse.

Truly, Azagoth had been good to her. The big, scary Grim Reaper had done nothing but be nice. Oh, sure, he'd been a jackass at first, but then, she'd been a little hostile too. And to know that he'd been down here so long, unable to feel anything...it broke her heart.

Granted, being unable to feel was probably what kept him sane. Having to deal with evil twenty-four seven would make anyone who was sensitive to emotion crazy.

Several hours later, she'd found nothing helpful, and a small part of her was glad.

As she shoved the last book she'd thumbed through back onto a shelf, Cat poked her head through the doorway, and Lilliana jumped, startled by her own guilt. "I didn't mean to scare you," Cat said. "Can I bring you anything more to eat or drink?"

"Thank you, no." She studied the other woman, wondering just how intimate the relationship between them should be. Azagoth had hired her, but Lilliana could really use a friend down here.

Problem was, she didn't know how to go about it. She'd never had many friends. Time travelers had a tendency to illicit distrust in others. Lilliana's supervisor claimed it was because, deep down, others knew they wouldn't be able to resist the temptation to change history, and there was nothing angels hated more than reminders that they were so flawed.

Finally, Lilliana just threw it out there. "I was thinking about taking a walk. Would you like to join me?"

Cat grinned, flashing petite fangs that came standard issue for both Unfallen and True Fallen angels. "I'd be happy to."

"Really?" Lilliana blurted. "Why?"

Flames from the hearth cast an orange light on Cat's red hair, creating a gentle halo around her head, and for a moment, Lilliana could picture her as a full angel, her green eyes glinting with impish humor.

"I owe you and Azagoth for saving me," she said simply. "I like it here."

"You...*like* it?"

She nodded. "Very much. No one is hunting me, the *griminions* aren't bad once you get to know them, and Zhubaal is kind of hot."

Okie-dokie, then. They walked outside into the ever-present gray blah, and even though the chill in the air didn't bother her, she rubbed her arms. Everything outside of Azagoth's manor just *looked* cold and inhospitable.

"I've been exploring the surrounding buildings," she said to Cat. "They were once occupied, and there's a lot of stuff that was left behind."

"Who used to live here?"

"I have no idea," Lilliana said. "Azagoth has been a little tight-lipped."

"He's very odd. But in a good way," Cat added quickly. She said something else, but Lilliana's concentration had taken a sudden detour.

"Cat." She gripped the other female's shoulder, shutting her up. "Do you see that?"

Cat followed Lilliana's gaze to a patch of ground near the fountain in the center of the courtyard. "That's weird. Why would that one bit of land be—"

"Green," Lilliana whispered. "It's grass."

As they stood there, bright green blades of grass popped up, expanding outward, swallowing up the blackened earth as it went. When the grass reached a scraggly, leafless gray bush, color began to push up the thick, dead stems, and at the very tips of the branches, little pink buds popped out.

"What's going on?"

"Emotion," Lilliana breathed. "It makes sense. Azagoth said it himself. *I am Sheoul-gra.*" He'd said he'd been corrupted by evil, his emotions stripped away. And now, with his emotions starting to open up, his realm was reflecting that. Holy shit. "Where is he? I have to show him this."

Cat cringed. "He gave me a message for you. I forgot. I'm sorry I didn't tell you right away."

"It's okay." As she spoke, Lilliana couldn't take her eyes off of the transformation taking place in front of her. "What's the message?"

"He said he had to go to the Inner Sanctum. He didn't know when he'd be back."

Lilliana finally looked over at Cat. "Did he say why?"

"All I know is that a seriously yummy guy with a blue Mohawk came to visit, and they left together."

"Ah. That would be Hades." Too bad she hadn't been there to meet him. She was curious about the fallen angel who Azagoth had appointed as his Soul Keeper.

"*The* Hades?" Cat asked. "Wow. He's like a rock star. Does he come up from the Sanctum often?"

"I have no idea." Lilliana started walking, giving the new green patches a wide berth. Stepping on the fresh new life struck her as a jerk thing to do.

"Do you think Azagoth would let me see the Inner Sanctum?"

Lilliana jerked in surprise. "Why would you want to? By all accounts, it's a cesspool of suffering."

"I want to be reminded of why I want to earn my way back into Heaven."

Lilliana nearly tripped over her own feet. Overdosing on evil seemed like an extreme way to keep yourself on the straight and narrow path, but she supposed it was better than the alternative.

They wandered through the buildings Lilliana hadn't gotten to the other day. She'd planned to search for something to help with the *chronoglass*, but she was so curious about everything that searching for something specific took a backseat to simply exploring. They found classrooms complete with history books—human, demon, and angel. They found indoor and outdoor training and sports facilities. They even found what appeared to have been gardens. What *was* this place?

"This is such a waste," Cat said sadly. "These buildings were meant to be filled."

Yes, but with who? Or what?

Eventually, they made their way back to the main building, but Azagoth hadn't yet returned. Lilliana helped Cat cook dinner, and while they ate, Cat insisted that they watch a movie called *Magic Mike*. There hadn't been any magic, but *dayum*...Lilliana would never look at a male stripper the same way again.

As the credits rolled, Cat gathered their dinner plates. "I think I'm going to see if Zhubaal wants some company," she said with a sly smile that all but announced her lusty intent. "And maybe if you're lucky, Azagoth will be back soon."

Strangely, Lilliana hoped so. Not because the movie had pushed every one of her horny buttons, but because she was actually starting to like the guy.

*He's an asshole father.*

Okay, there was that. But what if he wasn't entirely to blame for whatever had gone down with Methicore? Now that she had a little distance, she could see a bit more clearly, and the guy had definitely struck her as a bit of an ass. But what could he have done to deserve the things his father had said to him?

Her own father's harsh words clanged in her ears as she showered and put on her nightgown and robe. Had she tried too hard to build a relationship with him? Had she not tried hard enough?

Frustrated by the questions she asked herself way too often, she shoved a pile of clean, folded clothes inside the wardrobe. The box holding the necklace Azagoth had given her tumbled out, and the shiny silver chain skittered across the floor.

Picking it up, she admired the delicate little key pendant and finely-wrought clasp. He'd given it to her with an order to wear it, but she hadn't, and he hadn't nagged her about it or gotten angry. But then, with his emotional void, she supposed he wouldn't have thrown a fit about it. Still, it had seemed important to him.

And it really was pretty...

She fastened it around her neck, and the cold silver warmed instantly on her skin.

As she climbed into bed, it didn't escape her notice that Azagoth's body did the same thing.

# Chapter Thirteen

Azagoth hadn't come home last night.

Inexplicably irritated, because yeah, why *wouldn't* someone be upset about getting an uninterrupted night's sleep, Lilliana skipped breakfast and stormed into his office, expecting to find him there.

Nothing. The fire roared in the hearth and his computer was humming softly, but the soul tunnel was closed and Azagoth was nowhere to be found.

Even more annoyed now, she went to the library, but he wasn't there, either. Fine, she thought as she stared at the *chronoglass*. She should use it. Go someplace without Azagoth, just as he'd done.

But even as she thought it, she knew she wouldn't do it. In all her years of existence, she'd never seen such unfettered joy in anyone, and she'd certainly never given it. Being able to give someone a gift like that made her feel good. Really good.

The door burst open and over six and a half feet of dangerously handsome male strode into the library. Black military-style pants and a black turtleneck made Azagoth seem even larger, sleeker, and deadlier, but then, he'd never come across as anything less than one hundred percent lethal grace. Raw power radiated from him like heat from one of Sheoul's lava lakes.

His eyes smoldered as he took in her jeans and pink tank top, and she felt the blood rush to her face at the memory of the last time he'd looked at her like that.

It was yesterday, when he'd made her come, right here where she was standing.

"Morning."

"Yes," she grumbled. "It is."

He cocked a dark eyebrow. "Something wrong? Is Cat not working out? I can find someone else—"

"No!" she said quickly, and then dialed it back a little. "No. I like Cat."

"Then what's bothering you?"

She hesitated. At what point in their relationship should she start questioning his whereabouts? Her relationship with Hutriel had never reached that point. He'd blown his lid the first time she'd asked him why he was late for their dinner date, and after that, she'd only asked to piss him off. Which it did. Every single time.

"Lilliana?" he asked softly. "Are you going to tell me what's going on?"

Feeling a bit like a fishwife, she blurted, "Where have you been?"

"Didn't Cat tell you? I went to the Inner Sanctum with Hades."

"She told me," Lilliana assured him. He'd mentioned not being one for second chances, and she definitely didn't want to get Cat fired. "But I didn't expect you to be gone all night. Why did it take so long?"

His expression turned grave. "I had business to take care of."

"That's it? Just...business?"

"I'm the Grim Reaper, Lilli. I have business with demons sometimes."

*Lilli.* He'd called her that yesterday too, when she'd had her hand curled around his erection, her palm stroking the stiff length as he moaned in ecstasy.

*"Fuck," he breathed. "Oh, damn...Lilli..."*

No one had ever given her a nickname. Warmth suffused her, but she let herself linger on the name only for a moment before getting back to the subject at hand.

"What in the world can dead demons do for you?" she asked.

"Newly acquired demons have information I want and need. It's how I make bargains and find new souls to take. Trust me, you don't want details."

No doubt he was right. Still... "If I did want details, would you tell me?"

"Yes." He gave her a look that chilled her to the bone, and she knew for sure she didn't want to know the particulars of what he did with the souls. "But please don't ask."

*You got it, buddy.*

She wasn't sure where to go from there, but Azagoth seemed to have no such problem. He strode over to her, hauled her against him, and laid a kiss on her that had her melting into him like softened butter.

"I missed you," he whispered huskily against her lips. "All I could think about was getting back to you and finishing what we started here in the library. You made me feel, Lilli. For the first time in...fuck, I don't know, I felt something other than the cold."

Oh, yes, she felt it too, in the bulge nudging at her center. Instantly, her breasts grew heavy and a warm rush of wetness blossomed between her legs.

"Azagoth?" she murmured, as he kissed a hot path from her mouth to her ear. "Have you been outside?"

"No." He nibbled her earlobe and her knees nearly gave out. "Why?"

He didn't know about the new growth out there, the signs of hope that were sprouting out of the black ash of his realm. But it wasn't enough to tell him...she wanted to show him.

"No reason." She moaned as he traced the shell of her ear with his tongue. "Maybe we could take a walk?"

Pulling back, he looked down at her. "A walk? Here?" He jerked his head toward the *chronoglass*. "How about somewhere more interesting. Where to today?"

She hadn't actually thought about it. The last two journeys had been designed to thoroughly annoy him, but he'd been ecstatic. She no longer wanted to fool around like that. He deserved better.

"Maybe you should suggest a time and place," she offered. "Surely there's someplace you want to go."

With tenderness that shocked her even though he'd been nothing but gentle with her, he grazed a knuckle over her cheek. "I've been locked inside my realm for thousands of years. Anywhere you take me is going to be amazing."

She snorted. "Oh, I doubt that. London during the Black Death was a drag." Taking his hand, she guided him to the mirror. "Where do you want to go?"

"A beach," he said without hesitation. "On the Oregon coast. I've always wanted to see the tide pools." He squeezed her hand. "No, wait. Let's do that tomorrow. I feel like going somewhere tropical."

Ooh, tropical. She'd been a tropical waters girl since she'd tasted her first coconut. "I know just the place." An image appeared on the mirror's surface, blue waters and golden sand beckoning. Clinging tightly to Azagoth's hand, she stepped into the *chronoglass* and out into a sultry breeze.

Azagoth inhaled, and his entire body relaxed, as if the sun and air had drained every last drop of tension from him. "Where are we?"

"It's a private resort in the Caribbean." She gestured to the cliffs around them. "And this is a private alcove." Overhead, birds sailed on the currents, and in the distance, fish jumped out of the waves and made splashes as they hit the crystal water.

"It's perfect," Azagoth said. "If mortals come here, will they see us?"

"Nope. We're invisible to them. In reality, we are just as much here as they are, and we can manipulate objects. But when we do something that changes the world around them, their reality warps to fit our needs."

He kicked off his boots and sighed as his bare feet dug into the sand. "That makes no sense."

Time travel was complicated, with thousands of natural and mystical laws to fit every situation. It had taken her hundreds of years to learn just a fraction of them. She'd have to break her explanation down to the most basic level.

"Okay, let's say I take the last French fry off some guy's plate at Denny's. He either won't remember that there was a French fry there, or he'll believe he ate it. That's the angelic warp in action. Or maybe I steal someone's car. The angelic warp will wipe any witness memories away, and the owner of the car will report it stolen. But as long as I'm inside the vehicle, the angelic warp will keep it visible yet...unnoticeable...until I get out of the car. But that's exactly why we're supposed to be observers only, and we get in a lot of trouble if we mess with humans. The Powers That Be don't like human memories to be messed with unless absolutely necessary." Which was hilarious, given that The Powers That Be had no problem with messing with the memories of angels.

"Can humans ever see you?"

Her gut dove to her feet. "Yes. When you break out of the *shrowd*. That's why it's forbidden to the extreme."

"How does Heaven find out when it happens?"

"The second you break out, alarm bells shriek in the Time

Travel Department. Approximately sixty seconds later, a team of angels will flash to the location of the breakout, and if the offending angel is still there, they either kill the responsible party or arrest them. Depends on the circumstances. Obviously, this doesn't happen very often."

He bent to pick up a shell, and she unabashedly ogled his backside. "How many times has it happened since you've been time traveling? I mean, besides you."

"What?" Damn, he had a fine ass. "Oh, right...just once." Except she *was* the once.

He rubbed his thumb over the shell's smooth curves, and her breasts tingled, as if they wanted in on that action. "What happened to him?"

"It was a her. And her fate is still up in the air." She pointed to a massive vessel on the ocean horizon. "There's a cruise ship. I could take you on one of those sometime. They have the most incredible lavish buffets, bars, activities, and ship-borne viruses."

"Sounds delightful."

She loved his understated sense of humor. "You know what would be delightful? Cocktails. Hold on." She flashed to a nearby beach bar and used a frowned-upon but not forbidden trick of planting a suggestion in the bartender's ear. A few minutes later, she was flashing away with two Mai Tais, complete with little umbrellas.

But when she materialized on the beach where she'd left him, she found only a pile of clothing. Then she heard splashing.

It was all she could do to not roll her tongue out like a welcome mat when she saw Azagoth naked and hip deep in the surf, his face turned to the sun and his hands dragging through his wet hair. Holy mother of hotness, he was sex on legs. If there had been people here—and they could see him—he'd have every woman on the beach drooling.

As it was, the only drooling going on was coming from Lilliana.

She watched him dive into a wave, his sinuous body barely rippling the surface as he arched like a dolphin. His long, muscular legs and spectacular ass glinted in the sunlight before disappearing into the ocean. He surfaced a few yards out, laughing in pure, unadulterated pleasure.

Lilliana had spent her entire life in Heaven amongst angels with a zest for living, but she'd never seen anyone come alive the way Azagoth did every time they passed through the *chronoglass*. It was as if he was a different person, and Lilliana really, really liked that person.

"Come on, angel!" he called out. "Water's great!"

"Nuh-uh," she teased, holding up the drinks. "Ice'll melt. Guess I'll have to drink them both."

She took the tips of both straws between her lips, and in an instant, Azagoth was in front of her, naked, dripping water, and gloriously aroused.

"If you really want to suck on something..." He waggled his brows, and she rolled her eyes, but the truth was that she enjoyed this playful side of him, and she loved that it brought out the playful side of her, too.

It was becoming harder and harder to think about leaving.

Shoving those thoughts into the back of her mind, she thrust Azagoth's drink at him. "Suck that, Soul Boy."

He narrowed his eyes. "Did you just call *me*, the Grim Fucking Reaper, *Soul Boy*?"

"I did," she teased. "What are you going to do about it?"

His voice became a low purr. "I do think I'll have to spank you."

A shiver of unabashed want trekked up her spine. "Promise?"

Three days ago, she wouldn't have believed she'd be flirting with Azagoth. Heck, she wouldn't have believed she'd be flirting with anyone. Hutriel had been too serious for flirting, and she'd been too busy since they'd broken up to even think about seeing anyone else.

"Mmm." His noncommittal response left her practically squirming with uncertain anticipation.

Azagoth's gaze never left her face as his lips closed on the straw. He sucked down the drink, his Adam's apple bobbing with each swallow. When he'd drained every last drop, he tossed the empty glass to the ground and stepped into her.

"Swim with me." His hand came up to her throat, and then froze. "My necklace," he murmured. "You're wearing it."

"It's beautiful."

His eyes darkened with emotion so pure and powerful that she felt it wrap around her heart like a warm blanket. "You honor me by wearing it by choice, not by command," he said softly. "But you don't have to wear it."

Her hand shook as she rested it on his. "I wanted to."

A rough, primitive sound rolled like thunder from inside his chest. His mouth came down hard on hers, and she met him with equal aggression, tangling her tongue with his and nipping at his lips.

As if a dam had broken, need flooded her body, swift and urgent. She'd known lust before, but this was wild, the kind she'd thought might actually be a myth.

She lifted her thigh to his hip and arched her sex against his. She just needed to get out of these pesky clothes—

Abruptly, the hair on the back of her neck stood up and a shrieking alarm clanged around inside her skull.

*Oh, shit.*

They weren't alone.

# Chapter Fourteen

The vibration that skittered over Azagoth's skin was almost orgasmic. In Sheoul-gra, evil was everywhere, permeating everything so thoroughly that unless a being was off-the-charts evil, he barely noticed.

But here in the human realm, evil stood out like a hell stallion in a herd of donkeys.

Reluctantly, he pulled away from Lilliana and turned to meet the source of the malevolent vibes.

Two fallen angels, both looking like they'd stepped out of a *Mad Max* movie, were walking toward them, their crude leather armor streaked with dried blood, their hands wrapped around sharp, wicked-looking swords. Teeth, bones, and scalps hung from their belts, and he didn't even want to know what was stuck between their teeth and crusted to their boots.

These were true killers, fallen angels so corrupted by darkness that murder was all they lived for. He didn't know what made some fallen angels turn into mindless beasts, but he encountered their type every once in a while when they came through his soul tunnel. They were defiant, antagonistic, and they scoffed when he threatened to send them to the worst places in the Inner Sanctum.

Later, much later, when Azagoth went to check up on their misery, they were different people. The information they willingly spewed had given him some of his greatest blackmail material.

Next to him, he felt Lilliana charge up her powers, but he could already tell that these two fucktwats coming toward them were stronger than she was. No problem, because he was going to take them apart in a matter of—

A lightning bolt slammed down in a surge of light, and the fallen angel on the left lit up like a neon sign. His scream joined the crash of the surf and the calls of the seabirds overhead. Stunning ruby-tipped black wings sprouted from Lilliana's back, arching high against the blue sky as she threw her hand out, sending another strike that knocked the enemy to the ground, his skin reddened and steaming.

Azagoth grinned. His female was a warrior. Time to finish off these fucks and have some victory sex.

"Okay, boys," he growled. "Time to die."

He let loose a barrage of fire bombs...at least, he tried to. The weakly little sparks died before they got ten feet from his fingertips. What the hell—

The non-crisped fallen angel snarled, and suddenly, Lilliana was slammed by an invisible force so powerful that she hit the rocky cliff thirty yards behind her. Blood spattered on the stones, and she crumpled to the sand in a broken lump.

Rage burned Azagoth's throat like he'd swallowed burning tar, and with a roar, he let out the beast he'd become, the thing that hid beneath his skin. As his bones popped and his features contorted, the fallen angel that attacked Lilliana streaked toward her, his gore-crusted weapon raised.

*"No!"* Azagoth's voice, so warped that he didn't recognize it, didn't faze the bastard.

Power sang through Azagoth as his wings erupted from his back. He shot into the air and came down on top of the fallen angel, his black, serrated talons ripping into the guy's flesh with the ease of a spoon through gelato.

A weapon struck him, and pain blasted through his chest, but he ignored it as he snapped his jaws closed on one thick arm. The limb tore away with a satisfying rip, and the fallen angel's scream was absolute music.

He lost himself to the sounds, tastes, and smells of the battle...until he heard another fight taking place. Out of the corner of his eye, he saw the fried fallen angel engaged in combat with Lilliana. Her summoned fire sword was holding up against the fallen angel's elemental staff, but Azagoth wasn't taking any chances.

With a final roar, he stabbed his claws through the guy's rib cage. The dude's scream came out gurgled as his blood filled his mouth. Tightening his grip, Azagoth yanked his hands apart, ripping the fallen angel in half.

At the same time, he raised his scaly tail and aimed the poisonous bone spur at the tip at the charred son of a bitch. As Crispy swung his staff at Lilliana's head, Azagoth struck. The tail spike skewered the fallen angel at the base of the skull, piercing the brain stem and delivering a lethal dose of toxin into his nervous system.

If the physical trauma didn't kill him, the poison would.

Crispy fell to the ground, body spasming, mouth open in a silent scream as white foam boiled out of his throat.

Awesome.

Lilliana stood there, eyes wide as she stared at the two dead fallen angels. They went even wider when she finally got a load of Azagoth. Her fear was palpable, shivering through him as if it was his own. Just days ago, he'd have been ecstatic to feel her emotions, no matter what they were, simply because he hadn't felt anything at all in so damned long.

But he hated that he was scaring her, and for the first time since becoming the Grim Reaper, he felt shame.

"I'm sorry," he said, his voice smoky and rough as it cleared his massive jaws and teeth. "It takes a few minutes to turn back."

She swallowed. Nodded. And then she made her summoned sword and wings disappear.

"It's okay," she breathed. "But I gotta say, you are one scary-ass bastard."

"You say the sweetest things," he rumbled.

She dropped her gaze to the dead fallen angels. "You really don't mess around, do you?"

He grinned, and then quickly hid it, because in this dragon-demon mash-up form, a grin was probably terrifying. "The beauty of all of this is that I get to see their souls again when they come through my tunnel later."

As if on cue, *griminions* materialized from out of nowhere and streaked to the bodies, which had just started to disintegrate.

"Hey, fellas," he said. "Feel free to play with these bastards while you're waiting for me to open the tunnel."

Their excited chatter sounded like squirrels on crack. They were cute little buggers sometimes.

He watched as the souls of the fallen angels rose out of their rapidly decaying bodies, only to be shackled by the *griminions* and ushered away in a poof of gray smoke. Their screams lingered in the air a little while longer.

"Did you see that?" he asked. "That was cool." Lilliana looked at him like he was crazy. "What? I've never seen souls rise and my *griminions* show up for the harvest. I'm always on the receiving end of the soul reaping."

Lilliana grimaced. "Let me repeat the scary-ass bastard thing." She held out her hand as if to touch him. "May I?"

He shrugged, making his twelve-foot leather wings flap in the breeze. Tentatively, Lilliana skimmed her fingers over the scaly skin of his forearm, and a strange rumble he'd never heard bubbled up from his skeletal chest. It took a moment to figure out what it was.

A purr. He was purring.

Lilliana didn't seem to be disturbed by the noise in the least, and if anything, she'd moved closer, was now running her hand up his arm to his shoulder.

"Is this okay?" she asked softly? "I'm not hurting you or anything, am I?"

"Hurting...*me?*" He stared down at her in amazement. He could bite her head off right now, before she could even blink, and she was worried that her sensual touch was hurting him?

"Well, you do have blood on you."

"It's not mine." The initial injury he'd taken from the non-crispy fallen angel had healed already, leaving only a thin, foot-long scar across his torso. In another five minutes, even that would be gone.

"Good," she murmured. "Can you change into this form at will?"

"Yes. But it comes out on its own when I'm angry." Not that he was angry often, given his numbness to emotions. But his inner beast took advantage of even mild anger now and then. "It came out this time because I don't seem to have any powers in this realm."

"It's the *shrowd*," she said. "Only angels with the ability to time travel can use their powers here."

"You could have mentioned that earlier," he muttered.

"Sorry," she said, even though she sounded anything but contrite as she explored the corded tendons in his neck.

He closed his eyes, marveling at the sensation of a female

touching him so...reverently. Sweet, savage hell, that felt good. Between the jacked-up high of the battle and Lilliana's feathery touch, a lance of lust shot through him.

And then, to his abject horror, his cock got interested in everything Lilliana was doing. With a hiss, he spun around, desperately trying to will his body to shift back.

"Azagoth?" Her hand came down between his shoulder blades, in the sensitive expanse just below his wings. "Are you okay?"

"Just...give me a minute."

Her hand fell away, and for a long, painful moment, he thought he'd offended her. But then she strode past him on her way toward the surf. A few feet away, she looked back over her shoulder with an impish smile on her face.

"I'm going swimming. Join me if you want to." She stripped as she walked, shedding clothes in a trail on the sand, and he was panting before her feet hit the water.

Suddenly, he didn't give a shit what he looked like. He needed that female, and he needed her now.

\* \* \* \*

Lilliana had only gone shin-deep in the water when she heard a whoosh and a splash behind her. Turning, she faced Azagoth, still in his beast form.

Damn, he was scary. At least two feet taller and a hundred pounds heavier than his usual form, he was the epitome of what humans would call a demon. From his massive, elongated jaws and serrated talons, to the black horns that jutted from his forehead and curled up over his skull, he was the stuff of nightmares.

No doubt he'd become those fallen angels' worst nightmare. And to make it all worse, they couldn't escape him in the afterlife, either. She almost felt sorry for them.

Almost. One of them could have been the bastard who'd killed her mother. So if Azagoth wanted to spend weeks in the Inner Sanctum with them, she was okay with that.

It occurred to her that she was thinking into the future, but this time, she couldn't get worked up about it. Not now. Not with this magnificent creature in front of her.

Azagoth's deep chest was heaving as he stared at her with intense, red eyes, and she probably should have been terrified, but after the initial shock of seeing him like this wore off, she'd been fascinated. He was beautiful in the way a cobra was, sleek and graceful, primitive and deadly.

He was also very, very turned on.

She tried not to stare. She really did. But Azagoth The Sleek and Deadly was sporting a baseball bat between his legs. Morbid curiosity made her want to touch it, to see if she could close both hands around the thickness.

"I can feel the change starting to happen," he rumbled. "So if there's anything you want to...explore...now's the time."

Oh, what the hell. This wasn't a stranger. It was Azagoth, even if he didn't look like he usually did, and if she was even *considering* staying with him, she had to accept all of him.

Stepping closer, she took his length into her hands. He hissed in pleasure as she gently stroked the ebony head and feathered her fingers down the rigid shaft. Sweet mother of sin, he was huge, so thick around that the tips of her thumbs and fingers barely met as she grasped him in both hands. When she reached the base of the smooth column, she dipped one hand lower, to his scrotum, and yup, there were the baseballs to match the bat.

"You're, um, well endowed," she whispered, her tongue so dry she could barely speak. Probably because all of her moisture had gone south, and even as her mouth dried up, her sex became soaked.

Was she really turned on by this? Her aching breasts and throbbing pelvis said yes.

Azagoth's big body trembled, and as she watched, his form crumpled in on itself until he was back in his usual form, panting, his eyes wild.

He stumbled back, averting her gaze, and alarm rang through her.

"Azagoth?" She moved toward him, but he turned away, leaving her to stare at his bare back. "What's wrong?"

"No one...no one has ever touched me like that."

"I can't believe no one has touched your penis."

He inhaled raggedly. "No, I mean, no one has touched *me* like that. Not in my demon form. Weren't you afraid I'd hurt you?"

"Why would I be? You were *you* in there. You weren't some mindless beast." She laid her hand on his shoulder. "Am I wrong? When you're in that form, can't you control yourself?"

His muscles flexed under her palm. "I'm in complete control unless I'm killing. But even then, my focus is limited to the one I'm fighting."

"See? That's why I wasn't afraid to touch you."

"But this is what thousands of years of corruption has done to me. I'm hideous."

"Not to me," she said softly.

He moved in a blur. One second he was staring at the sand, and the next, he was pressed against her, his arms wrapped around her back and shoulders, his hands digging into her hair. His lips came down on hers in a fierce, hot meeting of mouths.

"Lilli," he whispered, "thank you."

She had no idea what he was thanking her for, and it didn't matter. At this moment, she needed everything he could give her. It was as if she couldn't bear another second without him inside her.

Throwing her arms around his shoulders, she lifted herself up so her thighs wrapped around his waist and his sex rubbed against her core. He groaned into her mouth, the very male sound of need reverberating all the way to her breasts.

Arching, she used her entire body to stroke him, her sex grinding against his, her breasts rubbing over the smooth skin of his chest, her belly creating hot friction against his abs. Dear, sweet Lord, she was going to come right here, right now.

He took her down to the wet sand, where tiny waves lapped at her skin as he positioned himself over her. This was different than it had been in the library, when he'd been wracked with emotion he couldn't control. Now he was using his cool self-restraint to devastating effect, kissing and nibbling down her neck as he rocked slowly between her legs, his shaft sliding between her folds in languid thrusts.

She clung to him, digging her nails into his shoulders as he dragged his mouth lower to kiss her breasts and lave the stiff peaks with his tongue. Closing his mouth over one, he sucked, drawing upward with such delicious pressure that she groaned and arched, seeking more and at the same time, thinking it was way too much.

"I love how you respond to me," he murmured against her skin. "I love the sounds you make. The way you smell." He pushed her breasts together and licked up the deep valley between them. "The way you taste."

A gentle wave pushed between their bodies, lapping at the hot place where their bodies met, and she groaned again.

"If we had time, I'd lick you everywhere," he said, giving each breast a kiss. "But I can do that later."

She couldn't wait, but he was right. They had only minutes now, and she was anxious to feel him deep inside her, to know what his weight would feel like as he pumped against her.

"Please," she whispered. "I'm so ready." A sudden thought popped into her lust-soaked brain, and she gripped him fiercely. "Protection?"

He dragged his tongue up between her breasts. "I can turn my fertility on and off." He gave her a cocky smile. "It's one of the advantages of being me."

"Very handy," she admitted before giving his hair a playful tug. "Now, show me some more advantages."

"You got it." Reaching between their bodies, he guided his cockhead to her entrance. "This will hurt, sweetheart," he said. "But only for a second." He planted a gentle kiss on her lips. "If I could bear it for you, I would."

Tears stung her eyes. How could a male with such a fierce reputation be so caring? Azagoth was constantly surprising her, and she wondered how many more he had in store for her.

"I'm pretty tough," she croaked.

"That," he said softly, "is very clear."

He brought his thumb to his mouth and dragged his tongue across the tip before returning his hand between their bodies again. She felt a light, buzzing stroke over her clit, and she sighed with pleasure.

His thumb circled the pulsing nub as he pushed his penis against her opening. Sensation burst through her pelvis, making her dizzy with need. The pain came then, sharp and searing as he slammed his hips forward, breaking her barrier and filling her so full she thought she'd die.

But almost instantly the pain was gone, replaced by pleasure so wondrous she gasped.

Azagoth froze, his arms trembling. "I'm sorry," he rasped. "Are you okay?"

"Oh, yes," she said. "This is incredible."

"It only gets better." Dipping his head, he kissed her throat.

Then he began to move, and she nearly screamed at the ecstasy. Oh, dear Lord, this was exquisite. Every time he nearly pulled out, she tensed up, afraid of losing that amazing feeling of fullness. Every time he thrust deep again, she clenched, as if doing so would keep him there.

"You're so...fucking...tight," he ground out. "And you keep...ah, yes, squeeze me harder...fuck, yeah."

"Azagoth," she breathed. "More. I need more."

She felt him smile against her neck. "So do I, baby. So do I."

He picked up his speed, pumping harder and faster, until she was sliding forward with each thrust. All around them, the tiny waves lapped at their bodies, licking between her legs in her most sensitive spots, until it felt as though Azagoth's cock and tongue were both working her in sync with his thumb.

Groaning, she rolled her hips to take him even deeper, to get him moving faster...anything to ignite the climax building at her core.

It came in a detonation of ecstasy so intense she saw lights behind her eyes as her consciousness practically exploded from her body. She might as well have been shooting through time and space.

Azagoth lifted his head to stare into her eyes as he held himself above her, his body flexing and surging, the sunlight glinting off the fine sheen of sweat and seawater coating his skin.

"Mine," he growled, the tendons in his neck straining with each word. "You. Are. Mine."

His words triggered another orgasm, and she screamed as it took her even harder than the first one. Throwing back his head, he joined her with a feral shout that was surely heard in the Heavens. He drove into her with such power and erotic savagery that she left a deep groove in the sand as he propelled them forward, but she didn't care. Her climax kept her spiraling out of control, mindless with pleasure.

Finally, he jerked, his body spasming as the last of his hot jets spilled inside her.

Now she knew the reason she'd held on to her virginity. It might not have been a conscious thing, and maybe it was even fate. But whatever had kept her virginity intact, she now understood why.

She was meant for Azagoth.

# Chapter Fifteen

Azagoth hated that they had to return to his realm. Especially just seconds after the best sex he'd ever had. He'd barely withdrawn from Lilli's wet heat when the pull of the *chronoglass* dragged them back into the cold darkness of Sheoul-gra.

But this time, the well of emotional turmoil didn't writhe out of control like before. This time, he was able to grasp each one and wrestle it into submission as he wrapped Lilliana in a blanket and carried her to his shower, where he spent half an hour washing her.

And another half an hour making love to her on one of the benches.

He loved listening to her come. Loved tasting her as she orgasmed in his mouth over and over. And when he'd entered her again, it had been like the whole world was right.

For the first time since creating his realm, it now truly felt like home.

Even better, the necklace he'd given her hadn't been needed. Oh, it was still beautiful on her delicate, creamy skin, but its true purpose hadn't played a role at all.

When he'd decided he wanted a mate, he'd been concerned that he and the female would need an emotional connection, something he couldn't give her, nor she him. So he'd had the jewelry special made to operate within Sheoul-gra to transmit thoughts and emotions from his mate to him. He'd hoped he could feel her. Understand her.

All of that was happening naturally, and damn if that wasn't a miracle.

"I have a surprise for you, Soul Boy." Lilliana said as she

slipped her feet into flip-flops. She'd chosen a pair of shin-length white pants and a bright orange T-shirt, all of which would have been perfect for the beach earlier. He wondered if she was still basking in the tropical glow.

Because he sure as hell was.

"I like surprises," he said. "Good ones."

Smiling, she took his hand and led him out of the bedroom. "It's a good one."

He let her lead him outside the palace and onto the stone steps. "Where are we going—" He broke off with a breathless gasp.

The landscape had transformed. It still looked like a nuclear blast had devastated the area, but signs of rebirth and recovery were everywhere. Green grass was punching up through the blackened soil, and colorful buds were sprouting from tree branches that were no longer gnarled and as dark as licorice. The pulsing vines climbing the buildings had withered and died, replaced by grape vines that were spreading even as he stood there.

He stood, speechless, as a breeze, something he'd not experienced here in centuries, brought a light floral scent with it. He couldn't remember the last time the air out here had smelled of anything but decay.

"How," he croaked. "How did you do this?"

"I didn't. I think it's connected to your emotions. As you start feeling them, your realm is reflecting that."

Of course. The place had died as he'd grown more and more corrupted by evil, until there was nothing left. His domain had been as dead as he was, but now that he could feel life pulsing inside him once again, the world around him was feeling it too.

But Lilliana was wrong on one point. "You did do this, Lilli," he said, as he framed her face in his palms. "Without you, this wouldn't be happening. This *is* your doing."

Lowering his mouth to hers, he kissed her softly, drinking in the sweetness that was Lilli's soft, welcoming lips.

"Thank you," he murmured. "You've brought more to my world in a few days than anyone has given me in a lifetime."

She went taut, and he was about to ask what was wrong when the sound of a clearing throat interrupted his thoughts.

"My lord."

"Dammit, Zhubaal—"

"It's Hades," Zhubaal said from where he stood on the

temple's bottom step. "He has another situation."

Fuck. Ever since Azagoth had authorized the reincarnation of Lucifer's soul—at Satan's insistence—things in the Inner Sanctum had been chaos. Now every fallen angel wanted to be reincarnated, born as an *emim*—the non-winged but still powerful offspring of two fallen angels. The demon souls in the Inner Sanctum were antsy, sensing Lucifer's coming birth, something that could affect all of the realms...demon, human, and Heavenly...in game-changing ways.

The doors at the top of the stairs blasted open, and Hades strode out, his face and bare chest streaked with blood. His seizure-inducing color-shifting pants were oddly clean, but his boots were covered in stuff Azagoth didn't want to guess at. His blue Mohawk was pristine, though. The dude never let anything mess up his hair.

"Did he tell you?" Hades growled. "Riots. I'm dealing with riots. I think it's time you went Grim Reaper on a few asses."

"I'm sorry, Lilli," he sighed. "I have to go."

"Duty calls." She smiled sadly, and he shouldn't be thrilled by that, but he was. She was sorry to see him go. How great was that? Most people would sell their souls to get him out of their lives. Literally.

"I'll be back soon," he swore. He'd take care of whatever Hades was whining about, and afterward...there was something he needed to do. With his emotions coming back online, he wanted to connect with his children. Oh, thanks to Methicore, seeing any of them in person would be impossible...for now. But the bastard couldn't take away his ability to care for them, and maybe even to love them.

Because now he knew he could love. Knew it for sure.

He was in love with Lilliana.

# Chapter Sixteen

Two days passed without Azagoth. Two days in which Lilliana did nothing but worry. She'd done her best to keep busy, helping Cat with cooking, reading in the library, and her favorite, tending to the new plant growth outside.

Not once did she try to find a way to get the *chronoglass* out of Sheoul-gra. She figured she still had three weeks to decide if she was truly staying, and when it came down to it, she simply didn't want to think about leaving. Without the *chronoglass*, returning to the Heavenly realm would end in a life of lobotomized misery. With it, she could continue with the life she'd had, but really, what kind of life was that? She'd been busy but lonely. Happy but not content.

Could she be content here?

And where in the hell was Azagoth, anyway? Should she be worried? She didn't think he could be in any danger, but suddenly, a million scenarios spun through her head, many involving hostile takeovers in the Inner Sanctum. Azagoth was the ultimate power down here, but what if Hades and all of the demons trapped in the Sanctum rose up against him? Could he be held prisoner? Maybe even killed?

Okay, so now she'd gotten herself into a panic, and when Zhubaal passed her in the hallway as she was on her way to Azagoth's office, she grabbed his arm.

"Has Azagoth returned?"

Zhubaal snarled at her. "How should I know?"

"Isn't it your job to keep track of him?"

He yanked out of her grip. "He doesn't always inform me of every move he makes."

"Can you at least tell me if he's okay?"

"Of course he's okay." Impatience dripped from his voice. "He's Azagoth."

Zhubaal was really ill-tempered. She hoped Cat didn't get involved with him. "Does he go away like this a lot?"

"Sometimes."

So not an answer. "Okay, let's try this. Why is he there? What's going on?"

"It's not my place to share."

"Yeah? Well, he's my mate, so you *will* share."

A slow, sinister smile spread across his face. "You truly want to know?"

"No," she snapped, her patience worn out, "I asked because I don't want to know. What are you not telling me?"

His smile grew broader. "He went to the Inner Sanctum to visit a lover."

"What?" Her heart clenched. "Why?"

"Why does anyone visit a lover?"

Instant, crushing hurt left her dazed and sick to her stomach. "I don't believe you," she croaked.

He shrugged. "Ask him yourself when he gets back. Her name is Rhona."

Spinning around like he couldn't wait to get away from her, he took off, leaving her shaking with rage and jealousy. After all she and Azagoth had been through, after his assurances that she'd changed his life and helped him, he could do this to her?

*He's Azagoth. He's evil. What the hell did you expect?*

No, this was wrong. Zhubaal was lying. He was, after all, a fallen angel, and everything that came out of their mouths was suspect.

Still, tears stung her eyes as she jogged toward Azagoth's office. She had to see him. Had to find out if there was a way to get into the Inner Sanctum. Maybe a *griminion* could help.

But as she passed the entry to the great hall, she caught movement out of the corner of her eye.

Doubling back, she peeked through the doorway. Relief flooded her when she saw Azagoth standing in front of a huge stone she'd thought was a weird piece of boring art. But now it was transparent, its surface flickering like a TV screen.

A spy stone. Interesting. The things were fairly common, but few had the power to use them. She should have known Azagoth would be one of the few.

Frowning, she inched closer. What was he watching? There appeared to be a beach in the background, and as the screen narrowed and focused, a female in a skimpy swimsuit leaped for a volleyball.

The female, a curvy redhead, sent the ball sailing back over the net. She landed gracefully, her perky breasts bouncing all over the place and drawing every male eye around. Azagoth smiled, and Lilliana's throat burned. With a wave of his hand, the picture changed, this time focusing on a dark-haired female in tight yoga pants and a sports bra as she jogged through what looked like Central Park in New York City.

Azagoth's smile grew wider, and Lilliana's throat burned more. He reached out, touched his finger to the female's face, the reverence in his expression leaving Lilliana flushing miserably.

Suddenly, the picture went blank, and he strode off toward his office. Must be a bigwig soul coming through the portal. Lilliana wondered what kind of baddie was bad enough to drag him away from the females he'd been lusting after.

The bastard.

Irrational rage such as she'd never felt before, not even when her kidnapper threatened and abused her, singed the edges of her control. As if flames were searing her from the inside, she exploded in a fury that blackened her vision and her thoughts.

With a snarl, she rushed forward on a collision course with the stone. She hit it with her shoulder with as much force as she could muster. The thing tilted, teetered, and started to right itself.

"No!" Azagoth's furious voice startled her, but she'd committed, and now she was going to finish her mission.

She shoved the stone before it fell back into place, and with a crash, it hit the floor and shattered into a million pieces. A godawful roar echoed through the room, vibrating the air and making every statue, every portrait, tremble. Even the floor beneath her feet bucked, throwing her off balance as she raced toward the exit.

She didn't make it.

An icy hand clamped around the back of her neck, and suddenly she was being slammed onto the ground. As the stone floor came at her face, everything went black.

\* \* \* \*

Lilliana came to lying on the couch in Azagoth's office. He was sitting across from her in his desk chair, forearms braced on his knees, head hanging loosely on his slumped shoulders.

"Why did you do that?" he asked, his voice softer than she would have expected.

Azagoth had spread a blanket over her, and as she scooched into a sit, she shoved it away, not wanting any of his kindness right now. "You swore you wanted me."

"I do." He was still looking down between his spread knees, his tone even and showing no signs of anger.

Was he truly calm, or was he simply back to being unable to feel emotion? If the latter, he could be on the verge of killing her and she wouldn't know until it was over and she was nothing but a soul waiting to be reaped.

Or turned into one of his stone statues.

She shuddered. "If you want me," she shot back, "then why did you go to the Inner Sanctum to see a lover? And why were you looking at other females?"

His head came up sharply, his green eyes blazing. "A lover? You mean Rhona? Did Zhubaal tell you that?" At her nod, he cursed. "She hasn't been my lover for over a century. She seduced Methicore, and he killed her for it. I went to see her to get information."

Abruptly, Lilliana felt nauseous. If he was telling the truth, she'd just made a huge fool of herself.

Holding her stomach, as if that would stop the rolling that threatened to spill her breakfast, she asked, "What about the females you were watching in the stone?"

"They were my daughters," he said roughly. "That stone is—*was*—the only way I could see what was happening in my childrens' lives."

Oh...oh, shit.

Her breath came raw and scorching in her throat. "I thought...I thought you didn't care about them. Methicore said—"

"Methicore is a bastard who coveted what I have," he snapped. "This place used to be teeming with life, but he ruined it all."

This place? She'd known it used to be green and full of creatures, but...she inhaled a sharp breath. "Your outbuildings...someone used to live there."

"Your powers of observation are unsurpassed," he drawled.

Ignoring the well-deserved sarcasm, she continued. "You said you built them to create a unity of sorts with the human world. But you built them for people, didn't you? Who?"

"Memitim." A blast of cold came from him, and she tugged the blanket over her again, not because she was cold, but because she needed a shield between them, even if it was just a flimsy piece of flannel. "For any who wanted to stay here."

"You let them live here?"

"Let them? I *wanted* them here. They don't have the powers normal angels have, and they can't live in Heaven until they've Ascended to become full angels, so they're vulnerable to demons in the human realm. I gave them a safe place to live and to train for their duties."

"Then why did they leave?"

"Rebellion." Reaching over to his desk, he swiped the ever-present bottle of rum off a stack of papers. "I gave them sanctuary. A place to gather in safety and prepare for their eventual Ascension. I'd intended for Methicore to become my apprentice, to take over Sheoul-gra one day."

She blinked. "But you're immortal. You don't have to give this up."

He laughed bitterly. "Give this up? Really? Do you think I like being isolated? Would you want to spend all eternity alone?" He took a swig from the bottle and then heaved it into the fireplace. It shattered, the alcohol exploding in a massive *whoosh*. "I wanted out. That's why I've spent my entire time down here trading in information and death. I figured that eventually I'd find someone with the knowledge to get me what I wanted." His expression became a mask of rage through which she saw flickers of his inner beast. "Then, a few centuries ago, Methicore decided he wanted to overthrow me. He and hundreds of his brothers and sisters tried to kill me. Turned out they would rather rule this realm than play guardian to humans who need them."

She couldn't even begin to understand how it felt to be betrayed by your children like that. Especially after he'd offered them a safe place to live and gather as a family. What a bunch of ingrates. She'd have given anything to have a family.

"Not all of them rebelled," he continued. "A handful stuck

around to serve in this realm until a few years ago, when the first Horseman's Seal broke. It was chaos for them then. Their assigned humans were all in danger, and they were too busy to return to this realm. Many died. None came back. What little life was left here died."

*Now* Lilliana felt suddenly chilled, and she gathered the blanket more snugly around her. "None?"

"One of my daughters, Idess, visits, but only when there's an urgent matter. I can only hope that Methicore's plan to keep everyone away won't extend to her. She gave up her angel status to be with a Seminus demon mate, so Memitim rules shouldn't apply."

"You really love your children," she murmured.

He looked at her with bloodshot eyes. "I didn't," he said in a strained voice. "I felt mild affection for them. Until now. Until you unlocked the box of emotions I thought was sealed tight. Now I love them." He picked up a jagged piece of rock, and with horror she realized that it was a chunk of the spying stone she'd broken. "And now I'll never see them again."

Oh...God. She swallowed, desperate to keep breakfast down. "You can get another stone, right?" Her voice was shaky, hollow, shot to hell.

"Yes, but they only work to spy on those who have given their permission. By now, Methicore has probably poisoned them all against me."

"I'm sorry," she whispered. "I'm so sorry. I've never felt jealousy before, and I didn't know how to handle it. That's not an excuse, I know, but please believe me when I say I'm sorry." She took a deep breath and met his gaze, desperate to make him see her regret. "And I'm very sorry that I judged you as a father. I think I carried my issues over to you."

He narrowed his eyes. "Your issues?"

"My father...he was..." She started to say, "Like you," but Chaniel was nothing like Azagoth. "He was a sperm donor. Nothing more. After my mother died, he wouldn't have anything to do with me. The bastard left me to be raised an orphan at the battle angel academy."

"He what?" Azagoth's jaw clenched so hard she heard bone pop. "I hope he has since pleaded for your forgiveness. And that you told him to fuck off."

She almost laughed at that. No way she'd have told him off.

She'd have taken any scrap he'd have given her. "He refuses to see me."

Azagoth's eyes sparked crimson. "He doesn't deserve to be a father. He wouldn't deserve even a viewing stone."

The reminder of the stone she'd broken made his expression go hard and flat again, and she shoved to her feet, prepared to fall to her knees and beg his forgiveness if that's what it took. "Azagoth—"

"Don't." He bounded from his chair and away from her. "I can't deal with you right now."

He might as well have driven a stake through her heart, that's how badly his words hurt. "Do you want me to leave?" she asked, before realizing he didn't know she had a thirty-day window.

"Even if you could, no." He smiled sadly. "I told you I want you, and that hasn't changed. If anything, I want you even more. You're all I have left." He backed up, lifting his hands in an almost defensive gesture. "But stay away from me. Just for now."

With that, he slammed out of the office, and that's when she lost it.

So much for breakfast.

# Chapter Seventeen

Lilliana paced across the twenty-foot diameter pentagram at the base of the portal out of Sheoul-gra, trying to work off the events of yesterday and the sleepless night alone in the giant bed, with reminders of other females all around her in Azagoth's sex furniture. Without him there, all she could think about was how he'd used each and every item, and how she'd yet to banish those ghosts from the bedroom.

Now it might be too late.

Azagoth had disappeared after leaving her in his office, and according to Zhubaal, he'd gone to visit his "lover" again.

She'd punched him. Right in the nose. She'd believed Azagoth when he told her about his past relationship with Rhona, and Zhubaal wasn't going to plant doubt in her head again.

Zhubaal was very clear on that now.

She only wished she could be as clear on how she felt about the situation she currently found herself in.

She had messed everything up. Thanks to her impulsiveness, she'd severed Azagoth's last connection with his children. And thanks to her deception, he'd grown to care for her, and if she was honest with herself, she had to admit that she cared for him, too.

She hadn't intended for any of this to happen, hadn't considered the collateral damage involved in her grand plan to abscond with the *chronoglass*.

If she left now, it might be the best thing for him. After all, their relationship was based on lies. She couldn't handle it anymore. She'd reached a tipping point, one that was very close to toppling. She had to commit—to either staying...or leaving.

"Hi Lilliana."

Startled, Lilliana whirled around. An Adonis-faced angel stood in the center of the pentagram, his crisp business suit as flawless as his distinguished salt-and-pepper hair and olive skin.

"Hutriel," she gasped.

"It's good to see you."

She wished she could say the same, but she really did not like her ex. "Why are you here?"

His periwinkle eyes flashed imperiously. "I come with news from Raphael."

Oh, shit. She had a sneaky suspicion she wasn't going to like this news. "Well, spit it out."

He stiffened in that haughty way of his. "I'm an angel of the Order of Virtues. I outrank you by three Orders. In addition, I'm an angel of good standing, while you..." He sneered at Azagoth's manor. "You are a shameful wrongdoer undeserving of my company. You will address me with respect."

"I give respect when it's earned," she said bluntly. "You lost mine a long time ago, and I don't see it happening again soon, Rod of God."

He used to love to point out that his name meant, "*rod of God*", as if it made him important. He was a rod, all right, but he probably wouldn't appreciate the alternative use of the word.

The egotistical rod.

"I don't like your attitude," he ground out.

"And I no longer care what you like or don't like." She crossed her arms over her chest. "So tell me why you're here or go away."

His mouth pursed so tight she thought his teeth would break. "Raphael wants to know what's taking you so long."

"I have a month. It's only been a few days. Tell him to hold his horses."

Rod of God's eyes nearly bugged out of his head. "That's an archangel you're speaking about."

"He hasn't earned my respect either. So why don't you march your suck-up self back to Raphael and tell him..." Tell him what? That she'd changed her mind? *Had* she changed her mind? For sure? "Tell him I need more time. And I could use some help, as well. With my limited powers, the *chronoglass* is too heavy to move."

"That's not his problem."

"No, it's yours," she said. "You're the one who has to go back and tell him to bite me."

"You're very brave down here in Azagoth's realm. Will you be so mouthy once you're face to face with Raphael in his chambers?"

She'd deal with that when—and if—she stole the *chronoglass*.

"I don't know. Will you be so mouthy when you're face to face with Azagoth?"

He snorted. "It's really too bad you're not going to stay here. You deserve him."

"How do you know I'm not staying?"

He laughed, a full-on belly laugh. "Come now, Lilliana. I know how you like your freedom. It's why you left me, isn't it?"

She shrugged. "Mostly I left you because you're a controlling asshole. It's funny how Azagoth is talked about as if he's a soulless monster, but he's been better to me in a few days than you were in a hundred years."

"Good...Lord," he breathed. "You actually like him. You're *falling* for him." He stared at her, horror spreading over his perfect features as the truth of her situation began to solidify in his mind. "You've fucked him, haven't you? You...whore."

"You haven't changed a bit. Still a judgmental dick." Done with him, just like she'd been all those decades ago, she spun around and started toward the building. Walking away was as easy this time as it had been then. "Tell Raphael to suck an egg."

He moved in a flash to snare her wrist and yank her back to him. Teeth bared, he snarled. "Find a way to steal the *chronoglass*, Lilliana. Raphael feels that giving you too much time has made you slack off. You now have two days to do it."

She inhaled sharply. "What?"

"Two days, Whore of Sheoul-gra." His eyes flared with exaggerated astonishment even as his fingers dug painfully hard into her flesh. "Oh, you don't like that name? Because that's what everyone is going to call you if you stay here. So get your ass in gear, or—"

A roar shattered the air, and suddenly Hutriel went airborne in a bloody explosion. A fine pink mist hung in the air as his wrecked body hit the ground inside the portal's pentagram ring.

Lilliana pivoted toward the owner of that bloodcurdling roar, and her heart slammed hard into her rib cage. Azagoth, fully eviled-out, was pounding down the stairs three at a time, his massive, sharp teeth bared, his wings extended, his eyes glowing with crimson death.

"You dared to touch my mate?" His words were warped,

guttural, and dripping with murder. He snarled, and Hutriel screamed as dozens of bones in his body snapped. "You. Will. Die."

"Azagoth, no!" She leaped to intercept, but Hutriel, still inside the portal circle, disappeared in a glittery shower of sparks, barely escaping with his life.

He rounded on her, but his voice had tempered. "Who was he?"

"Take off your demon face," she said in a low, soothing tone, "and we'll talk."

His nostrils flared, and a muffled, soft growl rumbled in his chest. He stared at the empty space where Hutriel used to be, his clawed hands flexing as if he was regretting the missed opportunity to rip the angel apart.

"Come on," she urged quietly. "Shift back."

Azagoth remained like that for a few seconds, and then he paced in a circle for a minute, until finally, he morphed back into his usual body. As he turned back to her, his tall, elegant form outfitted in black slacks and a matching button-down, she couldn't help but think that the civilized clothing only heightened the awareness that underneath it all, he was death in human skin.

"Who. Was. He."

"He was my ex," she replied. "Hutriel."

Azagoth's nostrils flared and his eyes flickered with red sparks. "Why was he here?"

*Oh, because he needed to tell me to hurry up and steal your chronoglass.*

"He wanted to wish me good riddance," she said, hoping he didn't notice the tremor in her voice. She hated lying to him, but at this point, the truth was only going to cause more pain, and she couldn't do that to him again.

She'd done enough of that already.

"He grabbed you." Once more, flickers of his inner beast formed as shadows in his expression. Quickly, she took his hand and pulled him to her, drawing him hard against her body, where she'd needed him to be since yesterday.

"We fought." She slid her hand behind his neck and massaged him there, digging deep into muscles so tight they felt like bricks. "It's what we do. But I don't want it to be that way with you."

"He touched you. I can...*smell* him." With a growl, he hauled her even closer to him as he dipped his mouth to her ear. "I need to be inside you. I need to mark you. Brand you. Make him disappear forever."

Oh...oh, damn. "Yes," she whispered.

And with that, she knew for sure she wasn't leaving.

# Chapter Eighteen

Azagoth was in a state of animalistic need. The desire he felt for Lilli was so basic, so primal that, just like his killing urge, he knew better than to fight it. He swept her up and headed inside his manor on a direct course for his bedroom, and Hades help anyone who was stupid enough to get in his path.

Only one *griminion* came close to making that mistake, but he leaped out of the way with a squeak and scurried into his living quarters as Azagoth stalked down the hall. Lilliana's lips were kissing hot paths along his neck and jaw, driving him insane. When he reached the bedroom, he kicked open the door, not caring that it cracked down the middle.

Once inside the bedroom, he set her on the floor, but when he lowered his head to kiss her, he caught another whiff of her former lover. Possessive anger lit him up as he gripped the flirty purple sundress she was wearing and ripped it in half.

"You've had a very busy couple of days, haven't you?" He dropped the shredded dress to the floor and hooked his finger under the delicate lace of her panties. "Meeting with your ex, destroying my viewing stone, punching Zhubaal in the face."

"I'm not sorry about Zhubaal," she said. "He's a jerk. And I certainly didn't invite Hutriel for a visit." She laid her hand over his and pushed it deeper inside her underwear, until his fingers brushed her cleft. "But I swear, I'm so sorry about the spy stone."

He let his fingers play a bit, stroking over the flawless hills of her sex. Countless years of bedding angels had taught him that gentle touches while talking soothed the savage beast—both his and theirs.

"What led you to think I wanted someone besides you?"

"Zhubaal said...it's not important. And then I saw you looking at females," she said, going breathless as he slipped a finger between her folds. "Then there's all of this sex furniture stuff. You used it on other females, and I have to just sit here and look at it."

He supposed he understood that. If the situation were reversed and he'd been subjected to constant reminders of Hutriel the Silver-haired Douchebag, he'd be on edge, too.

"I'll toss it. All of it." He dropped to his knees and used a fang to slash her underwear open. Damn, he'd never get tired of the sight of her like this. Bare. Her flesh parted just enough to invite his tongue. "After," he growled as he put his mouth to her waiting sex.

She allowed him a single, mouthwatering lick before stepping away from him. "No. You want to erase Hutriel, and I want to do the same with all of your females." She marched over to the St. Andrew's Cross, her glorious backside swinging. With a lithe spin, she put her spine to the wood and snapped her wrists into the restraints. "Do it. Let's banish all of our demons. You know, figuratively."

He inhaled in an attempt to get a bead on where her emotions were, but all he got was a blast of lust that made his knees wobble as he came to his feet.

*Real smooth, buddy. Real fucking smooth...*

It was crazy how this female had torn down his defenses, made him feel things he hadn't felt in a long time. Or ever.

He looked around at the bedroom, at all of the equipment he kept, and suddenly he didn't want Lilliana's exquisite skin touching any of it. He'd used it for a purpose he'd never again need it for. It had to go.

Well, maybe the spanking bench could stay.

Summoning all his control, he unbuttoned his shirt. Slowly. Taking his time while Lilliana hung from the St. Andrew's Cross, her breasts rising and falling faster and faster every time a button popped.

"Do you want to know why I have all of this stuff?" he asked.

Licking her lips, she nodded.

He inhaled deeply, hating that his breath was shaky. He didn't want to admit this, but she needed to hear it, and he wanted to make sure she never doubted him again.

"Heaven sent me seventy-two females a year."

"Yes," she ground out. "I know that. All of Heaven knows that."

He probably shouldn't like the note of jealousy in her voice, but hey, he was evil.

Turning away, he stared at the Monet on the wall. "Seventy-two females who didn't want to be here. Much like you." Silence churned between them as the truth of what he'd said thickened the air like a rancid stew. "Well, that's not entirely accurate. Usually two or three of the bunch were eager to experience me. The rest..." Pivoting back to her, he waved his hand dismissively. "The rest closed their eyes and prayed. Literally *prayed*. Do you have any idea how unpleasant that is?"

"I can't imagine," she said softly. "But what does that have to do with all of this...stuff?"

"I told you that I couldn't feel any emotions of my own, but I discovered that the more they felt, the more I felt. Remember when I told you I took Thanatos's tattoos just so I could feel something?" At her nod, he continued. "The only other time I could ever feel anything was when I was inside an angel. The more she was worked up, the better for both of us." He trailed a finger over the wood near where Lilliana's wrist was circled by the leather cuff. "All of this allowed me to play until even the most timid female begged for my cock."

She growled. "I did *not* need to hear that."

Oh, yeah, he fucking loved that little twinge of jealousy. "And I didn't need to see Hutfuckriel touching you." That wasn't fair and he knew it, but the fact that he was actually experiencing jealousy was awesome. Right now, *every* emotion was awesome, simply because he could feel them at all. "But that's over. All of it is over, isn't it?"

"Yes," she whispered.

"Good. Now, let's try something more deserving of your behavior." He released the restraints.

"B-behavior?"

Smiling, he took her by the shoulders and swung her around to the spanking bench. He bent her over, locking her wrists into the cuffs. His cock strained behind the fly of his pants, and he unzipped, springing it from its fabric prison.

"Are you ready?" he asked as he took his erection in his hand and gave it a few strokes.

He was dying for this, but he wanted her to be dying for it, too, the way she'd been on the beach and in the shower. But instinctively, he knew this was a cleansing of sorts, a way for them to banish their pasts. He wanted intimacy. He wanted the sex to mean something.

This could be a new start for them both.

He stroked himself as he gave her a swat on her perky ass. She hissed, but as he rubbed the pink handprint on her ivory skin, she pushed into his palm.

"Yes," she moaned. "Please."

"Another then," he murmured, swatting her harder.

This time she whispered a soft, "Oh, yeah. More. We are so keeping this bench."

He gave her three more slaps in rapid succession, and his cock thickened to the point of exquisite pain as her ass reddened and grew hotter with every blow. Her arousal was like an airborne aphrodisiac, entering his lungs and spreading through his body like wildfire.

"Azagoth," she pleaded, her breathless voice pushing him to the edge of his control. "I need to come."

"You got it." He positioned himself behind her and nearly moaned at the way she lifted her hips in anticipation. Her juices glistened between her swollen folds, and when he cupped her mound, her honey coated his fingers.

Still stroking himself, he slid his fingers into her slit and rubbed back and forth. She whimpered, pushing into his hand as far as the restraints would allow.

"Don't worry," he whispered. "I'll release you. We'll start this way, but I want to end with you on your back. I want to look into your eyes when I come."

She cried out, so close to orgasm he could feel the tremors building between her legs. Gently, he eased his thumb into her silken opening.

"When you first came here, did you think we'd end up like this?"

"Never." The honesty in her voice was tinged with an odd note of remorse. Did she feel bad about not wanting to come here?

Didn't matter. What mattered was that she was here now, and he had all eternity to show her that she'd made the right decision to join him in Sheoul-gra.

His cock throbbed as he pressed it against her slit. Very slowly, he nudged the head inside her, her slippery desire easing the passage into her tight channel. Suddenly, her emotions slammed into him, a mixture of yearning and guilt. He shook his head, wanting them gone. He could feel now; he didn't have to borrow her emotions.

But they wouldn't subside. What the hell? He gripped her hips, holding both of them steady as he struggled to clear his head.

A glint of silver caught his eye, and suddenly, it all made sense.

The key pendant. Designed to transmit strong emotion, it was doing exactly that.

Another blast of her guilt hit him hard enough to make him groan. He needed to remove the necklace and use the rest of the night to assuage whatever regrets she had. He never wanted her to have a negative emotion again.

He'd get her a new pendant. One that wasn't enchanted.

*You only have thirty days to get out with the chronoglass before we close the door on Sheoul-gra, and you're stuck with Azagoth forever.*

He froze as Lilliana's thoughts, her very memories, slammed into him like a lava troll's meaty fist. Stunned, he could only stare blankly as the unbelievable truth pinged around inside his head and clawed at his heart. She'd betrayed him. She'd lied from the very beginning.

The warmth that had been nudging at his flesh, that had been starting to thaw his body, iced over.

"Damn you," he rasped, his voice as raw as the wound she'd just inflicted. "You came here to steal the *chronoglass.*"

"Azagoth...no...wait—"

*"Damn you!"* Snarling, he gripped the necklace and yanked hard. The delicate chain snapped, and tiny links flew everywhere. Before she could say another word, he flipped the switch on the cuffs and released her.

"Get out." Bypassing the ripped garment on the floor, he threw open her wardrobe, ripped a sunny yellow sundress from a hanger, and hurled it at her. And wasn't he a gentleman for making sure he kicked her to the curb with undamaged clothing.

*Idiot.*

Lilliana caught the garment with shaking hands. "Please, just listen—"

"Listen?" he shouted. *"Listen?* To what? More lies? You've deceived me from the moment you crossed the threshold into my realm. You destroyed the only connection I had with my children, and now I find out you've lied about why you came here."

Pain, sharper than any he'd ever experienced, cleaved through his heart and he nearly doubled over. How could she do this to him? How could she betray him like this? She'd used him, exploited his desperation, just like Lilith had all those years ago.

"Get the fuck out of my realm," he gritted through clenched teeth. "and tell the archangels that if they dare to send another angel to me, for any reason, I'll send that angel back in pieces." He bared his teeth and advanced on her, forcing her to scramble backward toward the door. For the first time since she'd stepped foot in his realm, he got off on her fear. Craved it. Reveled in it. "Go. Before those pieces are yours."

\* \* \* \*

Lilliana tried to not cry as she fled down the hall toward the building's exit, tripping and careening off walls as she attempted to put on the dress while running at full speed. She'd screwed up badly. She'd hated Azagoth in the beginning, but he'd been nothing but good to her. And once she'd understood his lack of emotions, his coldness had not only made sense, but had been understandable.

She should have told him the truth the very moment she realized she was having second thoughts about why she'd come here. Instead, she'd swept her deception under the rug and hoped he'd never find out.

*Fool. Of course he found out. This is his realm. He knows all. Sees all.*

Wait...how *had* he found out?

Not that it mattered. What was done was done, and as the tears rolled down her cheeks in hot streaks, she cursed Raphael. Hutriel. Herself.

"Lilliana!"

Cat's voice rang out as Lilliana shoved open the door to outside. Only the knowledge that Cat might very well be screwed out of a job halted Lilliana in her tracks.

Cat jogged over. "What's wrong? Where are you going?"

"I'm leaving," Lilliana said. Well, she tried to say it, but the sobs muffled her words. "I'm sorry, Cat. I'm so sorry. Your job—"

The fallen angel threw her arms around Lilliana and hugged her tight, which only made her cry harder. "Screw the job. I don't want you to go."

*Get your head on straight. Pull yourself together for her sake. You can fall apart later.*

Easing back from Cat, Lilliana dabbed at her wet face with the hem of her dress. "Listen to me. Stay out of Azagoth's way for a while. If he fires you..." Lilliana couldn't believe she was about to say this, given the fact that she was an angel and this went against everything angels believed, but things had changed since she got here. *She* had changed. "There's a demon hospital called Underworld General. Go there. Try to get a job. You'll be safe from the fallen angels trying to drag you into Sheoul."

Cat nodded, her eyes filling with tears. "Don't go."

A tormented roar, barely muffled by the building, rang out, stirring up a malevolent wind that reeked of rot and danger. "I have to." She squeezed the female's hand. "Promise me you'll do as I said."

Cat's bottom lip trembled. "I promise."

Breathing a sigh of relief, Lilliana released Cat. "Be safe. And thank you for everything."

Hastily, before Azagoth made good on his word to send her to Heaven in pieces, Lilliana flew down the stairs and hit the ground running. As she stepped into the portal that would transport her out of here, she looked out over Azagoth's kingdom.

All the new life, all the vibrant color and fresh air, was dying. Her last thought before the portal whisked her away was about Azagoth.

If his realm was dying, what was happening to him?

# Chapter Nineteen

Azagoth stood in the library amongst shattered glass, his body trembling, his heart aching, his soul screaming. Pain surged through him in great waves that threatened to make him black out, but fate was a cruel bitch, and he remained as alert and sensitive to agony as ever.

His Lilli had betrayed him. Had plotted to steal his *chronoglass* and leave him. He looked down at the shards on the floor. Now she'd never get it. In a great fit of irrational fury, he'd destroyed it the way she'd destroyed him.

He could still feel her, and crazily, *stupidly*, he hoped she'd go to their bedroom and wait for him. Maybe try to convince him that he was wrong about her. That she loved him and couldn't leave.

He wasn't sure how he'd react to that, but a big part of him would be relieved.

Suddenly, something inside him extinguished, as if a flame had gone out. Or as if his breath had been forcefully expelled from his lungs.

Lilliana was gone.

Agony overwhelmed him. His breath scorched his throat with every desperate inhale. She'd left him, and his world was crumbling around him. Literally. The building was shaking, books falling from their shelves, cracks popping in the walls.

With a great roar, he fell to his knees. He screamed in utter misery, and only later realized he was screaming her name.

\* \* \* \*

Lilliana spent a full day in Heaven. Now she was down to twenty-two hours before Raphael's ticking time bomb was set to go off and she'd have to submit to the time-travelectomy procedure.

Or she'd be shut inside Sheoul-gra forever.

With a person who wanted to tear her to pieces.

So far, she'd been able to get around without anyone knowing she was back behind the pearly gates, and hopefully no one had gone into the Time Travel Department's artifact room yet.

Twenty-two hours.

She took one last look at the cottage she'd called home, at the eclectic decor from time periods all over the human world. She'd either never see this place again, or she'd return with no energy or passion for life.

But then, she didn't need to have her time travel ability ripped away for the latter to happen.

*Twenty-two freaking hours.*

Taking a deep, bracing breath, she flashed herself out of Heaven and to as close as she could get to Underworld General Hospital, which turned out to be its underground parking lot.

There weren't many cars, but there was a blond male in a black paramedic uniform scrubbing out the inside of one of two black ambulances near the entrance. Lilliana had no idea what had happened inside the vehicle, but it looked more like a mobile slaughterhouse than a rolling medical unit.

"Excuse me."

"What?" came the gruff response.

"I'm looking for someone named Idess."

"Inside."

How helpful. "I can't go inside." No angel could enter the demon hospital, thanks to some sort of anti-angel ward. Apparently, no one could commit violence inside, either, thanks to another spell. Those wily demons had thought of everything.

"Guess you're out of luck."

Okay, now she was getting irritated. Stepping to the side of the rig, she slammed her fist into the center of the Underworld General symbol, leaving one hell of a dent.

"Luck is irrelevant," she said. "I can't enter the hospital, and I need help. Is it not your job to render assistance?"

Very slowly, he turned around, his fangs and silver eyes flashing. Surprise flickered at the sudden realization that he was a dhampire, a rare vampire-werewolf cross. She'd studied them in their Scottish homeland during one of her time travel assignments. She'd be fascinated to meet one in person if she wasn't so annoyed. And in a serious time crunch.

"*Medical* assistance," he said. "Are you bleeding to death, having a cardiac incident, or suffering from a splinter in your little finger? No? Then fuck off."

Steam built in her veins. Tales of Underworld General staff arrogance reached the farthest corners of Heaven, but she'd always thought they were exaggerated. Turned out, not so much.

She slapped her palm against the side of the rig again, using a bit of angel power to make the sound crash through the enclosed parking lot like a sonic boom. Dhampire boy jumped high enough that he nearly brained himself on the roof.

"I'm approximately one insult away from rendering you down to a greasy stain of dhampire fat on the asphalt, so hear me, and hear me well," she said, using the same power to make her voice resonate all the way to the paramedic's marrow. "This is about Idess's father. If you're at all aware of who he is, if you've only heard *whispers* regarding his identity, you will drop that bottle of cleaner and fetch her. Now."

The male, whose name tag read *Conall*, studied her for a moment. "You could have lead the conversation with the threat and saved us both a lot of time, not to mention damage to the rig." He leaped out of the truck, and as he strode away, boots clapping on the pavement in heavy thuds, she swore she heard him mutter, "Fucking angels."

She waited impatiently, watching a few vehicles come and go through the hidden portal in the lot's concrete wall. Finally, just as she was contemplating climbing into the ambulance and turning on the siren, Conall returned with a stunning female whose caramel hair had been piled on top of her head in a messy knot.

"I'm Idess," she said. "You're here about Azagoth?"

Lilliana glanced over at the paramedic, who stood protectively by Idess. "Can we have some privacy, please?"

Idess nodded at the dhampire, and after shooting Lilliana a look that promised pain if she caused trouble, he hopped inside the ambulance and went back to his gruesome work.

"Your father needs you," Lilli began. Might as well get to the point. "One of your brothers, Methicore, arranged to have Sheoul-gra cut off to all Memitim. His viewing stone is broken, and he has no way to contact his children, let alone see them. I think you're the only one who can access his realm now."

"Methicore," she hissed. "That son of a bitch has been causing trouble for centuries." She eyed Lilliana. "How do you know all of this? Who are you?"

"I was supposed to mate him."

Idess's eyes flared. "Supposed to? Wait...*mate* him? What about the seventy-two angels? What the hell is going on?"

"I'll explain it all later. Right now your father is in trouble, and I don't have much time. I need your help. *He* needs your help."

For a long moment, Idess stood there, staring at Lilliana. Finally, she said, "Why is this important to you?"

No matter what she said, she was going to sound stupid, so she might as well put it all out there. "Because he deserves a chance to be happy. And...I love him."

Conall's head whipped around and he stared at her like she was insane, but Idess merely looked curious.

"Are you trying to win him back?" she asked.

Lilliana shook her head. "I would love a second chance, but even if that doesn't happen, I want to fix what I broke, and you're the only person who can help me do that. Please. Not for me, for him."

Idess glanced at her watch. "My lunch break is in ten. Let's grab a bite somewhere and figure this out." She gave Lilliana a wary glance. "How do I know this isn't a trick? No offense, but a lot of angels have turned out to be..."

"Lying assholes?"

Idess snorted. "Yeah."

"Do you know Reaver?" When Idess nodded, Lilliana breathed a sigh of relief. "He can vouch for me."

Idess's expression lit up. "If Reaver is cool with you, then so am I. Welcome to the family, Lilliana."

Lilliana appreciated the welcome, and the family thing sounded awesome. But she doubted it would happen. Hell, she was lucky Azagoth hadn't killed her. There was no way he'd forgive her.

*Betray me and you'll see exactly how unforgiving I can be. There are no second chances.*

# Chapter Twenty

Azagoth stood in the courtyard outside of his palace, staring into the murky waters swirling around in the black-streaked fountain. What had, for a few short days, been pristine white was now smeared with sooty residue. The once-crystal water had stagnated, its surface so thick with slime that it resembled industrial sludge.

His belly hurt and his heart ached, and his throat was raw from screaming. He missed Lilliana as much as he hated her. No, that wasn't entirely accurate. He missed her more than he hated her. And truth be told, he didn't hate her...he hated what she'd planned to do.

"Father."

The familiar voice came from out of nowhere, and he wheeled around. Idess stood on the stone pathway that led from the portal, dressed in jeans and a fitted violet silk blouse with matching strappy sandals. The desire to hug her damned near made him tremble.

But so did the fear that she was the rotten icing on the cake, here to tell him to fuck off like everyone else. Bracing himself, he waited.

"I spoke with Lilliana," she said, and his heart shot into his throat. "She's worried about you."

He snorted. "She should be worried about herself. After the archangels relieve her of her time travel ability, she's going to be miserable." He should be happy about that, but no, the thought of her suffering only dragged him deeper into the pit of despair he'd dug for himself. "How is it that you spoke with her?"

"She came to me at Underworld General. She told me what Methicore did. And she gave me this." Idess reached into her purse and withdrew a polished sapphire globe about the size of a softball. "She stole it from the Time Travel Department."

"What is it?"

"It's a miniature viewing stone. It's practically useless to Heaven because it requires permission from those you want to spy on...and who in their right mind consents to that?" She shrugged. "But somehow Lilliana convinced hundreds of my brothers and sisters to give permission. It's not the same as them being able to visit, but it's better than nothing. Some of them even sent messages and invitations to contact them. They're all about Skype."

He had no idea what to say, even if he could speak. His voice was gone, clogged by the emotion in his throat. Idess handed the shiny ball to him, the solid weight of it sitting heavy on his soul. Lilliana had done this even after the way he'd treated her?

*You treated her that way because she lied to you. She deceived you.*

Somehow, none of that seemed to be important right now, which was strange, because he had *never* treated betrayal lightly. Had anyone else done what she did, they'd be gracing his great hall right now, frozen in a screaming statue.

"Father," Idess said softly. "I know this is none of my business, but I think you should cut her some slack."

He rolled the globe around in his palms, strangely comforted by the fact that Lilliana had once held it in her own graceful hands. "You don't know what she did." His voice was humiliatingly hoarse.

"Yes, I do. She came down here to steal the *chronoglass* and return to Heaven." Idess dropped her bag on the ground and gazed out at the devastated landscape. "Did she ever tell you why she was given the choice to come here or have her ability taken away?"

"She broke out of the *shrowd*."

"Yes, but did she tell you why she did that?"

He frowned. She'd always skirted around the issue or changed the subject, never lighting on talk of her punishment or the *shrowd* for long. "No, she didn't."

"She did it because she was taken prisoner by an angel named Stamtiel. He forced her to travel into the past to search for some sort of holy object he could use to wrest power away from one of the archangels. She refused, even when he tortured her."

His breath burned in his throat, and his voice turned smoky with the depth of his anger. "He tortured her?"

"Badly. He wrecked her, Father. To save herself, she agreed to do his bidding, but it was a trick. She went into the past and then broke out of the *shroud* in hopes that angels would rescue her. They did, but they were angels from the past. What she did was highly illegal, and it caused a lot of problems. Memories had to be wiped, and getting her back to the present was a long, involved process that required more memory alterations."

"So she was punished for escaping her torturer?"

Idess nodded. "You know how Heaven operates. Rules are rules, and they can't be broken for any reason."

Bastards. "Why would she tell you all of this but not tell me?"

"She didn't tell me. I asked Reaver to do a little digging, and he discovered all of that. The reason she didn't tell you is that she doesn't remember the worst of it."

"Why not?"

"She was in bad shape," Idess explained. "The angels knew she needed to be punished, but even they felt sorry for her, so they altered her memories. She knows she was kidnapped and that she escaped, but she has no recollection of the horrors Stamtiel inflicted on her." Idess pursed her lips in disgust. "Father, she came here to steal your property, but somehow, she managed to fall for you, and given her past, if she can't consciously remember it, that's kind of a miracle."

He squeezed his eyes shut, but his vicious actions replayed on the back of his eyelids. "I'm such a fool."

"Males always are," she muttered.

"Did you give your..." He held up the orb, afraid to even ask if she'd consented to allow him to check up on her from afar.

For a moment, Idess looked perplexed. "Why would I?"

"You're siding with Methicore, then."

She grimaced. "Hardly. I didn't infuse my permission into the globe because I'm not Memitim. I can visit your realm anytime I want to. And if you want to see me, send one of your *griminions*. Or heck, send an e-mail. I'll come, Father."

He gaped at her. "You'd visit me? For no reason other than that I requested it?"

"Of course." She shrugged. "I didn't know you wanted me here or I'd have come more often. And when my son is born, I'll bring him, too."

He sucked in a sharp breath. "You're pregnant?"

"Soon," she said. "With all the apocalyptic crap that happened recently, Lore and I wanted to wait until we knew we wouldn't be bringing a child into a shitty world. It's still shitty, but between Lore's family, the Horsemen, and Reaver and Harvester, I know my son will have a powerful, loving family to depend on. And, of course, you."

He hugged her, something he'd never done before. It was awkward and stiff at first, but when she relaxed into him, an emotional earthquake rocked him. This was his first true connection with one of his children, and he hoped it wouldn't be the last.

He tried not to think of the children he might have had with Lilliana as he reluctantly pulled back.

"Thank you, Idess," he said, his voice thick with the force of what he felt for her. "You've already done so much, but I have one favor to ask of you."

"Anything."

"Tell her...tell her I love her."

Idess stepped away. "I can't do that," she said, and his heart sank. "But you can tell her yourself."

She turned, and he followed her gaze to the steps of his mansion, where Lilli was standing...in a flowing white gown, just as she'd been dressed when she'd first arrived. Her hair was long and loose, the way he liked it, and peeking out from under the hem of the gown were her bare toes, painted bright cherry red.

He closed the distance between them in less time than it took to blink. Then he stood there like a dolt on the step beneath hers. He'd had so much to say to her just a few seconds ago, and now he was completely blank.

"Hi," she said.

He couldn't even manage that. Dolt.

"Um..." She cleared her throat. "I'm not sure where to start. I originally came here with every intention of stealing your *chronoglass* and leaving." Her eyes grew liquid, and it took every ounce of restraint he had not to reach for her. "And then I...I started falling for you. I put off taking the *chronoglass* so I could stay, and then I changed my mind, but by then..."

"By then it was too late," he finished. God, he was an ass. "I'm sorry too," he croaked. "I should have let you explain. I should have listened. Instead, all I could think about was how I'd let another female deceive me. I went back to that dark place from so long ago, and it wasn't fair to you. Please forgive me, Lilli. Please."

A tear dripped down her cheek. "Only if you forgive me."

He caught the tear with his finger, and damn, it felt good to touch her again. "It doesn't matter. None of it matters." His heart thumped against his rib cage. "Tell me you're here to stay. Tell me—"

She silenced him with a kiss. When she pulled away, she was smiling. "The window for me to leave closed sixty seconds after I got here."

He stepped back and nearly fell down the stairs. "Lilli, damn...you took a huge risk. What if you'd gotten here and I was in a rage? Or if I never forgave you?"

"Then I'd spend the rest of eternity making it up to you." She grinned. "I can be pretty persuasive. It wouldn't have taken an eternity. Besides, I figured I could hold that hour a day of time traveling over your head."

He grimaced. Ran his hand through his hair. Looked down at his shoes. They were dirty. "Ah...about that. I sort of destroyed the *chronoglass.*"

"You *what?*"

"I know. I'm an idiot. I just—"

Abruptly, she gripped his arm in a bruising hold. "Azagoth! Look."

Cranking his head around, he took in the new splendor of his realm. His daughter was gaping in disbelief as the scorched earth once again sprouted with lush, green grass. The gnarled, charred trees straightened, their blackened bark peeling away to leave healthy wood in its place. Leaves unfurled along branches that stabbed up into an infinitely blue sky. And all around, the fountains spewed crystal water against the backdrop of pristine white buildings.

"That's your doing, Lilli," he breathed, his love for her flowing through his veins and through the realm. "This is all because of you."

She sidled up close, drawing him to her with arms around his waist. "We've been over this. It's you. Because you can feel again."

"Yes," he said, as he dipped his head to kiss her, "I can feel." He could feel everything now. Love. Joy. Tenderness. Against the soft warmth of her lips, he whispered, "But all of the beauty infusing my realm is simply a reflection of what I see when I look at you."

# Chapter Twenty-One

Eight days had passed since Lilli returned to Sheoul-gra, but to Azagoth, the realm now seemed like Heaven.

He could tell she missed being able to time travel, but maybe he could arrange for an artifact that would allow her to get out of here every once in a while. He'd heard that some objects, such as the one her torturer had possessed, could transport the user to a very specific time and place.

Better than nothing, he supposed.

He'd been keeping her busy with plans for the newest Inner Sanctum level, and it wouldn't be long before construction would start. She'd also been tending to the new growth in the realm, but soon she was going to need a definitive purpose. He just hadn't figured out what. He definitely didn't want her involved in soul reaping or visiting any of the Inner Sanctum levels.

A tap on his office door brought him out of his planning, and he hoped it was Lilli, in from outside for a lunch break and, if he was lucky, a little between the sheets action. Or on the floor action. Or against the wall action. Or maybe if he was very lucky, she'd done something deserving of a spanking.

He wasn't particularly picky.

"Come," he called out.

The door burst open, and the Four Horsemen's Heavenly Watcher, Harvester, swept in, dressed in super-skimpy attire as usual. Her mate, Reaver, must love her barely-there black leather miniskirt and thigh-high boots. Azagoth needed to get that outfit for Lilliana, ASAP.

"Azagoth." Harvester brushed her long black hair back from

her face. "I assume you're calling in that favor I owe you?"

"I am." He sat back in his chair and folded his hands across his abs. "I need an angel to be dead."

She gave a haughty sniff. "You do realize I'm not a fallen angel anymore. I can't go around killing angels for fun. Not that I wouldn't like to, mind you. But sadly, Heaven frowns on angels who assassinate other angels."

"You will handle this," he said, allowing a thread of warning to weave into his voice. "When I allowed you into the Inner Sanctum to rescue Reaver, you agreed to bring me one item and one person of my choice. Stamtiel is my person."

She narrowed her eyes. "Stam? Heaven has been looking for him for years. Do you know where he is?"

He nodded. His network of spies and people who owed him favors had made fast work of his request to locate the bastard. "He abused Lilliana. I want his soul."

"Can't you send your *griminions* out to give him a heart attack or something?"

"Come now, Harvester. You know they can only kill demons and evil humans." And even then, there were rules he had to follow.

"Hmm." Tapping her chin with one blue-lacquered nail, she appeared to consider that. "Swear to me that if I agree, I will be free of my debt to you."

A strange request, since that was the deal they'd struck already, but what the hell. "I swear."

"Then I agree." She shrugged. "So how are things going with your...what should I call her...prisoner?"

He looked past her shoulder at the female just now entering the office. "Why don't you ask Lilli?"

Lilliana strode inside, giving Harvester a polite, but forced, smile. "Hello."

"Lilliana, this is Harvester."

Lilliana checked up short, as if she'd hit an invisible barrier. "H-Harvester," she stammered. "I, ah, know your Reaver." Wincing, she shook her head. Damn, she hadn't even been this flustered when she'd met him. "I mean mate. I mean, I know your mate, Reaver."

Harvester cocked her head and studied Lilli. "Have you fucked him?"

Lilliana choked. Maybe he should tell Harvester to stop

messing with her, but this was kind of amusing.

"N-no." Lilli waved her hands vehemently. "We're just friends."

"Oh," Harvester said brightly. "Then you can keep your head. And geez, don't be so nervous. Also, you should probably know that it was your friendship with Reaver that got you sent down here."

"What?" Lilli blurted breathlessly. "How?"

Harvester's smile was sour. "Raphael and Reaver have a...past. Now that Reaver has been raised to Radiant status, he's far more powerful than Raphael, and he can't strike at Reaver the way he wants to, so he's finding other ways to punish him. When you did Reaver's Christmas shopping, it gave Raphael a reason to go after you." Her tone turned apologetic, something Azagoth had never heard from the notoriously prickly angel. "You got caught in the crossfire. I'm sorry."

Lilli looked down, and for a long moment, Azagoth feared the worst. That she was wishing she'd never gotten involved in a power struggle between an archangel and a Radiant.

But when she looked up again, there was fire in her gorgeous eyes. "A couple of weeks ago, this would be upsetting news. But today? I think I'm very fortunate that Raphael has it in for Reaver."

Harvester rolled her eyes, but Azagoth's heart got all stupid happy. Then a thought occurred to him.

"Harvester," he began, "if you knew why Lilliana was sent here, then you must have known about Stamtiel."

Now her eyes went wide with exaggerated innocence. *"Moi?"*

He stared, and she huffed.

"Okay, fine. Yes, I knew. And I suspect that Raphael was involved in Lilliana's kidnapping as well. Stamtiel was Raphael's friend until he went rogue. Raphael denies that they are still friends, but he's also a lying bastard. I'd bet my shiny new halo that Raphael put Stamtiel up to kidnapping Lilliana, but I think her escape wasn't part of the plan. In any case, I'd already intended to destroy the bastard for what he did to her. You didn't need to call in my debt to you."

Now her odd request earlier, that her debt would be paid if she killed Stamtiel, made sense. If he'd known that she was already planning to kill Stammy, he wouldn't have wasted the request on her. Well, fuck. But he had to admire her cunning.

She turned to Lilliana. "I also knew you didn't sleep with Reaver. I was screwing with you. That, I'm not sorry for. Now," she said, "if we're through here, I have an angel to hunt down."

"See Zhubaal in his office." Azagoth stood. "He'll give you the information you need to find the son of a bitch."

Harvester nodded in farewell. "Oh," she said, as she strode out the doorway, "I almost forgot. Reaver left you a present outside."

The moment Harvester was gone, Lilli turned to him. "A present?"

Azagoth groaned. "I had Hades hold Reaver in the belly of a giant demon in Sheoul-gra's Sanctum for three months. The present is likely not a good one." He took her hand. "Let's go see what we're in for."

Once outside, he inhaled the air, thick with the fragrance of apple blossoms. He still couldn't believe the transformation. And then he saw it. Movement in one of the trees.

"Doves," Lilliana whispered. "There are doves in that tree." She pointed excitedly. "And rabbits. Look over there!"

"Animals." He stared in awe. He hadn't seen anything but demon critters since he'd come here. "But they can't survive here. Not with the demon animals."

Cat appeared next to them. "I helped Reaver bring in the animals," she said, but he barely heard, too stunned by this new turn of events. Reaver should hate him, and yet...he was helping to make sure Lilliana was going to be happy here.

"He brought some other Unfallens to help clear the realm of demon creatures," Cat continued. "And we brought in several wolverines to help with the smaller things. And one of the Horsemen's mates, Cara, said she'll loan you a hellhound too, if you need it."

"No hellhounds," he said quickly. "They'll eat the Earth animals."

"She said she can tell it not to," Cat's voice held a note of admiration. "Apparently, they listen to her."

Still, a hellhound would be a last resort. The things were vicious, unpredictable and, frankly, they were assholes.

Harvester exited the building and trotted down the stairs. "Are you two dense? The animals aren't the surprise."

"You're such a pleasant person," he muttered.

She grinned. "Right?" She glanced over at Lilliana. "Do you

think you could make use of that?"

Lilli blinked. "Of what?"

Harvester pointed at the portal, and Lilliana gasped. "A *chronoglass*! Oh, my God. Where did you get it? *How* did you get it?"

Harvester held up her hands in a *not-me* gesture. "It was Reaver's doing. Idess overheard Azagoth say he broke his, and when she told Reaver, he made it a mission to secure one. I'm pretty sure he stole it from the Time Travel Department, but hey, it's yours now."

Lilliana broke away from them and dashed to the *chronoglass*, where she hugged it. Actually *hugged* the thing.

"Thank you, Harvester." He lowered his voice, even though Lilli was out of earshot. "I know you don't owe me anything anymore, but if you happen to run into an angel named Chaniel, I would consider it a personal favor if you would beat the crap out of him."

"Who is Chaniel?"

"Lilliana's father."

One shoulder rolled in a shrug as she started for the portal. "Consider it done."

Lilliana let go of the *chronoglass* long enough for Harvester to transport out of there. The angel waggled her fingers at them as her body started to dematerialize. "See ya."

Lilliana and Azagoth lingered for a few minutes after Harvester left, both so enthralled with the amazing work the Unfallens were doing. Azagoth still couldn't believe that not only had Reaver arranged all of this, but that people were actually volunteering to help clean up his realm.

"Azagoth?" Lilli squeezed his hand.

"Hmm?"

"Why do you think Unfallen are suddenly being grabbed and dragged to Sheoul?"

"I don't know." He watched a cottontail rabbit do some kind of spazzy hop and sprint. "Fallen angels have always made doing that a sport."

"But according to Cat, they're being hunted." She looked over at the unused buildings. "I was thinking that since the buildings aren't being used..."

Of course! His Lilli was brilliant. Besides giving her a purpose and the Unfallens a safe place to live, it would breathe even more life into the place.

"That's a great idea," he said. "And bonus, there'll be a lot of people who will owe me in the future." She gave him an exasperated look. "What? I'm evil."

She heaved a long-suffering sigh, but the faint smile on her glossy lips gave her away. "I don't think you're half as evil as you believe yourself to be. Come on," she said, tugging him toward the *chronoglass*. "Let's get it into your library. And then, I think we deserve a vacation."

"Where to?"

"Anywhere in the world you want to go."

There were so many places for him to choose from, but when it came down to it, he didn't need to leave to discover the world.

Lilliana *was* his world, and finally, for the first time in his life, he was content right where he was.

\* \* \* \*

Six months flew by before Lilliana knew it. Of course, in the grand scheme of an angel's life, six months was like a thousandth of a second.

And that's what it had felt like.

Even on the bad days, when Azagoth had to deal with some new, intense emotion he wasn't prepared for, time flew by. She didn't feel the need to escape into the *chronoglass* every day, and in fact, she and Azagoth hadn't gone anywhere in a week.

She loved her life in Sheoul-gra, and as long as she didn't visit the Inner Sanctum, she could almost pretend Sheoul-gra was a paradise.

A paradise full of *griminions*, fallen angels, and demons who came and went as they worked out deals with Azagoth.

Demons aside, she wouldn't give up her life here for anything. She was even doing good work with the nearly one hundred Unfallen angels who now called Sheoul-gra's outer buildings their home.

Every day she helped them to improve themselves and work their way toward making up for whatever sin had gotten them kicked out of Heaven. When they became discouraged, she reminded them that Reaver, now one of the most powerful angels in existence, used to be Unfallen. It was rare that a fallen angel could earn his or her way back into Heaven, but it happened, and she wouldn't give up. Not on the Unfallens. Not on anything.

This was her realm. Her future. And Azagoth was her mate. She was made for him and he for her.

And as she lay next to him in the huge bed where they both slept in the middle, she fingered the new, *un*enchanted key necklace he'd given her and realized that freedom wasn't about wide, open spaces. It was about being able to make choices.

And she chose Azagoth.

Forever.

Sign up for the 1001 Dark Nights Newsletter
and be entered to win a Tiffany Key necklace.
There's a contest every month!

Go to www.DarkNights.com to subscribe.

As a bonus, all newsletter subscribers will receive a free
1001 Dark Nights story:

*The First Night*
by Shayla Black, Lexi Blake & M.J. Rose

Turn the page for a full list of the
1001 Dark Nights fabulous novellas...

# 1001 Dark Nights

FOREVER WICKED
A Wicked Lovers Novella
by Shayla Black

CRIMSON TWILIGHT
A Krewe of Hunters Novella
by Heather Graham

CAPTURED IN SURRENDER
A MacKenzie Family Novella
by Liliana Hart

SILENT BITE: A SCANGUARDS WEDDING
A Scanguards Vampire Novella
by Tina Folsom

DUNGEON GAMES
A Masters and Mercenaries Novella
by Lexi Blake

AZAGOTH
A Demonica Novella
by Larissa Ione

NEED YOU NOW
by Lisa Renee Jones

SHOW ME, BABY
A Masters of the Shadowlands Novella
by Cherise Sinclair

ROPED IN
A Blacktop Cowboys ® Novella
by Lorelei James

TEMPTED BY MIDNIGHT
A Midnight Breed Novella
by Lara Adrian

THE FLAME
by Christopher Rice

CARESS OF DARKNESS
A Phoenix Brotherhood Novella
by Julie Kenner

*Also from Evil Eye Concepts:*
TAME ME
A Stark International Novella
by J. Kenner

# Acknowledgments from the Author

I very much want to extend a special thanks to Liz Berry and M.J. Rose for inviting me to be part of this amazing project. I've been dying to write Azagoth's story for a long time, and I can't thank Liz and M.J. enough.

I also want to send huge, squishy hugs to Liz, M.J., Lara Adrian, Lorelei James, Lexi Blake, Shayla Black, Cherise Sinclair, and Julie Kenner for their amazing support during a very hard time (the bracelet is gorgeous, ladies!) You touched me more than I can say!

On a similar note, hugs and thanks to Jillian Stein and the ladies of the Book Obsessed Chicks club. You are all so special, and I love you!

# About Larissa Ione

Air Force veteran Larissa Ione traded in a career as a meteorologist to pursue her passion of writing. She has since published dozens of books, hit several bestseller lists, including the New York Times and USA Today, and has been nominated for a RITA award. She now spends her days in pajamas with her computer, strong coffee, and supernatural worlds. She believes in celebrating everything, and would never be caught without a bottle of Champagne chilling in the fridge…just in case. She currently lives in Wisconsin with her U.S. Coast Guard husband, her teenage son, a rescue cat named Vegas, and her very own hellhound, a King Shepherd named Hexe.

**For more information about Larissa, visit
www.larissaione.com.**

# Revenant
## Demonica, Book 11
### By Larissa Ione
### Coming December 16, 2014

## HELL HATH NO FURY...

For five thousand years, Revenant believed he was alone in the world, a fallen angel beyond any redemption. Now he finds he has a twin brother who had all the light and love Revenant was denied. Caught in a tug of war between Heaven and Hell, he must weigh his thirst for revenge against his desire for a mysterious female named Blaspheme-a female whose very origins could deliver him into salvation... or destruction.

## LIKE AN ANGEL SCORNED

Blaspheme has a deadly secret: she's the forbidden offspring of an angel and a fallen angel. Hunted by both heavenly and satanic forces, she has survived only by laying low and trusting no one. When Revenant claims he can save them both, how can she possibly believe him? But the powerful angel is persistence incarnate and for Blaspheme, there's no place she can hide in Heaven or Hell where he won't find her...

\* \* \* \*

Revenant was one fucked up fallen angel.

No, wait...*angel*. He'd only *believed* he was a fallen angel.

For five thousand fucking years.

But he wasn't an angel, either. Maybe technically, but how could someone born and raised in Sheoul, the demon realm some humans called Hell, be considered a holy-rolling, shiny-haloed angel? He might have a halo, but the shine was long gone, tarnished since his first taste of mother's milk, mixed with demon blood, when he was only hours old.

*Five thousand fucking years.*

It had been two weeks since he'd learned the truth and the memories that had been taken away from him were returned. Now he remembered everything that had happened over the centuries.

He'd been a bad, bad angel. Or a very, very good *fallen* angel, depending on how you looked at it.

Toxic anger rushed through his veins as he paced the parking lot outside Underworld General Hospital. Maybe the doctors inside had some kind of magical drug that could take his memories away again. Life had been way easier when he'd believed he was pure evil, a fallen angel with no redeeming qualities.

Okay, he probably still didn't have any redeeming qualities, but now, what he did have, was conflicted feelings. Questions. A twin brother who couldn't be more opposite of him.

With a vicious snarl, he strode toward the entrance to the emergency department, determined to find a certain False Angel doctor he was sure could help him forget the last five thousand years, if only for a couple of hours.

The sliding glass doors swished open, and the very female he'd come for sauntered out, her blue and yellow duckie spotted scrubs clinging to a killer body. Instant lust fired in his loins, and fuck yeah, screw the drugs, she was exactly what the doctor ordered.

*Take her twice and call me in the morning.*

He watched her long legs eat up the asphalt as she walked, and he imagined them wrapped around his waist as he pounded into her. The closer she came, the harder his body got, and he cursed with disappointment when she dropped her keys and had to stop to pick them up. Then he decided she could drop her keychain as often as she wanted to, because he got a fucking primo view of her deep cleavage when her top gaped open as she bent over.

She straightened, looped the keychain around her finger, and started toward him again, humming a Duran Duran song.

"Blaspheme." He stepped out from between two black ambulances, blocking her path.

She jumped, a startled gasp escaping full crimson lips made to propel a male to ecstasy. "Revenant." Her gaze darted to the hospital doors, and he got the impression she was plotting her escape route. How cute that she thought she could get away from him. "What are you doing lurking in the parking lot?"

Lurking? Well, some might call it that, he supposed. "I was on my way to see you."

She smiled sweetly. "Well, you've seen me. Buh-bye." Pivoting, her blond ponytail bouncing, she headed in the opposite direction.

Back to the hospital.

He flashed around in front of her, once again blocking her path. "Come home with me."

"Wow." She crossed her arms over her chest, which only drew his attention to her rack. *Niiice.* "You get right to the point."

He shrugged. "Saves time."

"Were you planning to wine and dine me at least? You know, before the sex."

"No. Just sex." Lots and lots of sex.

He could already imagine her husky voice deepening in the throes of passion. Could imagine her head between his legs, her mouth on his cock, her hands on his balls. He nearly groaned at the imaginary skin flick playing in his head.

"Oh," she said, her voice dripping with sarcasm. "You're a charmer, you are."

Not once in his five thousand years had anyone ever called him a charmer. But even uttered with sarcasm, it was the nicest thing anyone had ever said to him.

"Don't do that," he growled.

"Do what?" She stared at him like he was a loon.

"Never mind." Dying to touch her, he held out his hand. "You'll love my play room."

She wheeled away like he was offering her the plague instead of his hand. "Go to hell, asshole. I don't date fallen angels."

"Good news, then, because it's not a date." And he wasn't a fallen angel.

"Right. Well, I don't fuck fallen angels either." She made a shooing motion with her hand. "Go away."

She was rejecting him? The sudden reality was like a blow that left him completely off balance. No one rejected him. *No one.*

She started to take off again, and a strange agitation fermented in his chest. This wasn't right. He had his sights set on her, and she was supposed to surrender. This was something new. Something…titillating. The agitation morphed into a sensation he welcomed and knew well; the jacked-up high of the hunt.

Instantly, his senses sharpened and focused. His sense of smell brought a whiff of her vanilla-honey scent. His sense of hearing brought her rapid, pounding heartbeat. And his sense of sight narrowed in on the tick of her pulse at the base of her throat.

The urge to pounce, to take her down and get carnal right here, right now, was nearly overwhelming. Instead, he moved in slowly, enjoying how she backed up, but he didn't catch the scent of fear from her.

"What are you doing?" She swallowed as she bumped up against a massive support beam.

"I'm going to show you why you need to come home with me." He planted both palms on the beam on either side of her head and leaned in until his lips brushed the tender skin of her ear. "You won't regret it."

"I already told you. I don't fuck fallen angels."

"So you said," he murmured. "Do you kiss them?"

"Ah…N—"

He didn't give her the chance to finish her sentence. Pulling back slightly, he closed his mouth over hers.

Strawberry gloss coated his lips as he kissed her, and he swore he'd never liked fruit as much as he did right now.

Her hands came up to grip his biceps, tugging him closer s she deepened the kiss. "You're good," she whispered against is mouth.

"I know," he whispered back.

Suddenly, pain tore into his arms as her nails scored his kin. "But you're not that good."

Before he could even blink, she shoved hard and ducke out from under the cage of his arms. With a wink, she strutted way, her fine ass swinging in her form-fitting scrub bottom. She stopped at the door of a candy apple red Mustang and gav him a sultry look that made his cock throb.

"Give up now, buddy. I can out-stubborn anyone." She hopped into her car and peeled out of her parking stall, leaving him in the dust.

\* \* \* \*

Blaspheme was practically hyperventilating as she drove through New York City's crowded streets, wishing she'd taken the Harrowgate to work today. But no, she'd chosen to drive from her Brooklyn apartment one last time, a sentimental stupidity that had not only taken up precious time, but had run her straight into

Revenant.

Gods, he'd looked like a giant goth biker, wrapped in leather and chains, his massive boots sporting wicked talons at the tips. Even the backs of his fingerless gloves were adorned with metal studs at the knuckles. She'd always hated the tough guy bullshit, but Revenant had fucking *owned* it. She got the impression that he lived his life that way; if he wanted it, he owned it.

He wasn't going to give up on her, was he? At least, not without a fight, which she was going to have to give him. She couldn't afford to have a fallen angel sniffing around, not when she had a massive secret to hide.

Cursing, she fumbled through her purse for her cell phone and dialed her contact from the moving company. Sally answered on the second ring.

"Hi, Bonnie," Sally said, using the name Blaspheme used when dealing with humans. "The movers said they'll be done loading your apartment for the second shipment to London by the end of the day."

"Good," Blas said. "I should be there in an hour—" The Call Waiting beep interrupted. "Can I get back to you? My mother is ringing in."

Sally's cheerful, "No problem," was followed by a promise to make sure the movers would take wonderful care of Blaspheme's things and not to worry, and a moment later, Blaspheme's mother was on the other line.

"Hi, Mom." Blaspheme slammed on her brakes to avoid rear-ending a piece of shit truck that apparently hadn't come equipped with a turn signal *or* brake lights. She shot the driver the finger through her front windshield.

"Blas." Her mother's raspy voice came from right next to Blaspheme.

Screaming, Blas dropped the phone. "Holy shit!"

She opened her mouth again to yell at her mother for popping into the car from out of nowhere, but when she saw the blood, her voice cut out. Deva, short for Devastation, sat in the passenger seat, every inch of her body covered in blood. The broken end of a bone punched through her left biceps, and a deep, to-the-femur burn had devastated her right leg.

"Oh, gods," Blaspheme gasped. "What happened?"

Her mother lifted her trembling hand from her abdomen, and

Blas got an eyeful of bowels poking through the laceration that stretched from just above her navel to her hipbone.

"I—" Deva sucked in a rattling breath…and slumped, unconscious, against the window.

# Also from Larissa Ione

~ DEMONICA/LORDS OF DELIVERANCE SERIES ~
Pleasure Unbound (Book 1)
Desire Unchained (Book 2)
Passion Unleashed (Book 3)
Ecstasy Unveiled (Book 4)
Eternity Embraced ebook (Book 4.5) (NOVELLA)
Sin Undone August (Book 5)
Eternal Rider (Book 6)
Supernatural Anthology (Book 6.5) (NOVELLA)
Immortal Rider (Book 7)
Lethal Rider (Book 8)
Rogue Rider (Book 9)
REAVER (Book 10)
AZAGOTH (Book 10.5)
REVENANT (Book 11)

~ MOONBOUND CLAN VAMPIRES SERIES ~
Bound By Night (book 1)
Chained By Night (book 2)

## On behalf of 1001 Dark Nights,
## Liz Berry and M.J. Rose would like to thank ~

Doug Scofield
Steve Berry
Richard Blake
Dan Slater
Asha Hossain
Chris Graham
Kim Guidroz
BookTrib After Dark
Jillian Stein
and Simon Lipskar

7156303R00094

Printed in Great Britain
by Amazon.co.uk, Ltd.,
Marston Gate.